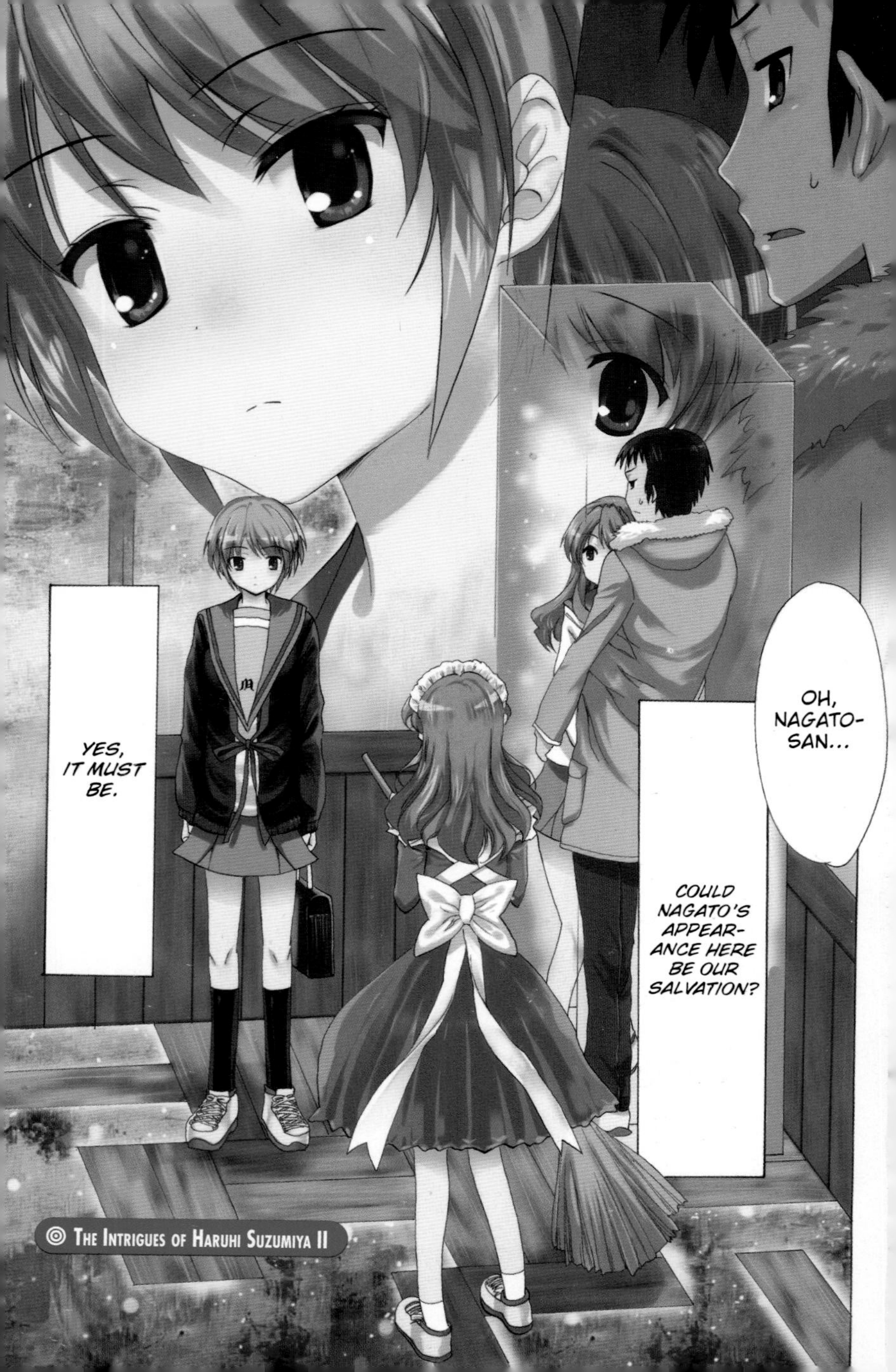
OH, NAGATO-SAN...
COULD NAGATO'S APPEARANCE HERE BE OUR SALVATION?
YES, IT MUST BE.
THE INTRIGUES OF HARUHI SUZUMIYA II

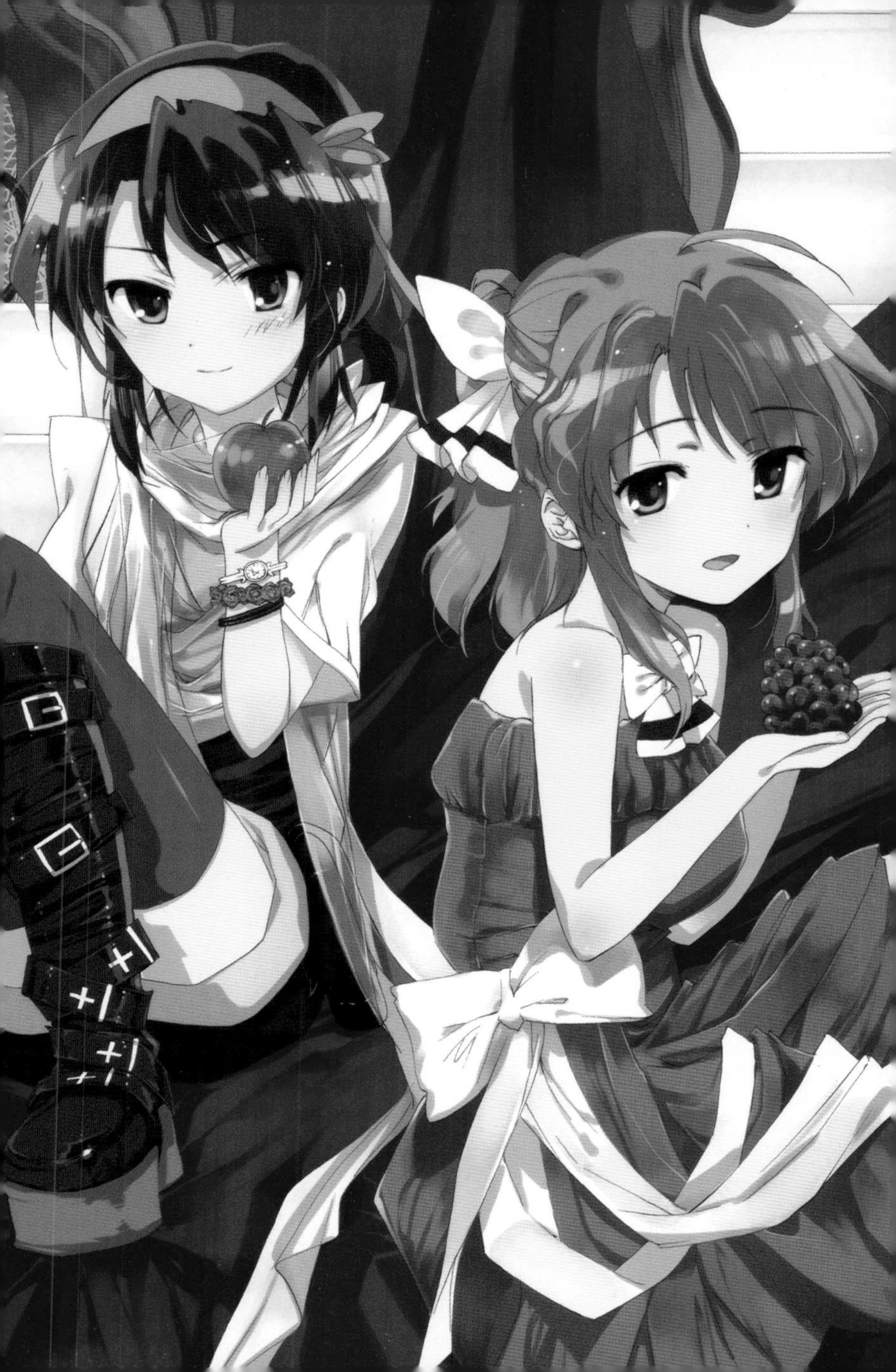

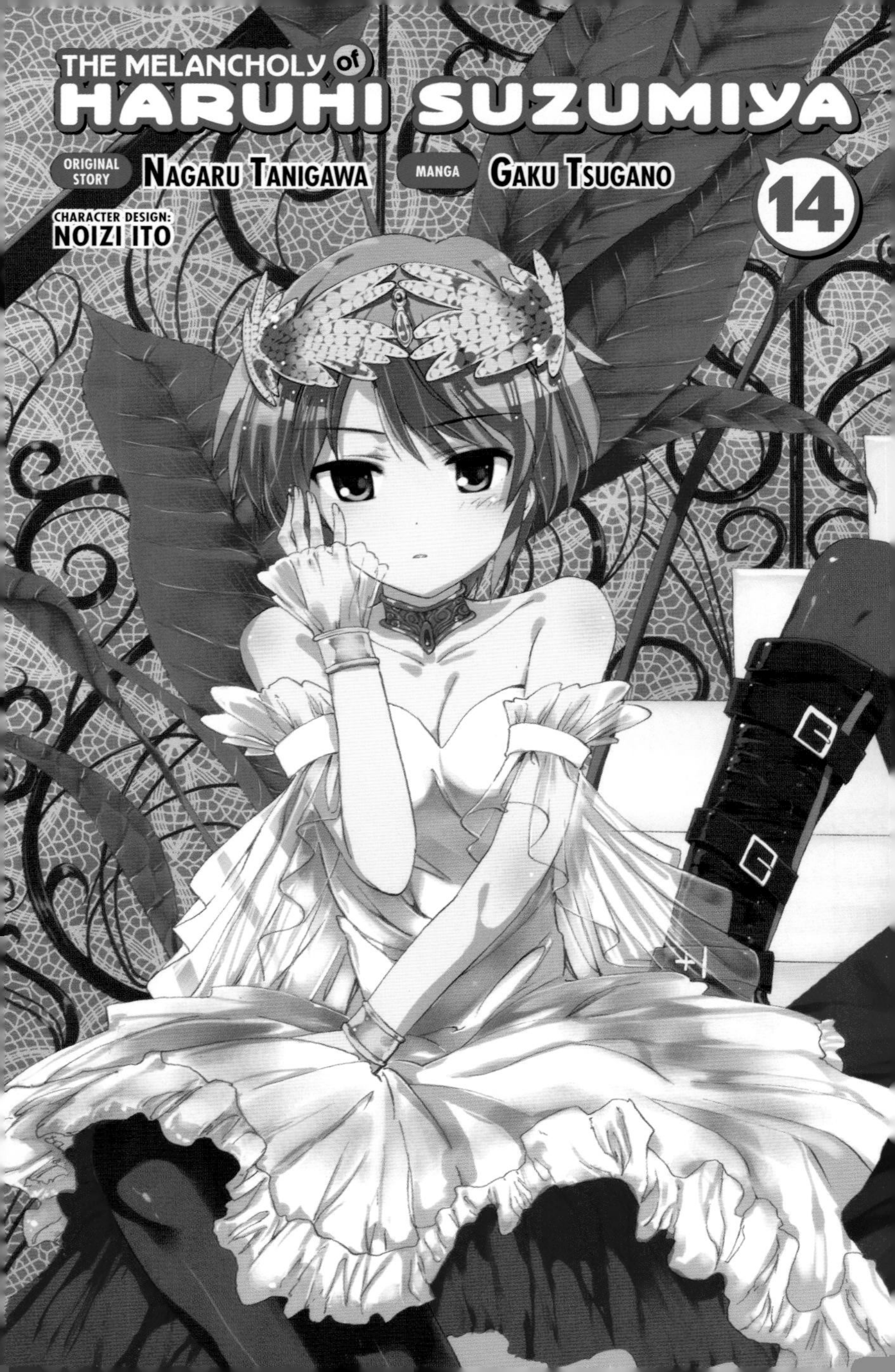
THE MELANCHOLY of
HARUHI SUZUMIYA
ORIGINAL STORY
NAGARU TANIGAWA
MANGA
GAKU TSUGANO
14
CHARACTER DESIGN:
NOIZI ITO

CONTENTS

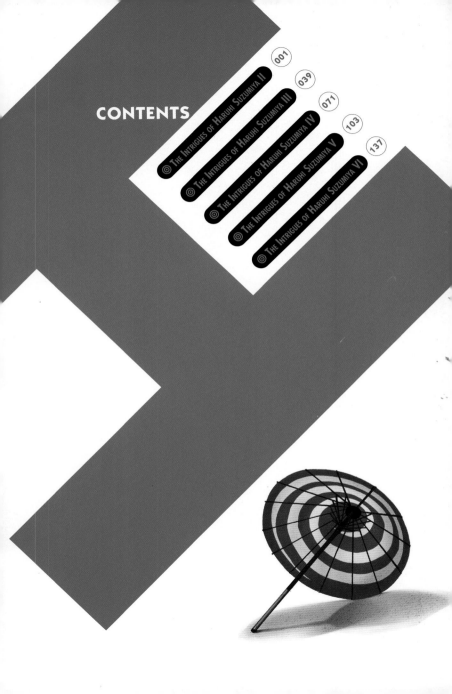

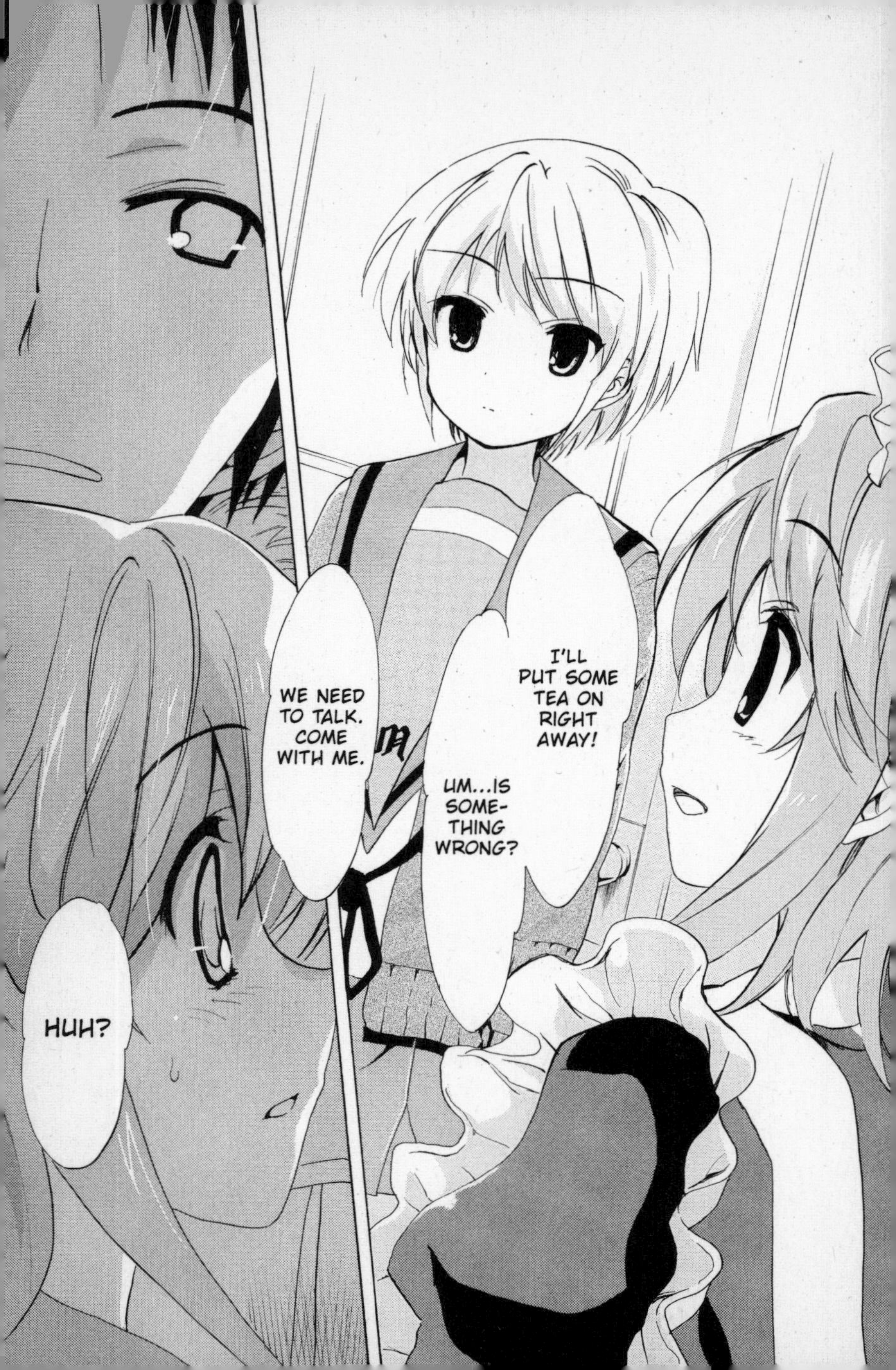
I'LL PUT SOME TEA ON RIGHT AWAY!
UM...IS SOMETHING WRONG?
WE NEED TO TALK. COME WITH ME.
HUH?

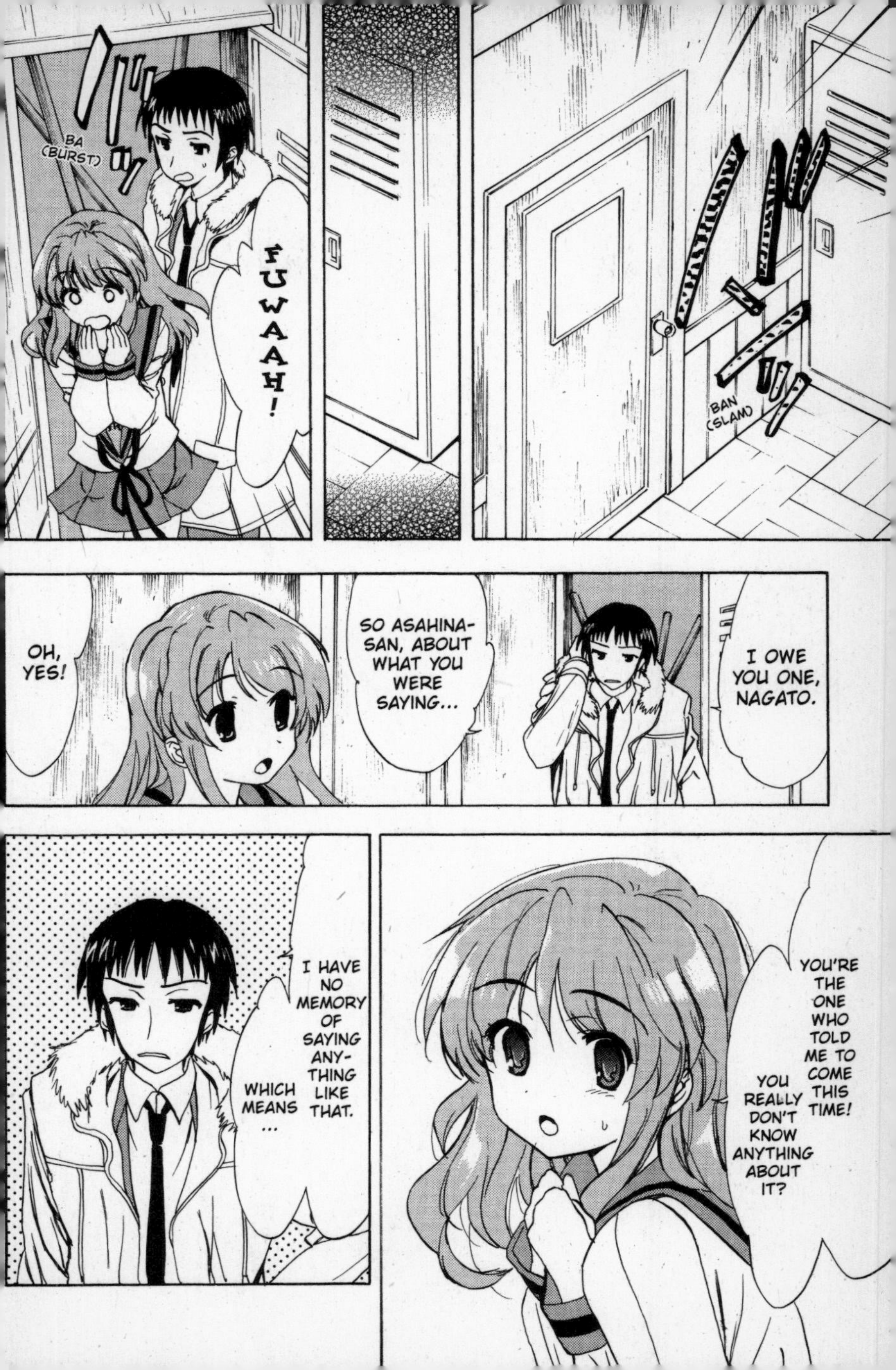
BAN (SLAM)
BA (BURST)
FUWAAH!
I OWE YOU ONE, NAGATO.
SO ASAHINA-SAN, ABOUT WHAT YOU WERE SAYING...
OH, YES!
YOU'RE THE ONE WHO TOLD ME TO COME THIS TIME!
YOU REALLY DON'T KNOW ANYTHING ABOUT IT?
I HAVE NO MEMORY OF SAYING ANYTHING LIKE THAT.
WHICH MEANS ...

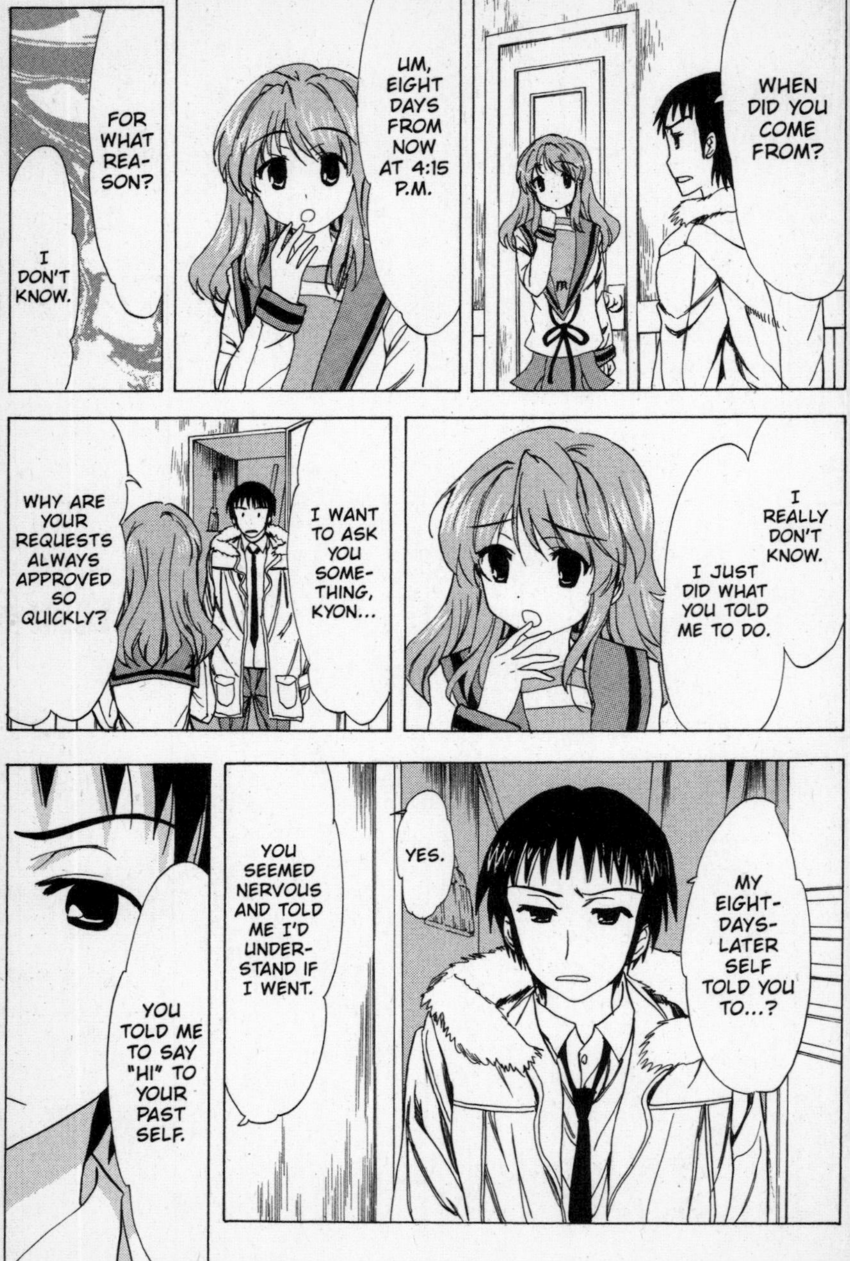
WHEN DID YOU COME FROM?
UM, EIGHT DAYS FROM NOW AT 4:15 P.M.
FOR WHAT REASON?
I DON'T KNOW.
I REALLY DON'T KNOW.
I JUST DID WHAT YOU TOLD ME TO DO.
I WANT TO ASK YOU SOMETHING, KYON...
WHY ARE YOUR REQUESTS ALWAYS APPROVED SO QUICKLY?
MY EIGHT-DAYS-LATER SELF TOLD YOU TO...?
YES.
YOU SEEMED NERVOUS AND TOLD ME I'D UNDERSTAND IF I WENT.
YOU TOLD ME TO SAY "HI" TO YOUR PAST SELF.

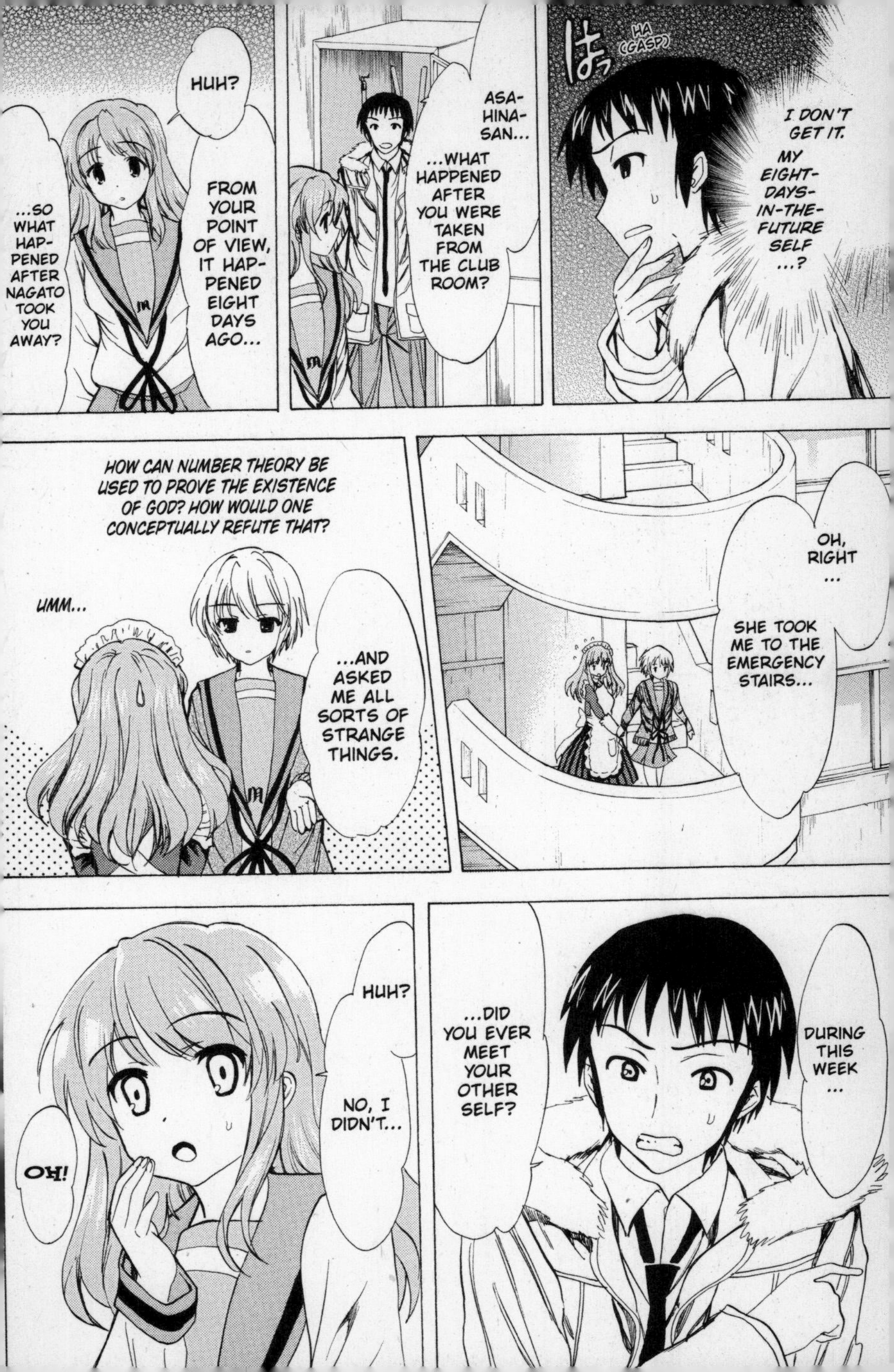
はっ
HA (GASP)
I DON'T GET IT.
MY EIGHT-DAYS-IN-THE-FUTURE SELF ...?
ASA-HINA-SAN...
...WHAT HAPPENED AFTER YOU WERE TAKEN FROM THE CLUB ROOM?
HUH?
FROM YOUR POINT OF VIEW, IT HAPPENED EIGHT DAYS AGO...
...SO WHAT HAPPENED AFTER NAGATO TOOK YOU AWAY?
OH, RIGHT ...
SHE TOOK ME TO THE EMERGENCY STAIRS...
...AND ASKED ME ALL SORTS OF STRANGE THINGS.
HOW CAN NUMBER THEORY BE USED TO PROVE THE EXISTENCE OF GOD? HOW WOULD ONE CONCEPTUALLY REFUTE THAT?
UMM...
DURING THIS WEEK ...
...DID YOU EVER MEET YOUR OTHER SELF?
HUH?
NO, I DIDN'T...
OH!

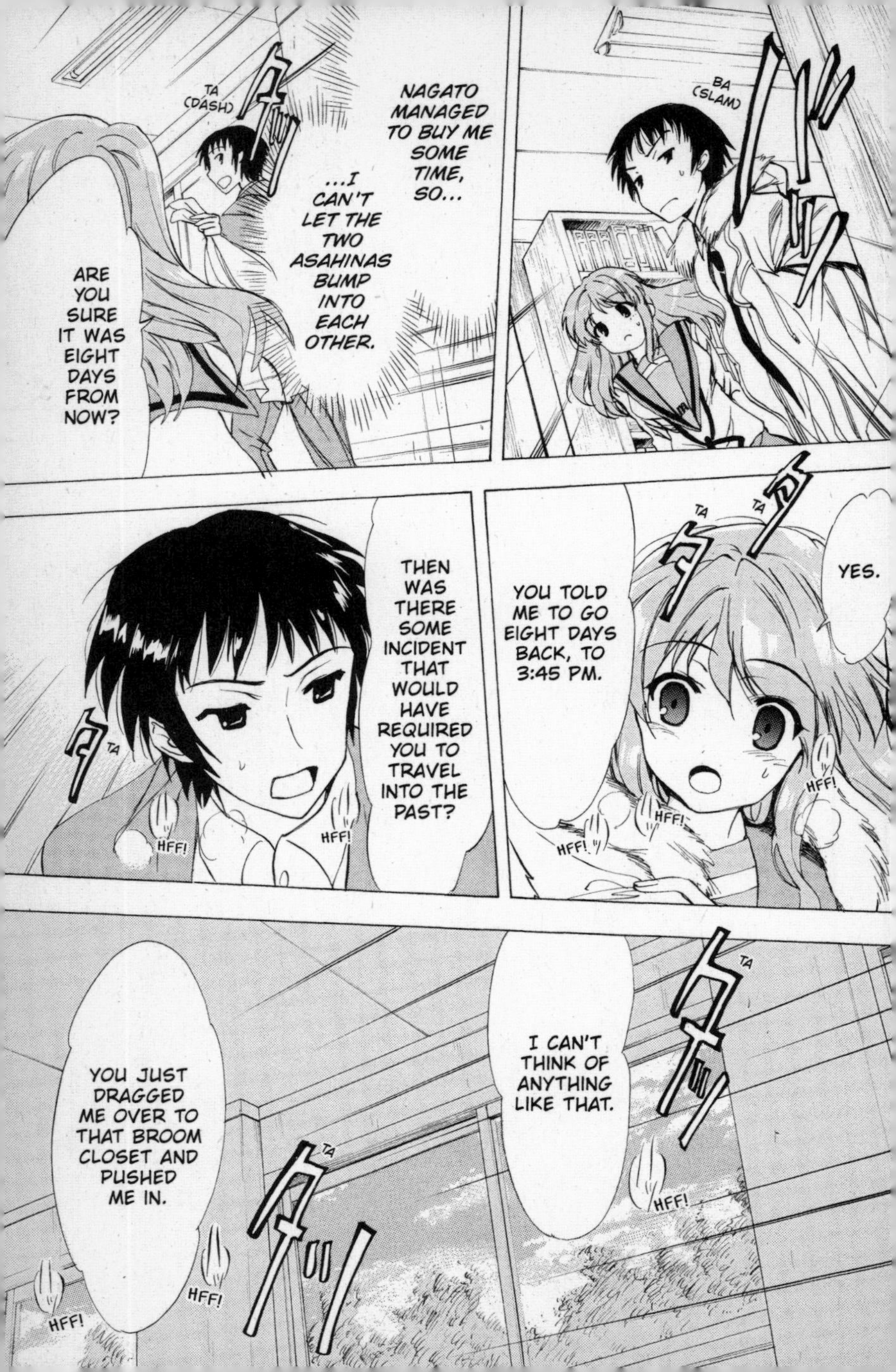
BA (SLAM)
NAGATO MANAGED TO BUY ME SOME TIME, SO...
...I CAN'T LET THE TWO ASAHINAS BUMP INTO EACH OTHER.
TA (DASH)
ARE YOU SURE IT WAS EIGHT DAYS FROM NOW?
YES.
TA
TA
YOU TOLD ME TO GO EIGHT DAYS BACK, TO 3:45 PM.
HFF!
HFF!
HFF!
THEN WAS THERE SOME INCIDENT THAT WOULD HAVE REQUIRED YOU TO TRAVEL INTO THE PAST?
TA
HFF!
HFF!
TA
I CAN'T THINK OF ANYTHING LIKE THAT.
HFF!
YOU JUST DRAGGED ME OVER TO THAT BROOM CLOSET AND PUSHED ME IN.
TA
HFF!
HFF!

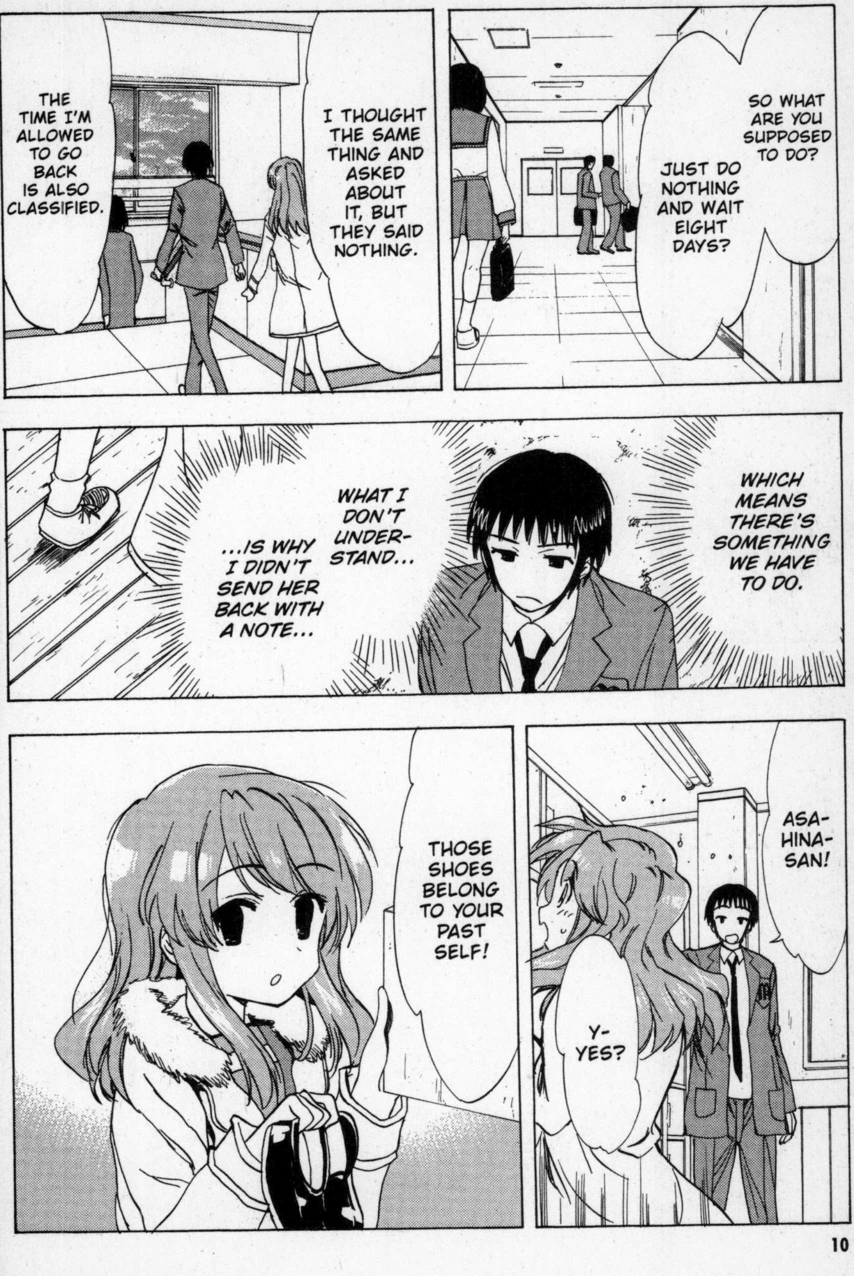
SO WHAT ARE YOU SUPPOSED TO DO?
JUST DO NOTHING AND WAIT EIGHT DAYS?
I THOUGHT THE SAME THING AND ASKED ABOUT IT, BUT THEY SAID NOTHING.
THE TIME I'M ALLOWED TO GO BACK IS ALSO CLASSIFIED.
WHICH MEANS THERE'S SOMETHING WE HAVE TO DO.
WHAT I DON'T UNDER-STAND...
...IS WHY I DIDN'T SEND HER BACK WITH A NOTE...
ASA-HINA-SAN!
Y-YES?
THOSE SHOES BELONG TO YOUR PAST SELF!

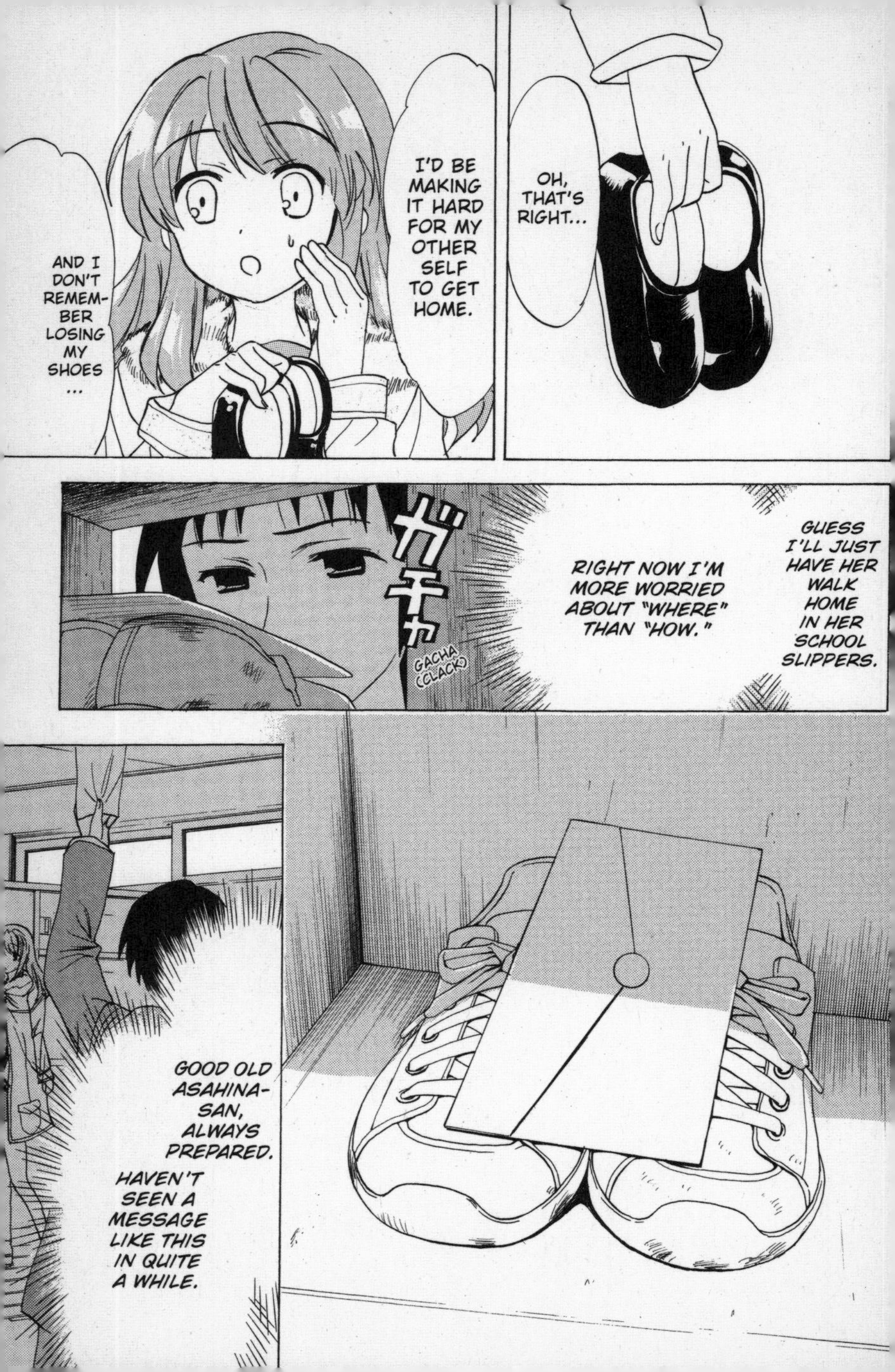
OH, THAT'S RIGHT...
I'D BE MAKING IT HARD FOR MY OTHER SELF TO GET HOME.
AND I DON'T REMEMBER LOSING MY SHOES...
GUESS I'LL JUST HAVE HER WALK HOME IN HER SCHOOL SLIPPERS.
RIGHT NOW I'M MORE WORRIED ABOUT "WHERE" THAN "HOW."
ガチャ
GACHA (CLACK)
GOOD OLD ASAHINA-SAN, ALWAYS PREPARED.
HAVEN'T SEEN A MESSAGE LIKE THIS IN QUITE A WHILE.

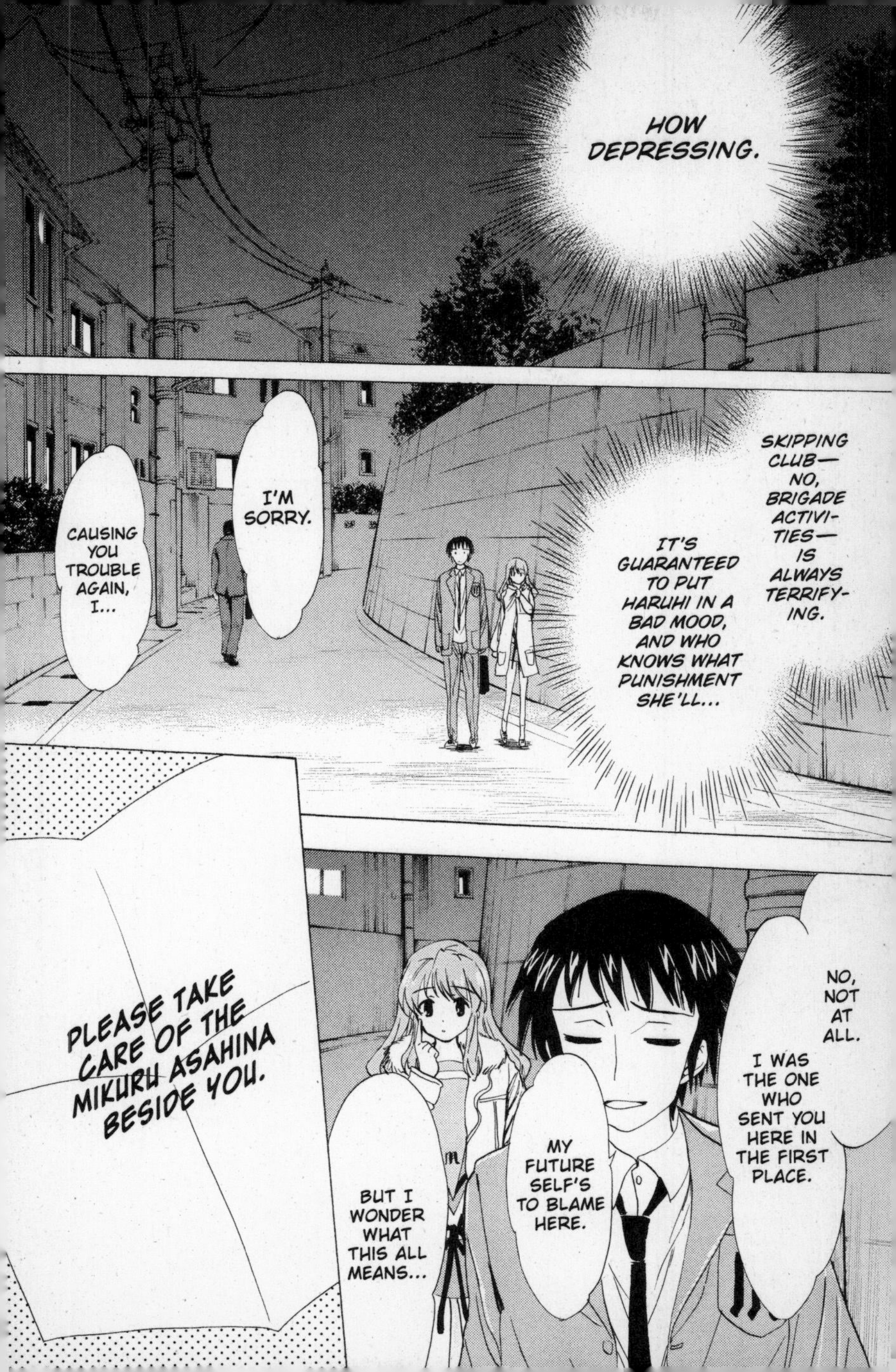
HOW DEPRESSING.
SKIPPING CLUB—NO, BRIGADE ACTIVITIES—IS ALWAYS TERRIFYING.
IT'S GUARANTEED TO PUT HARUHI IN A BAD MOOD, AND WHO KNOWS WHAT PUNISHMENT SHE'LL...
I'M SORRY.
CAUSING YOU TROUBLE AGAIN, I...
NO, NOT AT ALL.
I WAS THE ONE WHO SENT YOU HERE IN THE FIRST PLACE.
MY FUTURE SELF'S TO BLAME HERE.
BUT I WONDER WHAT THIS ALL MEANS...
PLEASE TAKE CARE OF THE MIKURU ASAHINA BESIDE YOU.

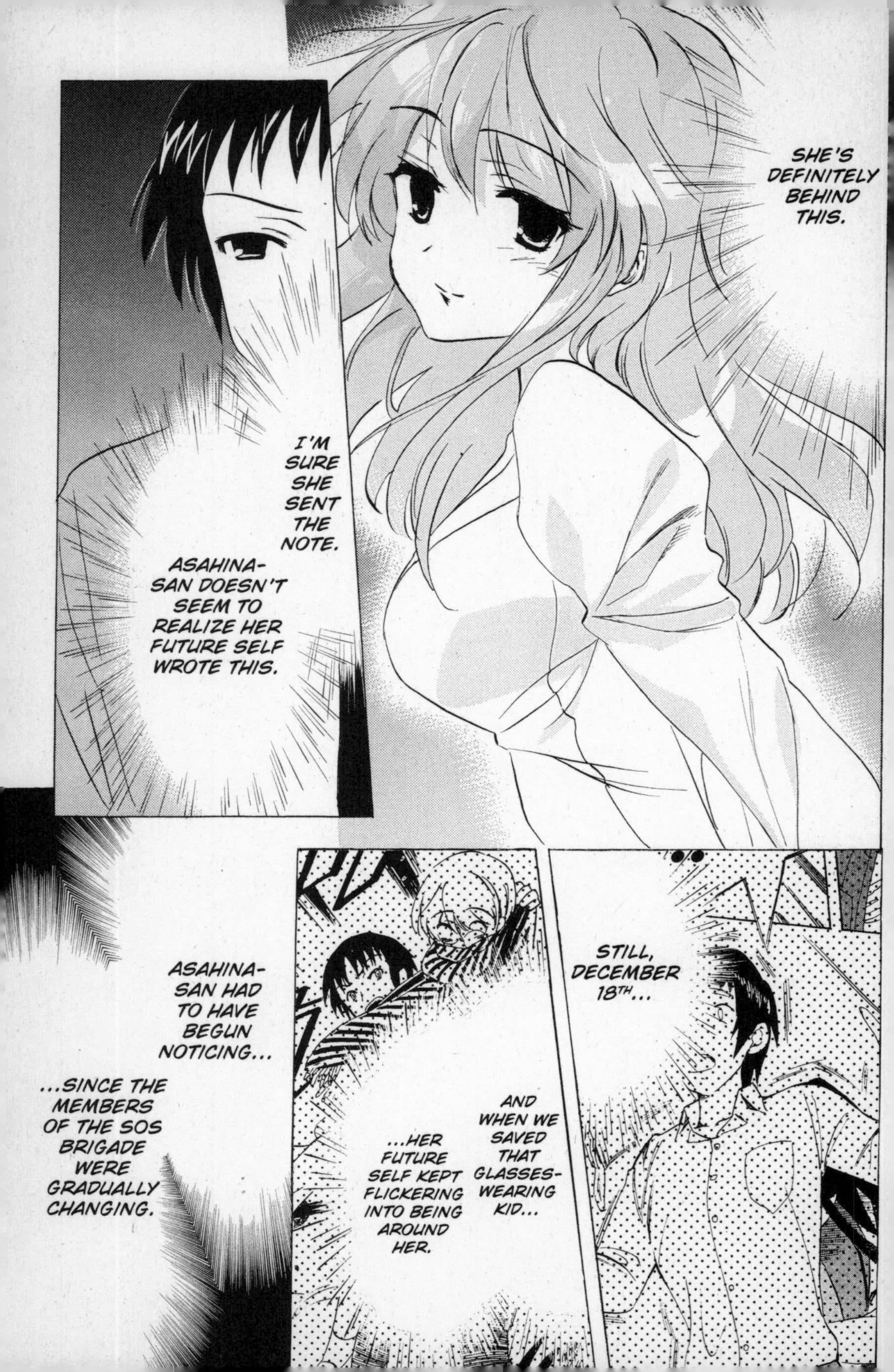
SHE'S DEFINITELY BEHIND THIS.
I'M SURE SHE SENT THE NOTE.
ASAHINA-SAN DOESN'T SEEM TO REALIZE HER FUTURE SELF WROTE THIS.
STILL, DECEMBER 18TH...
AND WHEN WE SAVED THAT GLASSES-WEARING KID...
...HER FUTURE SELF KEPT FLICKERING INTO BEING AROUND HER.
ASAHINA-SAN HAD TO HAVE BEGUN NOTICING...
...SINCE THE MEMBERS OF THE SOS BRIGADE WERE GRADUALLY CHANGING.

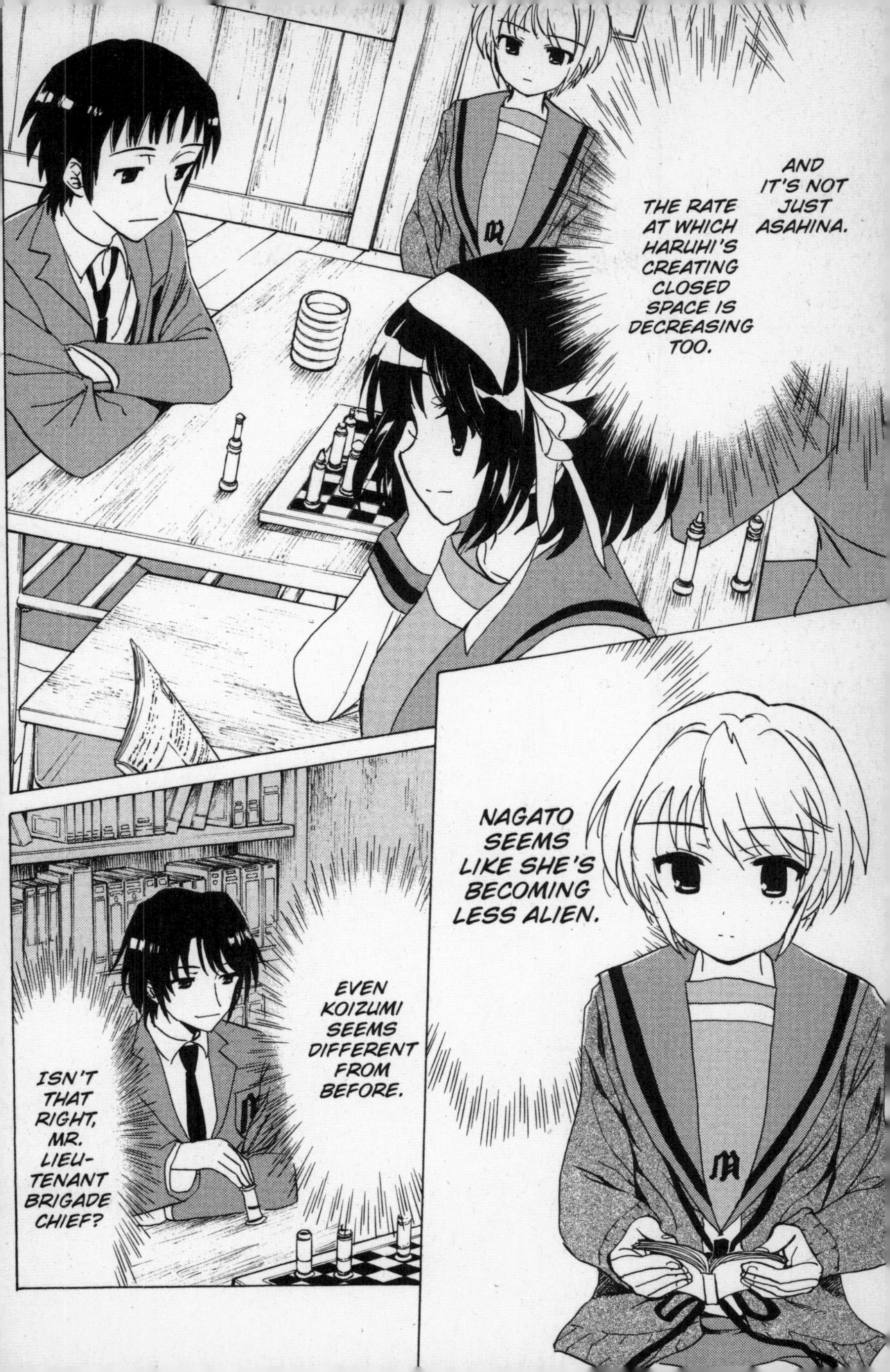
AND IT'S NOT JUST ASAHINA.
THE RATE AT WHICH HARUHI'S CREATING CLOSED SPACE IS DECREASING TOO.
NAGATO SEEMS LIKE SHE'S BECOMING LESS ALIEN.
EVEN KOIZUMI SEEMS DIFFERENT FROM BEFORE.
ISN'T THAT RIGHT, MR. LIEU-TENANT BRIGADE CHIEF?

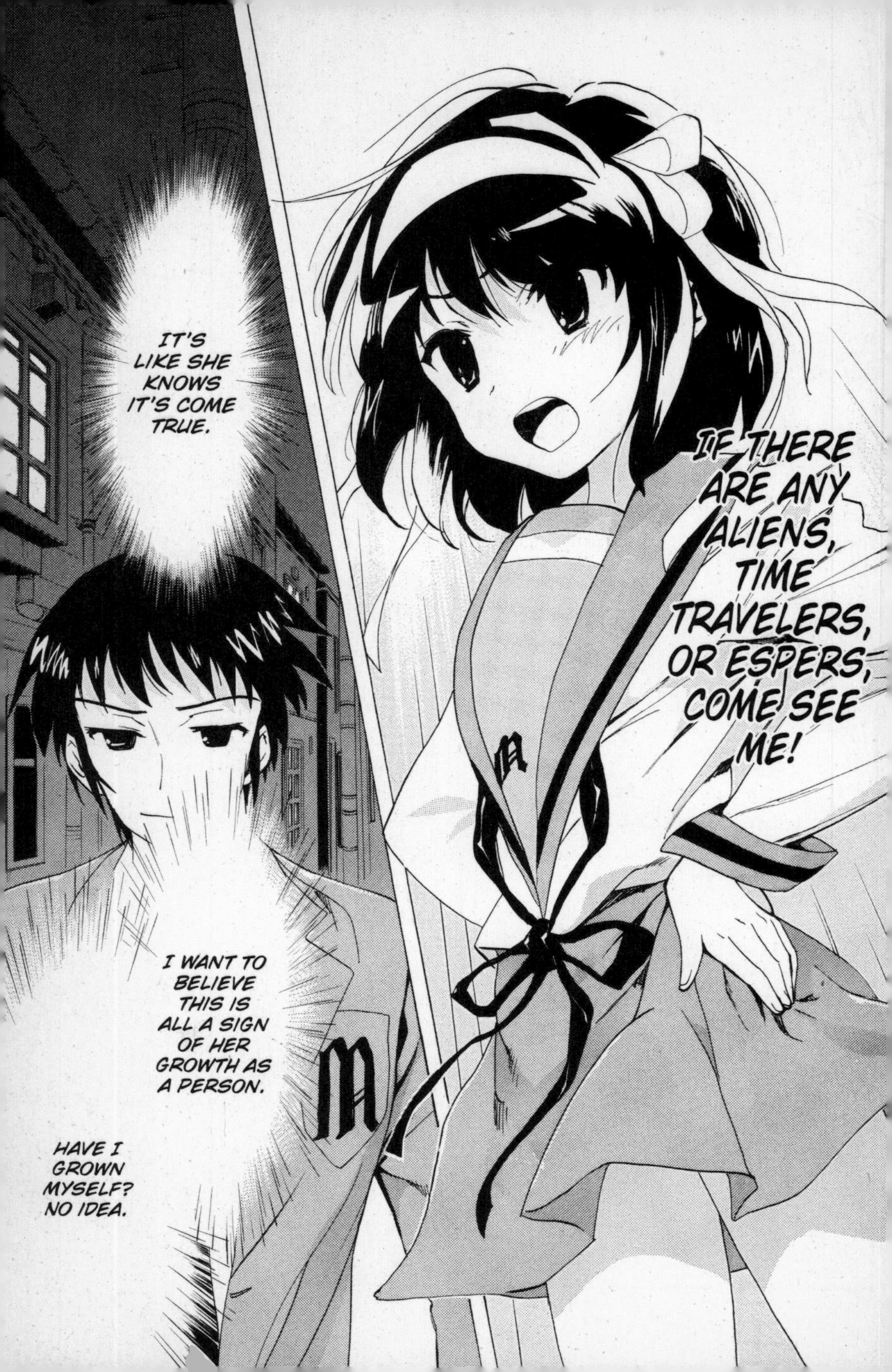
IF THERE ARE ANY ALIENS, TIME TRAVELERS, OR ESPERS, COME SEE ME!
IT'S LIKE SHE KNOWS IT'S COME TRUE.
I WANT TO BELIEVE THIS IS ALL A SIGN OF HER GROWTH AS A PERSON.
HAVE I GROWN MYSELF? NO IDEA.

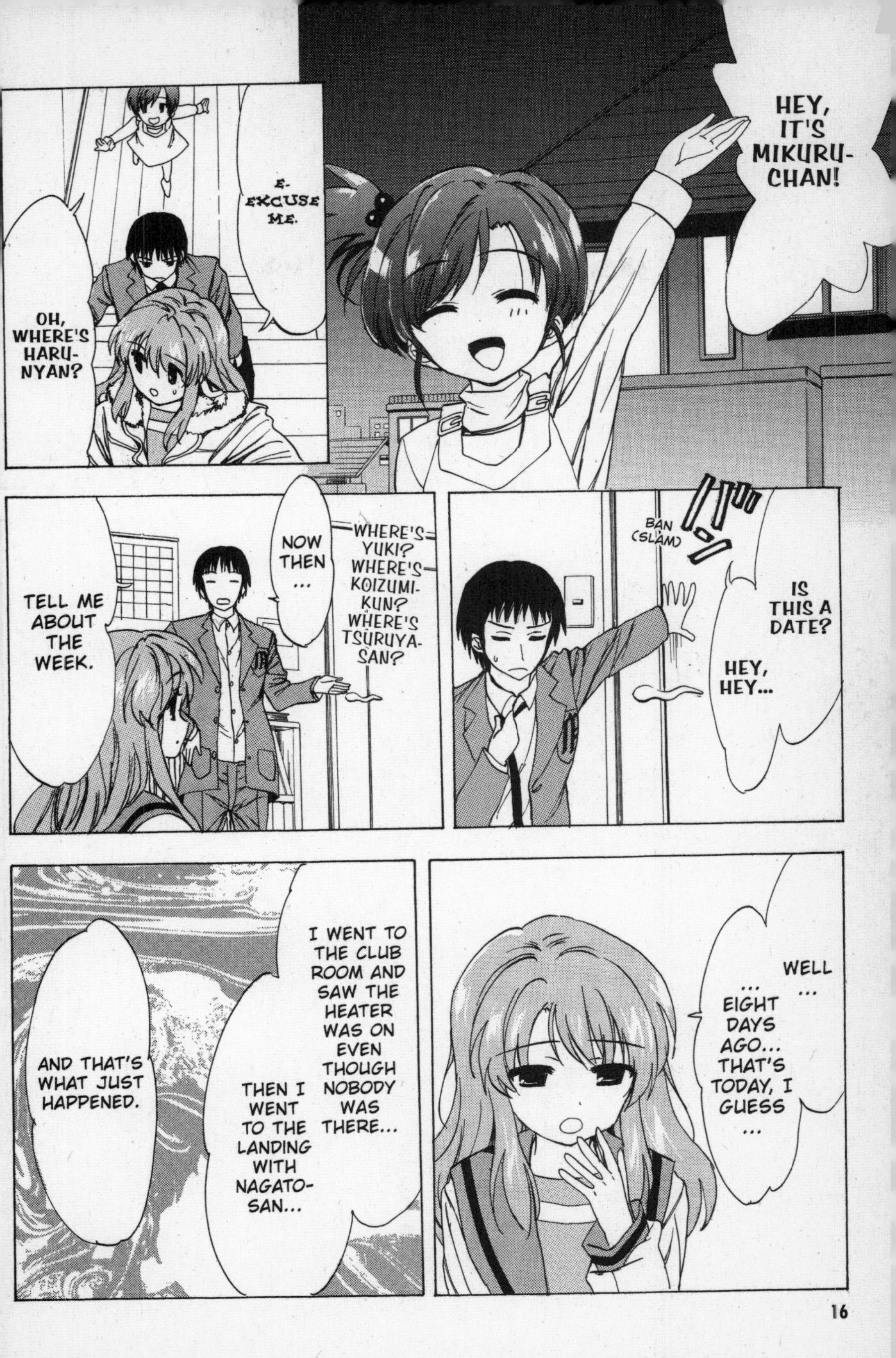
HEY, IT'S MIKURU-CHAN!
E-EXCUSE ME.
OH, WHERE'S HARU-NYAN?
BAN (SLAM)
IS THIS A DATE?
HEY, HEY...
NOW THEN ...
WHERE'S YUKI? WHERE'S KOIZUMI-KUN? WHERE'S TSURUYA-SAN?
TELL ME ABOUT THE WEEK.
WELL ... ...
EIGHT DAYS AGO... THAT'S TODAY, I GUESS ...
I WENT TO THE CLUB ROOM AND SAW THE HEATER WAS ON EVEN THOUGH NOBODY WAS THERE...
THEN I WENT TO THE LANDING WITH NAGATO-SAN...
AND THAT'S WHAT JUST HAPPENED.

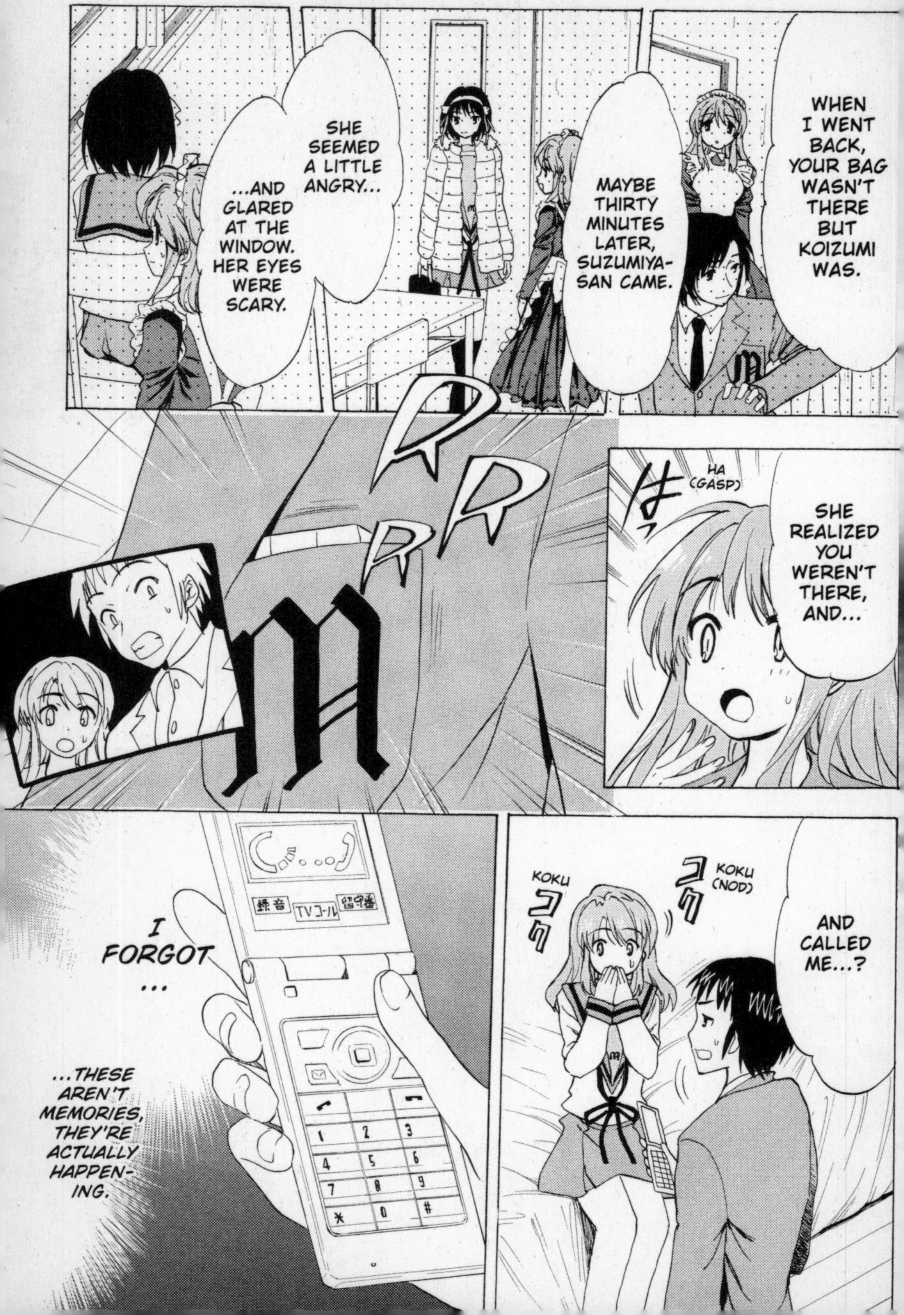
WHEN I WENT BACK, YOUR BAG WASN'T THERE BUT KOIZUMI WAS.
MAYBE THIRTY MINUTES LATER, SUZUMIYA-SAN CAME.
SHE SEEMED A LITTLE ANGRY...
...AND GLARED AT THE WINDOW. HER EYES WERE SCARY.
はっ
HA (GASP)
SHE REALIZED YOU WEREN'T THERE, AND...
RRR
コク
KOKU (NOD)
コク
KOKU
AND CALLED ME...?
録音
TVコール
留守番
I FORGOT...
...THESE AREN'T MEMORIES, THEY'RE ACTUALLY HAPPEN-ING.

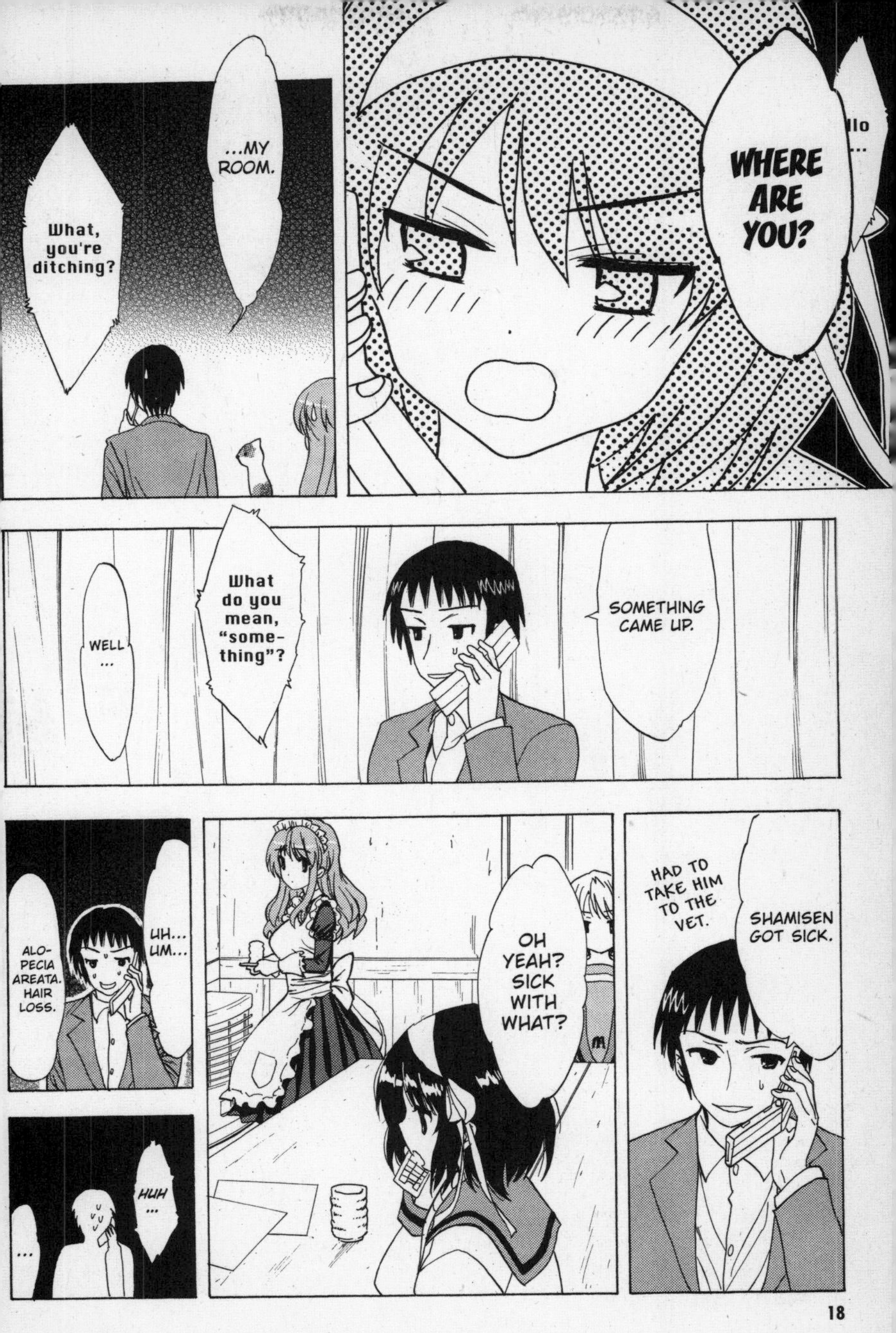
WHERE ARE YOU?
...MY ROOM.
What, you're ditching?
SOMETHING CAME UP.
What do you mean, "some-thing"?
WELL ...
SHAMISEN GOT SICK.
HAD TO TAKE HIM TO THE VET.
OH YEAH? SICK WITH WHAT?
UH... UM...
ALO-PECIA AREATA. HAIR LOSS.
HUH ...
...

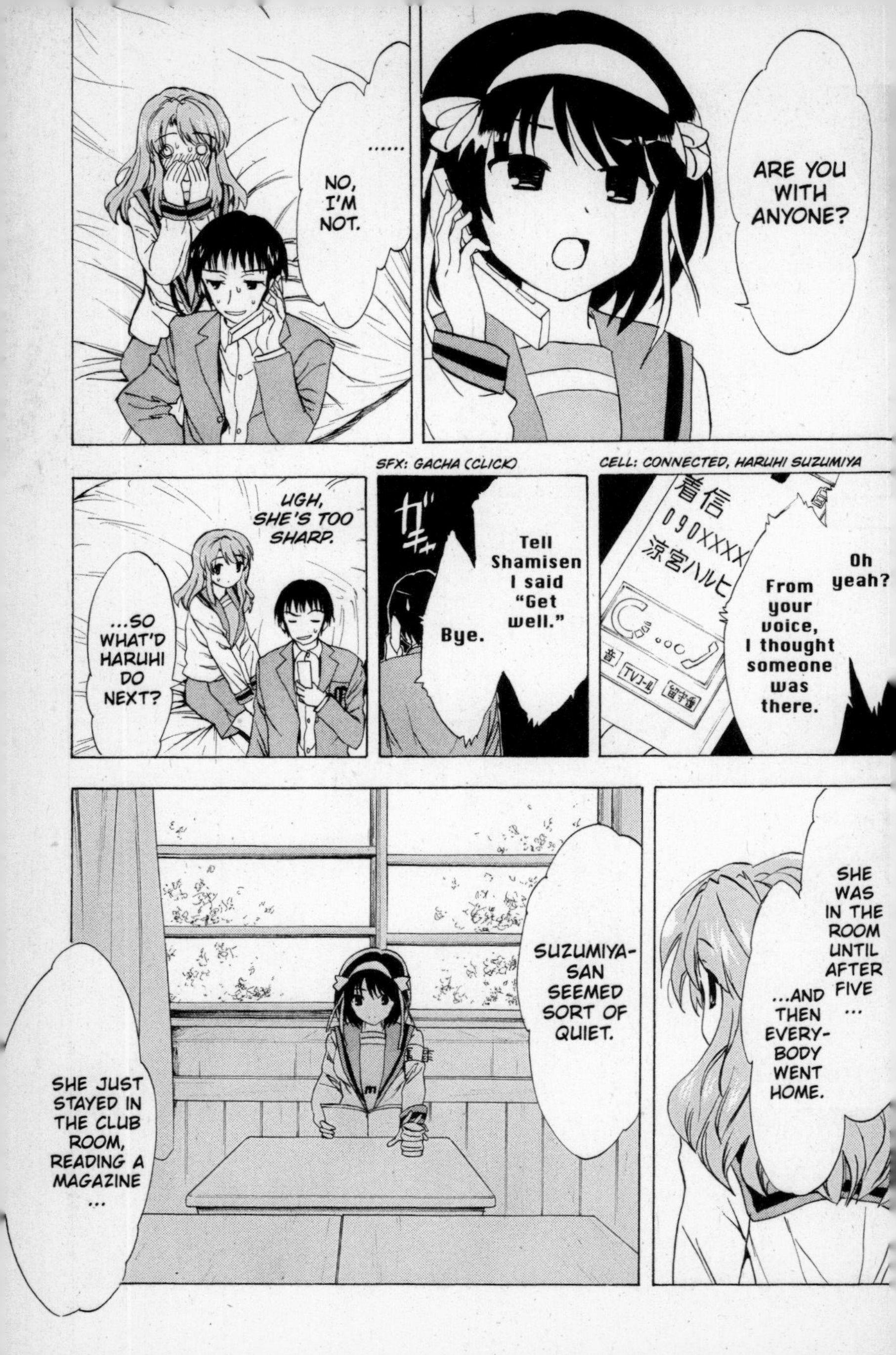
ARE YOU WITH ANYONE?
......
NO, I'M NOT.
CELL: CONNECTED, HARUHI SUZUMIYA
着信
090XXXX
涼宮ハルヒ
Oh yeah?
From your voice, I thought someone was there.
SFX: GACHA (CLICK)
ガチャ
Tell Shamisen I said "Get well."
Bye.
UGH, SHE'S TOO SHARP.
...SO WHAT'D HARUHI DO NEXT?
SHE WAS IN THE ROOM UNTIL AFTER FIVE ...
...AND THEN EVERYBODY WENT HOME.
SUZUMIYA-SAN SEEMED SORT OF QUIET.
SHE JUST STAYED IN THE CLUB ROOM, READING A MAGAZINE ...

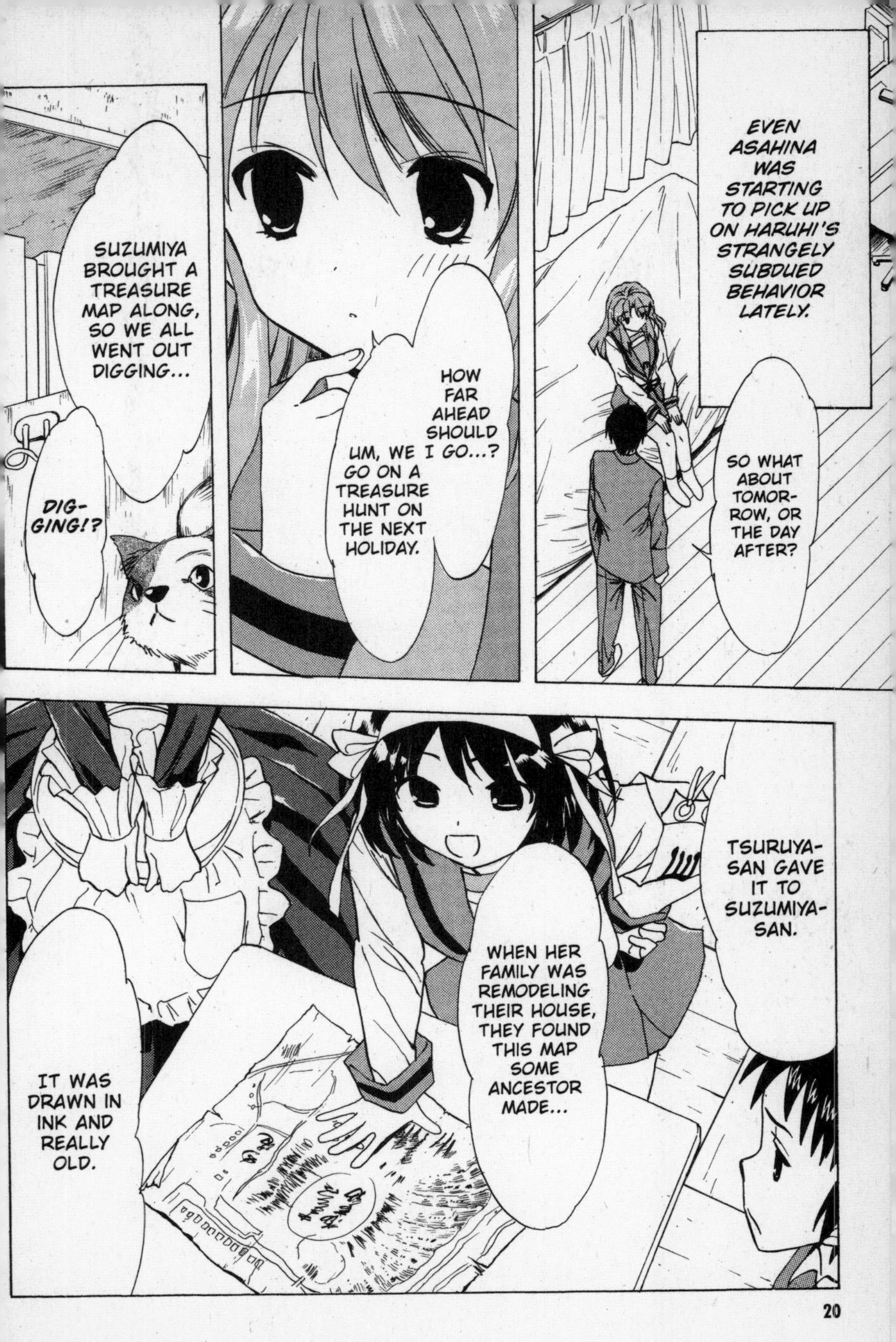
EVEN ASAHINA WAS STARTING TO PICK UP ON HARUHI'S STRANGELY SUBDUED BEHAVIOR LATELY.
SO WHAT ABOUT TOMOR-ROW, OR THE DAY AFTER?
HOW FAR AHEAD SHOULD I GO...?
UM, WE GO ON A TREASURE HUNT ON THE NEXT HOLIDAY.
SUZUMIYA BROUGHT A TREASURE MAP ALONG, SO WE ALL WENT OUT DIGGING...
DIG-GING!?
TSURUYA-SAN GAVE IT TO SUZUMIYA-SAN.
WHEN HER FAMILY WAS REMODELING THEIR HOUSE, THEY FOUND THIS MAP SOME ANCESTOR MADE...
IT WAS DRAWN IN INK AND REALLY OLD.

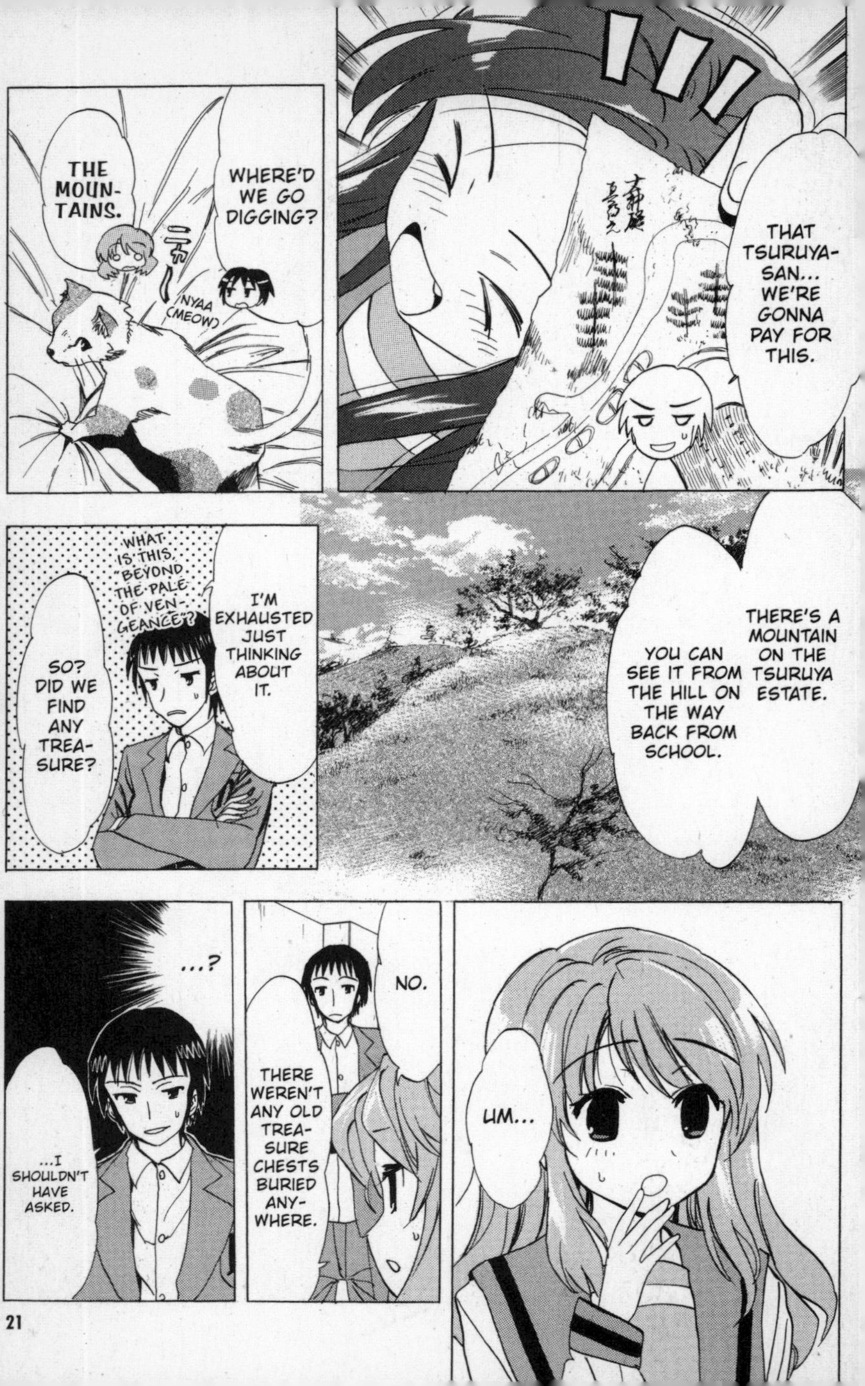
THAT TSURUYA-SAN... WE'RE GONNA PAY FOR THIS.
WHERE'D WE GO DIGGING?
THE MOUN-TAINS.
NYAA (MEOW)
THERE'S A MOUNTAIN ON THE TSURUYA ESTATE.
YOU CAN SEE IT FROM THE HILL ON THE WAY BACK FROM SCHOOL.
I'M EXHAUSTED JUST THINKING ABOUT IT.
WHAT IS THIS, "BEYOND THE PALE OF VEN-GEANCE"?
SO? DID WE FIND ANY TREA-SURE?
UM...
NO.
THERE WEREN'T ANY OLD TREA-SURE CHESTS BURIED ANY-WHERE.
...?
...I SHOULDN'T HAVE ASKED.

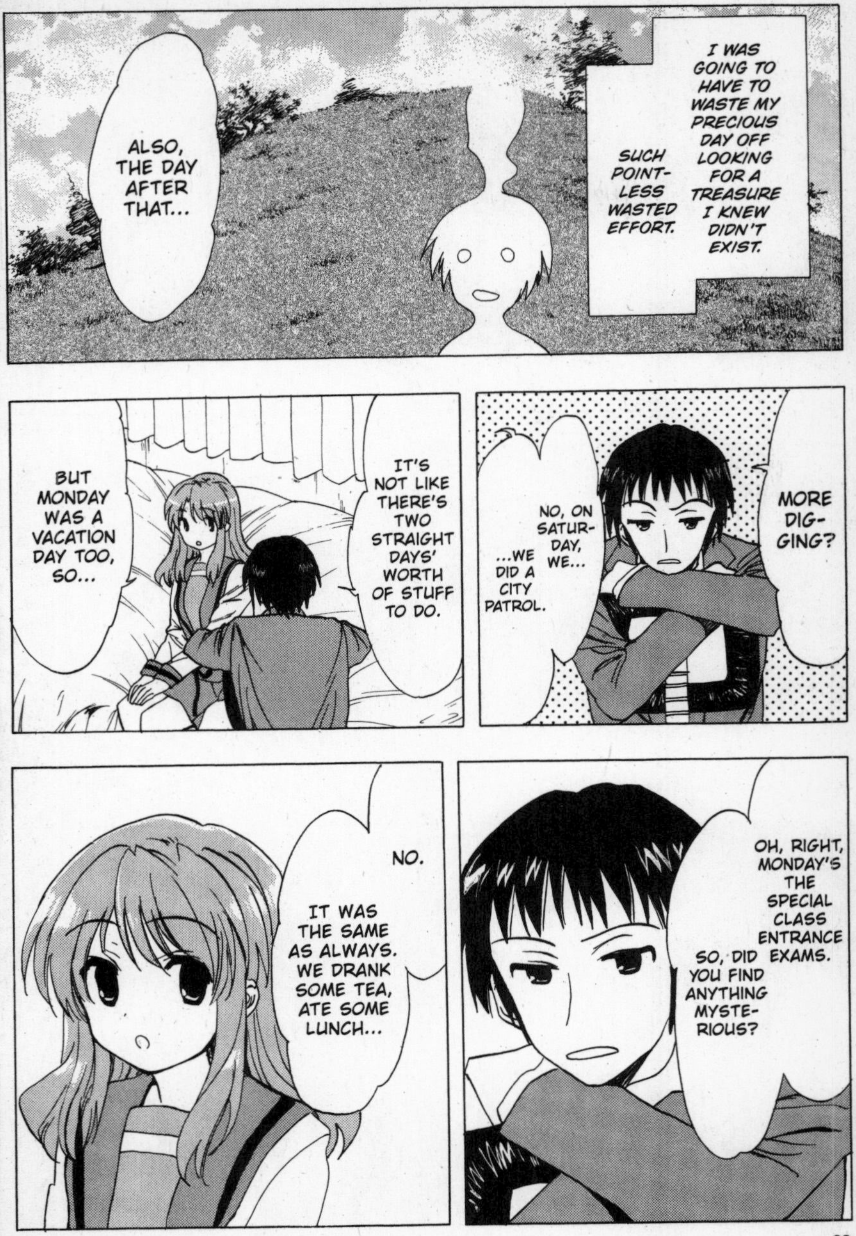
I WAS GOING TO HAVE TO WASTE MY PRECIOUS DAY OFF LOOKING FOR A TREASURE I KNEW DIDN'T EXIST.
SUCH POINTLESS WASTED EFFORT.
ALSO, THE DAY AFTER THAT...
MORE DIGGING?
NO, ON SATURDAY, WE...
...WE DID A CITY PATROL.
IT'S NOT LIKE THERE'S TWO STRAIGHT DAYS' WORTH OF STUFF TO DO.
BUT MONDAY WAS A VACATION DAY TOO, SO...
OH, RIGHT, MONDAY'S THE SPECIAL CLASS ENTRANCE EXAMS.
SO, DID YOU FIND ANYTHING MYSTERIOUS?
NO.
IT WAS THE SAME AS ALWAYS. WE DRANK SOME TEA, ATE SOME LUNCH...

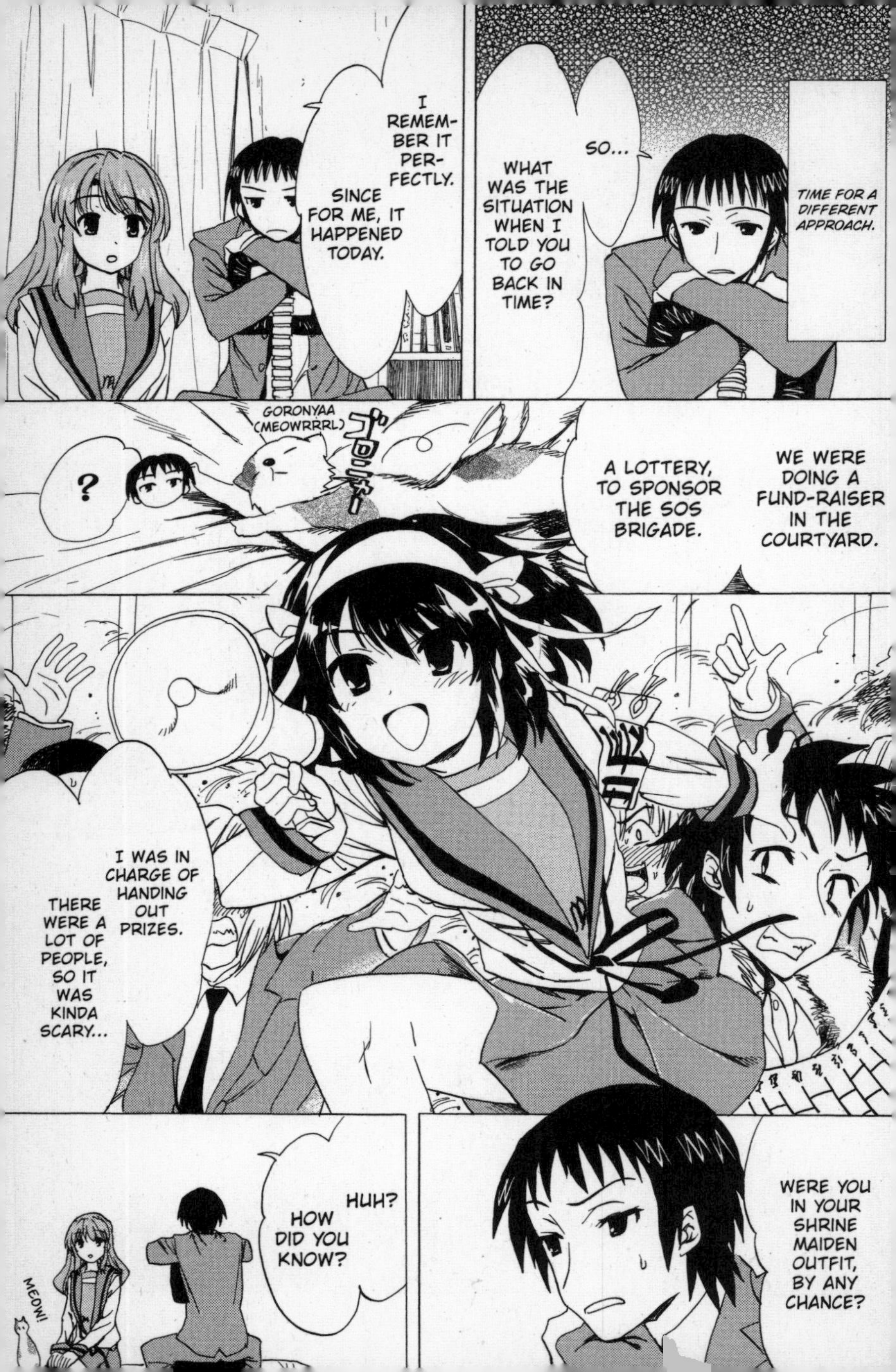

TIME FOR A DIFFERENT APPROACH.
SO...
WHAT WAS THE SITUATION WHEN I TOLD YOU TO GO BACK IN TIME?
I REMEMBER IT PERFECTLY.
SINCE FOR ME, IT HAPPENED TODAY.
WE WERE DOING A FUND-RAISER IN THE COURTYARD.
A LOTTERY, TO SPONSOR THE SOS BRIGADE.
GORONYAA (MEOWRRRL)
?
I WAS IN CHARGE OF HANDING OUT PRIZES.
THERE WERE A LOT OF PEOPLE, SO IT WAS KINDA SCARY...
WERE YOU IN YOUR SHRINE MAIDEN OUTFIT, BY ANY CHANCE?
HUH?
HOW DID YOU KNOW?
MEOW!

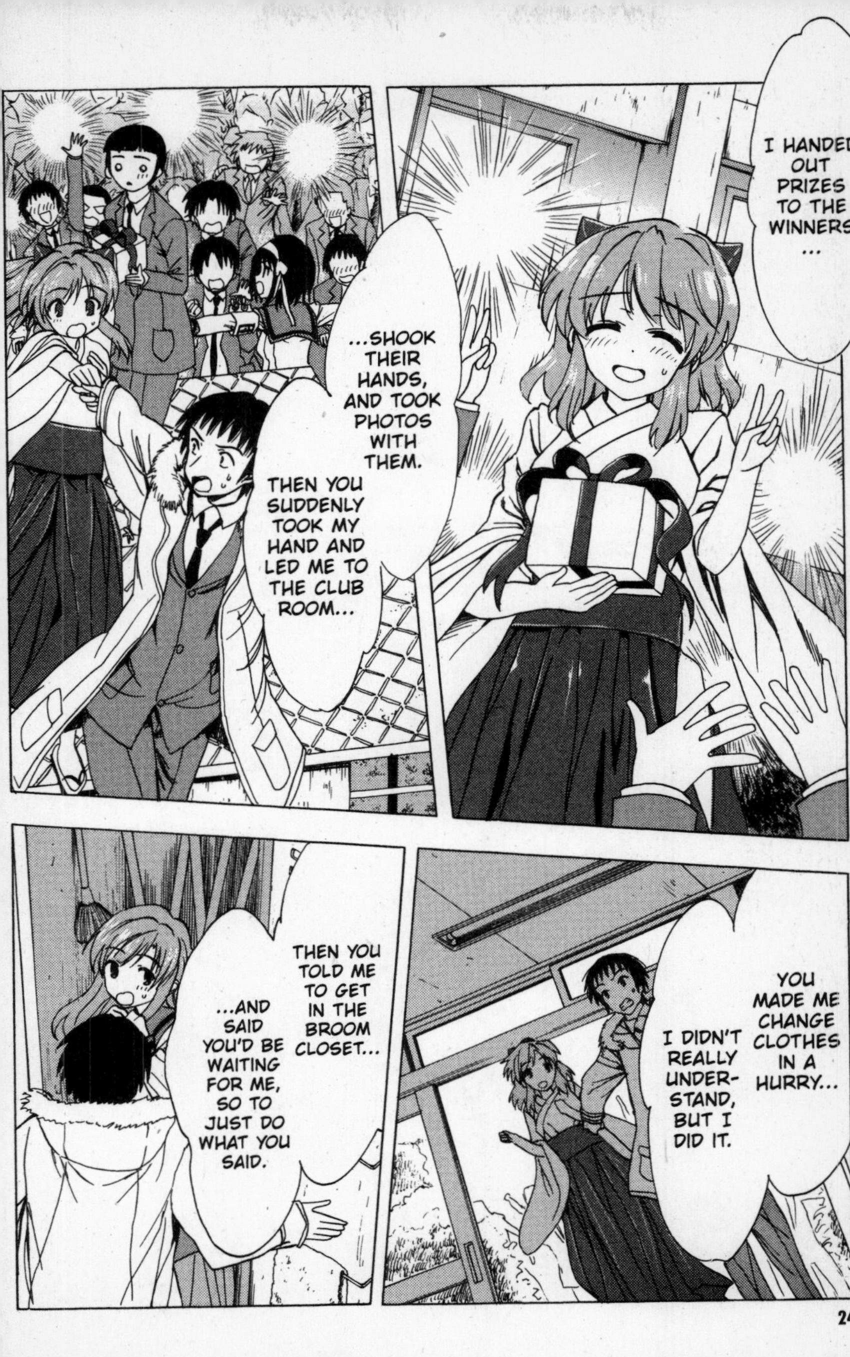
I HANDED OUT PRIZES TO THE WINNERS...
...SHOOK THEIR HANDS, AND TOOK PHOTOS WITH THEM.
THEN YOU SUDDENLY TOOK MY HAND AND LED ME TO THE CLUB ROOM...
YOU MADE ME CHANGE CLOTHES IN A HURRY...
I DIDN'T REALLY UNDER-STAND, BUT I DID IT.
THEN YOU TOLD ME TO GET IN THE BROOM CLOSET...
...AND SAID YOU'D BE WAITING FOR ME, SO TO JUST DO WHAT YOU SAID.

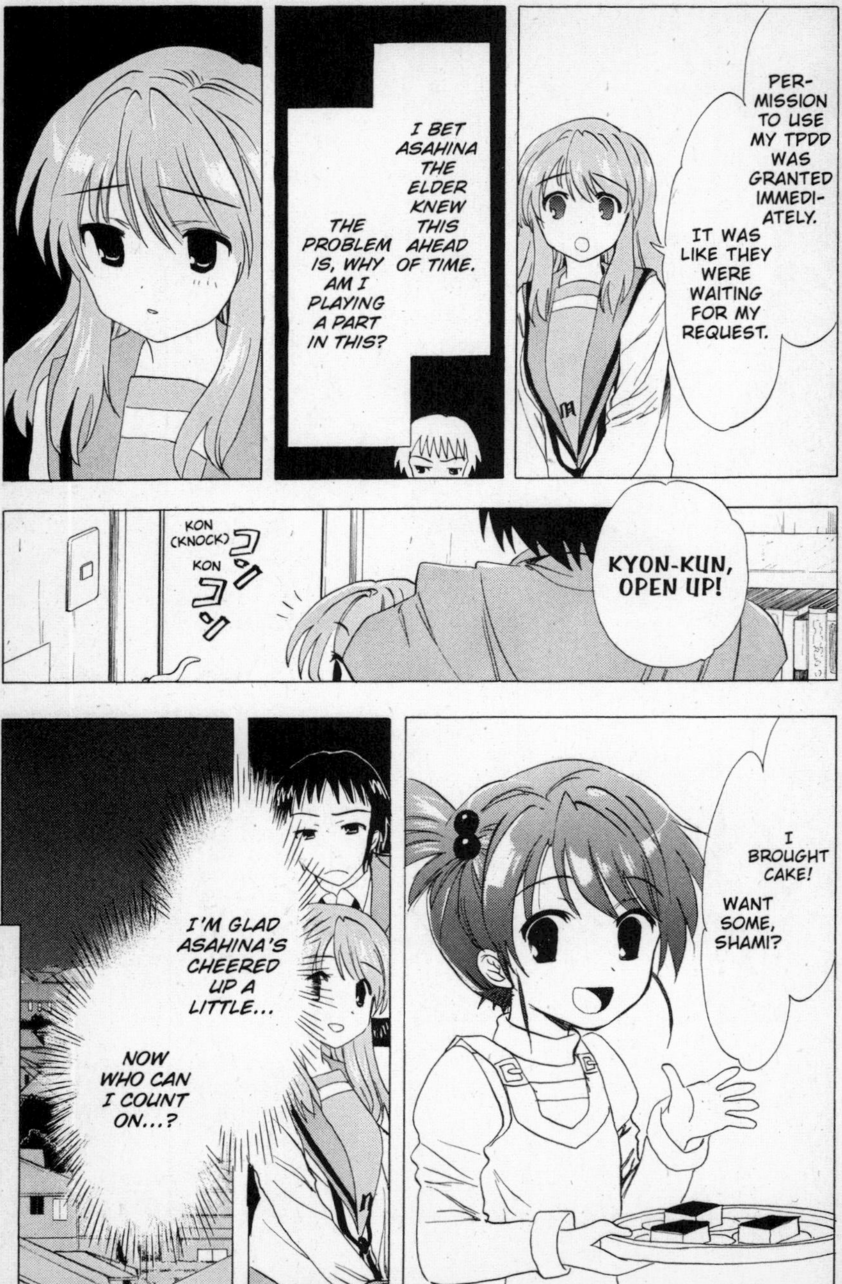
PER-MISSION TO USE MY TPDD WAS GRANTED IMMEDI-ATELY.
IT WAS LIKE THEY WERE WAITING FOR MY REQUEST.
I BET ASAHINA THE ELDER KNEW THIS AHEAD OF TIME.
THE PROBLEM IS, WHY AM I PLAYING A PART IN THIS?
KYON-KUN, OPEN UP!
KON (KNOCK) KON
I BROUGHT CAKE!
WANT SOME, SHAMI?
I'M GLAD ASAHINA'S CHEERED UP A LITTLE...
NOW WHO CAN I COUNT ON...?

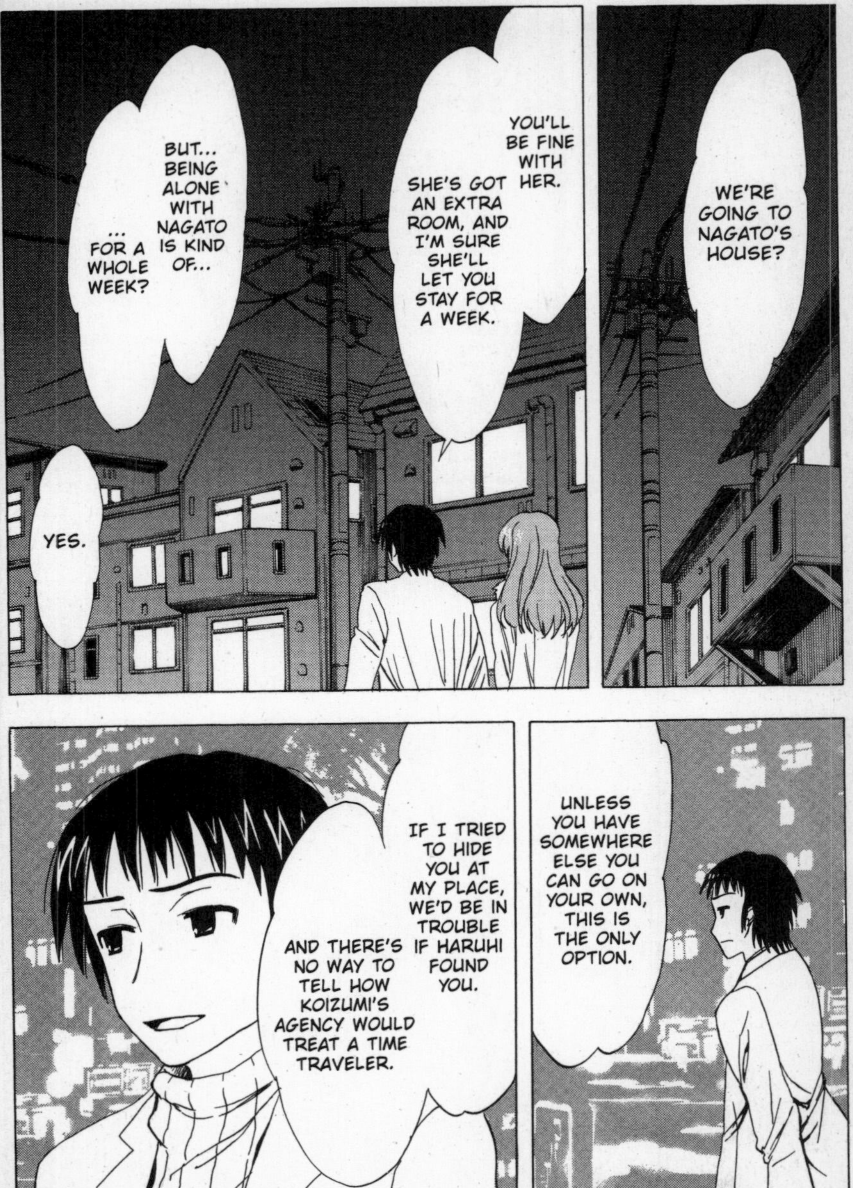
WE'RE GOING TO NAGATO'S HOUSE?
YOU'LL BE FINE WITH HER.
SHE'S GOT AN EXTRA ROOM, AND I'M SURE SHE'LL LET YOU STAY FOR A WEEK.
BUT... BEING ALONE WITH NAGATO IS KIND OF...
... FOR A WHOLE WEEK?
YES.
UNLESS YOU HAVE SOMEWHERE ELSE YOU CAN GO ON YOUR OWN, THIS IS THE ONLY OPTION.
IF I TRIED TO HIDE YOU AT MY PLACE, WE'D BE IN TROUBLE IF HARUHI FOUND YOU.
AND THERE'S NO WAY TO TELL HOW KOIZUMI'S AGENCY WOULD TREAT A TIME TRAVELER.

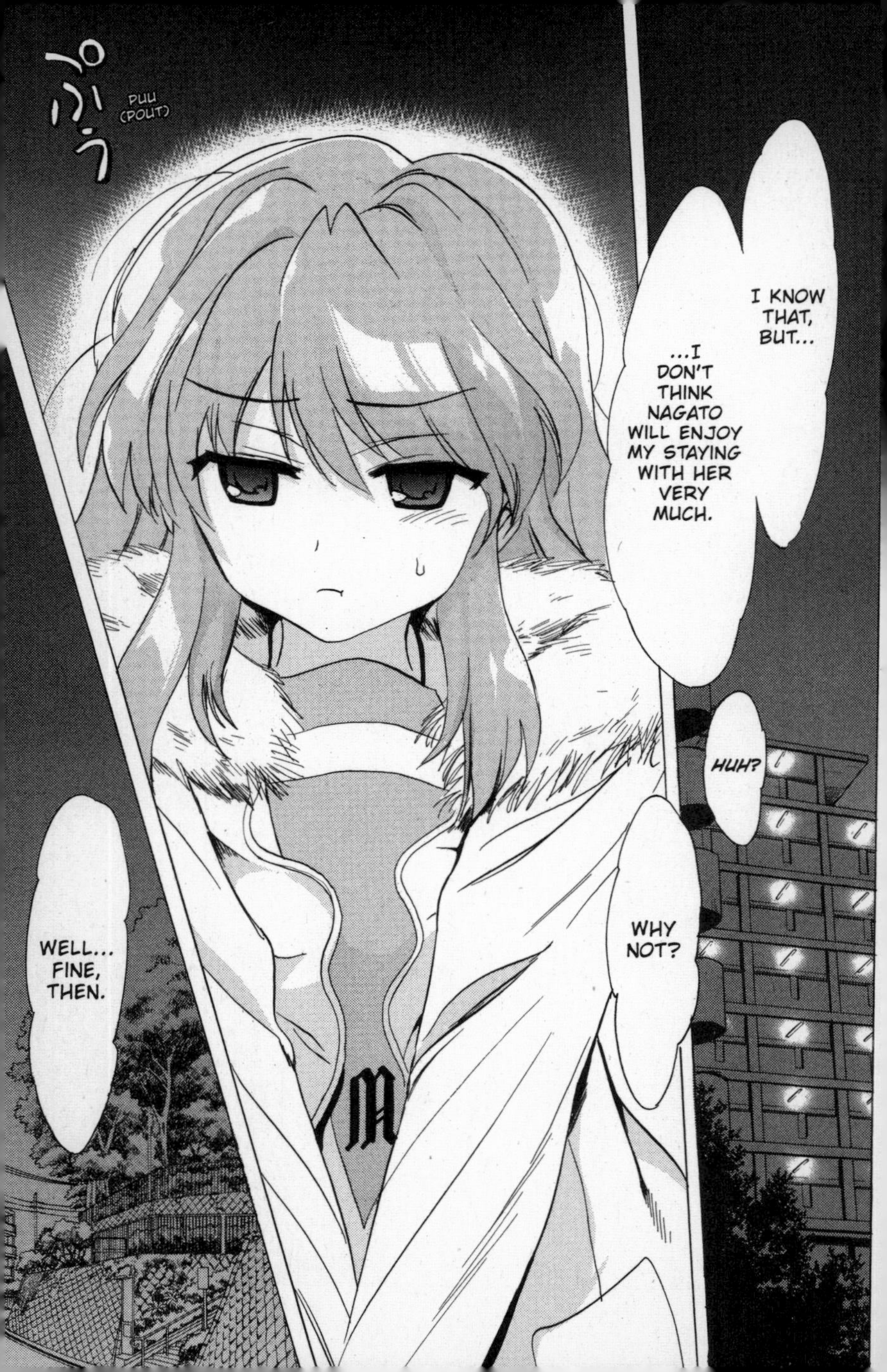
I KNOW THAT, BUT...
...I DON'T THINK NAGATO WILL ENJOY MY STAYING WITH HER VERY MUCH.
HUH?
WHY NOT?
ぷぅ
PUU (POUT)
WELL... FINE, THEN.

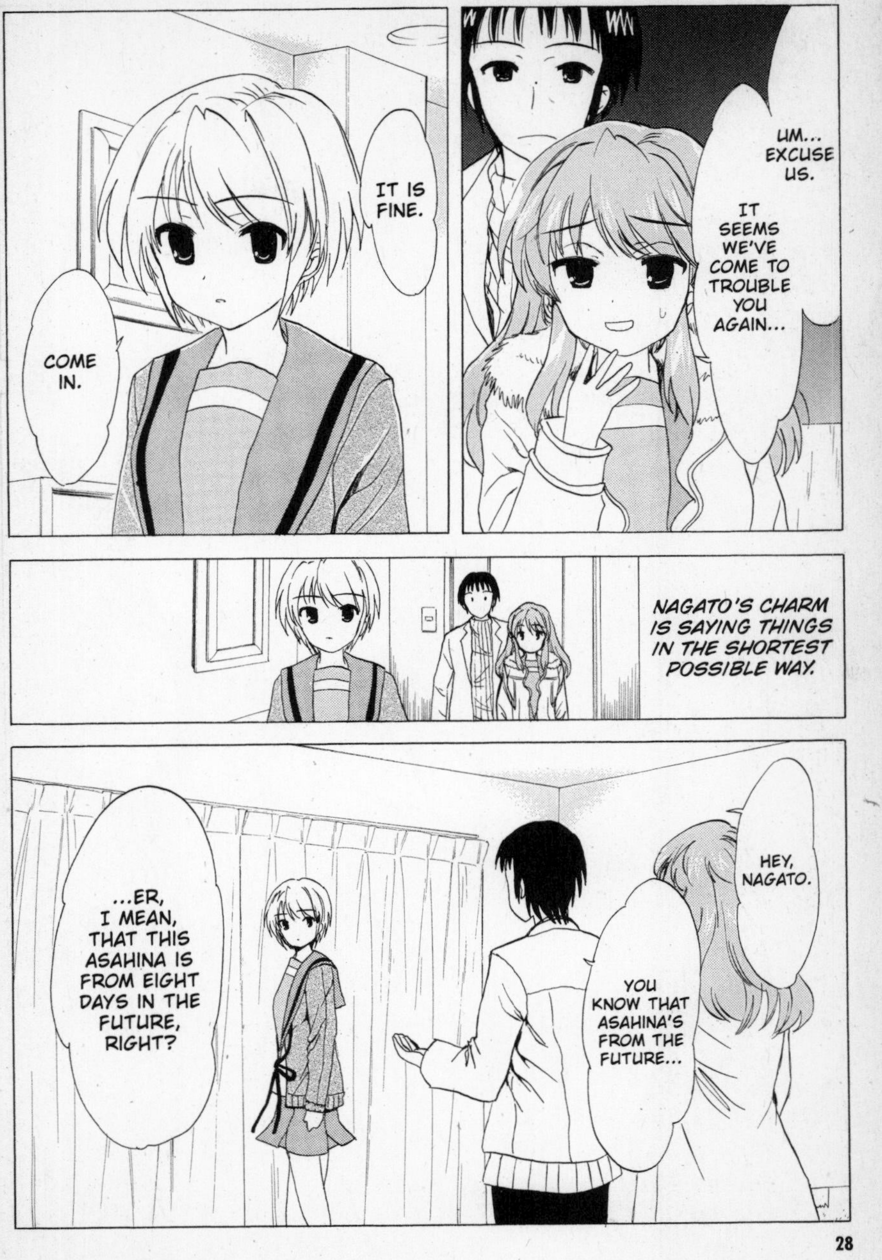
UM... EXCUSE US.
IT SEEMS WE'VE COME TO TROUBLE YOU AGAIN...
IT IS FINE.
COME IN.
NAGATO'S CHARM IS SAYING THINGS IN THE SHORTEST POSSIBLE WAY.
HEY, NAGATO.
YOU KNOW THAT ASAHINA'S FROM THE FUTURE...
...ER, I MEAN, THAT THIS ASAHINA IS FROM EIGHT DAYS IN THE FUTURE, RIGHT?

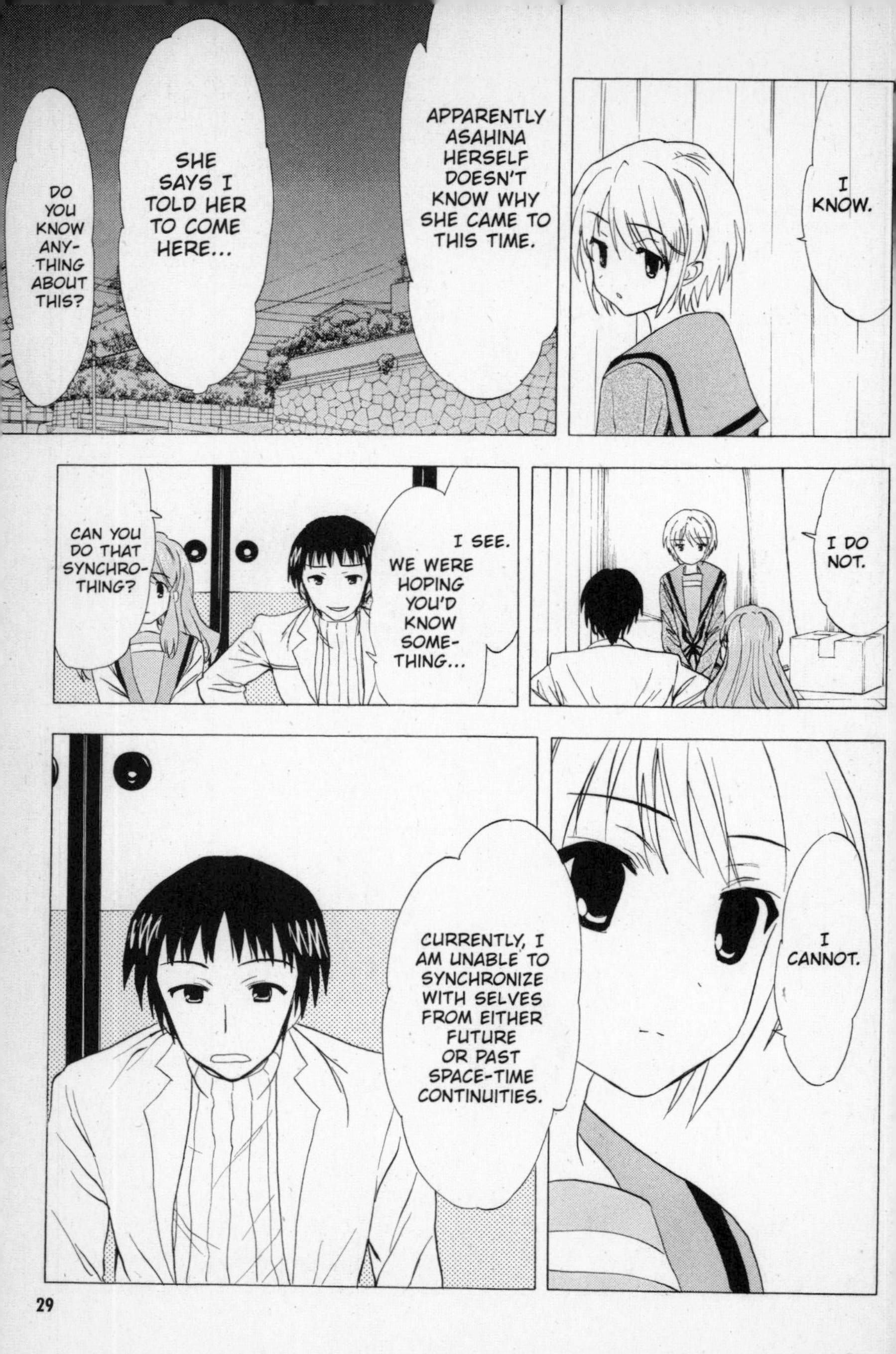
I KNOW.
APPARENTLY ASAHINA HERSELF DOESN'T KNOW WHY SHE CAME TO THIS TIME.
SHE SAYS I TOLD HER TO COME HERE...
DO YOU KNOW ANY-THING ABOUT THIS?
I DO NOT.
I SEE. WE WERE HOPING YOU'D KNOW SOME-THING...
CAN YOU DO THAT SYNCHRO-THING?
I CANNOT.
CURRENTLY, I AM UNABLE TO SYNCHRONIZE WITH SELVES FROM EITHER FUTURE OR PAST SPACE-TIME CONTINUITIES.

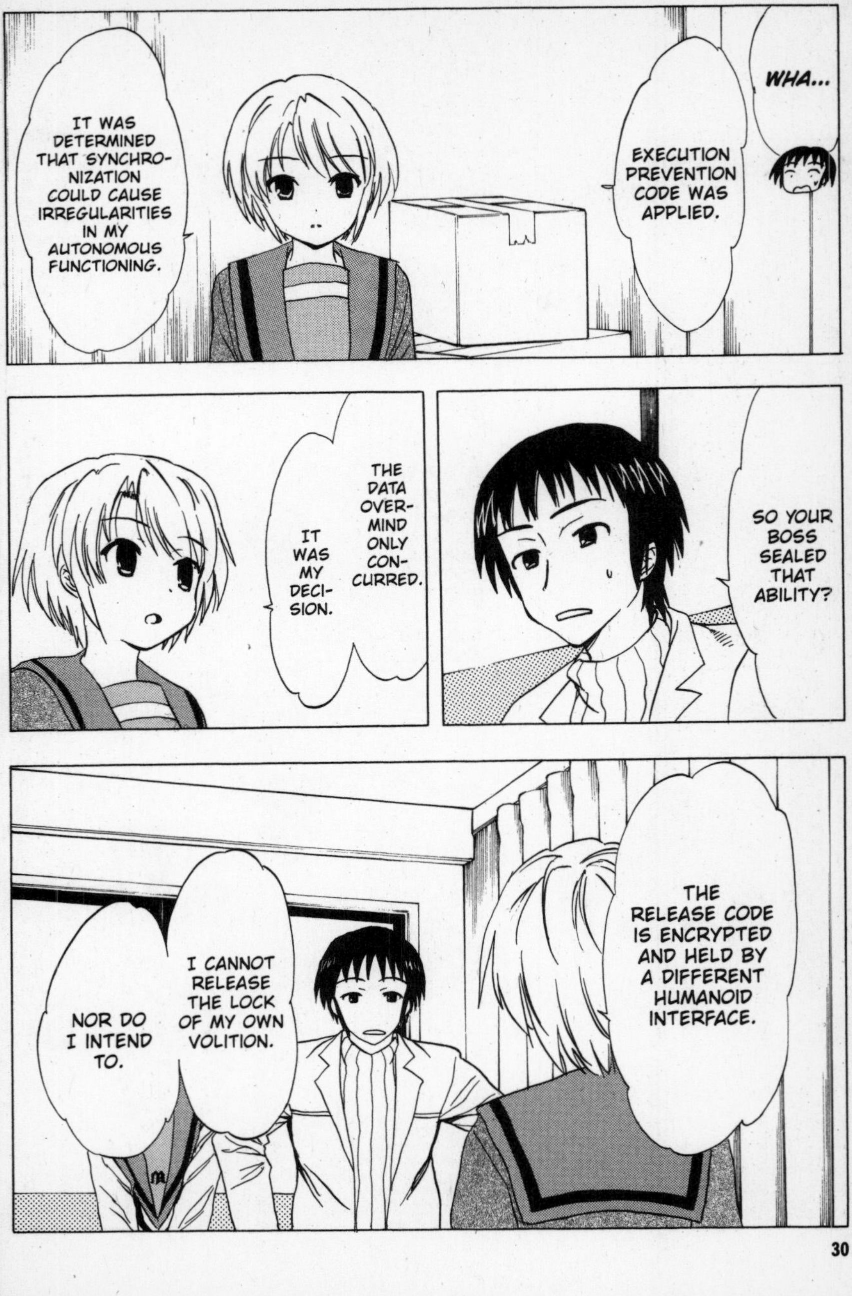
WHA...
EXECUTION PREVENTION CODE WAS APPLIED.
IT WAS DETERMINED THAT SYNCHRONIZATION COULD CAUSE IRREGULARITIES IN MY AUTONOMOUS FUNCTIONING.
SO YOUR BOSS SEALED THAT ABILITY?
THE DATA OVERMIND ONLY CONCURRED.
IT WAS MY DECISION.
THE RELEASE CODE IS ENCRYPTED AND HELD BY A DIFFERENT HUMANOID INTERFACE.
I CANNOT RELEASE THE LOCK OF MY OWN VOLITION.
NOR DO I INTEND TO.

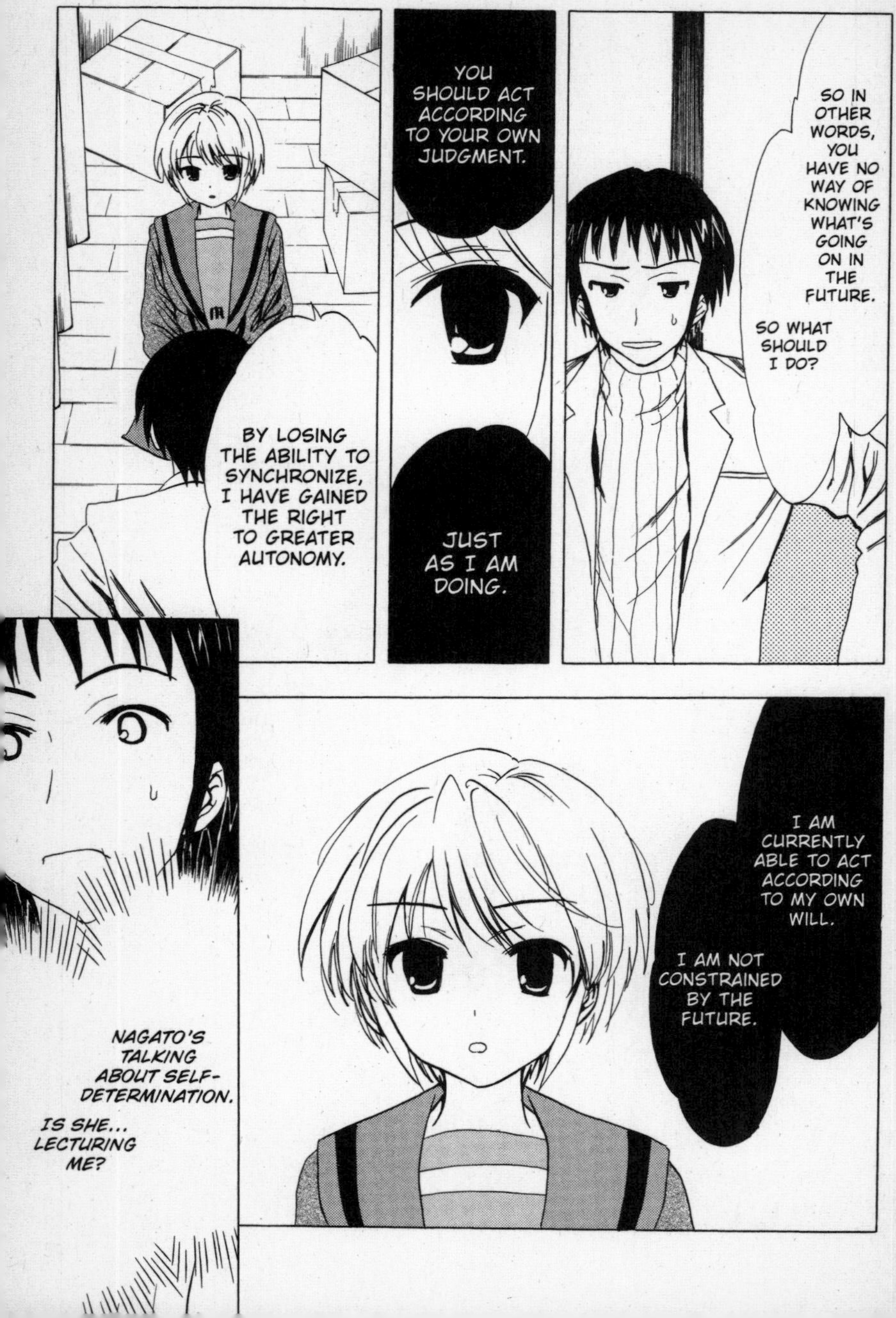
SO IN OTHER WORDS, YOU HAVE NO WAY OF KNOWING WHAT'S GOING ON IN THE FUTURE.
SO WHAT SHOULD I DO?
YOU SHOULD ACT ACCORDING TO YOUR OWN JUDGMENT.
JUST AS I AM DOING.
BY LOSING THE ABILITY TO SYNCHRONIZE, I HAVE GAINED THE RIGHT TO GREATER AUTONOMY.
I AM CURRENTLY ABLE TO ACT ACCORDING TO MY OWN WILL.
I AM NOT CONSTRAINED BY THE FUTURE.
NAGATO'S TALKING ABOUT SELF-DETERMINATION.
IS SHE... LECTURING ME?

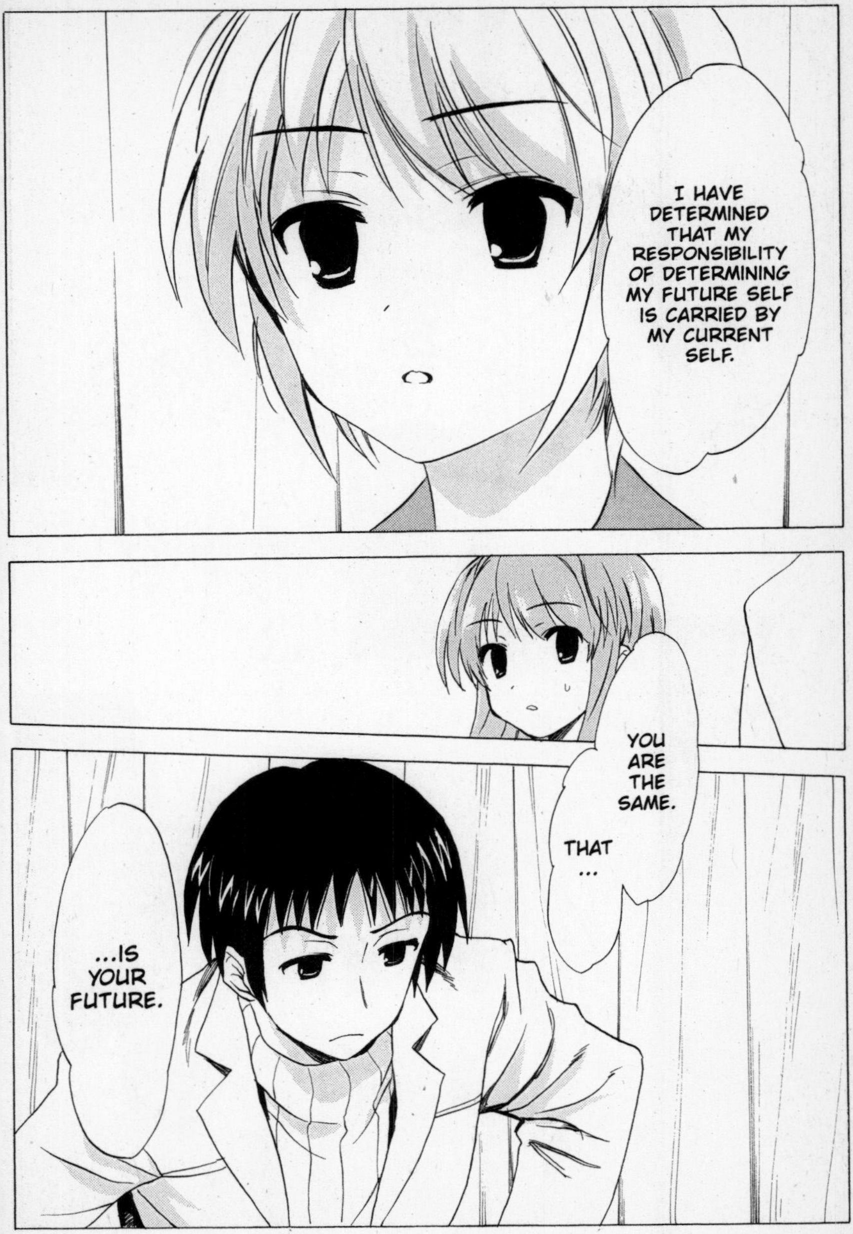
I HAVE DETERMINED THAT MY RESPONSIBILITY OF DETERMINING MY FUTURE SELF IS CARRIED BY MY CURRENT SELF.
YOU ARE THE SAME.
THAT ...
...IS YOUR FUTURE.

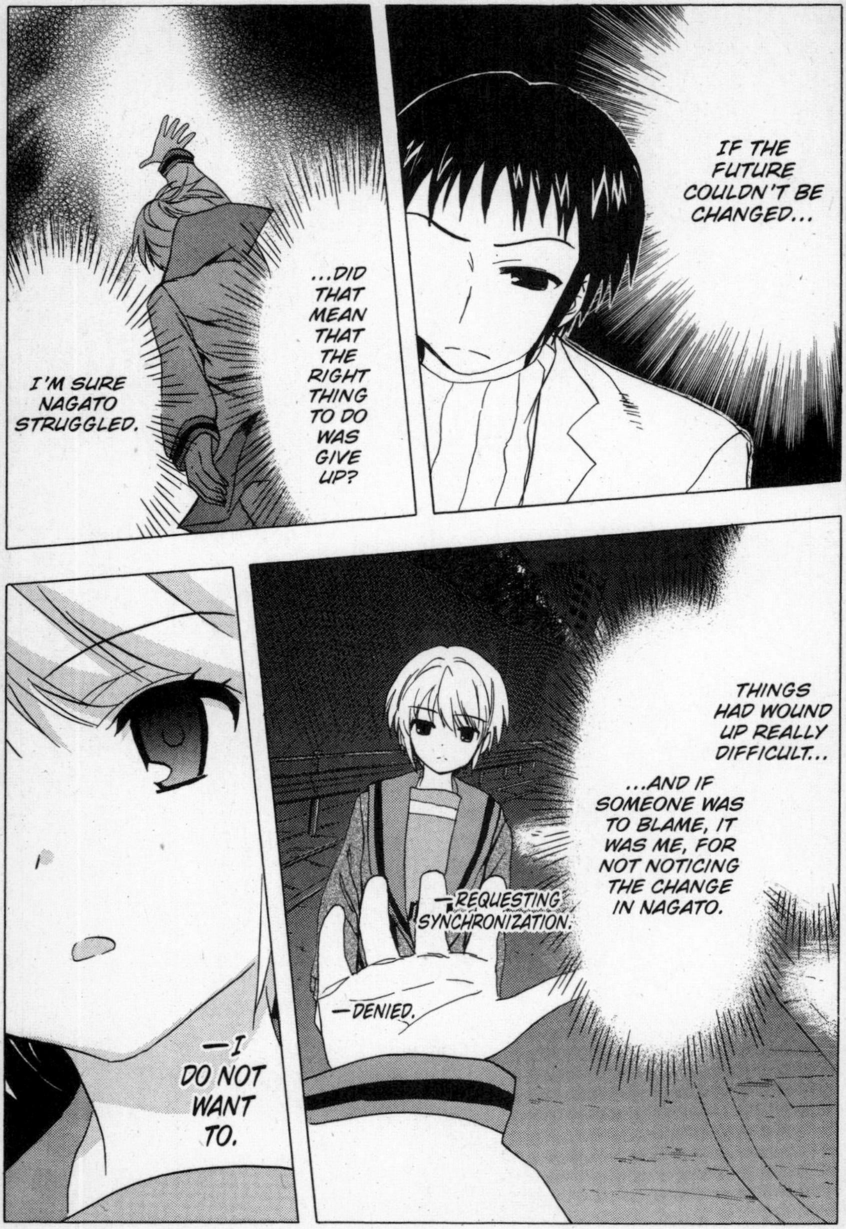
IF THE FUTURE COULDN'T BE CHANGED...
...DID THAT MEAN THAT THE RIGHT THING TO DO WAS GIVE UP?
I'M SURE NAGATO STRUGGLED.
THINGS HAD WOUND UP REALLY DIFFICULT...
...AND IF SOMEONE WAS TO BLAME, IT WAS ME, FOR NOT NOTICING THE CHANGE IN NAGATO.
—REQUESTING SYNCHRONIZATION.
—DENIED.
—I DO NOT WANT TO.

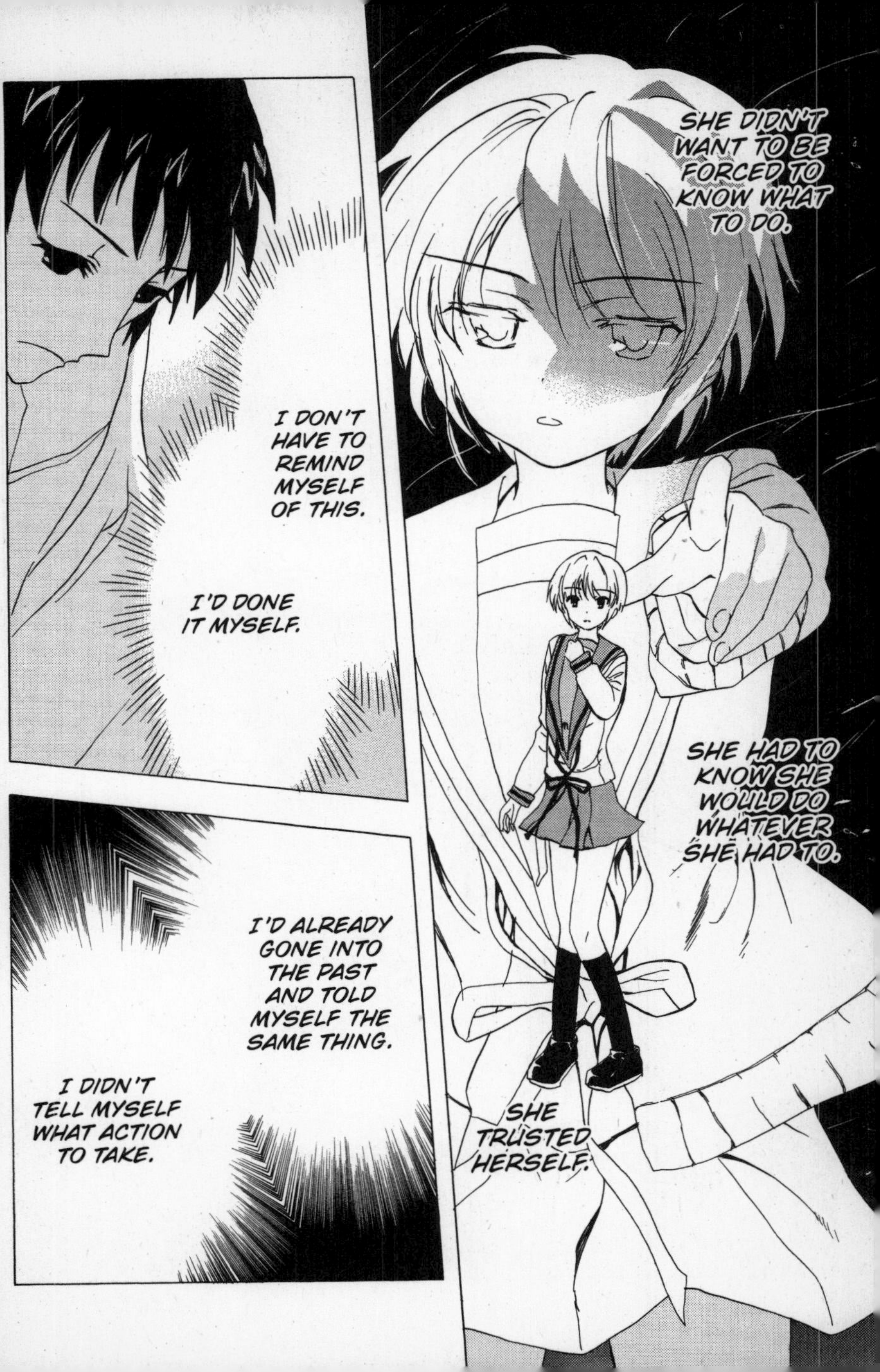
SHE DIDN'T WANT TO BE FORCED TO KNOW WHAT TO DO.
SHE HAD TO KNOW SHE WOULD DO WHATEVER SHE HAD TO.
SHE TRUSTED HERSELF.
I DON'T HAVE TO REMIND MYSELF OF THIS.
I'D DONE IT MYSELF.
I'D ALREADY GONE INTO THE PAST AND TOLD MYSELF THE SAME THING.
I DIDN'T TELL MYSELF WHAT ACTION TO TAKE.

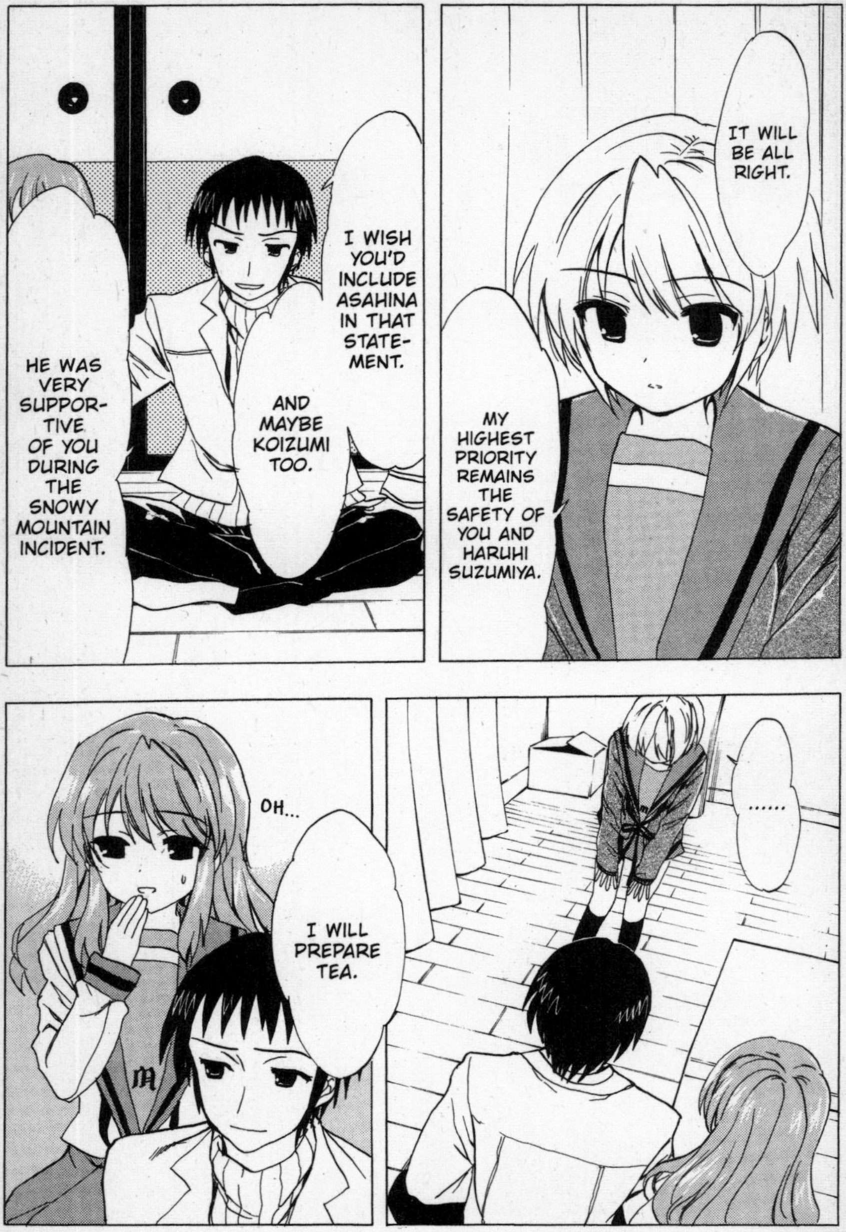
IT WILL BE ALL RIGHT.
MY HIGHEST PRIORITY REMAINS THE SAFETY OF YOU AND HARUHI SUZUMIYA.
I WISH YOU'D INCLUDE ASAHINA IN THAT STATE-MENT.
AND MAYBE KOIZUMI TOO.
HE WAS VERY SUPPOR-TIVE OF YOU DURING THE SNOWY MOUNTAIN INCIDENT.
......
OH...
I WILL PREPARE TEA.

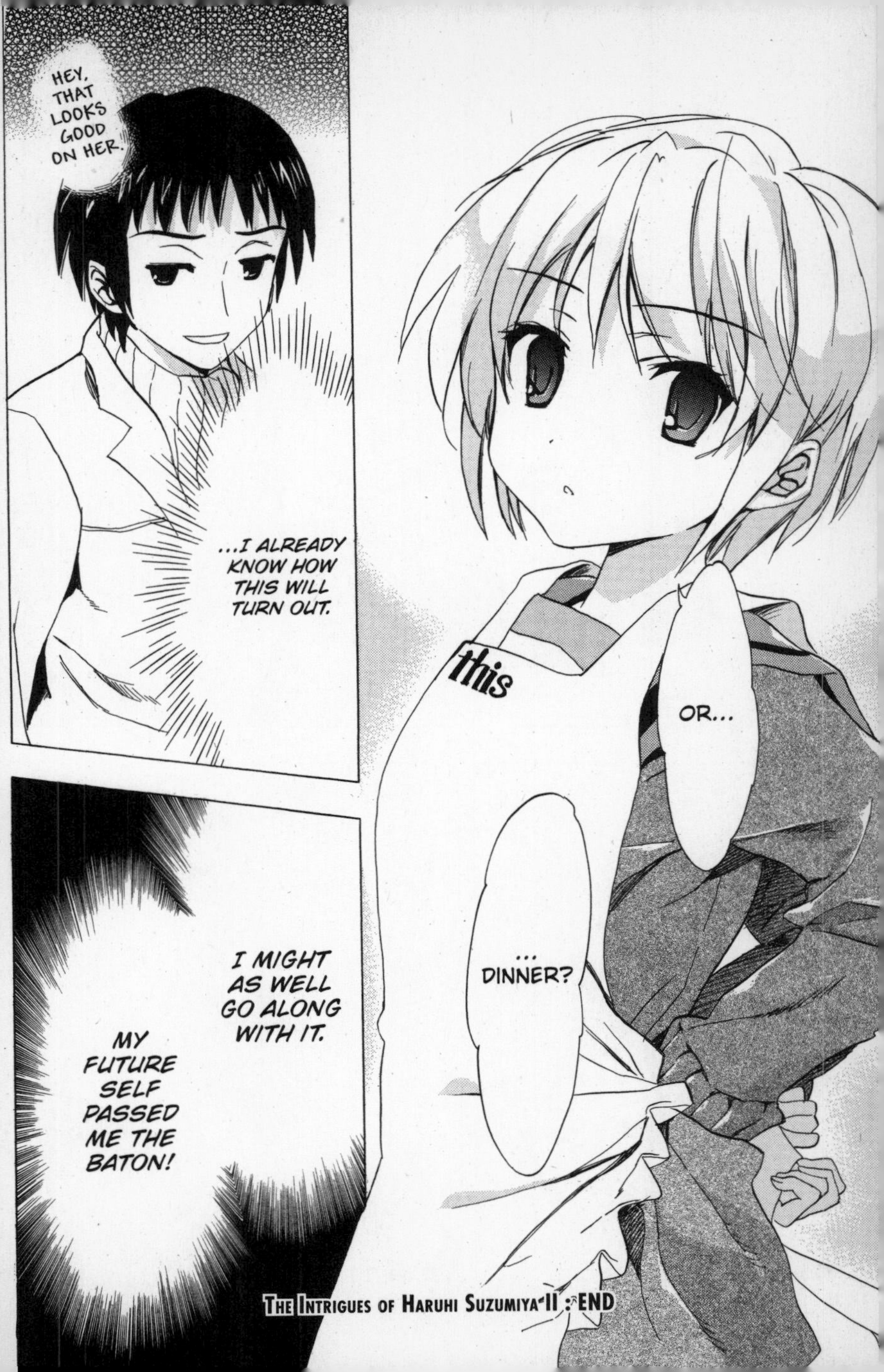
this
OR...
... DINNER?
HEY, THAT LOOKS GOOD ON HER.
...I ALREADY KNOW HOW THIS WILL TURN OUT.
I MIGHT AS WELL GO ALONG WITH IT.
MY FUTURE SELF PASSED ME THE BATON!
THE INTRIGUES OF HARUHI SUZUMIYA II : END

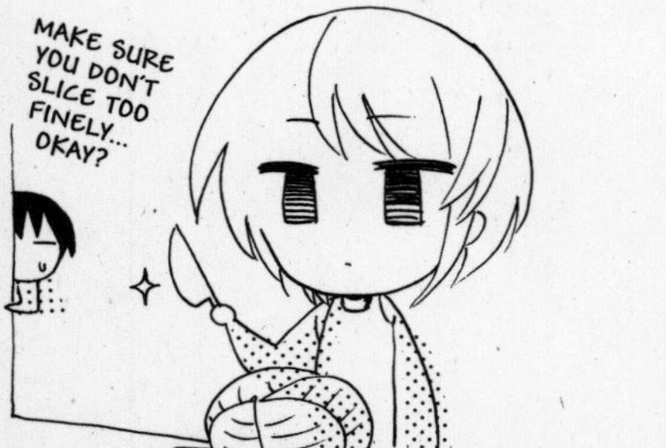
MAKE SURE YOU DON'T SLICE TOO FINELY... OKAY?

THE MELANCHOLY OF HARUHI SUZUMIYA

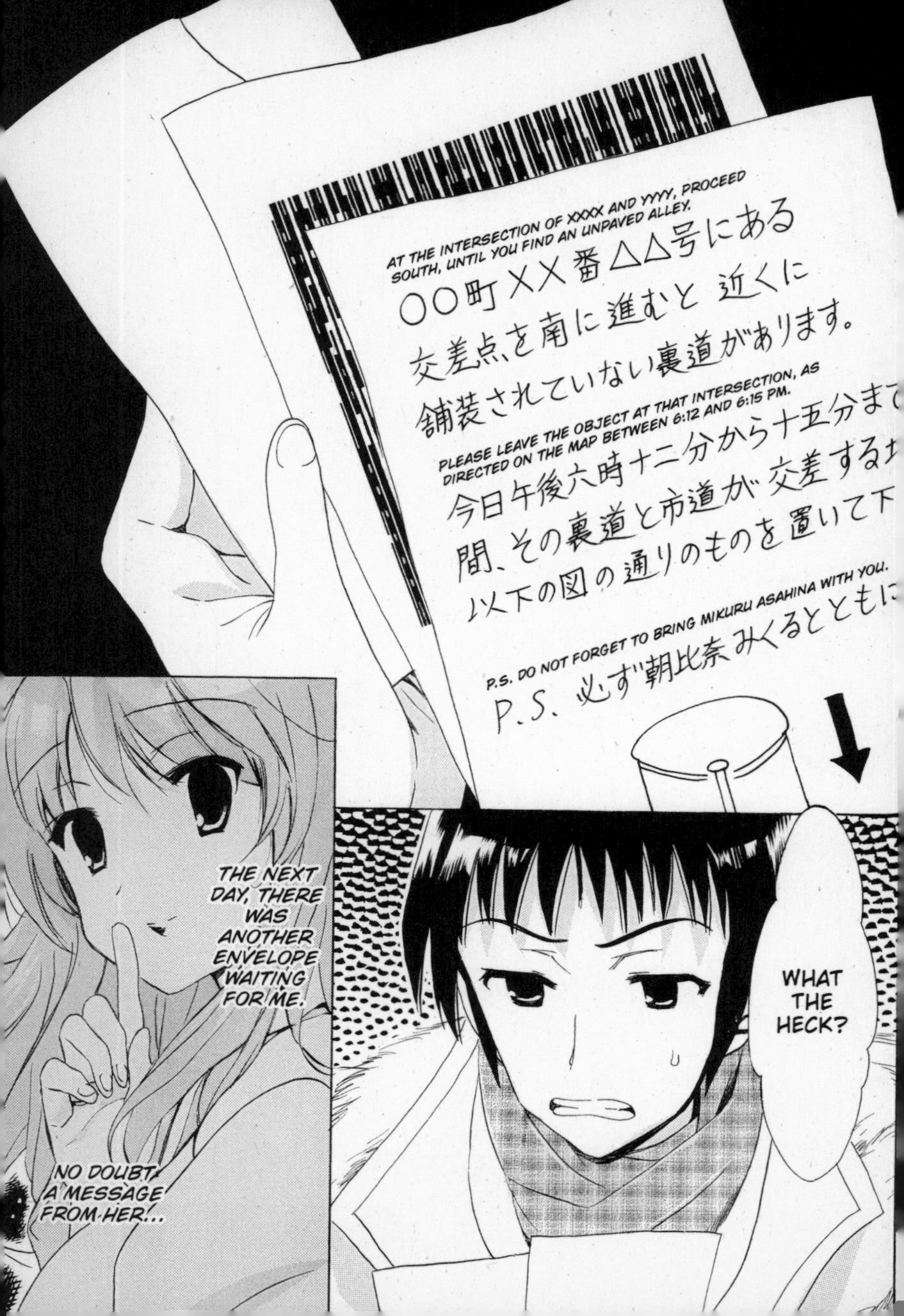
AT THE INTERSECTION OF XXXX AND YYYY, PROCEED SOUTH, UNTIL YOU FIND AN UNPAVED ALLEY.
〇〇町××番△△号にある
交差点を南に進むと近くに
舗装されていない裏道があります。
PLEASE LEAVE THE OBJECT AT THAT INTERSECTION, AS DIRECTED ON THE MAP BETWEEN 6:12 AND 6:15 PM.
今日午後六時十二分から十五分まで
間、その裏道と市道が交差する
以下の図の通りのものを置いて下
P.S. DO NOT FORGET TO BRING MIKURU ASAHINA WITH YOU.
P.S. 必ず朝比奈みくるとともに
WHAT THE HECK?
THE NEXT DAY, THERE WAS ANOTHER ENVELOPE WAITING FOR ME.
NO DOUBT A MESSAGE FROM HER...

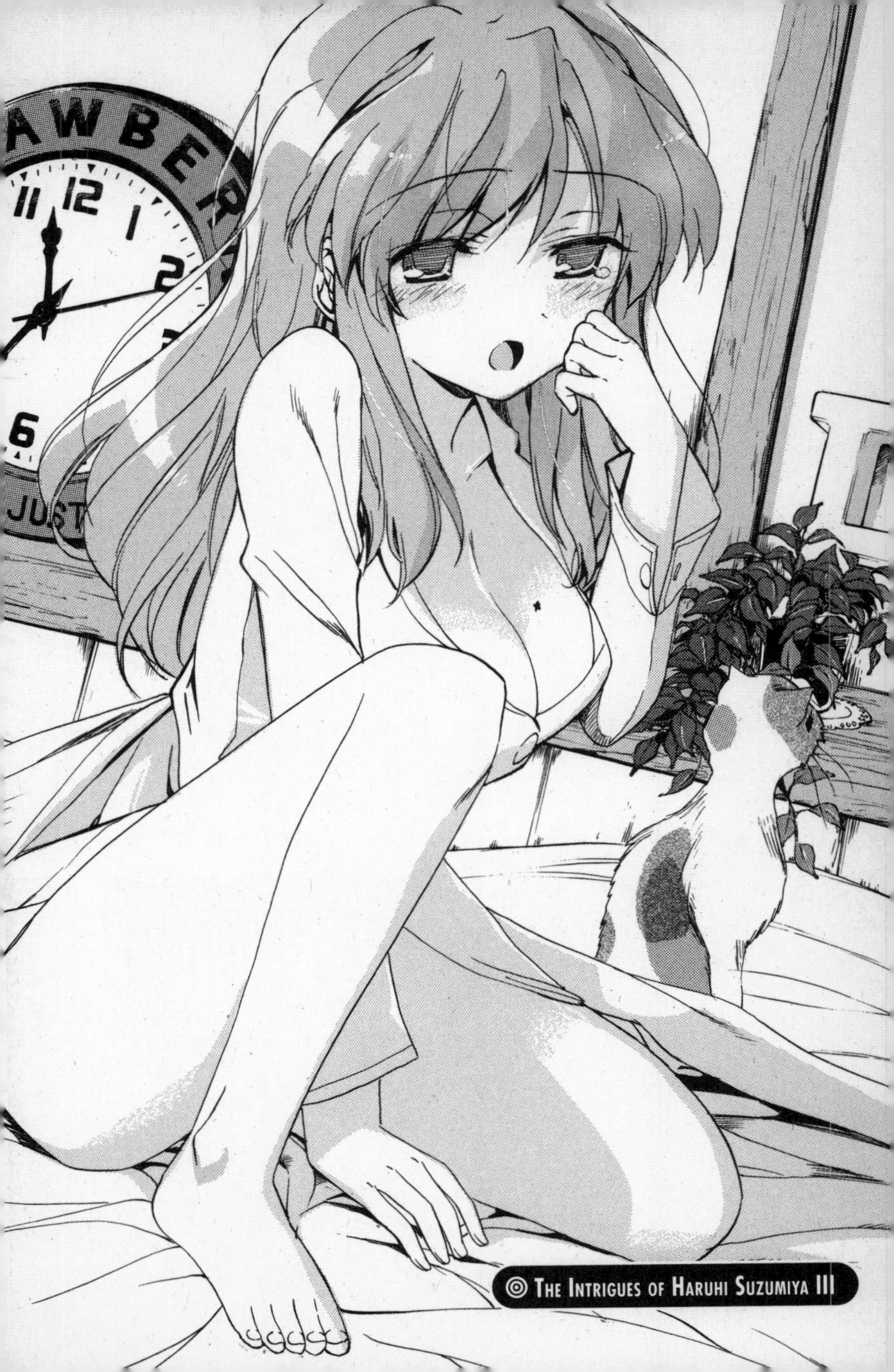
THE INTRIGUES OF HARUHI SUZUMIYA III

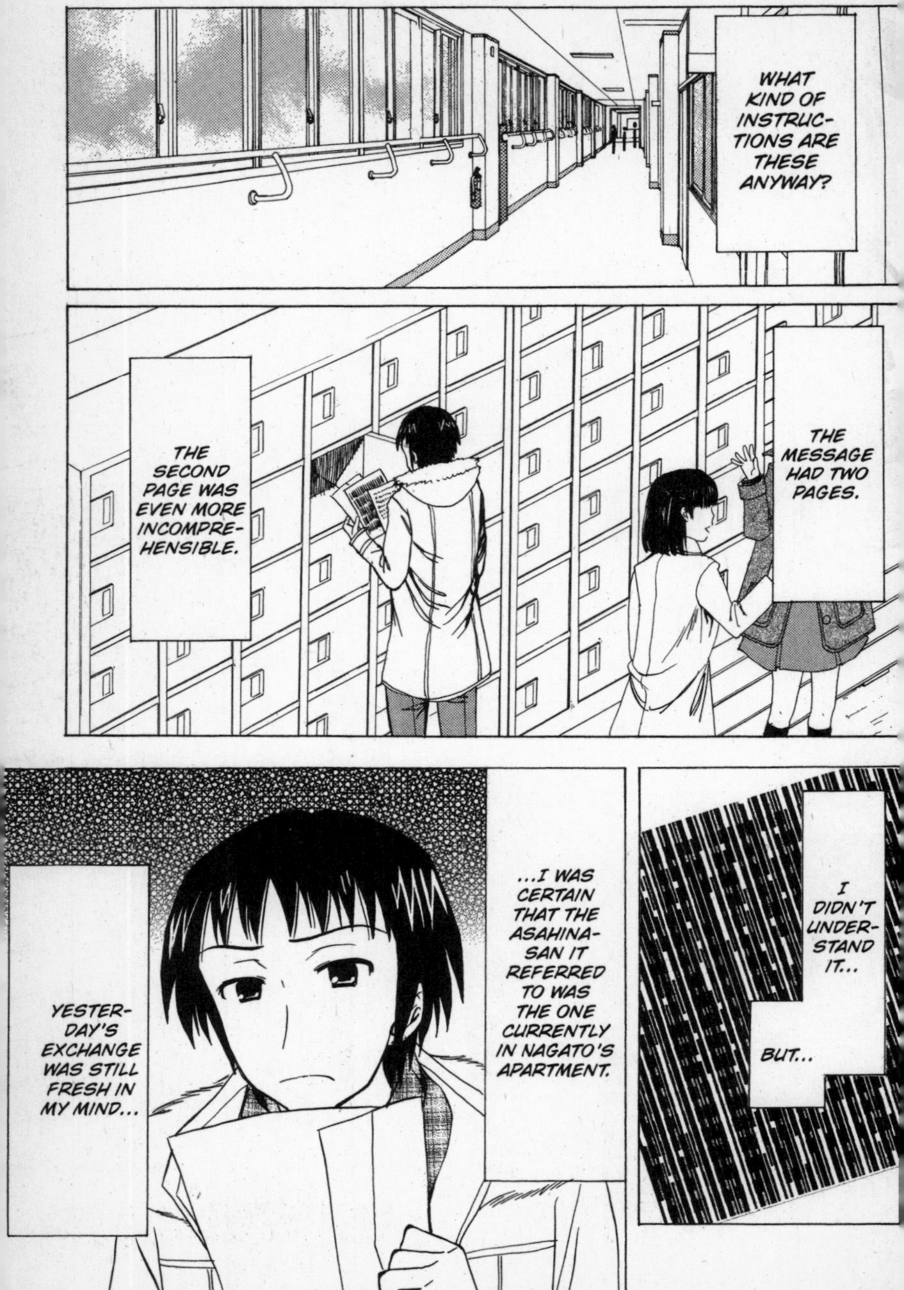
WHAT KIND OF INSTRUCTIONS ARE THESE ANYWAY?
THE MESSAGE HAD TWO PAGES.
THE SECOND PAGE WAS EVEN MORE INCOMPREHENSIBLE.
I DIDN'T UNDERSTAND IT...
BUT...
...I WAS CERTAIN THAT THE ASAHINA-SAN IT REFERRED TO WAS THE ONE CURRENTLY IN NAGATO'S APARTMENT.
YESTERDAY'S EXCHANGE WAS STILL FRESH IN MY MIND...

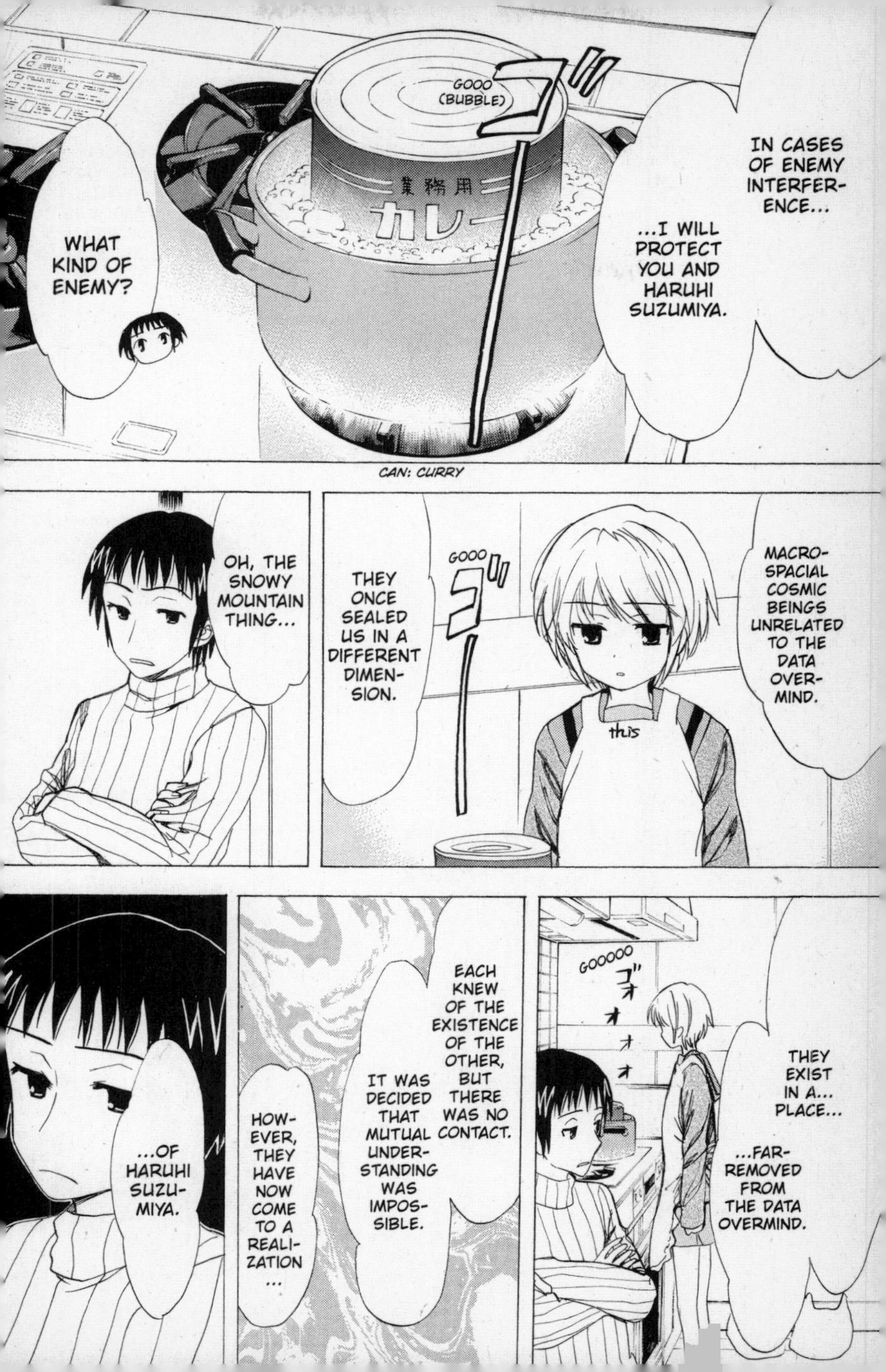
IN CASES OF ENEMY INTERFERENCE...
...I WILL PROTECT YOU AND HARUHI SUZUMIYA.
GOOO (BUBBLE)
WHAT KIND OF ENEMY?
CAN: CURRY
MACRO-SPACIAL COSMIC BEINGS UNRELATED TO THE DATA OVERMIND.
this
GOOO
THEY ONCE SEALED US IN A DIFFERENT DIMENSION.
OH, THE SNOWY MOUNTAIN THING...
THEY EXIST IN A... PLACE...
...FAR-REMOVED FROM THE DATA OVERMIND.
GOOOOO
EACH KNEW OF THE EXISTENCE OF THE OTHER, BUT THERE WAS NO CONTACT.
IT WAS DECIDED THAT MUTUAL UNDERSTANDING WAS IMPOSSIBLE.
HOWEVER, THEY HAVE NOW COME TO A REALIZATION...
...OF HARUHI SUZUMIYA.

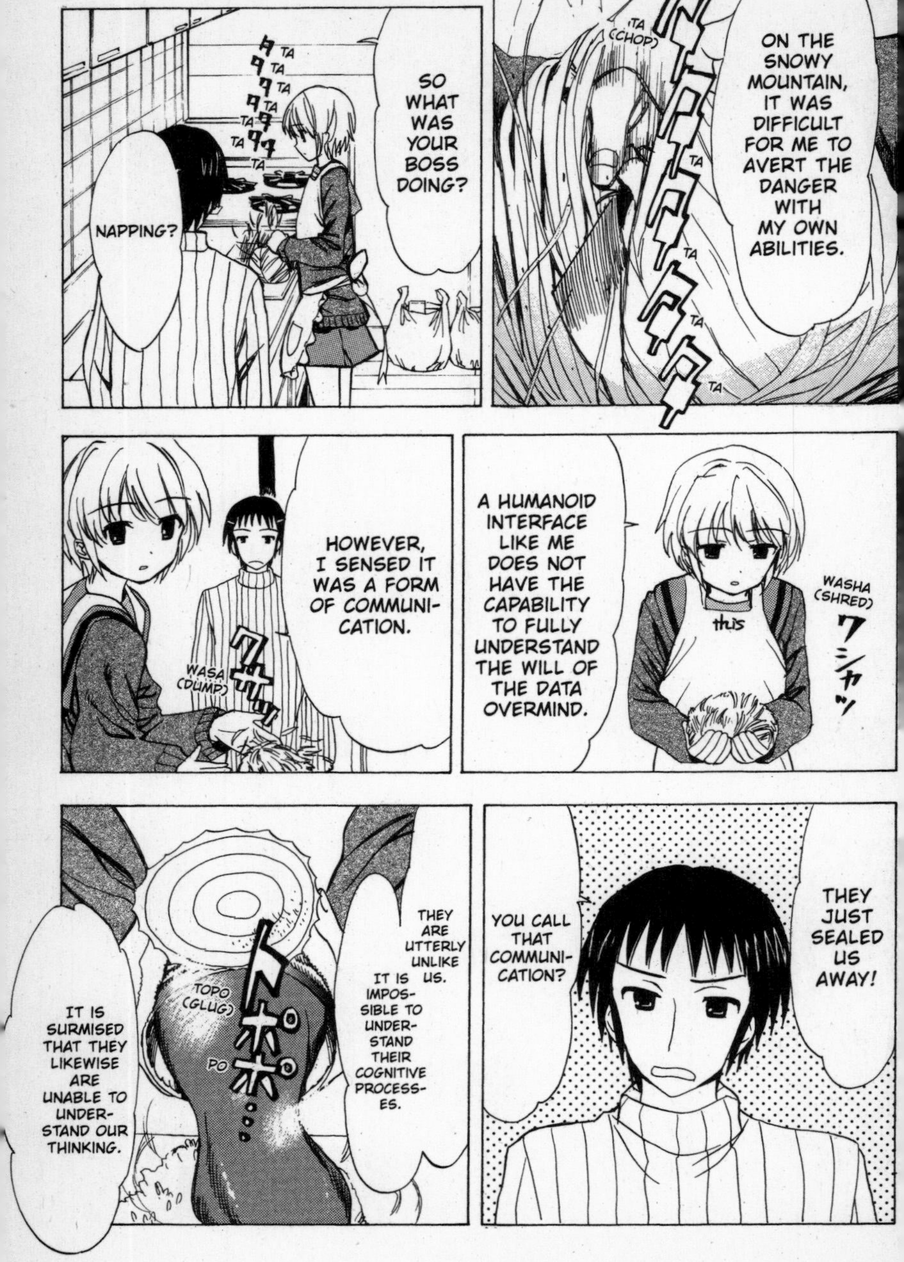
ON THE SNOWY MOUNTAIN, IT WAS DIFFICULT FOR ME TO AVERT THE DANGER WITH MY OWN ABILITIES.
TA (CHOP)
TA
TA
TA
TA
SO WHAT WAS YOUR BOSS DOING?
TA TA TA TA TA TA TA
NAPPING?
A HUMANOID INTERFACE LIKE ME DOES NOT HAVE THE CAPABILITY TO FULLY UNDERSTAND THE WILL OF THE DATA OVERMIND.
WASHA (SHRED)
HOWEVER, I SENSED IT WAS A FORM OF COMMUNICATION.
WASA (DUMP)
THEY JUST SEALED US AWAY!
YOU CALL THAT COMMUNICATION?
THEY ARE UTTERLY UNLIKE US.
IT IS IMPOSSIBLE TO UNDERSTAND THEIR COGNITIVE PROCESSES.
TOPO (GLUG)
PO
IT IS SURMISED THAT THEY LIKEWISE ARE UNABLE TO UNDERSTAND OUR THINKING.

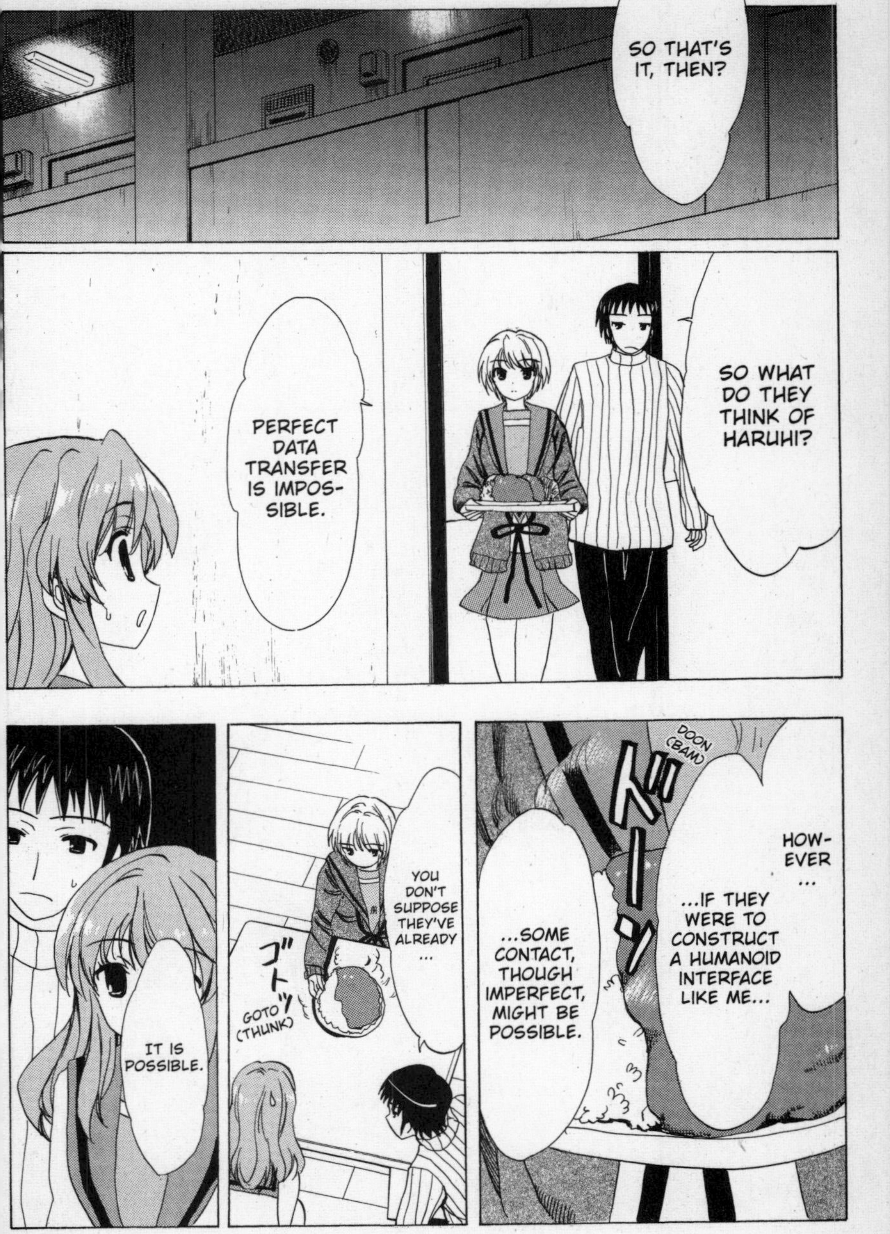
SO THAT'S IT, THEN?
SO WHAT DO THEY THINK OF HARUHI?
PERFECT DATA TRANSFER IS IMPOSSIBLE.
DOON (BAM)
ドーン
HOW-EVER...
...IF THEY WERE TO CONSTRUCT A HUMANOID INTERFACE LIKE ME...
...SOME CONTACT, THOUGH IMPERFECT, MIGHT BE POSSIBLE.
YOU DON'T SUPPOSE THEY'VE ALREADY...
ゴトッ
GOTO (THUNK)
IT IS POSSIBLE.

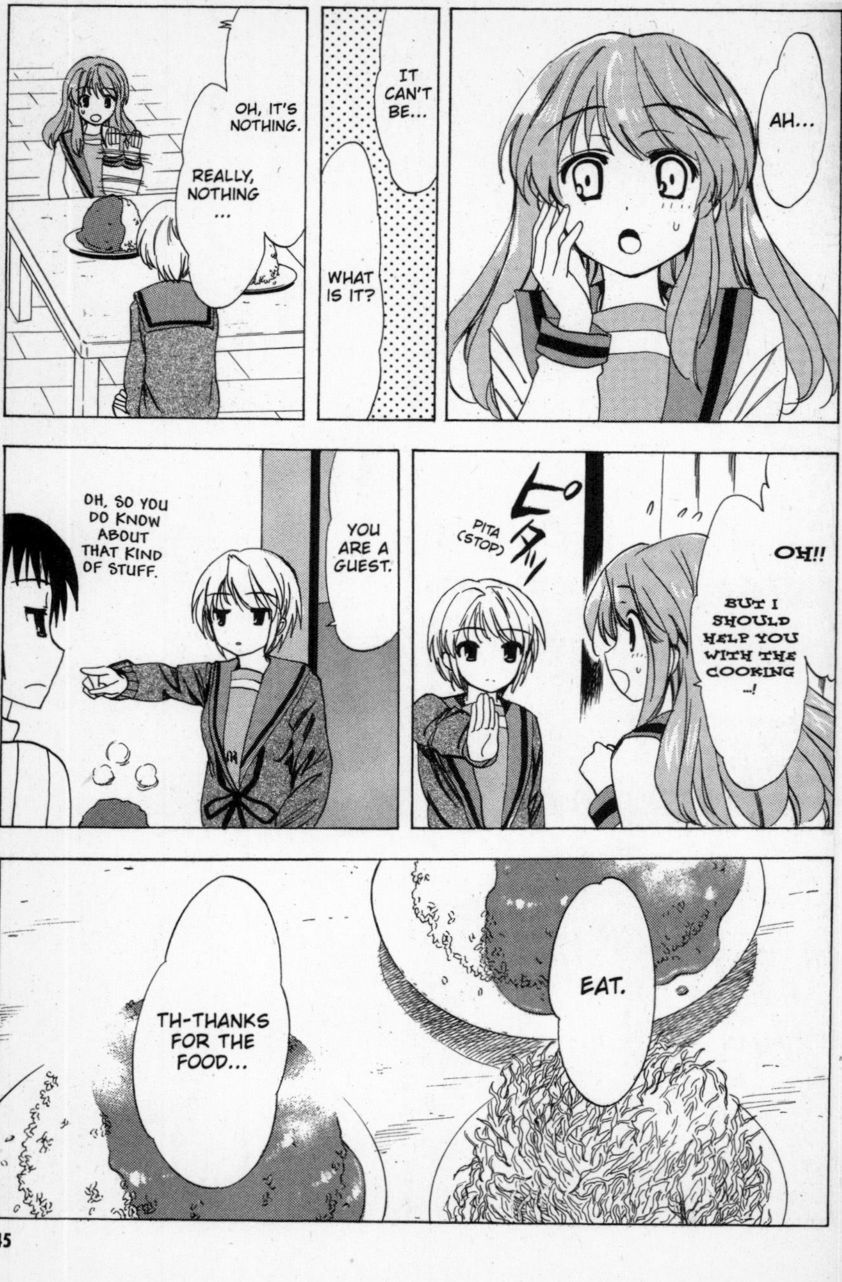
AH...
IT CAN'T BE...
WHAT IS IT?
OH, IT'S NOTHING.
REALLY, NOTHING ...
OH!!
BUT I SHOULD HELP YOU WITH THE COOKING ...!
PITA (STOP)
YOU ARE A GUEST.
OH, SO YOU DO KNOW ABOUT THAT KIND OF STUFF.
EAT.
TH-THANKS FOR THE FOOD...

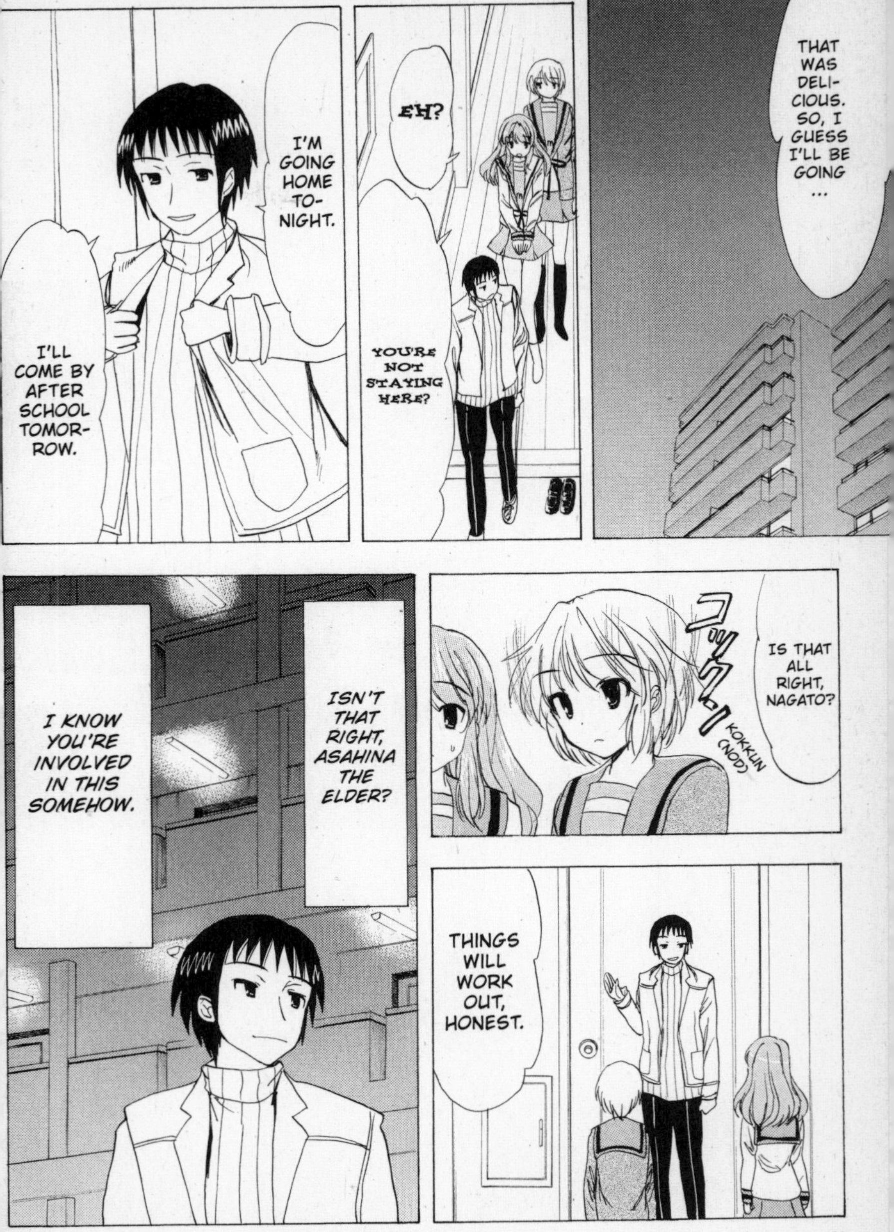
THAT WAS DELI-CIOUS. SO, I GUESS I'LL BE GOING ...
EH?
YOU'RE NOT STAYING HERE?
I'M GOING HOME TO-NIGHT.
I'LL COME BY AFTER SCHOOL TOMOR-ROW.
IS THAT ALL RIGHT, NAGATO?
KOKKUN (NOD)
THINGS WILL WORK OUT, HONEST.
ISN'T THAT RIGHT, ASAHINA THE ELDER?
I KNOW YOU'RE INVOLVED IN THIS SOMEHOW.

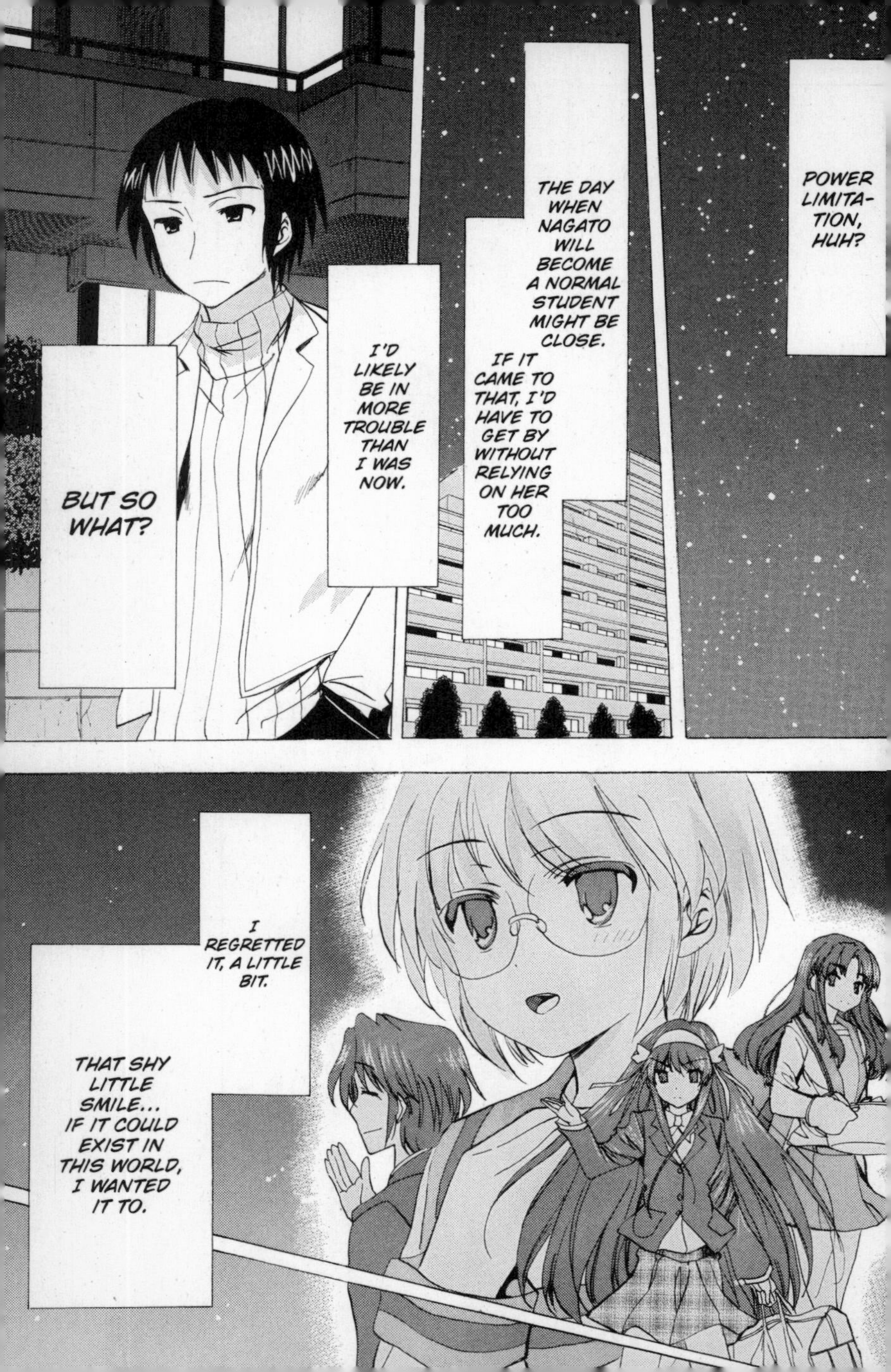
POWER LIMITATION, HUH?
THE DAY WHEN NAGATO WILL BECOME A NORMAL STUDENT MIGHT BE CLOSE.
IF IT CAME TO THAT, I'D HAVE TO GET BY WITHOUT RELYING ON HER TOO MUCH.
I'D LIKELY BE IN MORE TROUBLE THAN I WAS NOW.
BUT SO WHAT?
I REGRETTED IT, A LITTLE BIT.
THAT SHY LITTLE SMILE... IF IT COULD EXIST IN THIS WORLD, I WANTED IT TO.

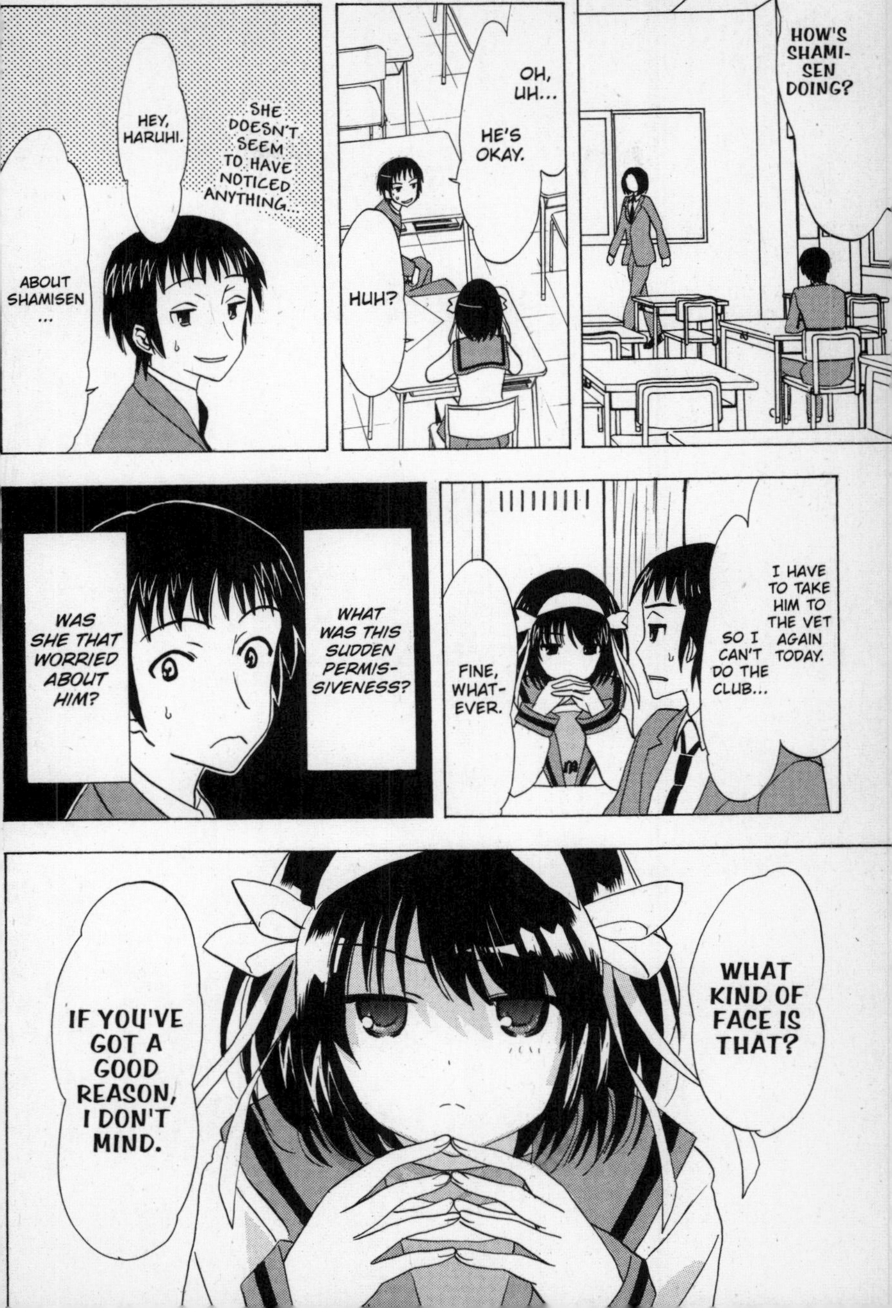
HOW'S SHAMISEN DOING?
OH, UH...
HE'S OKAY.
HUH?
SHE DOESN'T SEEM TO HAVE NOTICED ANYTHING...
HEY, HARUHI.
ABOUT SHAMISEN ...
I HAVE TO TAKE HIM TO THE VET AGAIN TODAY.
SO I CAN'T DO THE CLUB...
FINE, WHATEVER.
WHAT WAS THIS SUDDEN PERMISSIVENESS?
WAS SHE THAT WORRIED ABOUT HIM?
WHAT KIND OF FACE IS THAT?
IF YOU'VE GOT A GOOD REASON, I DON'T MIND.

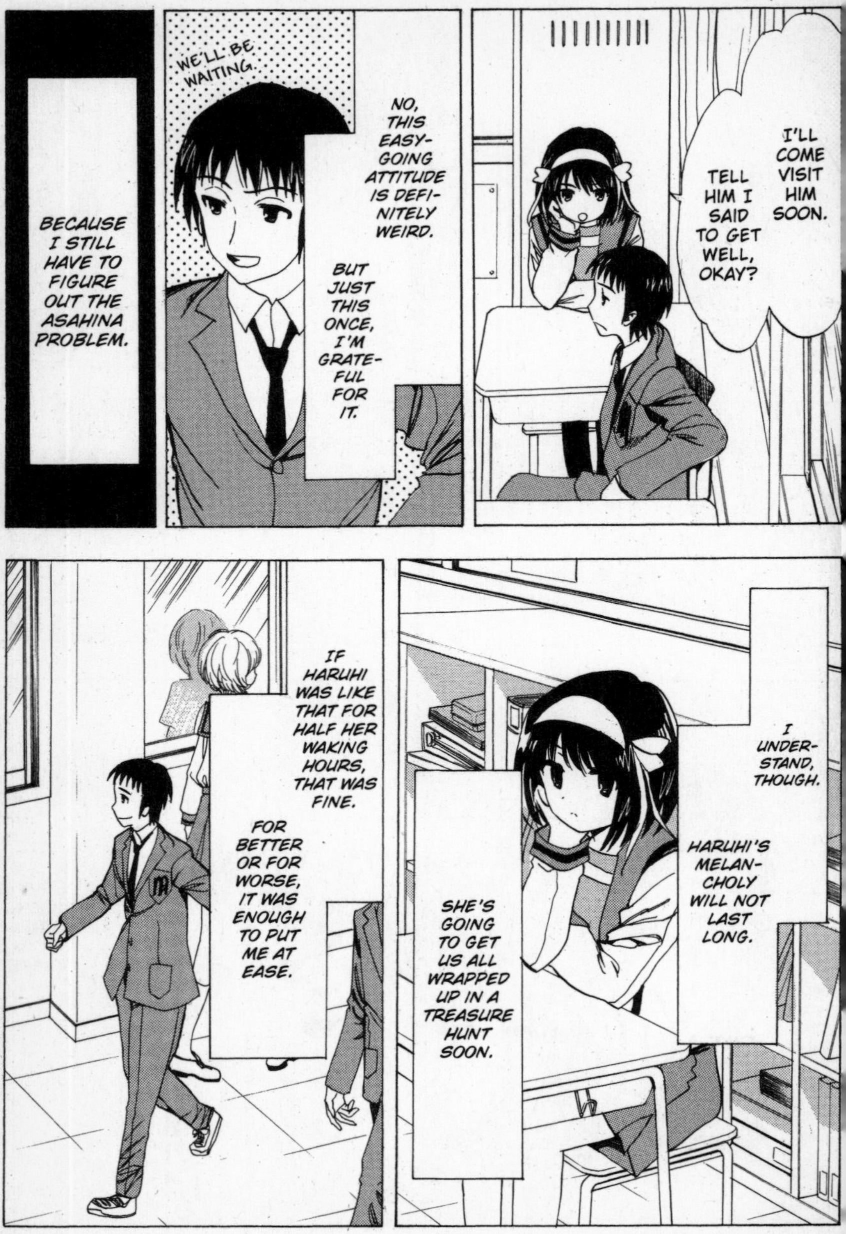

I'LL COME VISIT HIM SOON.
TELL HIM I SAID TO GET WELL, OKAY?
WE'LL BE WAITING.
NO, THIS EASY-GOING ATTITUDE IS DEFINITELY WEIRD.
BUT JUST THIS ONCE, I'M GRATEFUL FOR IT.
BECAUSE I STILL HAVE TO FIGURE OUT THE ASAHINA PROBLEM.
I UNDERSTAND, THOUGH.
HARUHI'S MELANCHOLY WILL NOT LAST LONG.
SHE'S GOING TO GET US ALL WRAPPED UP IN A TREASURE HUNT SOON.
IF HARUHI WAS LIKE THAT FOR HALF HER WAKING HOURS, THAT WAS FINE.
FOR BETTER OR FOR WORSE, IT WAS ENOUGH TO PUT ME AT EASE.

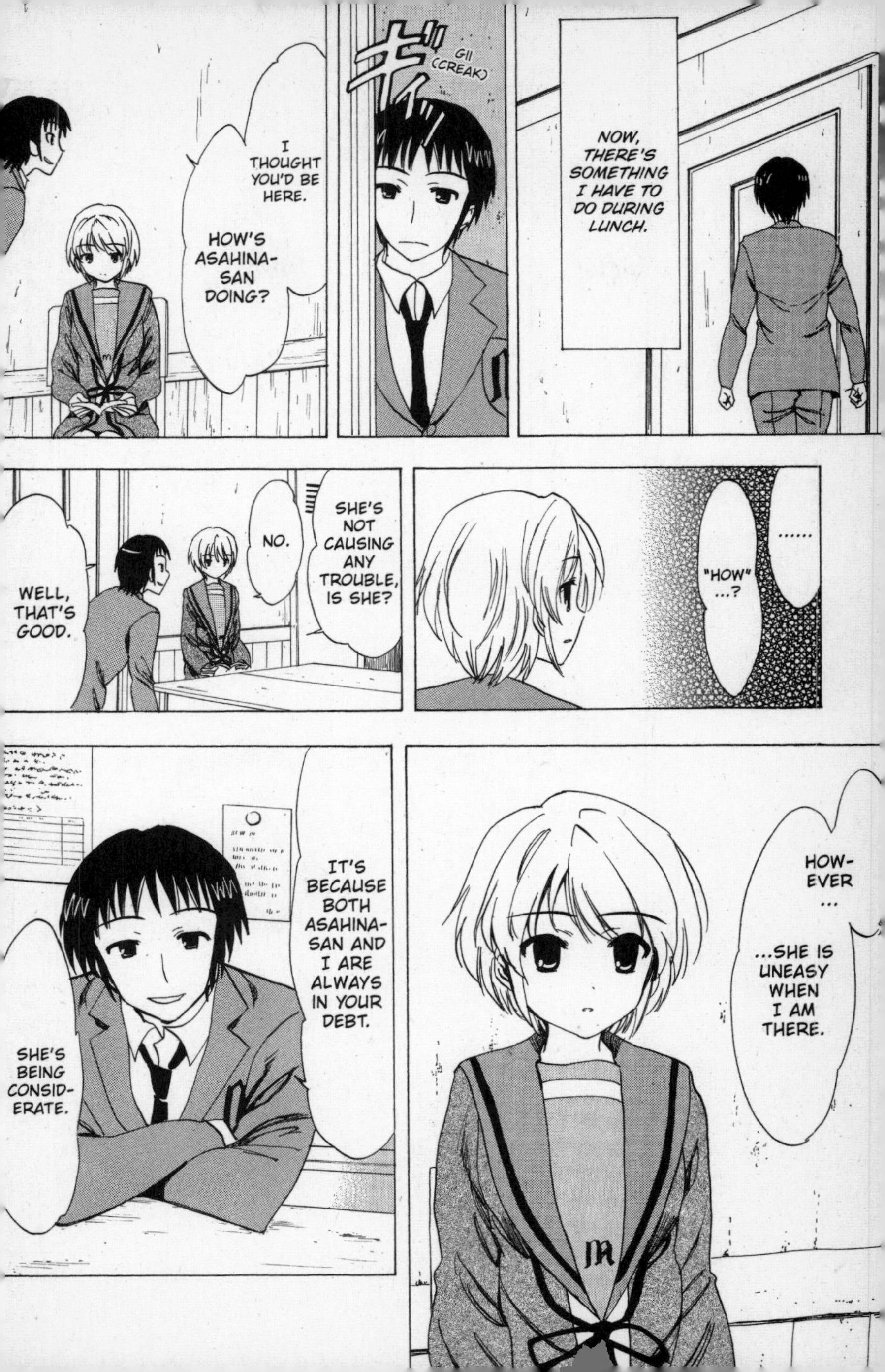
NOW, THERE'S SOMETHING I HAVE TO DO DURING LUNCH.
GII (CREAK)
I THOUGHT YOU'D BE HERE.
HOW'S ASAHINA-SAN DOING?
......
"HOW" ...?
SHE'S NOT CAUSING ANY TROUBLE, IS SHE?
NO.
WELL, THAT'S GOOD.
HOW-EVER...
...SHE IS UNEASY WHEN I AM THERE.
IT'S BECAUSE BOTH ASAHINA-SAN AND I ARE ALWAYS IN YOUR DEBT.
SHE'S BEING CONSID-ERATE.

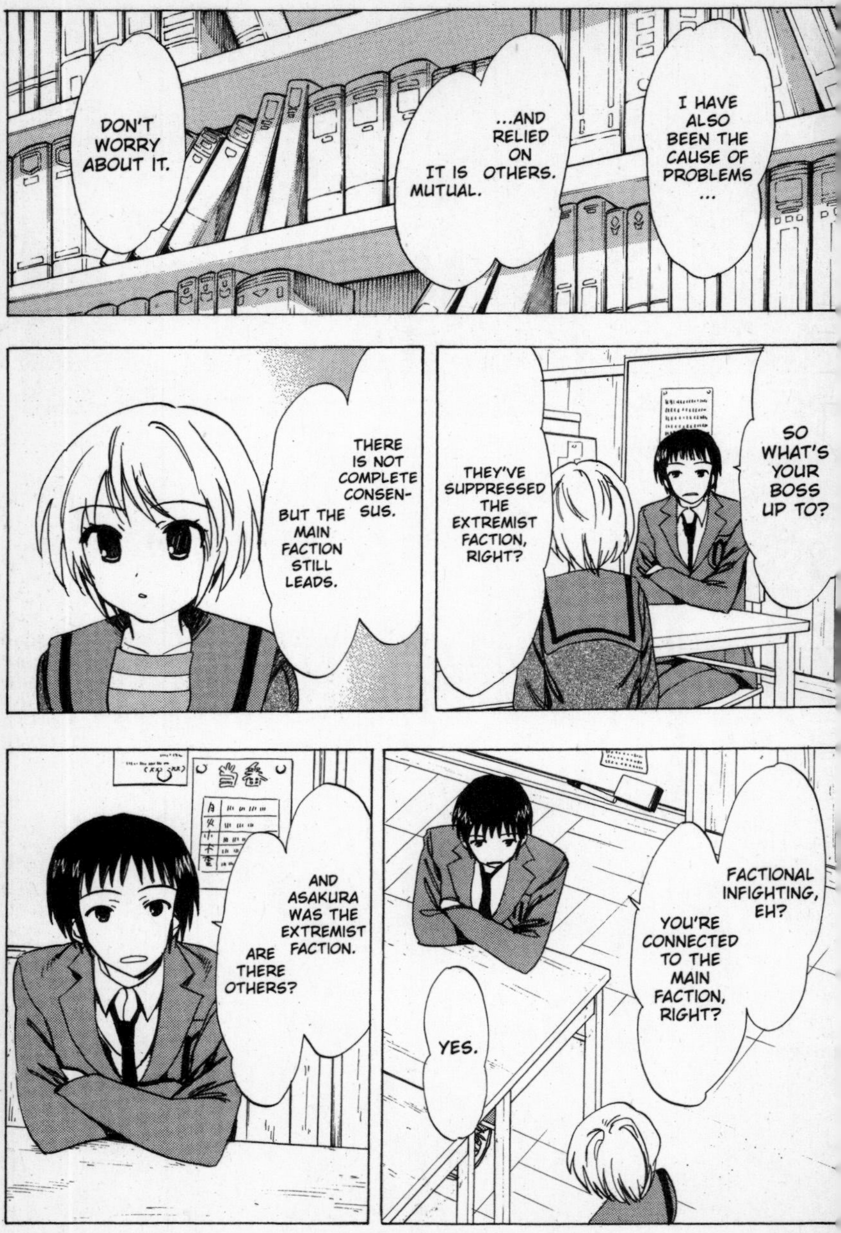

I HAVE ALSO BEEN THE CAUSE OF PROBLEMS ...
...AND RELIED ON OTHERS.
IT IS MUTUAL.
DON'T WORRY ABOUT IT.
SO WHAT'S YOUR BOSS UP TO?
THEY'VE SUPPRESSED THE EXTREMIST FACTION, RIGHT?
THERE IS NOT COMPLETE CONSENSUS.
BUT THE MAIN FACTION STILL LEADS.
FACTIONAL INFIGHTING, EH?
YOU'RE CONNECTED TO THE MAIN FACTION, RIGHT?
YES.
AND ASAKURA WAS THE EXTREMIST FACTION.
ARE THERE OTHERS?

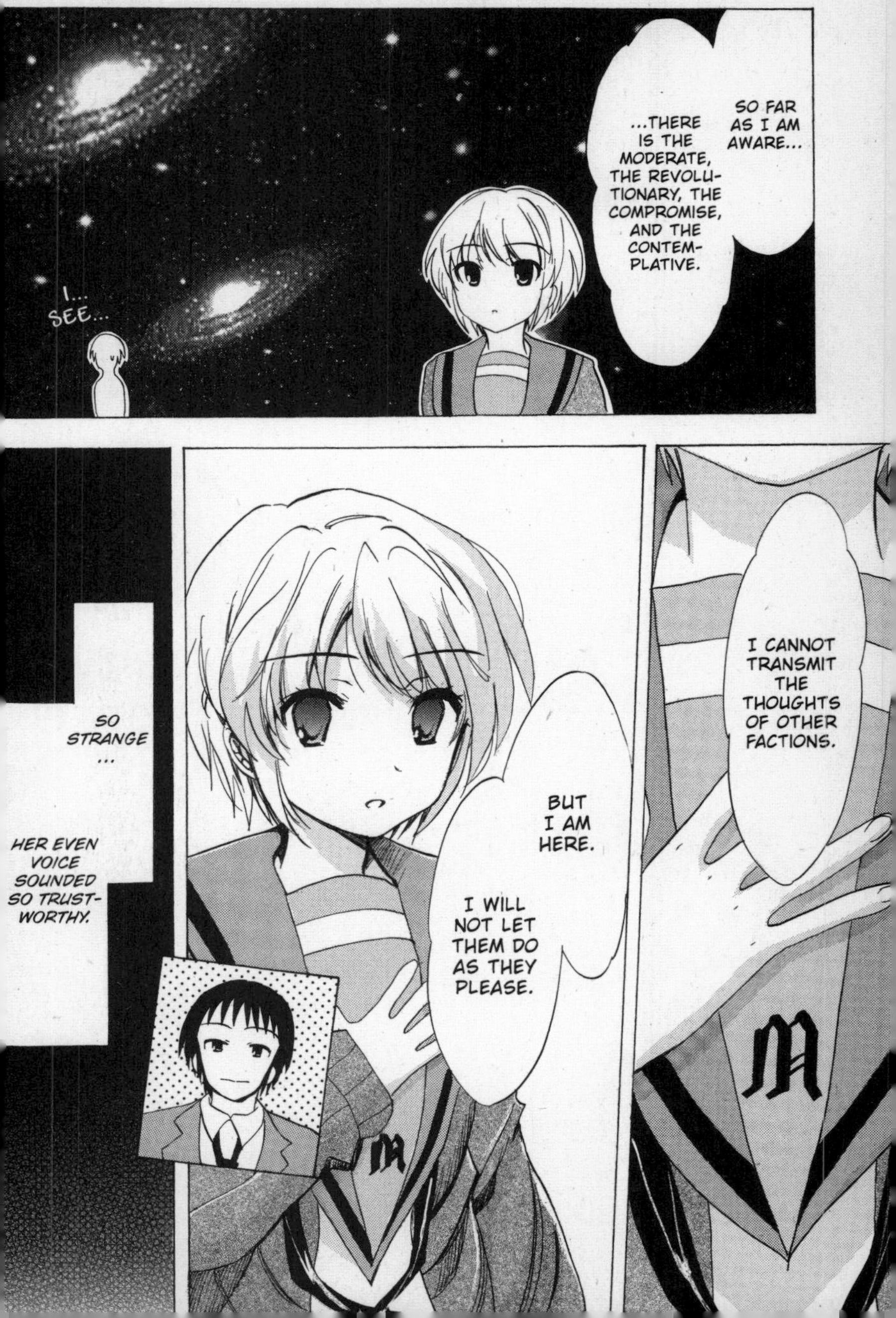
SO FAR AS I AM AWARE...
...THERE IS THE MODERATE, THE REVOLUTIONARY, THE COMPROMISE, AND THE CONTEMPLATIVE.
I... SEE...
I CANNOT TRANSMIT THE THOUGHTS OF OTHER FACTIONS.
BUT I AM HERE.
I WILL NOT LET THEM DO AS THEY PLEASE.
SO STRANGE...
HER EVEN VOICE SOUNDED SO TRUST-WORTHY.

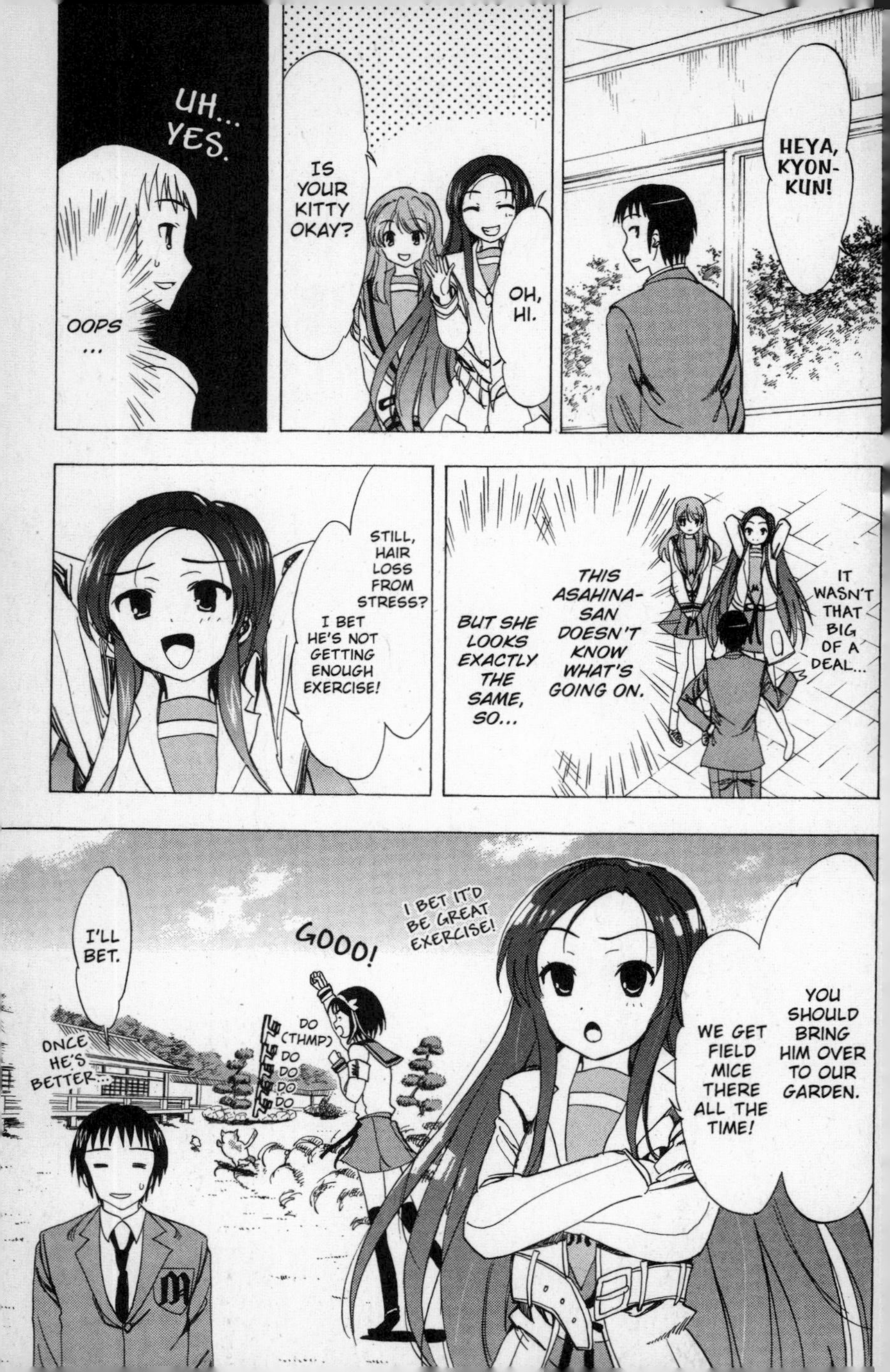
HEYA, KYON-KUN!
OH, HI.
IS YOUR KITTY OKAY?
UH... YES.
OOPS ...
IT WASN'T THAT BIG OF A DEAL...
THIS ASAHINA-SAN DOESN'T KNOW WHAT'S GOING ON.
BUT SHE LOOKS EXACTLY THE SAME, SO...
STILL, HAIR LOSS FROM STRESS?
I BET HE'S NOT GETTING ENOUGH EXERCISE!
YOU SHOULD BRING HIM OVER TO OUR GARDEN.
WE GET FIELD MICE THERE ALL THE TIME!
I BET IT'D BE GREAT EXERCISE!
GOOO!
DO (THMP) DO DO DO DO
I'LL BET.
ONCE HE'S BETTER...

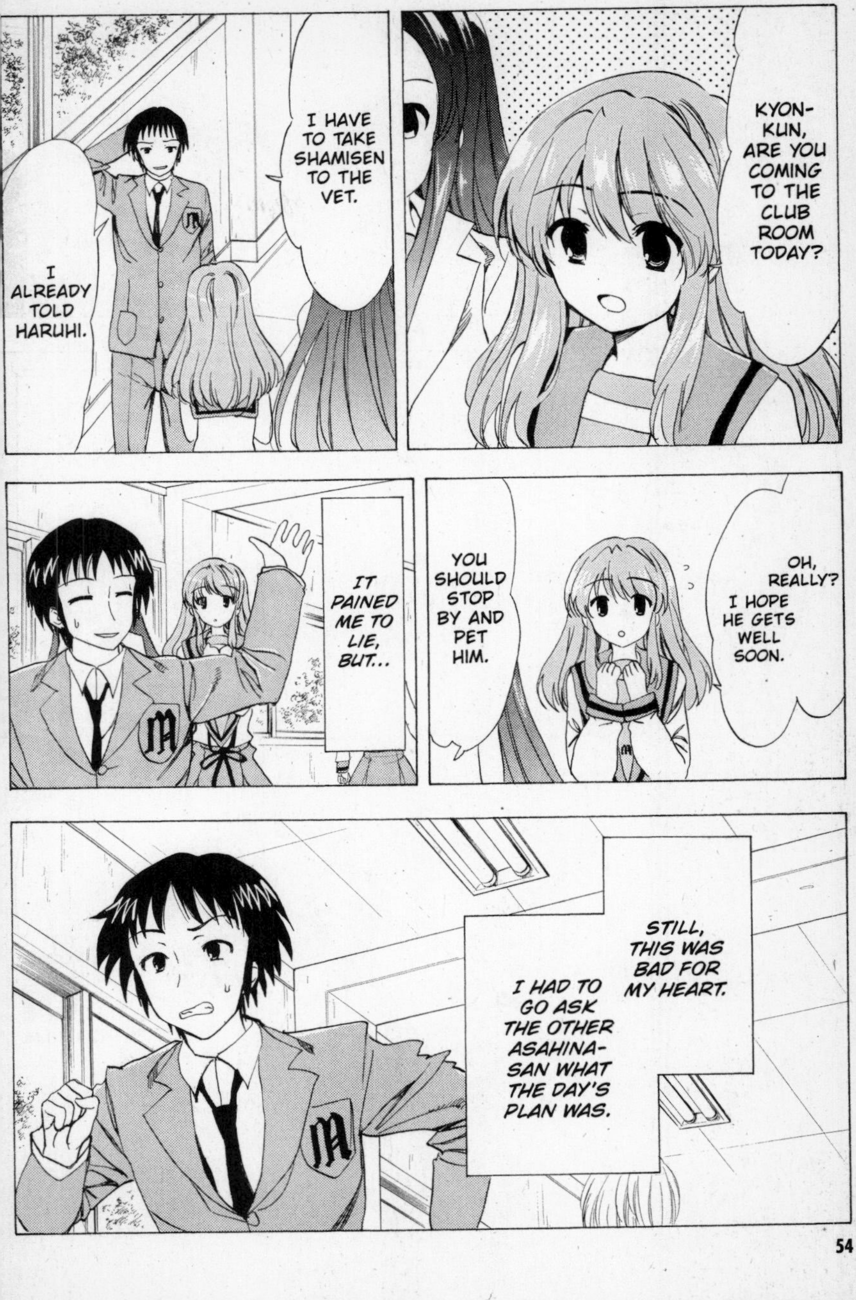
KYON-KUN, ARE YOU COMING TO THE CLUB ROOM TODAY?
I HAVE TO TAKE SHAMISEN TO THE VET.
I ALREADY TOLD HARUHI.
OH, REALLY? I HOPE HE GETS WELL SOON.
YOU SHOULD STOP BY AND PET HIM.
IT PAINED ME TO LIE, BUT...
STILL, THIS WAS BAD FOR MY HEART.
I HAD TO GO ASK THE OTHER ASAHINA-SAN WHAT THE DAY'S PLAN WAS.

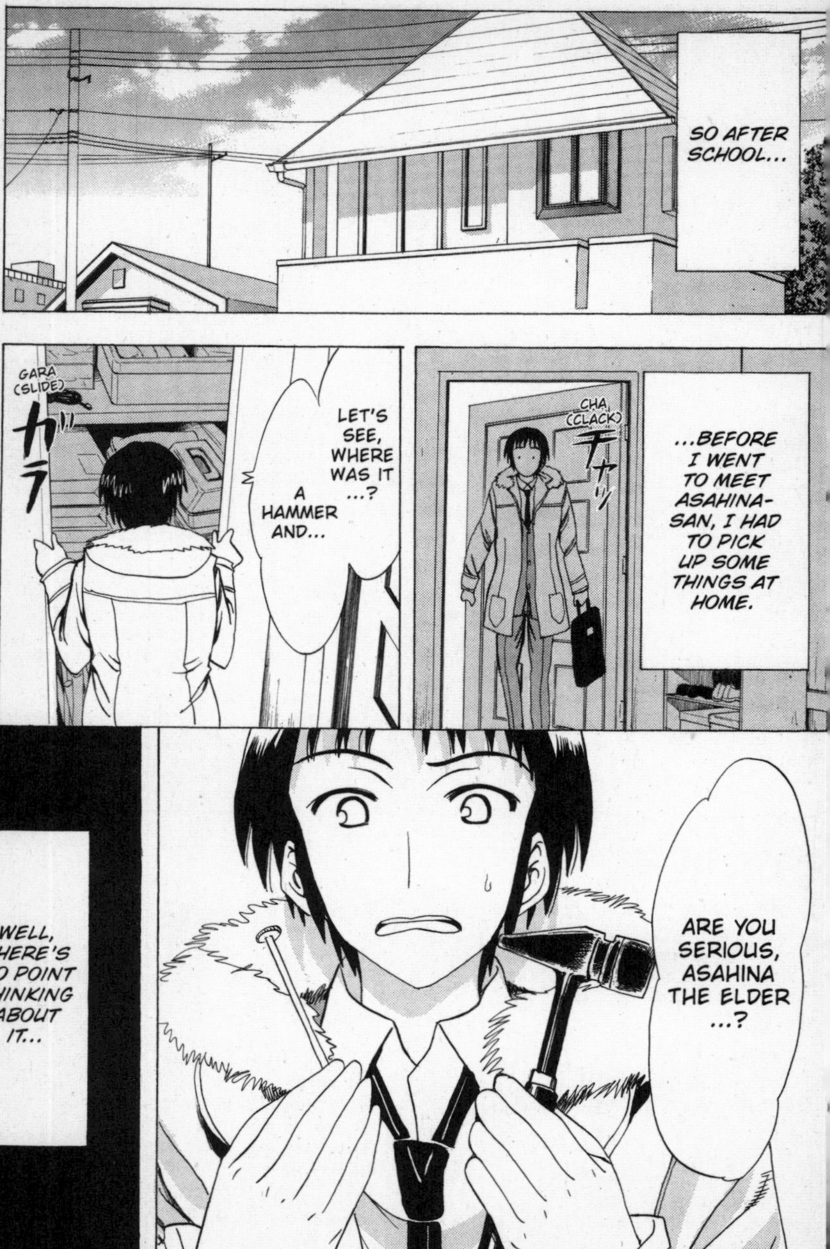
SO AFTER SCHOOL...
...BEFORE I WENT TO MEET ASAHINA-SAN, I HAD TO PICK UP SOME THINGS AT HOME.
CHA (CLACK)
チャッ
LET'S SEE, WHERE WAS IT ...?
A HAMMER AND...
GARA (SLIDE)
ガラ
ARE YOU SERIOUS, ASAHINA THE ELDER ...?
WELL, THERE'S NO POINT THINKING ABOUT IT...

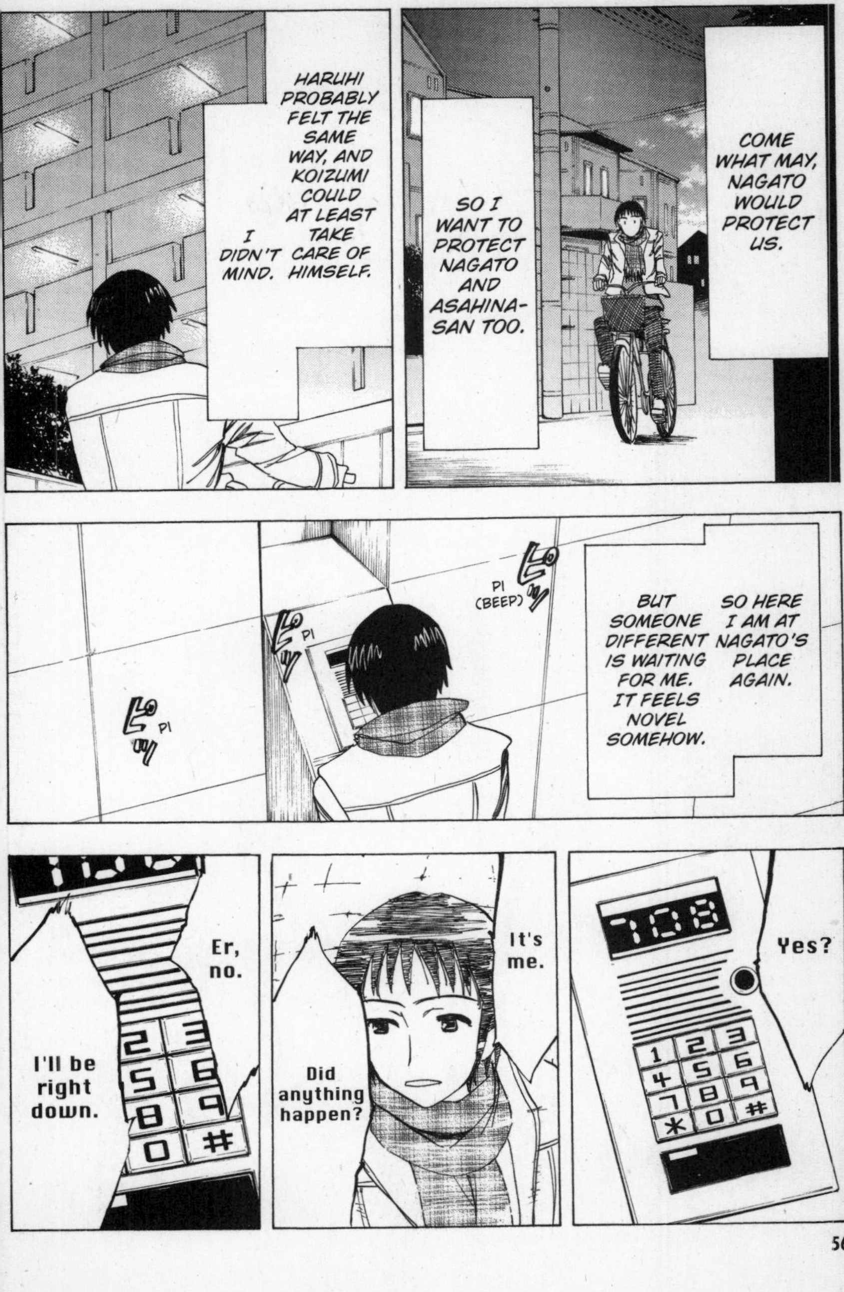
COME WHAT MAY, NAGATO WOULD PROTECT US.
SO I WANT TO PROTECT NAGATO AND ASAHINA-SAN TOO.
HARUHI PROBABLY FELT THE SAME WAY, AND KOIZUMI COULD AT LEAST TAKE CARE OF HIMSELF.
I DIDN'T MIND.
SO HERE I AM AT NAGATO'S PLACE AGAIN.
BUT SOMEONE DIFFERENT IS WAITING FOR ME. IT FEELS NOVEL SOMEHOW.
PI (BEEP)
PI
PI
708
Yes?
It's me.
Did anything happen?
Er, no.
I'll be right down.

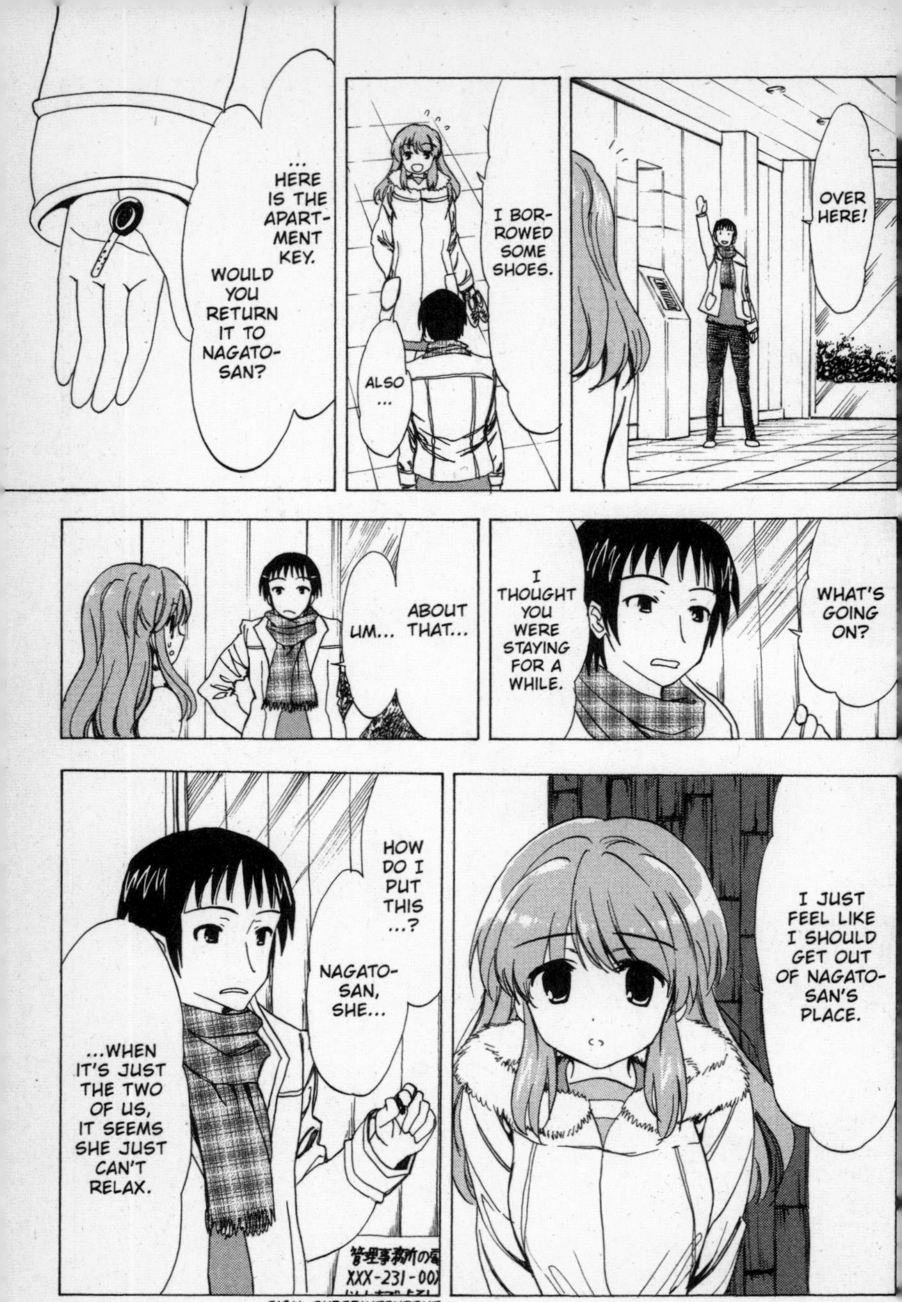
OVER HERE!
I BORROWED SOME SHOES.
ALSO ...
... HERE IS THE APARTMENT KEY.
WOULD YOU RETURN IT TO NAGATO-SAN?
WHAT'S GOING ON?
I THOUGHT YOU WERE STAYING FOR A WHILE.
UM... ABOUT THAT...
I JUST FEEL LIKE I SHOULD GET OUT OF NAGATO-SAN'S PLACE.
HOW DO I PUT THIS ...?
NAGATO-SAN, SHE...
...WHEN IT'S JUST THE TWO OF US, IT SEEMS SHE JUST CAN'T RELAX.
管理事務所の
XXX-231-00
SIGN: SUPERINTENDENT

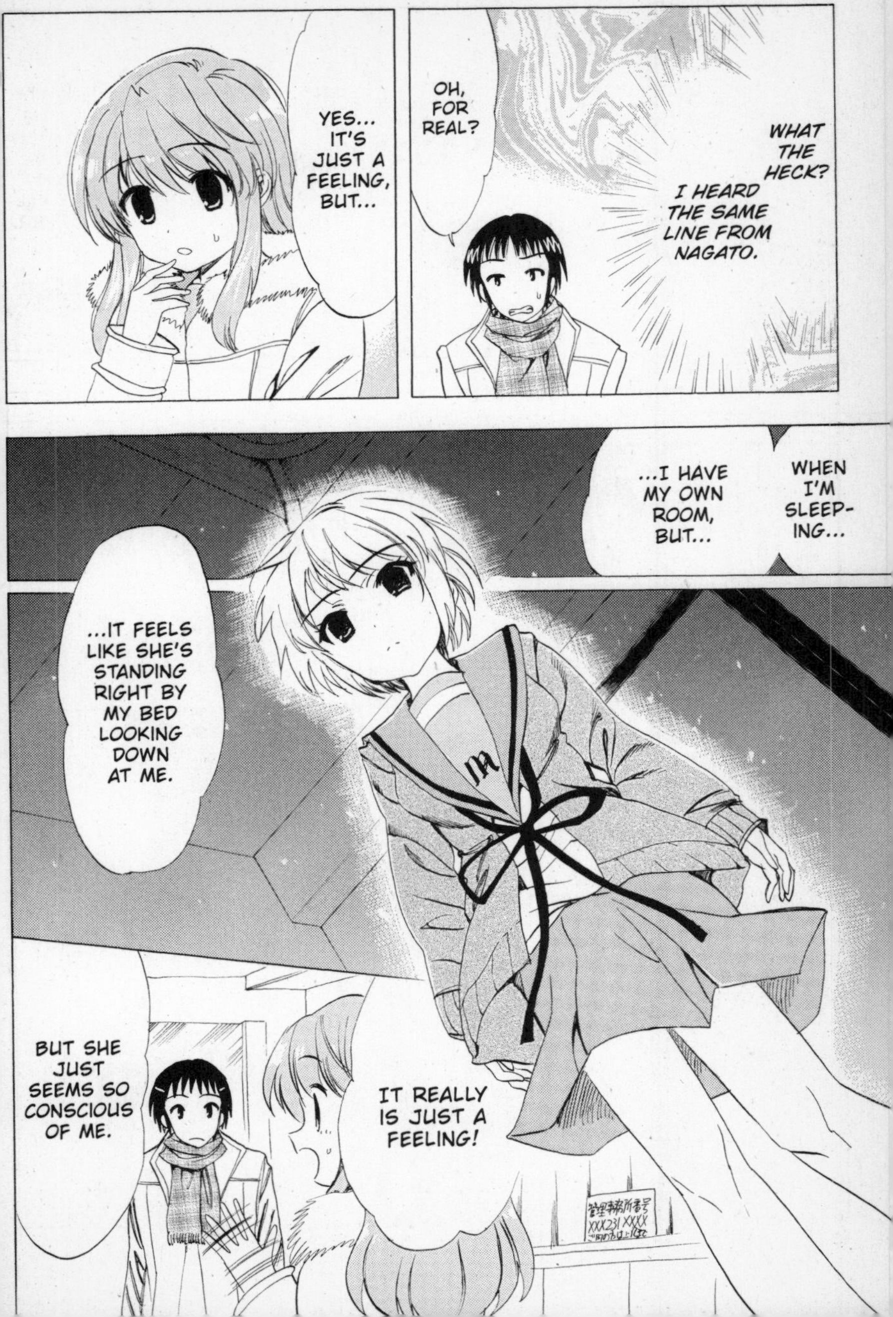
OH, FOR REAL?
WHAT THE HECK?
I HEARD THE SAME LINE FROM NAGATO.
YES... IT'S JUST A FEELING, BUT...
WHEN I'M SLEEP-ING...
...I HAVE MY OWN ROOM, BUT...
...IT FEELS LIKE SHE'S STANDING RIGHT BY MY BED LOOKING DOWN AT ME.
IT REALLY IS JUST A FEELING!
BUT SHE JUST SEEMS SO CONSCIOUS OF ME.

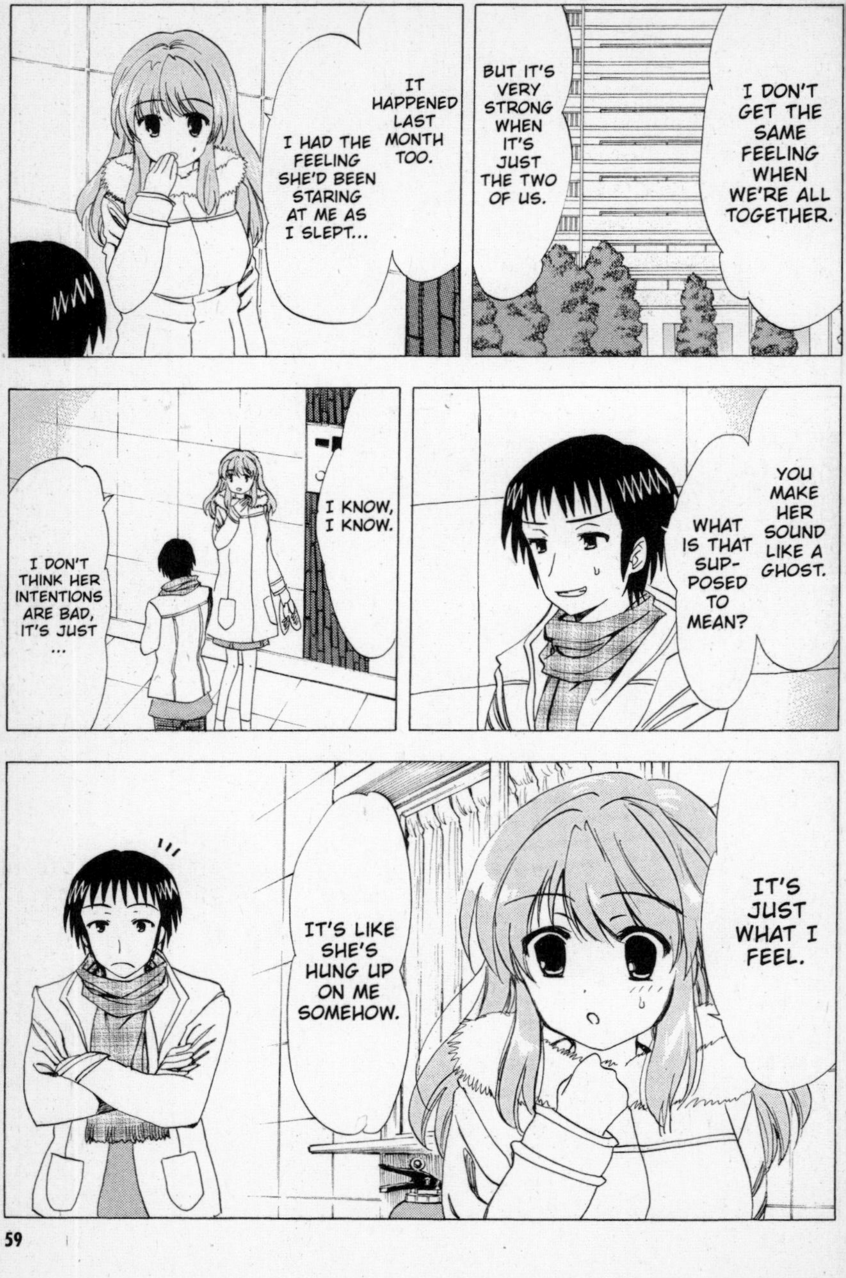
I DON'T GET THE SAME FEELING WHEN WE'RE ALL TOGETHER.
BUT IT'S VERY STRONG WHEN IT'S JUST THE TWO OF US.
IT HAPPENED LAST MONTH TOO.
I HAD THE FEELING SHE'D BEEN STARING AT ME AS I SLEPT...
YOU MAKE HER SOUND LIKE A GHOST.
WHAT IS THAT SUP-POSED TO MEAN?
I KNOW, I KNOW.
I DON'T THINK HER INTENTIONS ARE BAD, IT'S JUST ...
IT'S JUST WHAT I FEEL.
IT'S LIKE SHE'S HUNG UP ON ME SOMEHOW.

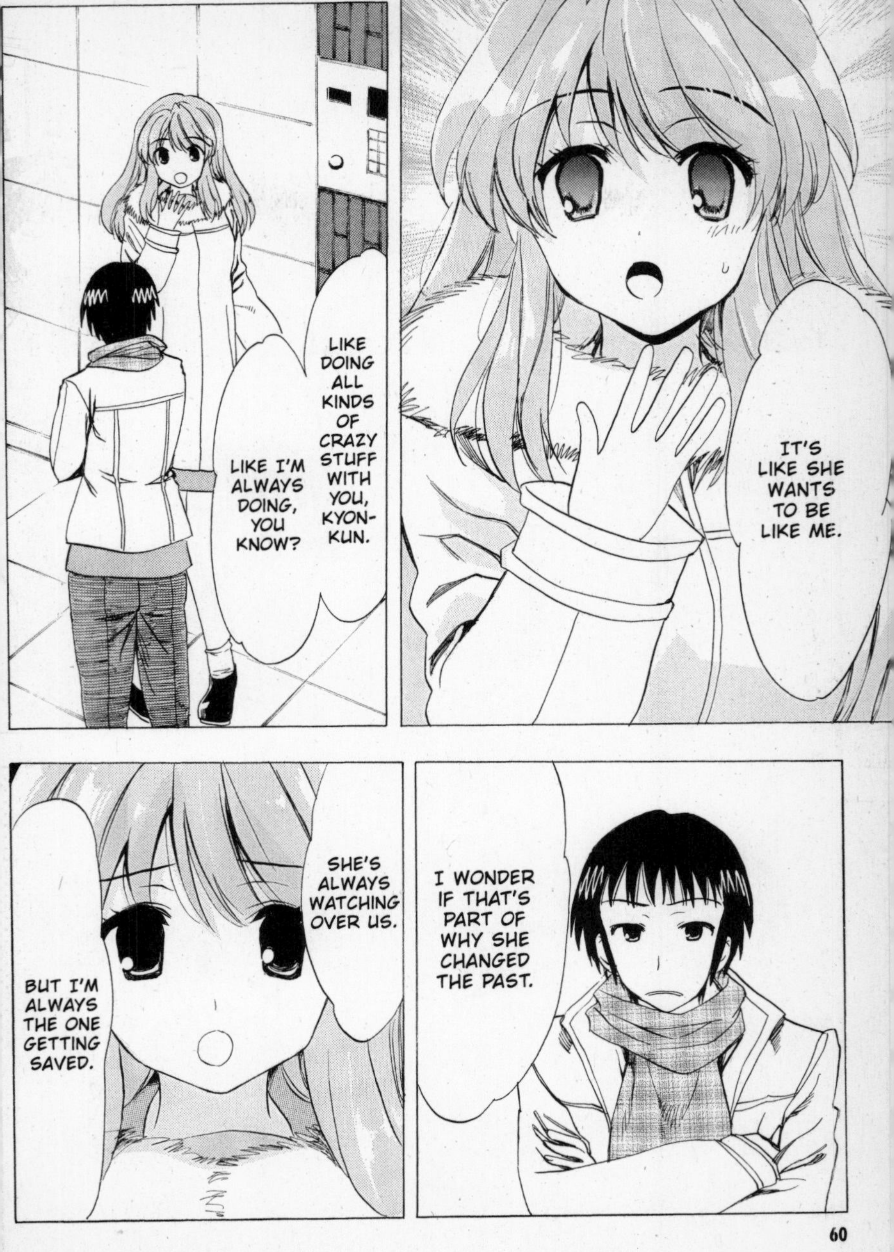
IT'S LIKE SHE WANTS TO BE LIKE ME.
LIKE DOING ALL KINDS OF CRAZY STUFF WITH YOU, KYON-KUN.
LIKE I'M ALWAYS DOING, YOU KNOW?
I WONDER IF THAT'S PART OF WHY SHE CHANGED THE PAST.
SHE'S ALWAYS WATCHING OVER US.
BUT I'M ALWAYS THE ONE GETTING SAVED.

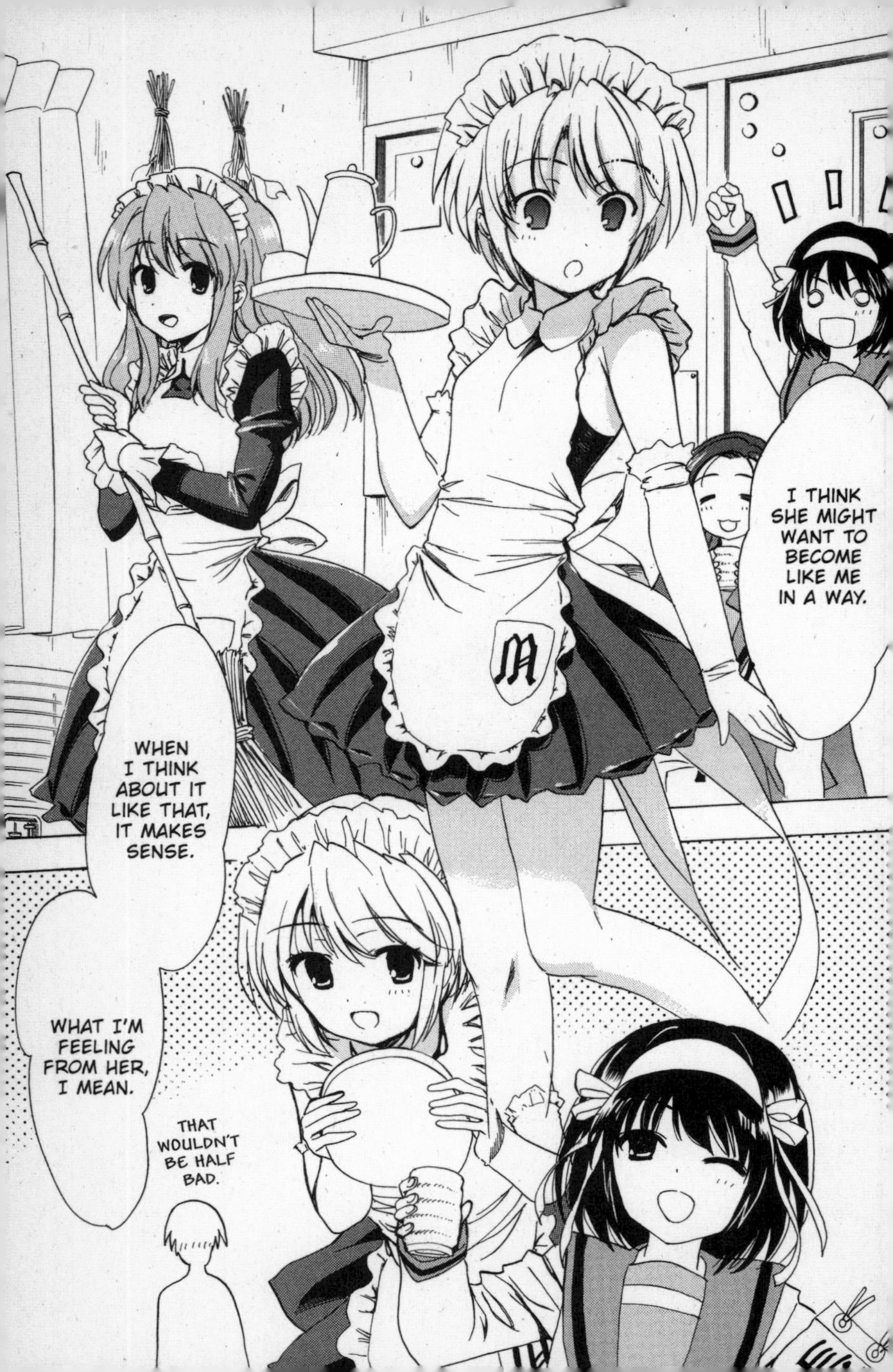
I THINK SHE MIGHT WANT TO BECOME LIKE ME IN A WAY.
WHEN I THINK ABOUT IT LIKE THAT, IT MAKES SENSE.
WHAT I'M FEELING FROM HER, I MEAN.
THAT WOULDN'T BE HALF BAD.

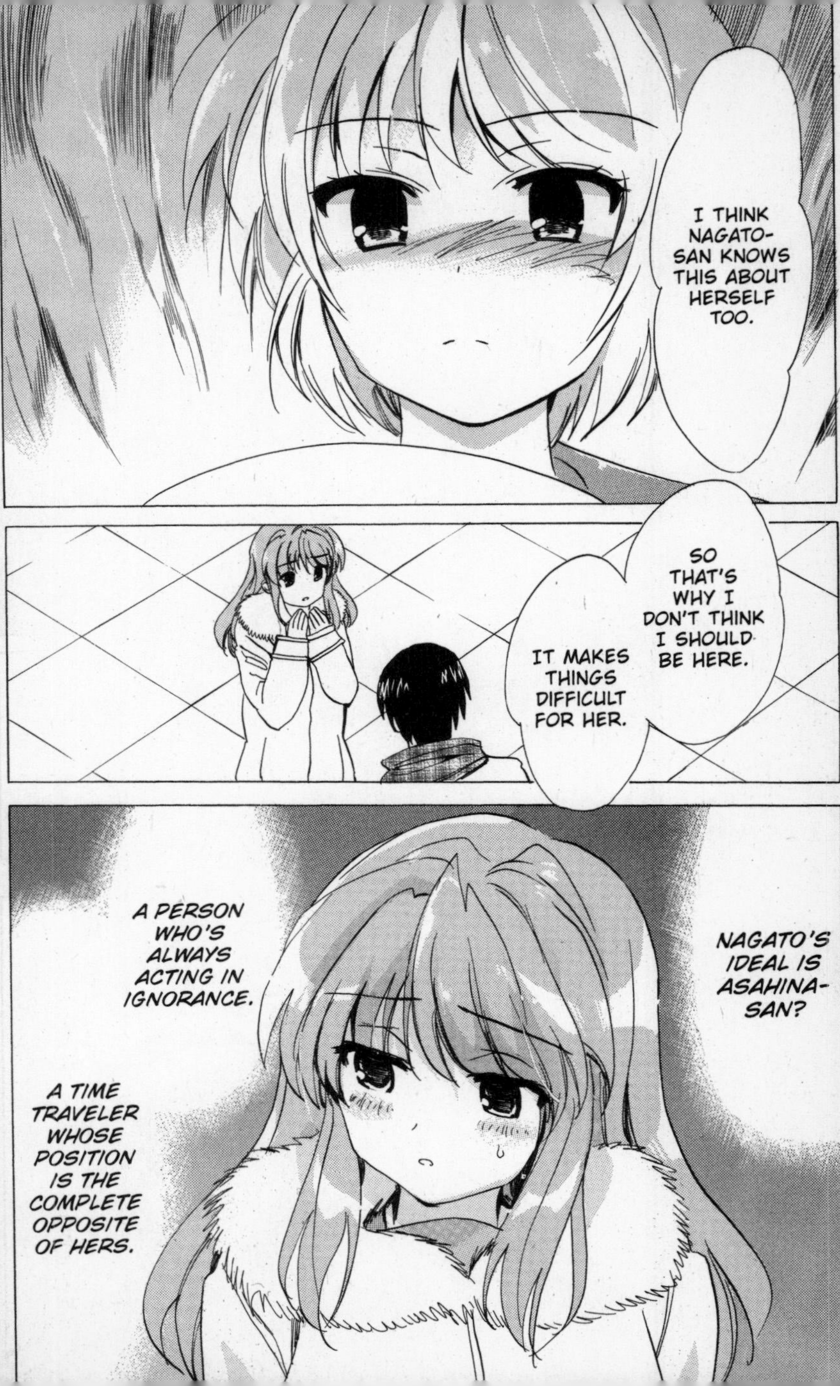
I THINK NAGATO-SAN KNOWS THIS ABOUT HERSELF TOO.
SO THAT'S WHY I DON'T THINK I SHOULD BE HERE.
IT MAKES THINGS DIFFICULT FOR HER.
NAGATO'S IDEAL IS ASAHINA-SAN?
A PERSON WHO'S ALWAYS ACTING IN IGNORANCE.
A TIME TRAVELER WHOSE POSITION IS THE COMPLETE OPPOSITE OF HERS.

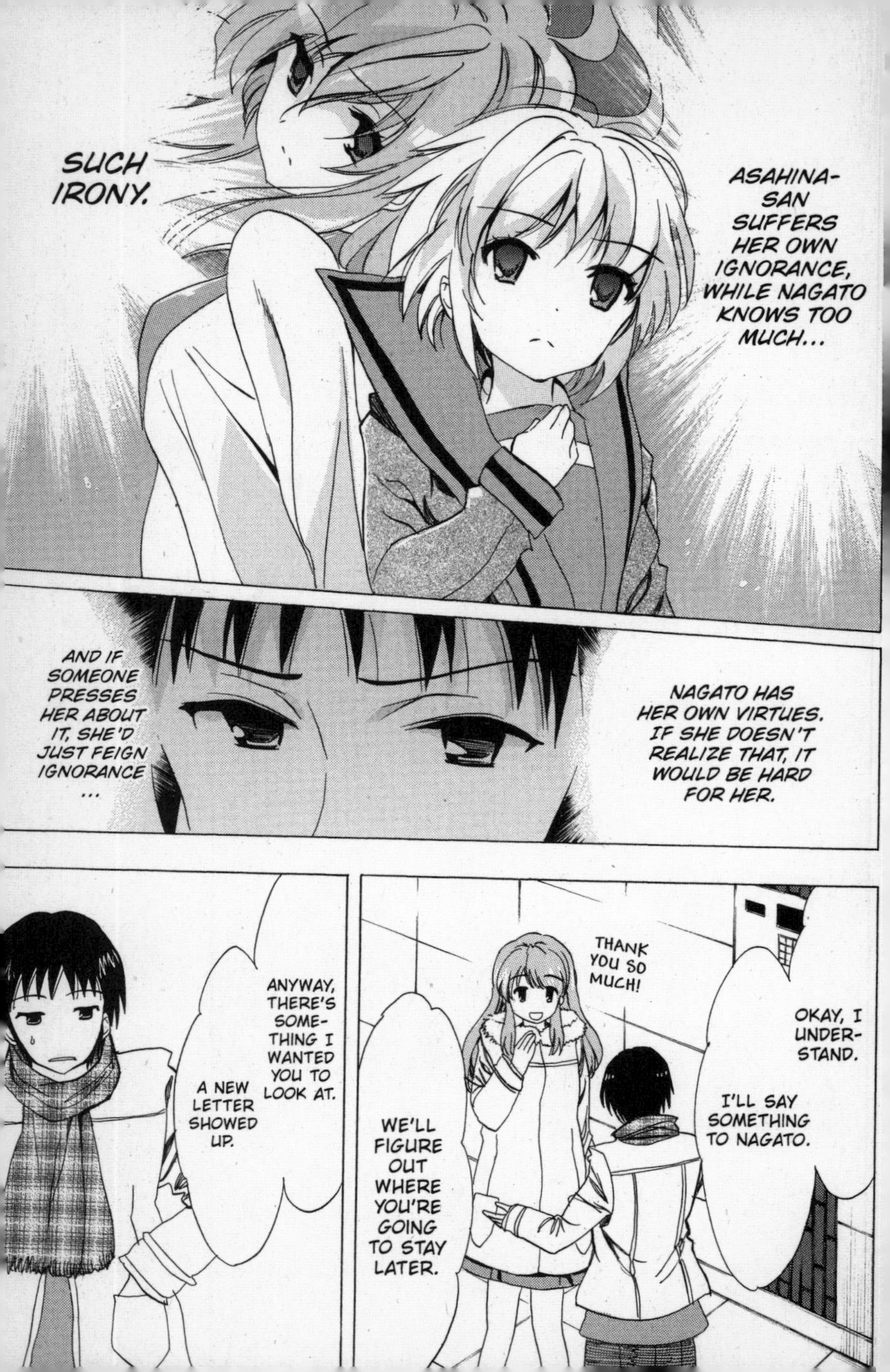
ASAHINA-SAN SUFFERS HER OWN IGNORANCE, WHILE NAGATO KNOWS TOO MUCH...
SUCH IRONY.
NAGATO HAS HER OWN VIRTUES. IF SHE DOESN'T REALIZE THAT, IT WOULD BE HARD FOR HER.
AND IF SOMEONE PRESSES HER ABOUT IT, SHE'D JUST FEIGN IGNORANCE...
OKAY, I UNDERSTAND.
I'LL SAY SOMETHING TO NAGATO.
THANK YOU SO MUCH!
WE'LL FIGURE OUT WHERE YOU'RE GOING TO STAY LATER.
ANYWAY, THERE'S SOMETHING I WANTED YOU TO LOOK AT.
A NEW LETTER SHOWED UP.

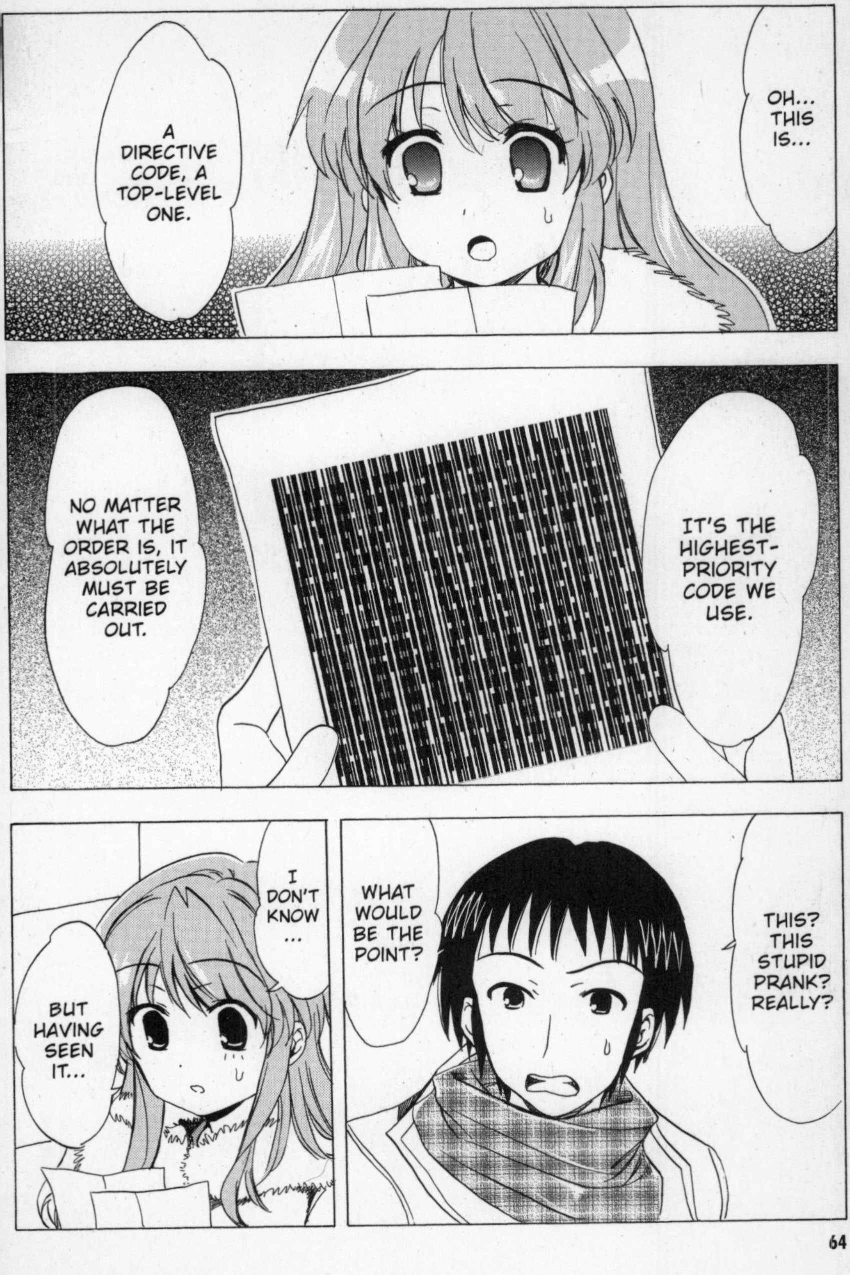
OH... THIS IS...
A DIRECTIVE CODE, A TOP-LEVEL ONE.
IT'S THE HIGHEST-PRIORITY CODE WE USE.
NO MATTER WHAT THE ORDER IS, IT ABSOLUTELY MUST BE CARRIED OUT.
THIS? THIS STUPID PRANK? REALLY?
WHAT WOULD BE THE POINT?
I DON'T KNOW ...
BUT HAVING SEEN IT...

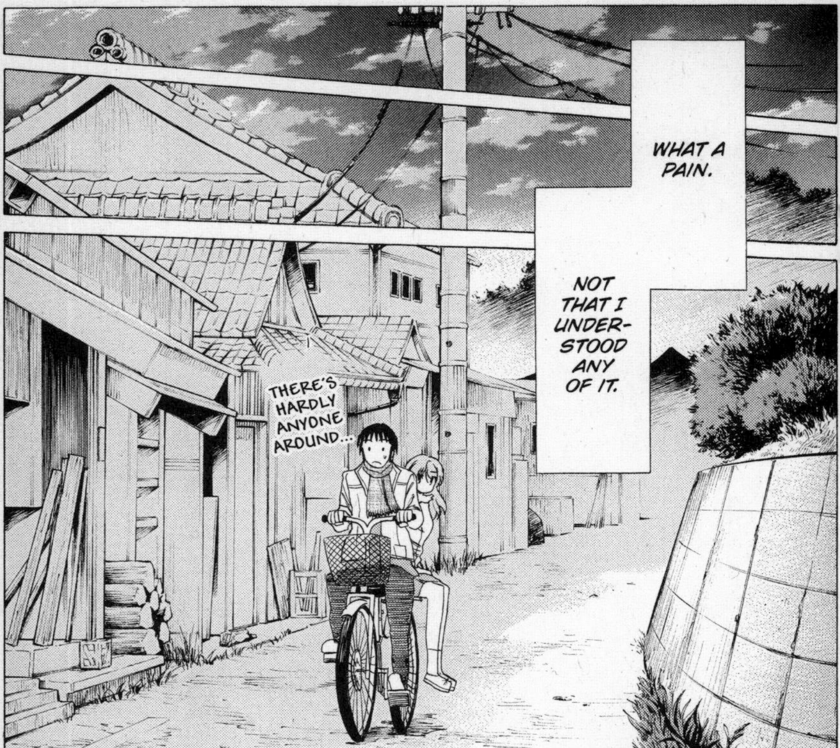
WHAT A PAIN.
NOT THAT I UNDERSTOOD ANY OF IT.
THERE'S HARDLY ANYONE AROUND...

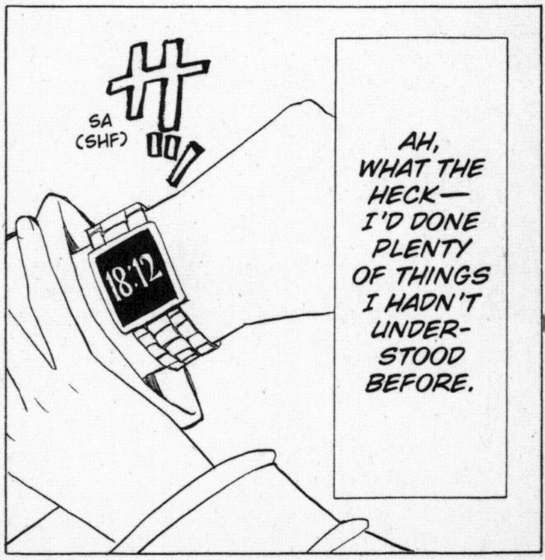
SA (SHF)
18:12
AH, WHAT THE HECK— I'D DONE PLENTY OF THINGS I HADN'T UNDERSTOOD BEFORE.

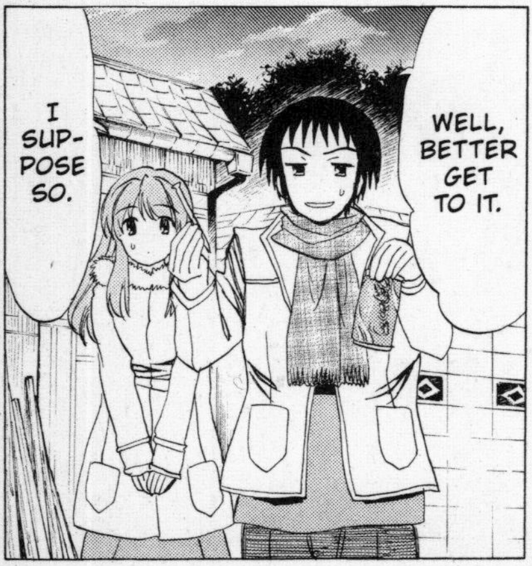
WELL, BETTER GET TO IT.
I SUPPOSE SO.

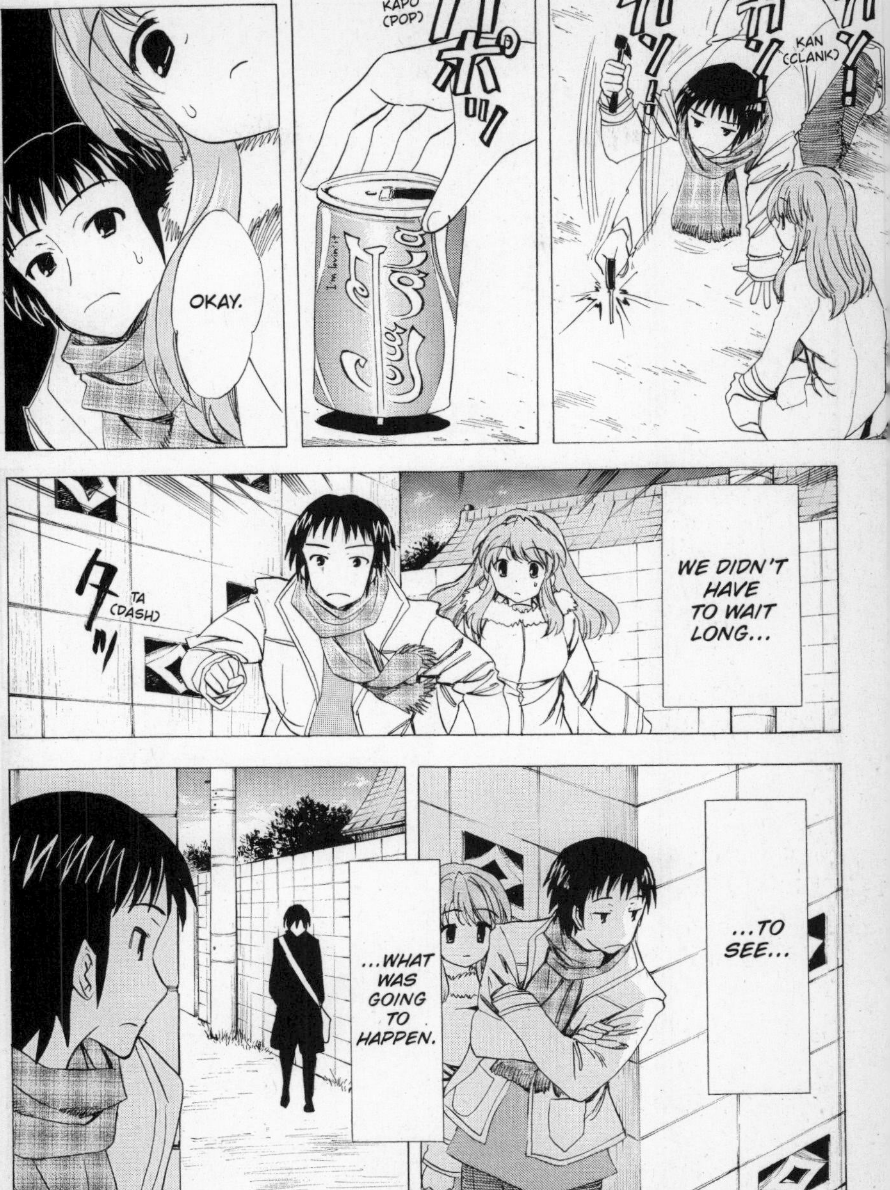
KAN (CLANK)
KAN
KAN
KAPO (POP)
OKAY.
WE DIDN'T HAVE TO WAIT LONG...
TA (DASH)
...TO SEE...
...WHAT WAS GOING TO HAPPEN.

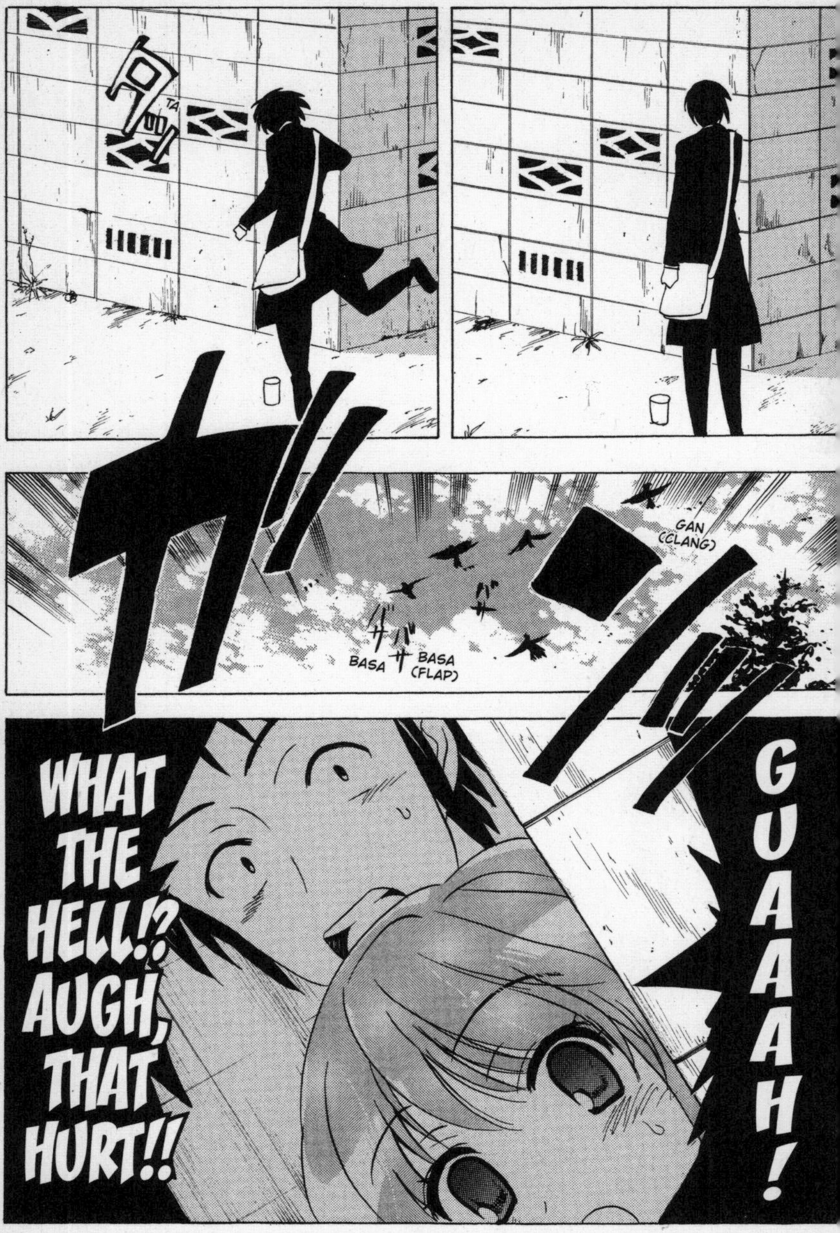
TA
GAN (CLANG)
BASA BASA (FLAP)
GUAAAH!
WHAT THE HELL!? AUGH, THAT HURT!!

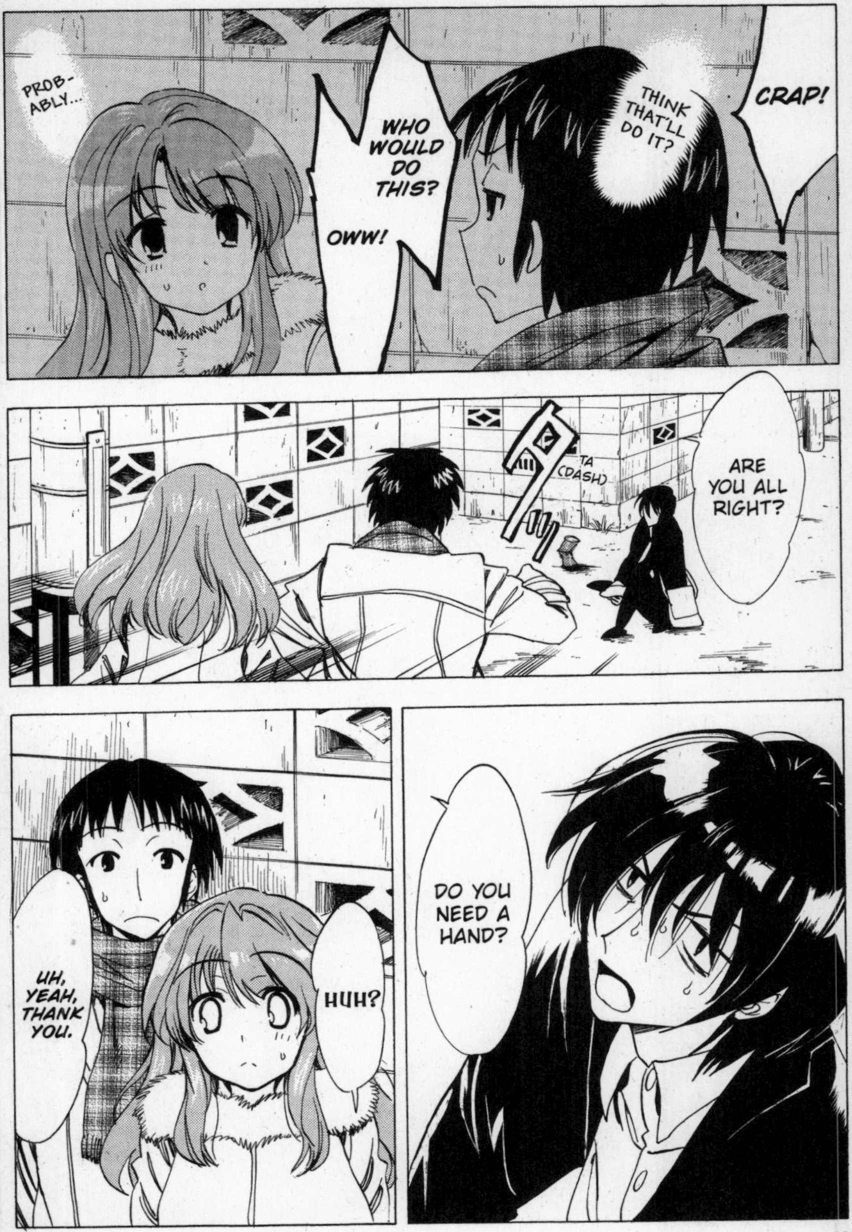
CRAP!
THINK THAT'LL DO IT?
WHO WOULD DO THIS?
OWW!
PROB-ABLY...
ARE YOU ALL RIGHT?
TA (DASH)
DO YOU NEED A HAND?
HUH?
UH, YEAH, THANK YOU.

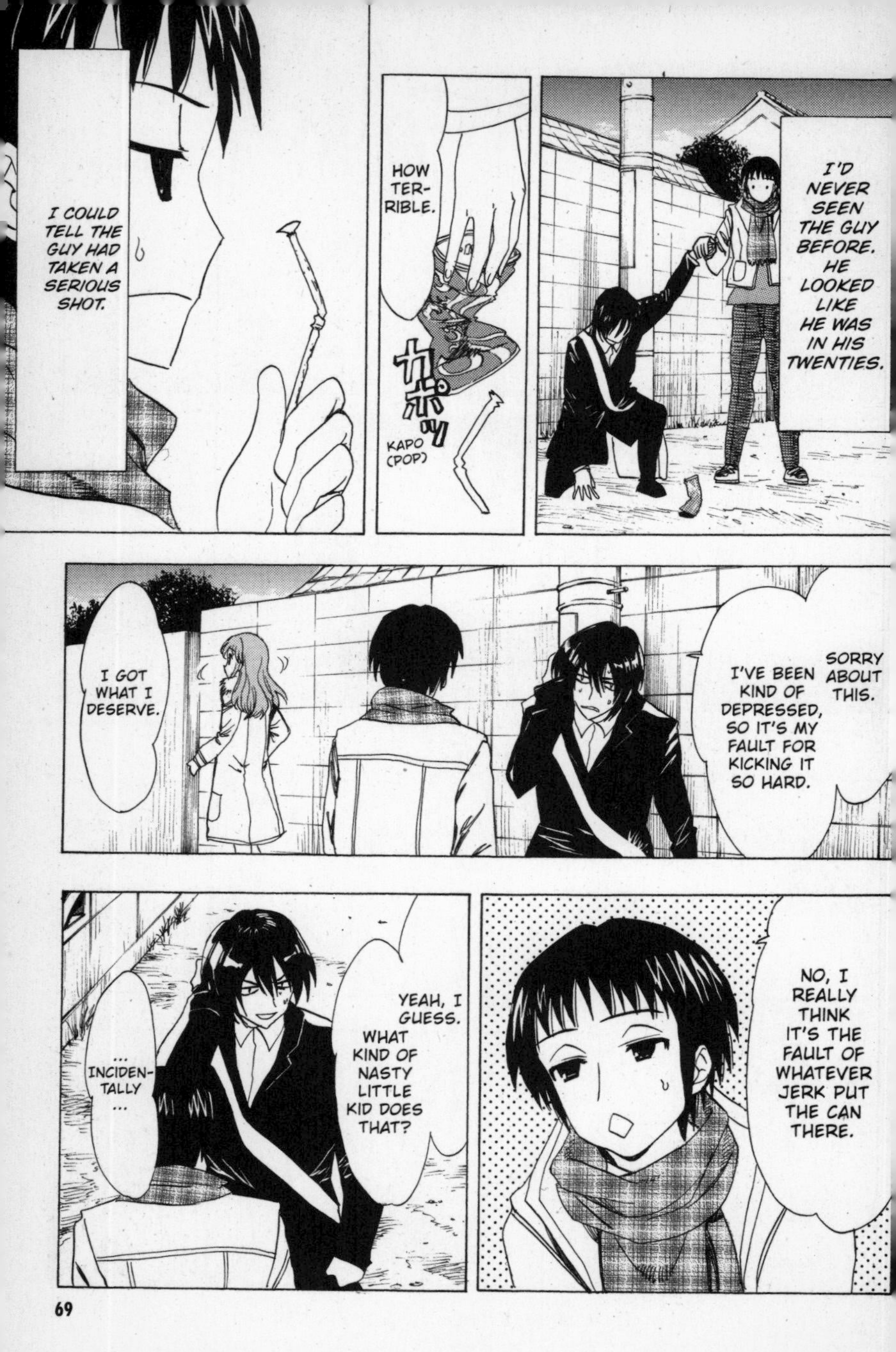
I'D NEVER SEEN THE GUY BEFORE. HE LOOKED LIKE HE WAS IN HIS TWENTIES.
HOW TERRIBLE.
カポッ
KAPO (POP)
I COULD TELL THE GUY HAD TAKEN A SERIOUS SHOT.
SORRY ABOUT THIS.
I'VE BEEN KIND OF DEPRESSED, SO IT'S MY FAULT FOR KICKING IT SO HARD.
I GOT WHAT I DESERVE.
NO, I REALLY THINK IT'S THE FAULT OF WHATEVER JERK PUT THE CAN THERE.
YEAH, I GUESS. WHAT KIND OF NASTY LITTLE KID DOES THAT?
... INCIDENTALLY ...

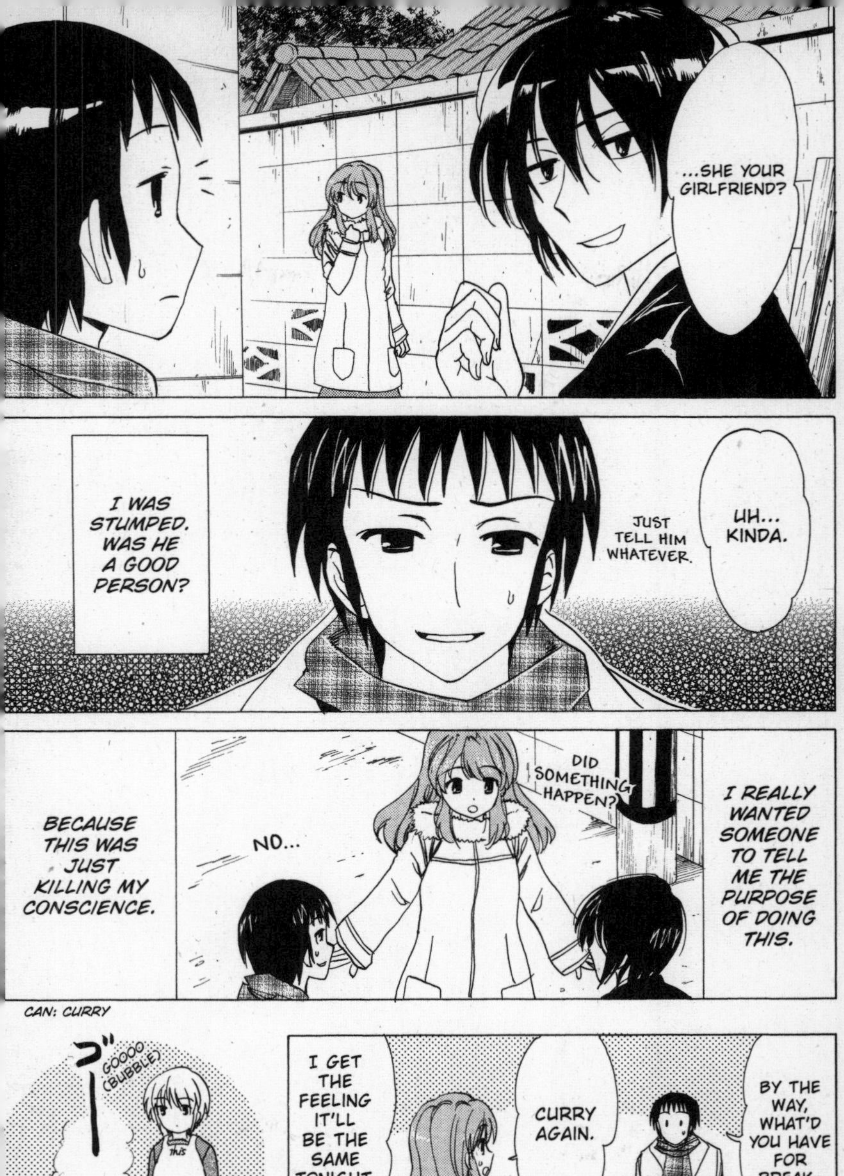
...SHE YOUR GIRLFRIEND?
UH... KINDA.
JUST TELL HIM WHATEVER.
I WAS STUMPED. WAS HE A GOOD PERSON?
I REALLY WANTED SOMEONE TO TELL ME THE PURPOSE OF DOING THIS.
DID SOMETHING HAPPEN?
NO...
BECAUSE THIS WAS JUST KILLING MY CONSCIENCE.
BY THE WAY, WHAT'D YOU HAVE FOR BREAKFAST?
CURRY AGAIN.
I GET THE FEELING IT'LL BE THE SAME TONIGHT.
ゴー
GOOOO (BUBBLE)
カレー
CAN: CURRY

THE INTRIGUES OF HARUHI SUZUMIYA III : END

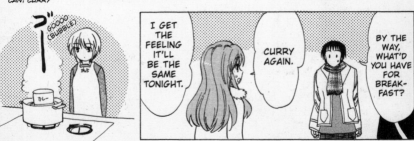

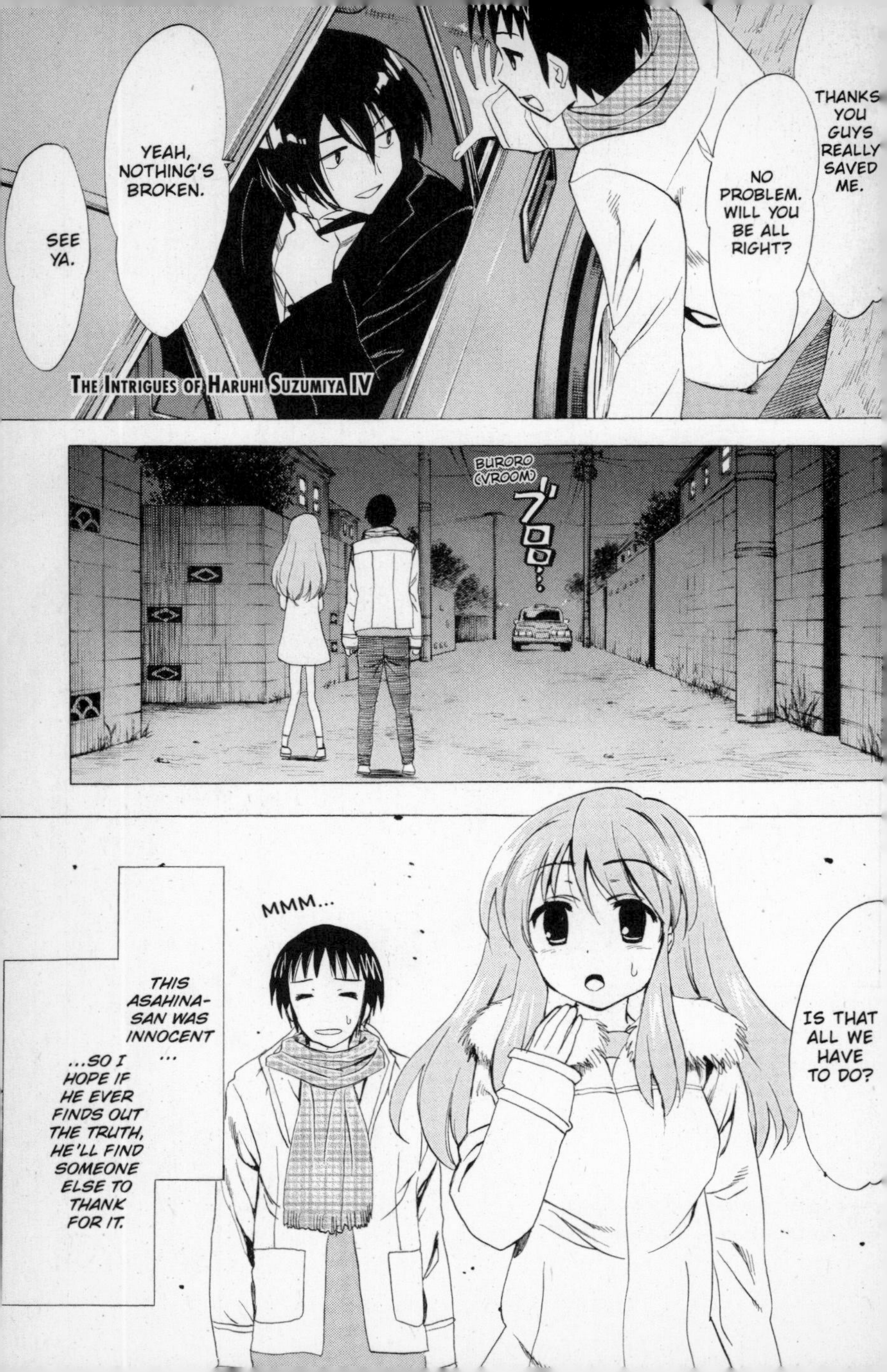
THANKS YOU GUYS REALLY SAVED ME.
NO PROBLEM. WILL YOU BE ALL RIGHT?
YEAH, NOTHING'S BROKEN.
SEE YA.
THE INTRIGUES OF HARUHI SUZUMIYA IV
BURORO (VROOM)
ブロロ…
IS THAT ALL WE HAVE TO DO?
MMM...
THIS ASAHINA-SAN WAS INNOCENT ...
...SO I HOPE IF HE EVER FINDS OUT THE TRUTH, HE'LL FIND SOMEONE ELSE TO THANK FOR IT.

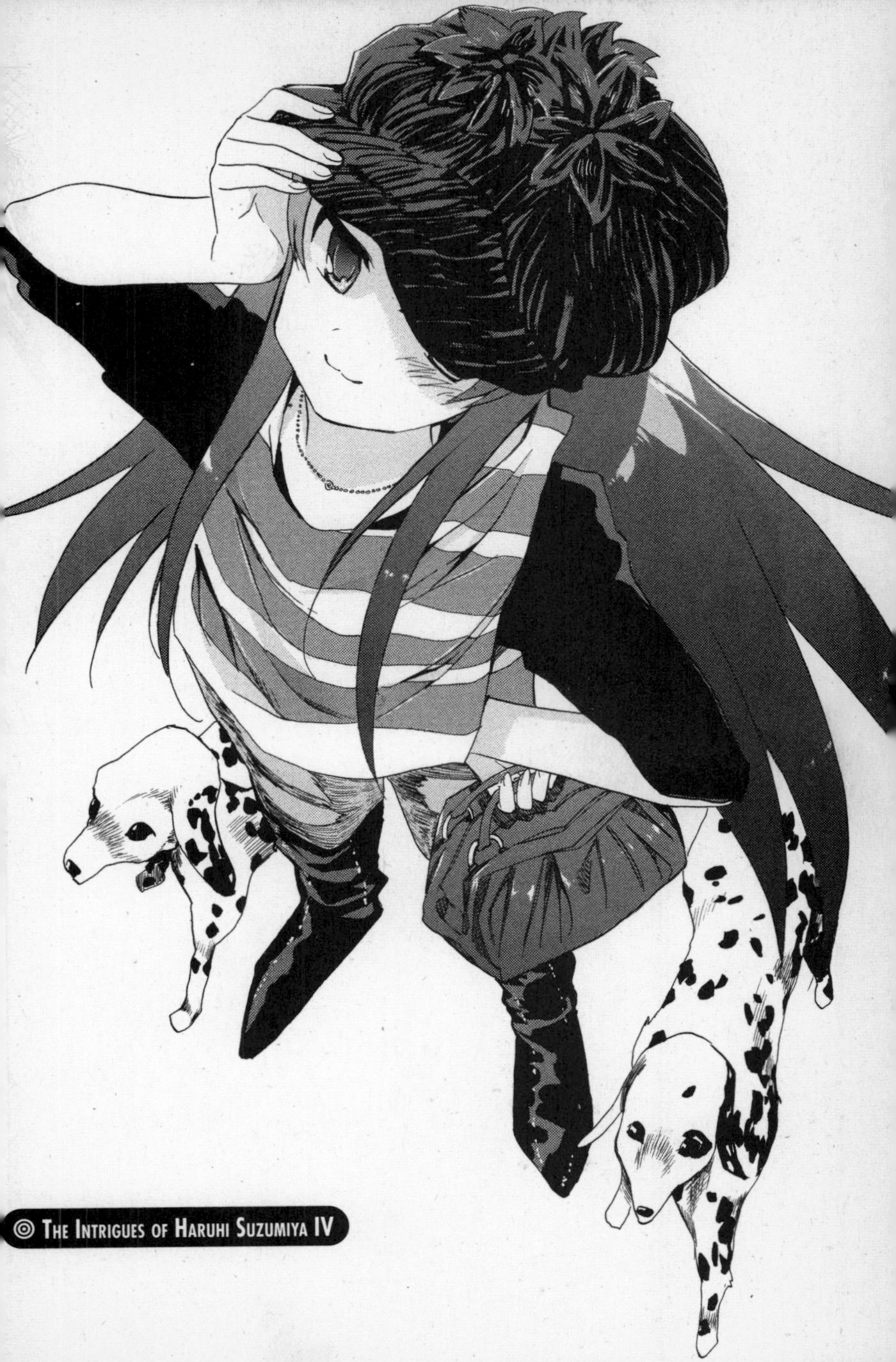

◎ The Intrigues of Haruhi Suzumiya IV

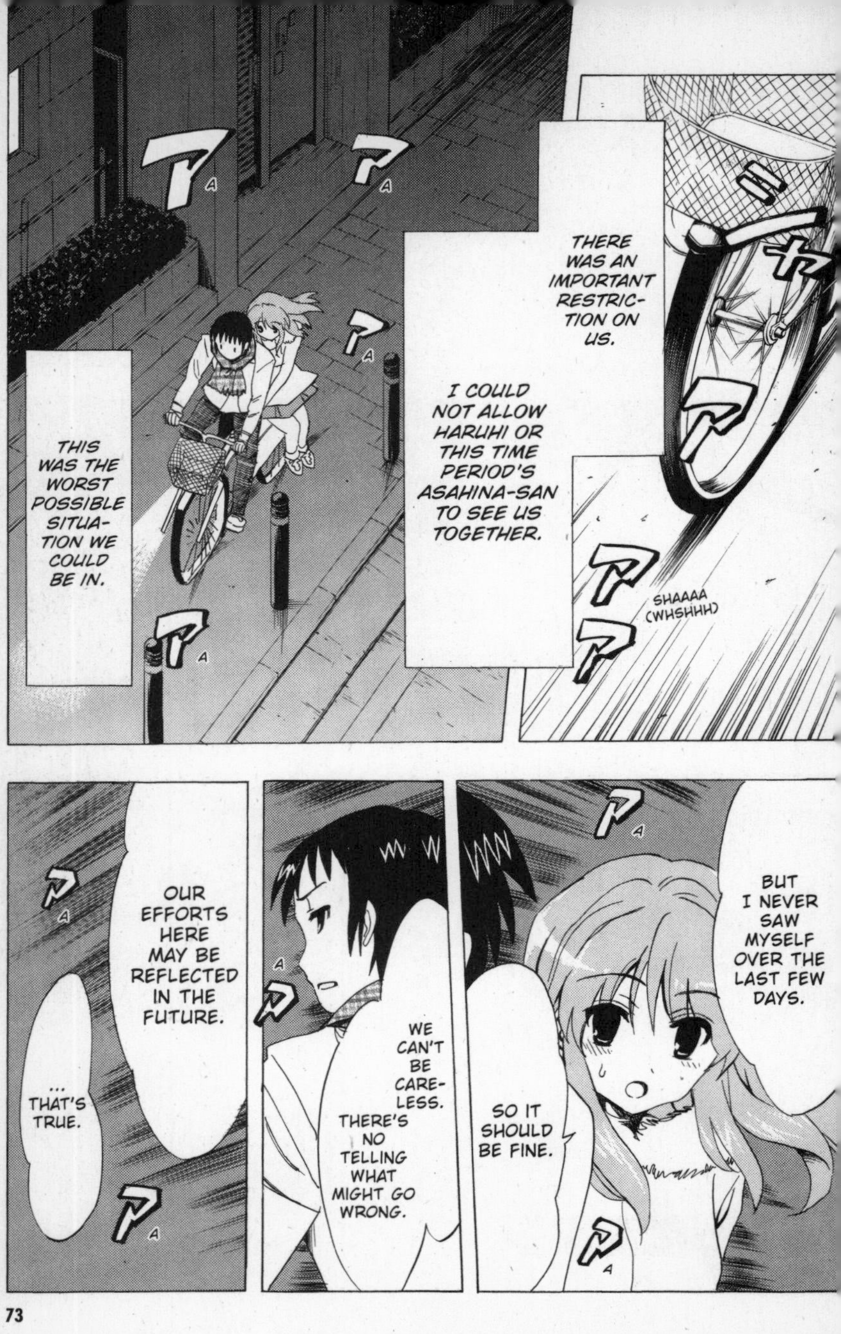
THERE WAS AN IMPORTANT RESTRICTION ON US.
SHAAAA (WHSHHH)
I COULD NOT ALLOW HARUHI OR THIS TIME PERIOD'S ASAHINA-SAN TO SEE US TOGETHER.
A
A
A
A
THIS WAS THE WORST POSSIBLE SITUATION WE COULD BE IN.
A
BUT I NEVER SAW MYSELF OVER THE LAST FEW DAYS.
SO IT SHOULD BE FINE.
A
A
WE CAN'T BE CARELESS.
THERE'S NO TELLING WHAT MIGHT GO WRONG.
A
OUR EFFORTS HERE MAY BE REFLECTED IN THE FUTURE.
... THAT'S TRUE.
A
A

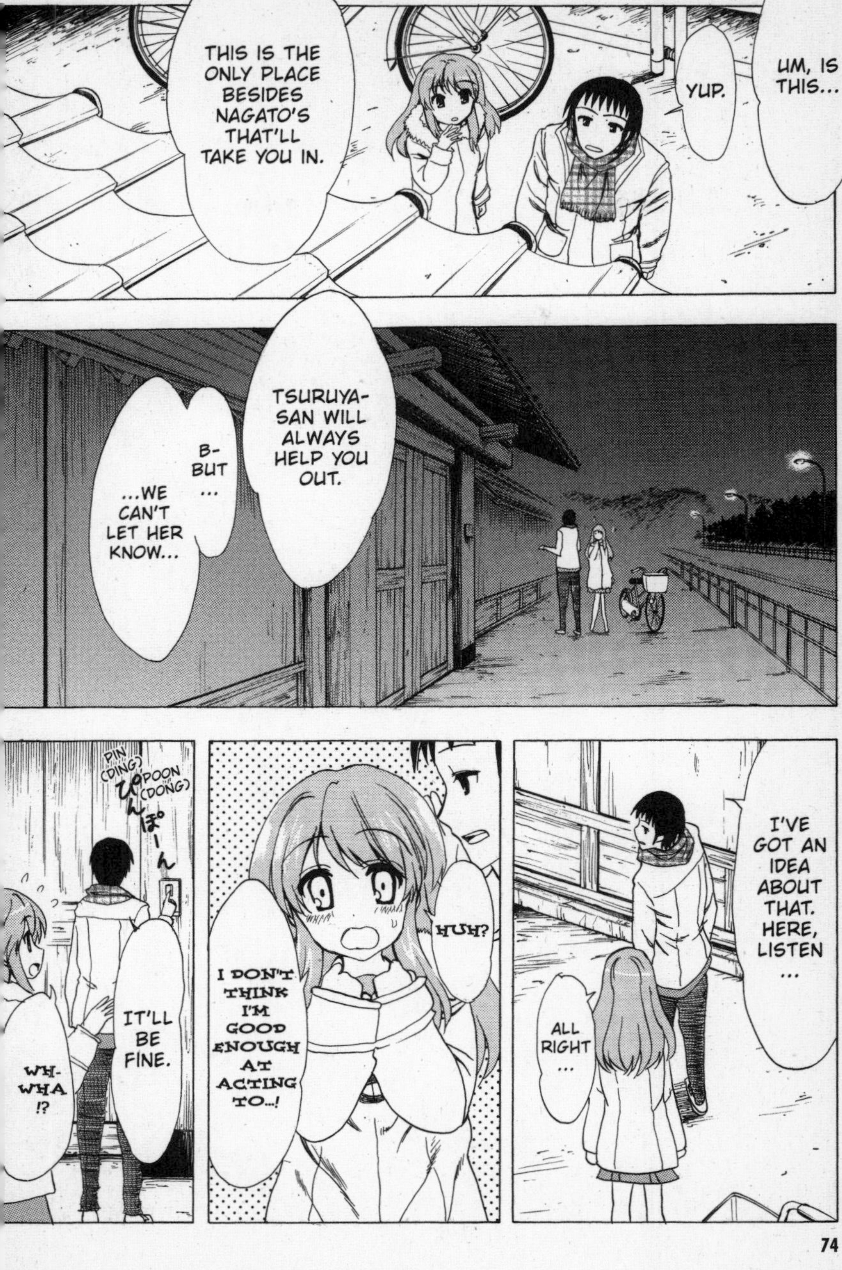
UM, IS THIS...
YUP.
THIS IS THE ONLY PLACE BESIDES NAGATO'S THAT'LL TAKE YOU IN.
TSURUYA-SAN WILL ALWAYS HELP YOU OUT.
B-BUT ...
...WE CAN'T LET HER KNOW...
I'VE GOT AN IDEA ABOUT THAT. HERE, LISTEN ...
ALL RIGHT ...
HUH?
I DON'T THINK I'M GOOD ENOUGH AT ACTING TO...!
ぴんぽーん
PIN (DING) POON (DONG)
IT'LL BE FINE.
WH-WHA !?

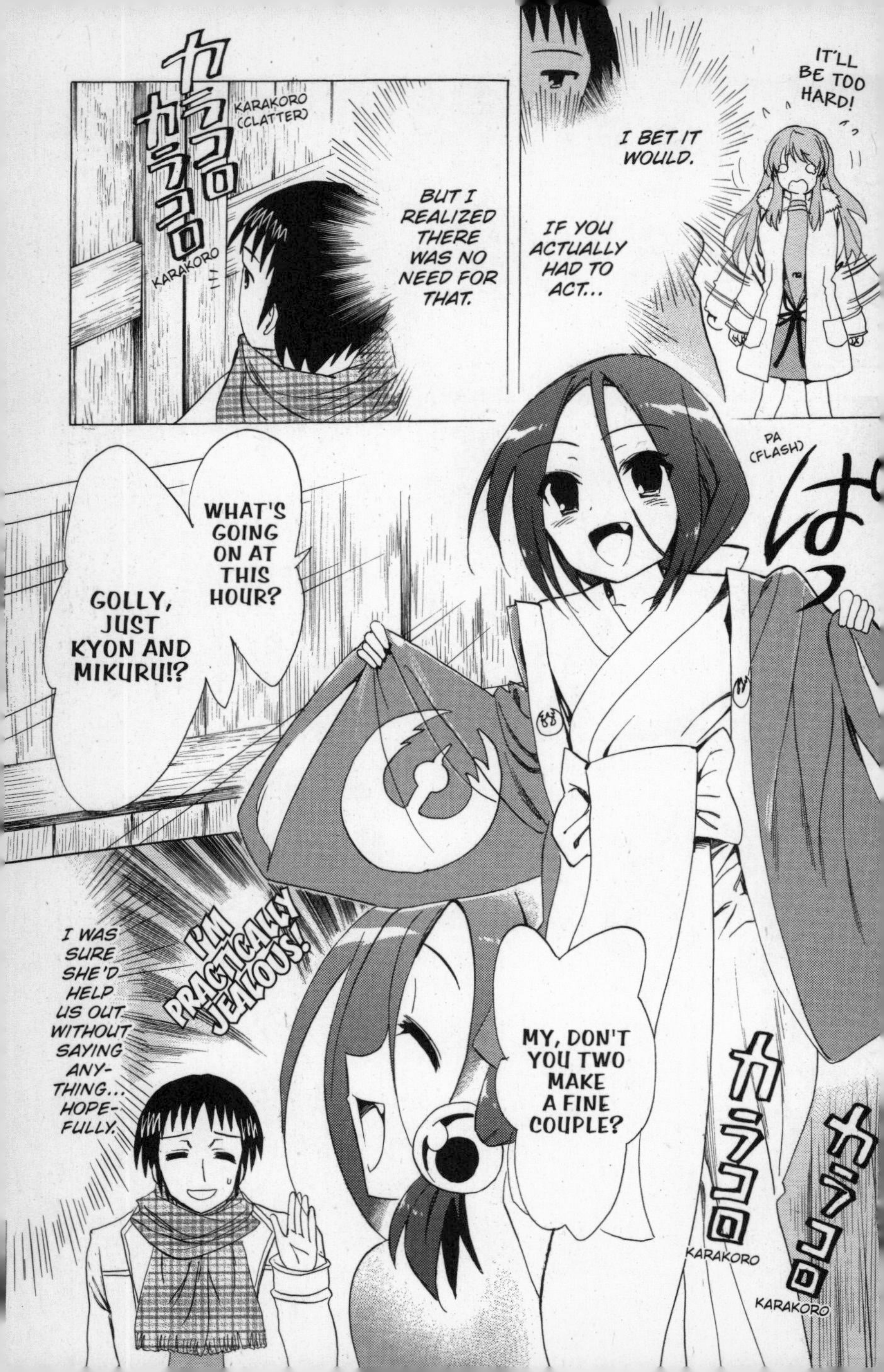
IT'LL BE TOO HARD!
I BET IT WOULD.
IF YOU ACTUALLY HAD TO ACT...
BUT I REALIZED THERE WAS NO NEED FOR THAT.
カラコロ
KARAKORO (CLATTER)
カラコロ
KARAKORO
ぱっ
PA (FLASH)
WHAT'S GOING ON AT THIS HOUR?
GOLLY, JUST KYON AND MIKURU!?
カラコロ
KARAKORO
カラコロ
KARAKORO
MY, DON'T YOU TWO MAKE A FINE COUPLE?
I'M PRACTICALLY JEALOUS!
I WAS SURE SHE'D HELP US OUT WITHOUT SAYING ANY-THING... HOPE-FULLY.

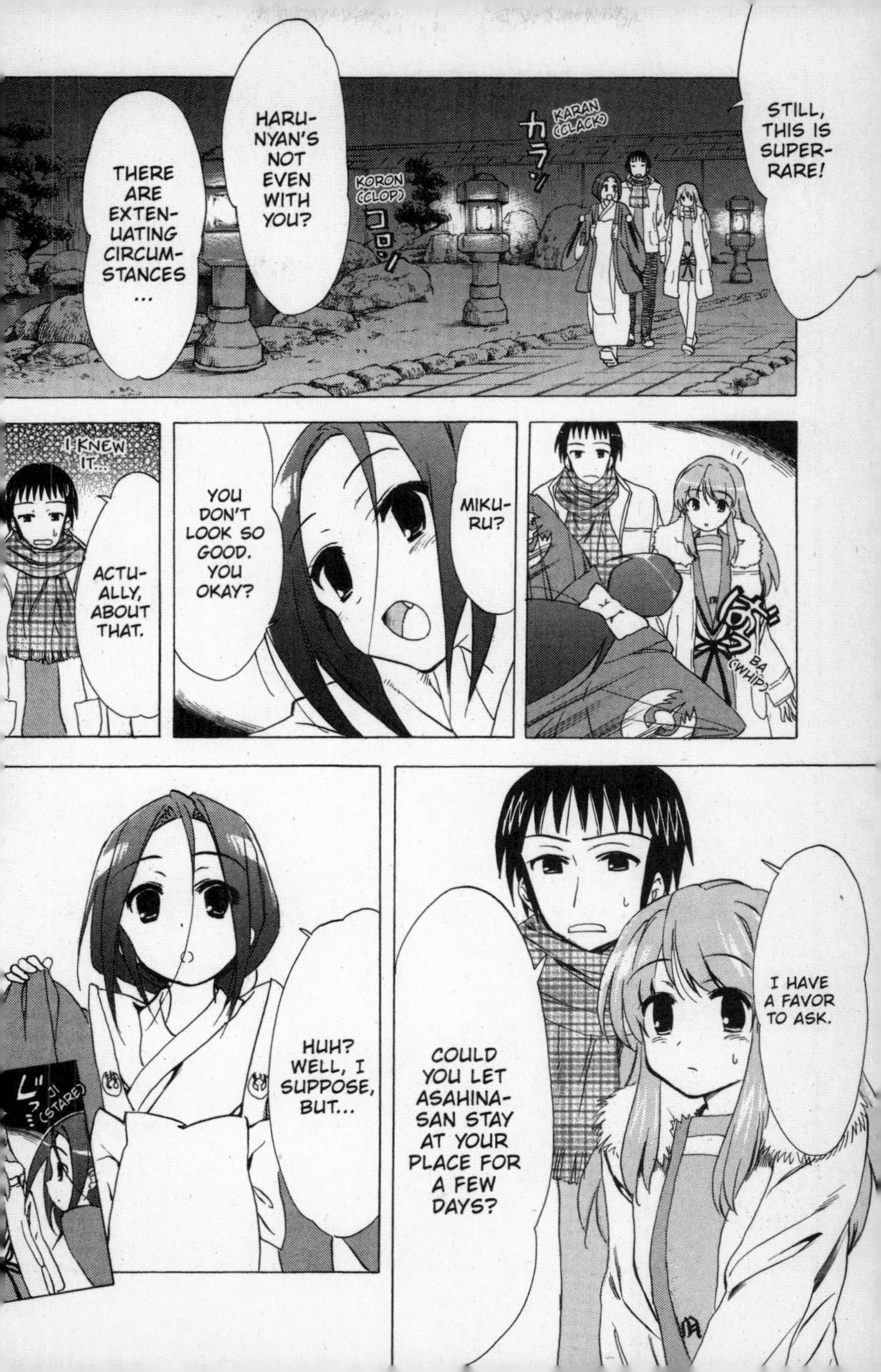
STILL, THIS IS SUPER-RARE!
KARAN (CLACK)
KORON (CLOP)
HARU-NYAN'S NOT EVEN WITH YOU?
THERE ARE EXTEN-UATING CIRCUM-STANCES...
BA (WHIP)
MIKU-RU?
YOU DON'T LOOK SO GOOD. YOU OKAY?
I KNEW IT...
ACTU-ALLY, ABOUT THAT.
I HAVE A FAVOR TO ASK.
COULD YOU LET ASAHINA-SAN STAY AT YOUR PLACE FOR A FEW DAYS?
HUH? WELL, I SUPPOSE, BUT...
JI (STARE)

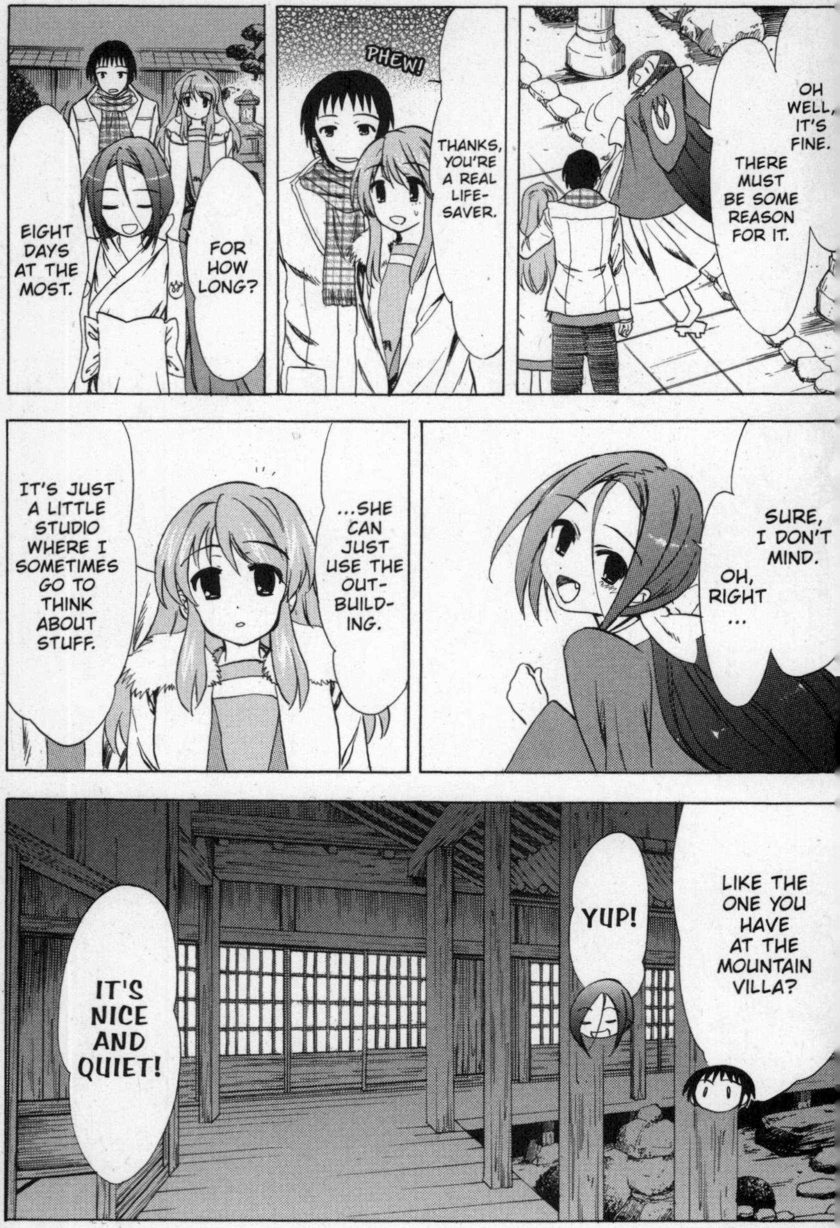
OH WELL, IT'S FINE.
THERE MUST BE SOME REASON FOR IT.
PHEW!
THANKS, YOU'RE A REAL LIFE-SAVER.
FOR HOW LONG?
EIGHT DAYS AT THE MOST.
SURE, I DON'T MIND.
OH, RIGHT...
...SHE CAN JUST USE THE OUT-BUILDING.
IT'S JUST A LITTLE STUDIO WHERE I SOMETIMES GO TO THINK ABOUT STUFF.
LIKE THE ONE YOU HAVE AT THE MOUNTAIN VILLA?
YUP!
IT'S NICE AND QUIET!

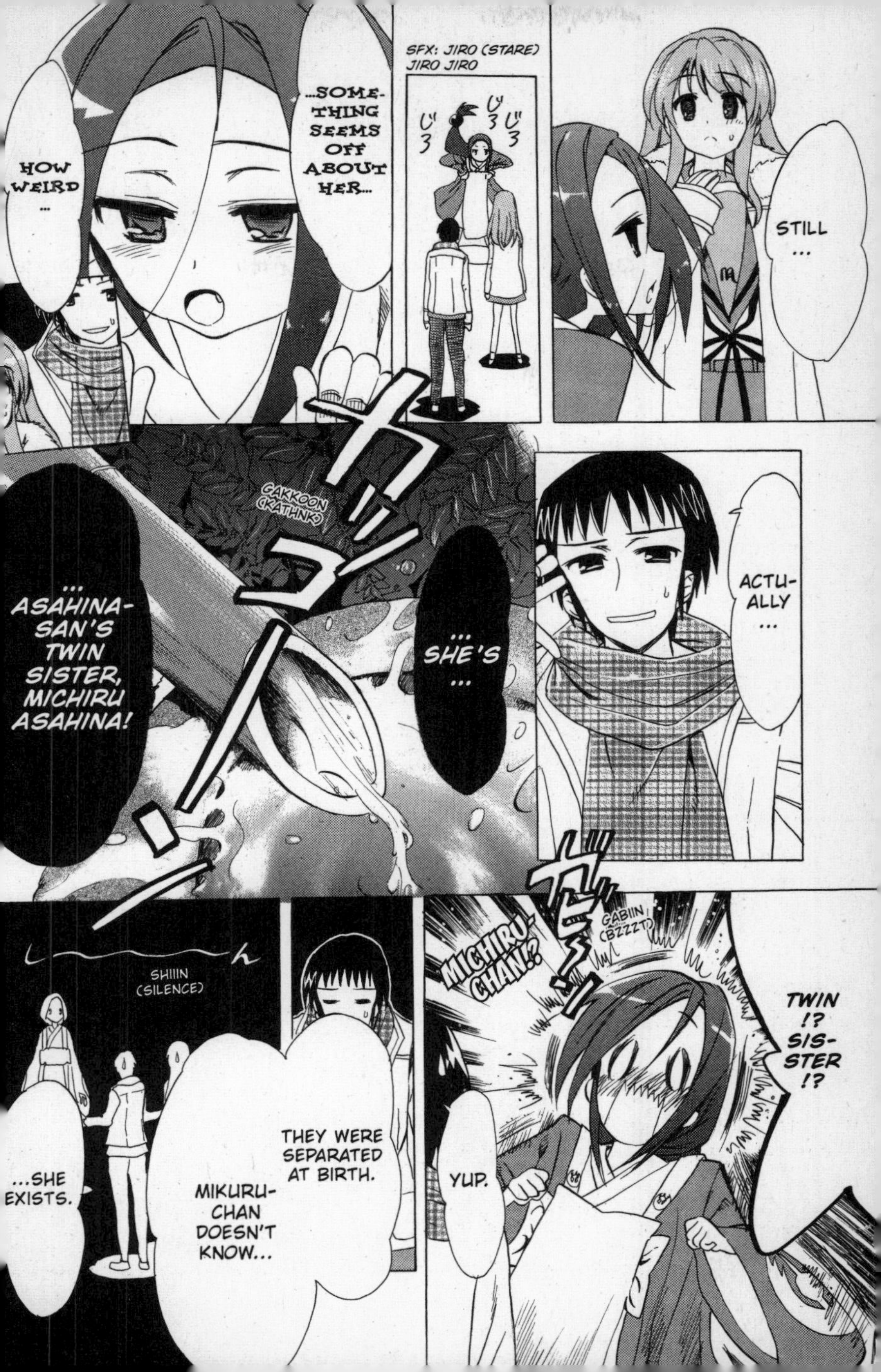
STILL ...
SFX: JIRO (STARE) JIRO JIRO
...SOME-THING SEEMS OFF ABOUT HER...
HOW WEIRD ...
ACTU-ALLY ...
... SHE'S ...
GAKKOON (KATHNK)
... ASAHINA-SAN'S TWIN SISTER, MICHIRU ASAHINA!
TWIN !? SIS-STER !?
MICHIRU-CHAN!?
GABIIN (BZZZT)
YUP.
THEY WERE SEPARATED AT BIRTH.
MIKURU-CHAN DOESN'T KNOW...
SHIIIN (SILENCE)
...SHE EXISTS.

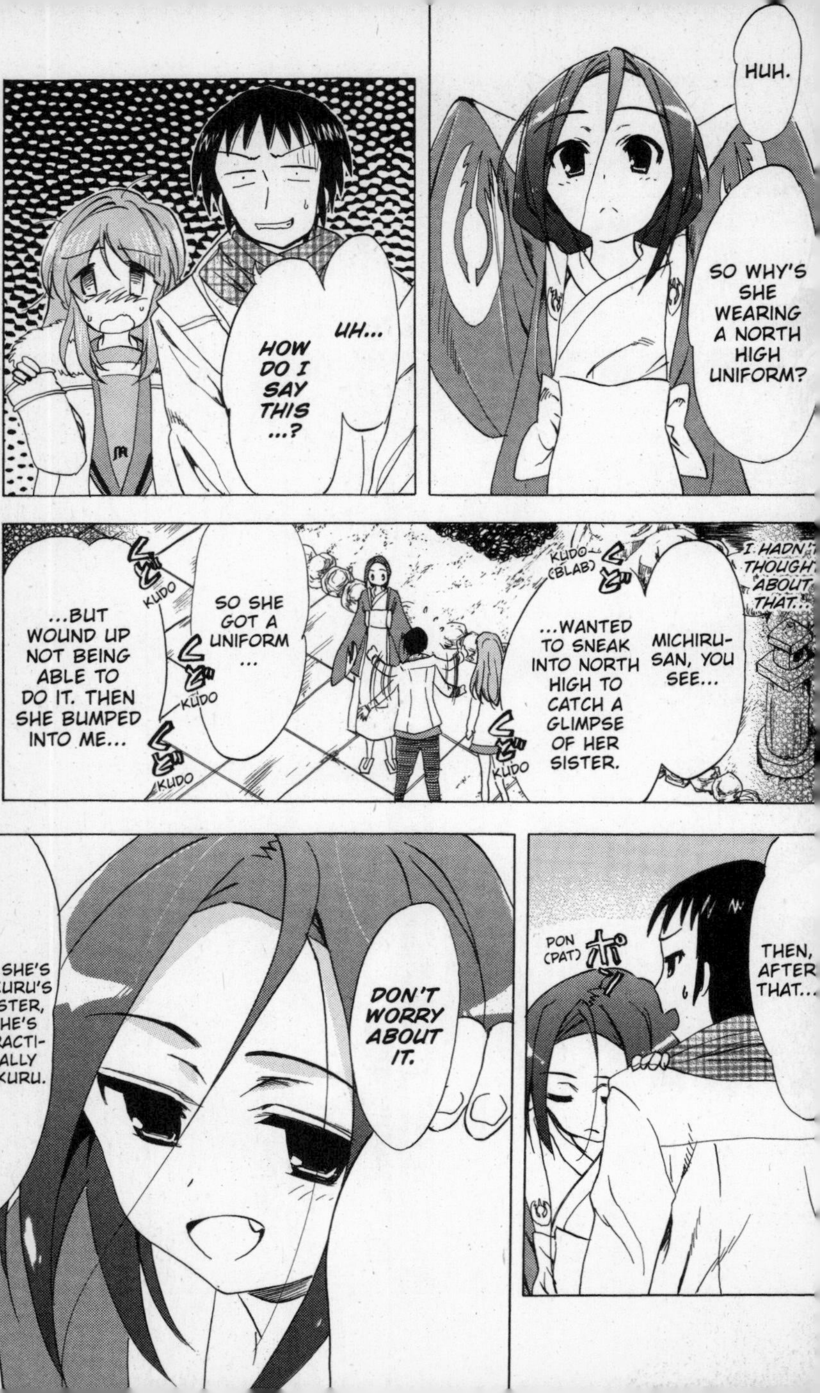
HUH.
SO WHY'S SHE WEARING A NORTH HIGH UNIFORM?
UH...
HOW DO I SAY THIS ...?
I HADN'T THOUGHT ABOUT THAT...
MICHIRU-SAN, YOU SEE...
KUDO (BLAB)
...WANTED TO SNEAK INTO NORTH HIGH TO CATCH A GLIMPSE OF HER SISTER.
KUDO
SO SHE GOT A UNIFORM ...
KUDO
...BUT WOUND UP NOT BEING ABLE TO DO IT. THEN SHE BUMPED INTO ME...
KUDO
KUDO
THEN, AFTER THAT...
PON (PAT)
DON'T WORRY ABOUT IT.
IF SHE'S MIKURU'S SISTER, SHE'S PRACTICALLY MIKURU.

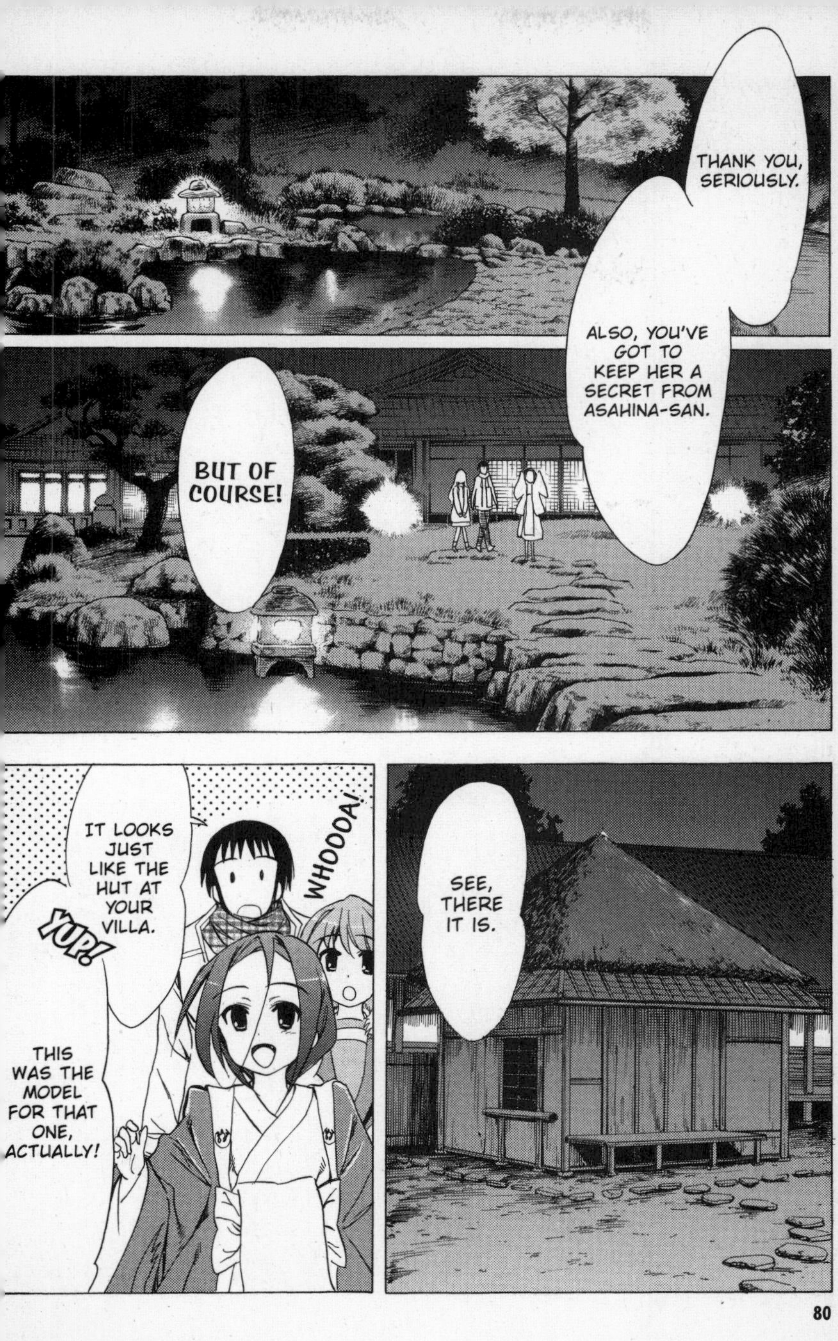
THANK YOU, SERIOUSLY.
ALSO, YOU'VE GOT TO KEEP HER A SECRET FROM ASAHINA-SAN.
BUT OF COURSE!
SEE, THERE IT IS.
WHOOOA!
IT LOOKS JUST LIKE THE HUT AT YOUR VILLA.
YUP!
THIS WAS THE MODEL FOR THAT ONE, ACTUALLY!

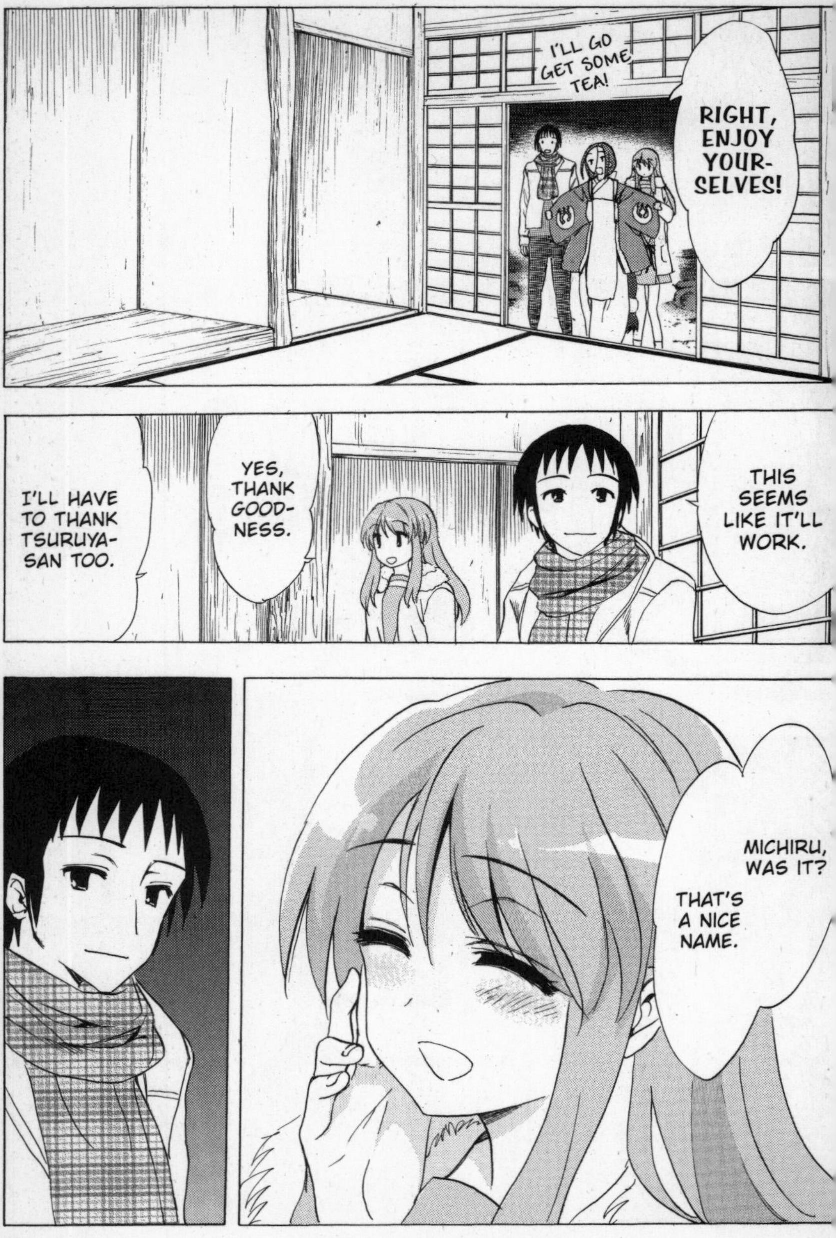
RIGHT, ENJOY YOUR-SELVES!
I'LL GO GET SOME TEA!
THIS SEEMS LIKE IT'LL WORK.
YES, THANK GOOD-NESS.
I'LL HAVE TO THANK TSURUYA-SAN TOO.
MICHIRU, WAS IT?
THAT'S A NICE NAME.

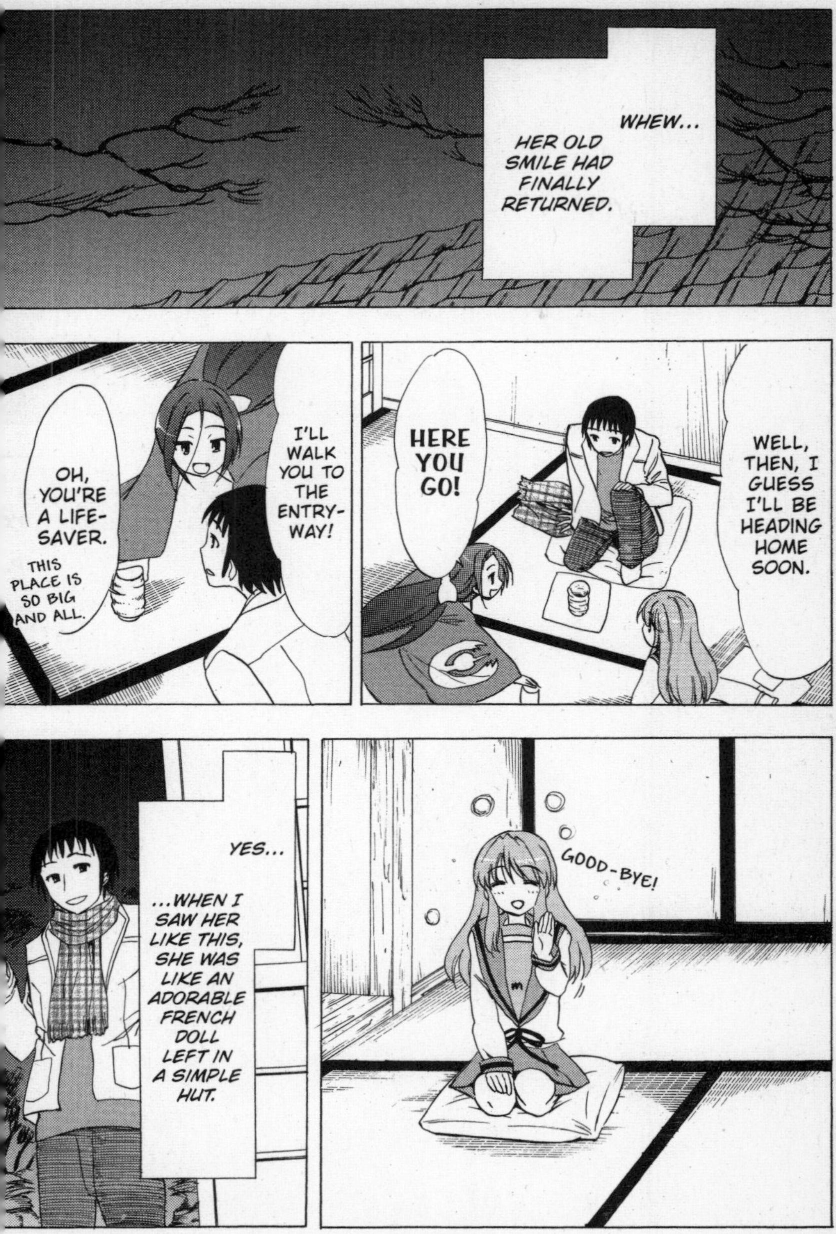
WHEW... HER OLD SMILE HAD FINALLY RETURNED.
WELL, THEN, I GUESS I'LL BE HEADING HOME SOON.
HERE YOU GO!
I'LL WALK YOU TO THE ENTRY-WAY!
OH, YOU'RE A LIFE-SAVER.
THIS PLACE IS SO BIG AND ALL.
GOOD-BYE!
YES...
...WHEN I SAW HER LIKE THIS, SHE WAS LIKE AN ADORABLE FRENCH DOLL LEFT IN A SIMPLE HUT.

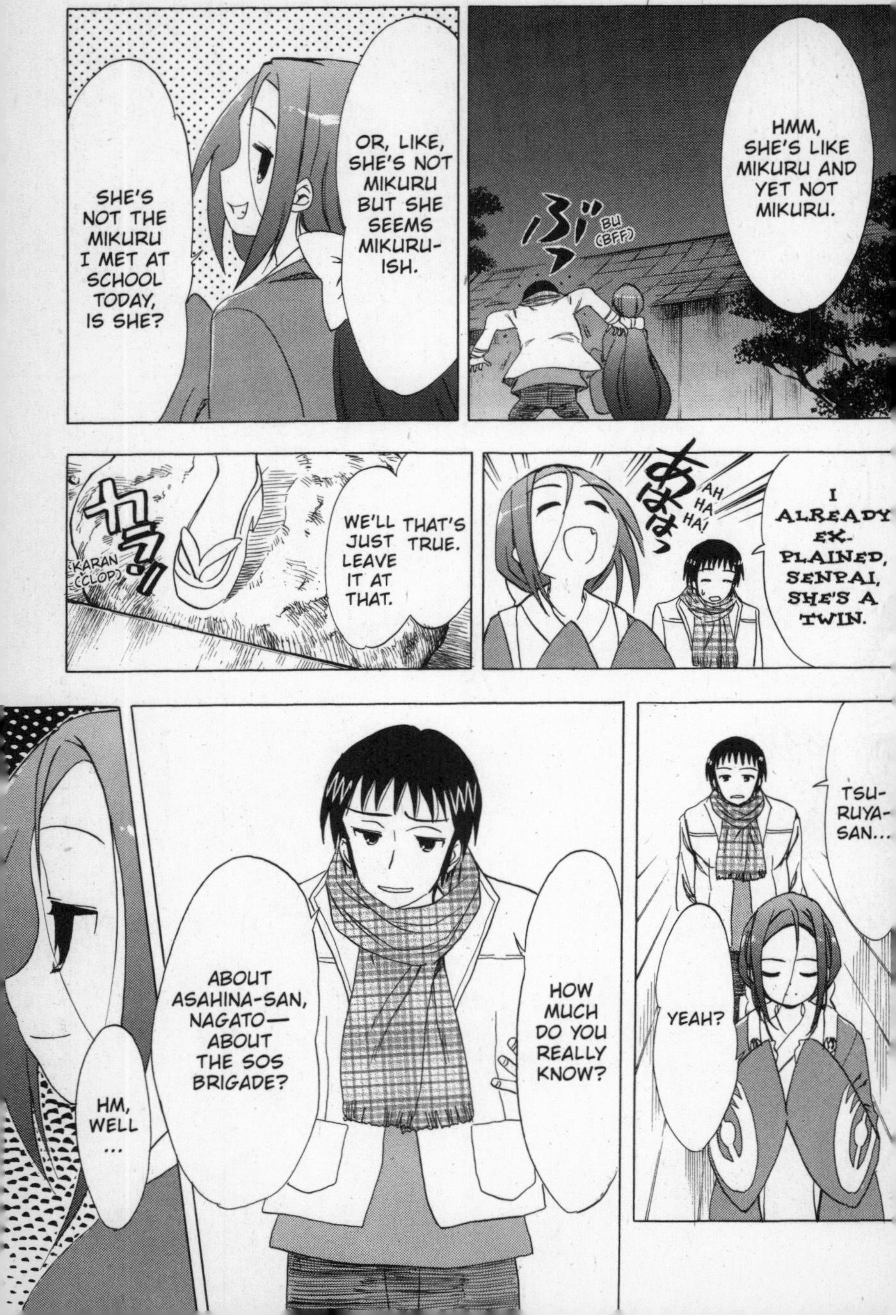
HMM, SHE'S LIKE MIKURU AND YET NOT MIKURU.
ぶっ
BU (BFF)
OR, LIKE, SHE'S NOT MIKURU BUT SHE SEEMS MIKURU-ISH.
SHE'S NOT THE MIKURU I MET AT SCHOOL TODAY, IS SHE?
I ALREADY EX-PLAINED, SENPAI, SHE'S A TWIN.
あははっ
AH HA HA!
THAT'S TRUE.
WE'LL JUST LEAVE IT AT THAT.
カラン
KARAN (CLOP)
TSURU-YA-SAN...
YEAH?
HOW MUCH DO YOU REALLY KNOW?
ABOUT ASAHINA-SAN, NAGATO—ABOUT THE SOS BRIGADE?
HM, WELL...

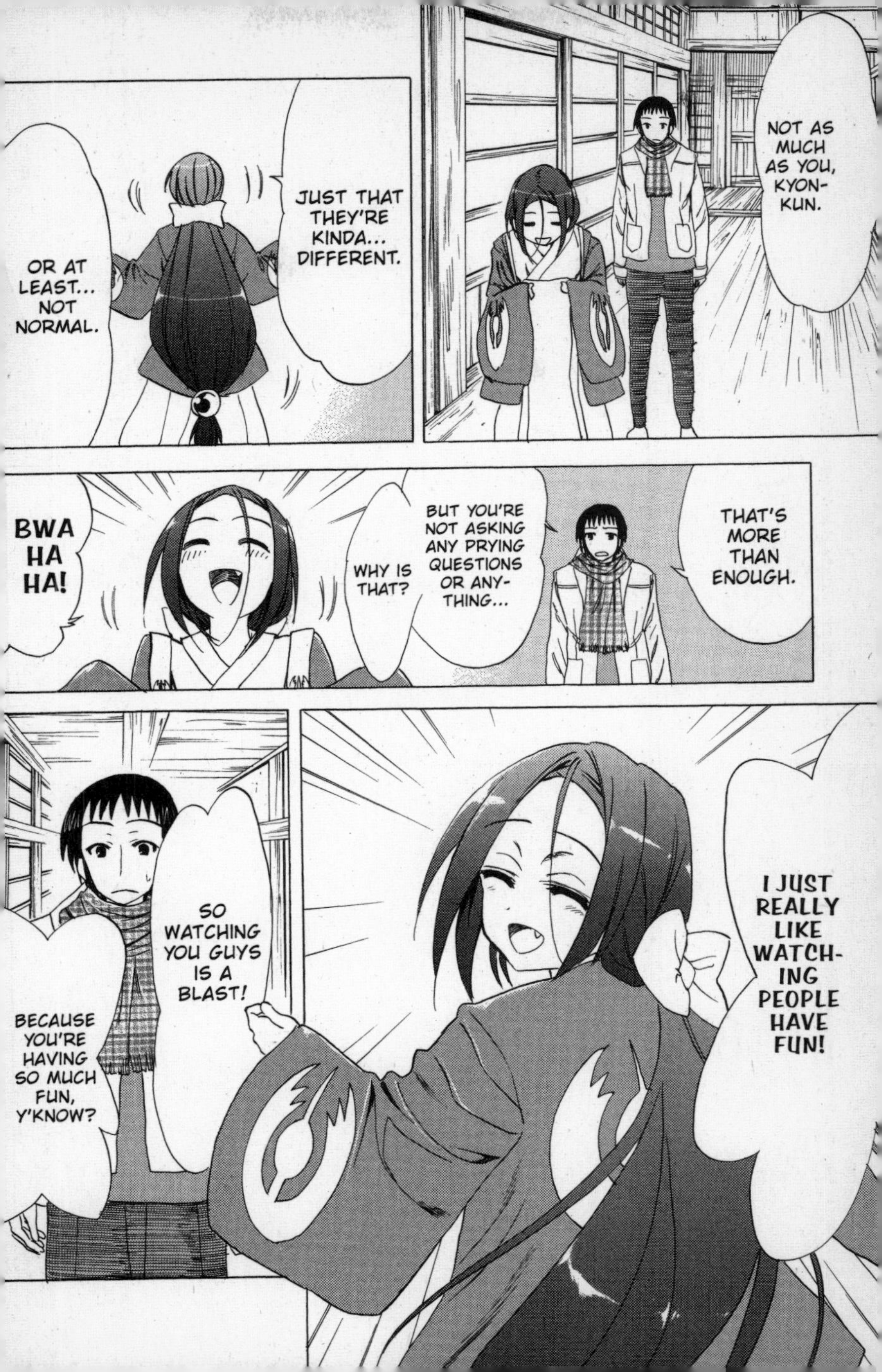

NOT AS MUCH AS YOU, KYON-KUN.
JUST THAT THEY'RE KINDA... DIFFERENT.
OR AT LEAST... NOT NORMAL.
THAT'S MORE THAN ENOUGH.
BUT YOU'RE NOT ASKING ANY PRYING QUESTIONS OR ANYTHING...
WHY IS THAT?
BWA HA HA!
I JUST REALLY LIKE WATCHING PEOPLE HAVE FUN!
SO WATCHING YOU GUYS IS A BLAST!
BECAUSE YOU'RE HAVING SO MUCH FUN, Y'KNOW?

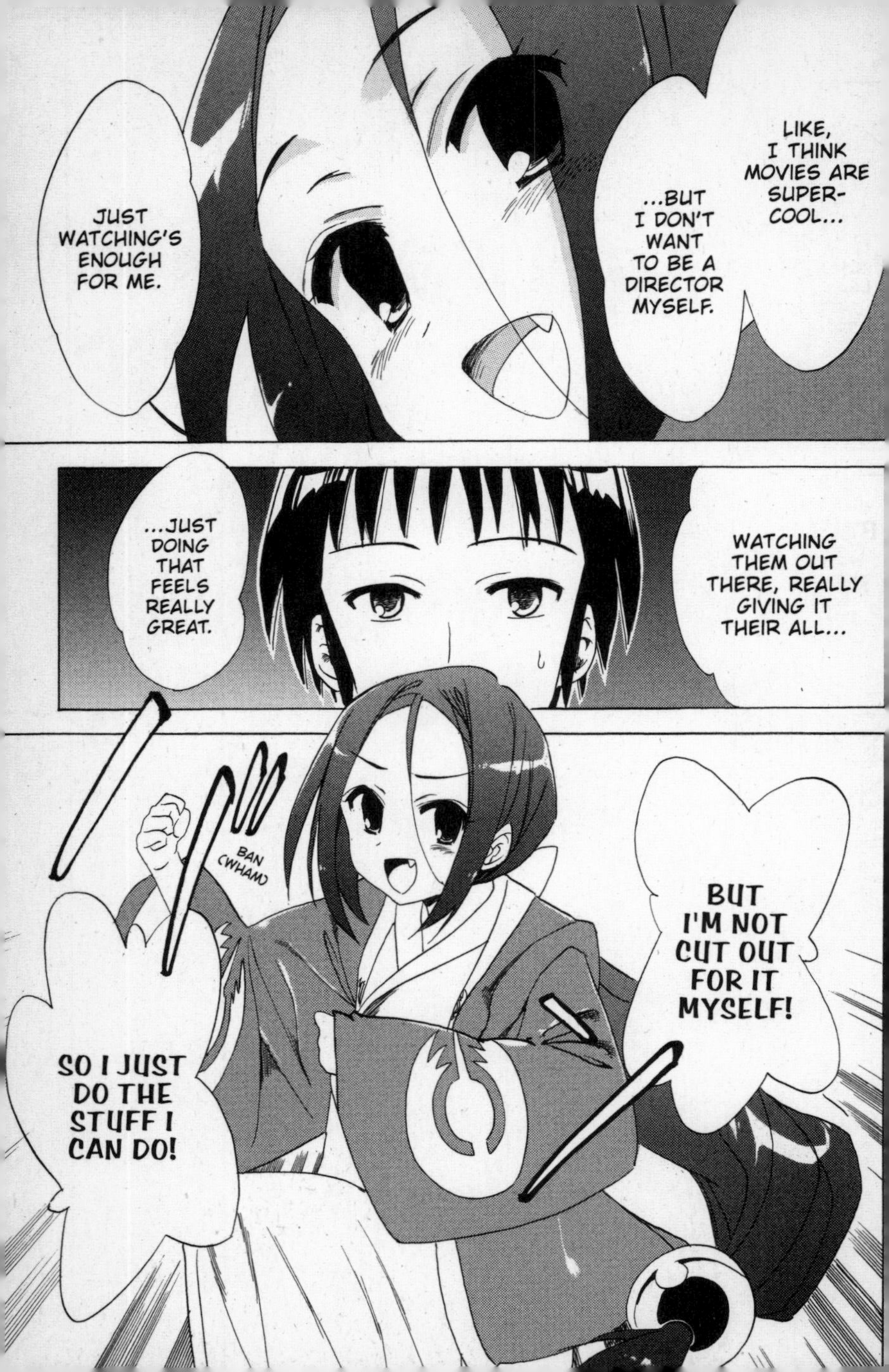
LIKE, I THINK MOVIES ARE SUPER-COOL...
...BUT I DON'T WANT TO BE A DIRECTOR MYSELF.
JUST WATCHING'S ENOUGH FOR ME.
WATCHING THEM OUT THERE, REALLY GIVING IT THEIR ALL...
...JUST DOING THAT FEELS REALLY GREAT.
BUT I'M NOT CUT OUT FOR IT MYSELF!
BAN (WHAM)
SO I JUST DO THE STUFF I CAN DO!

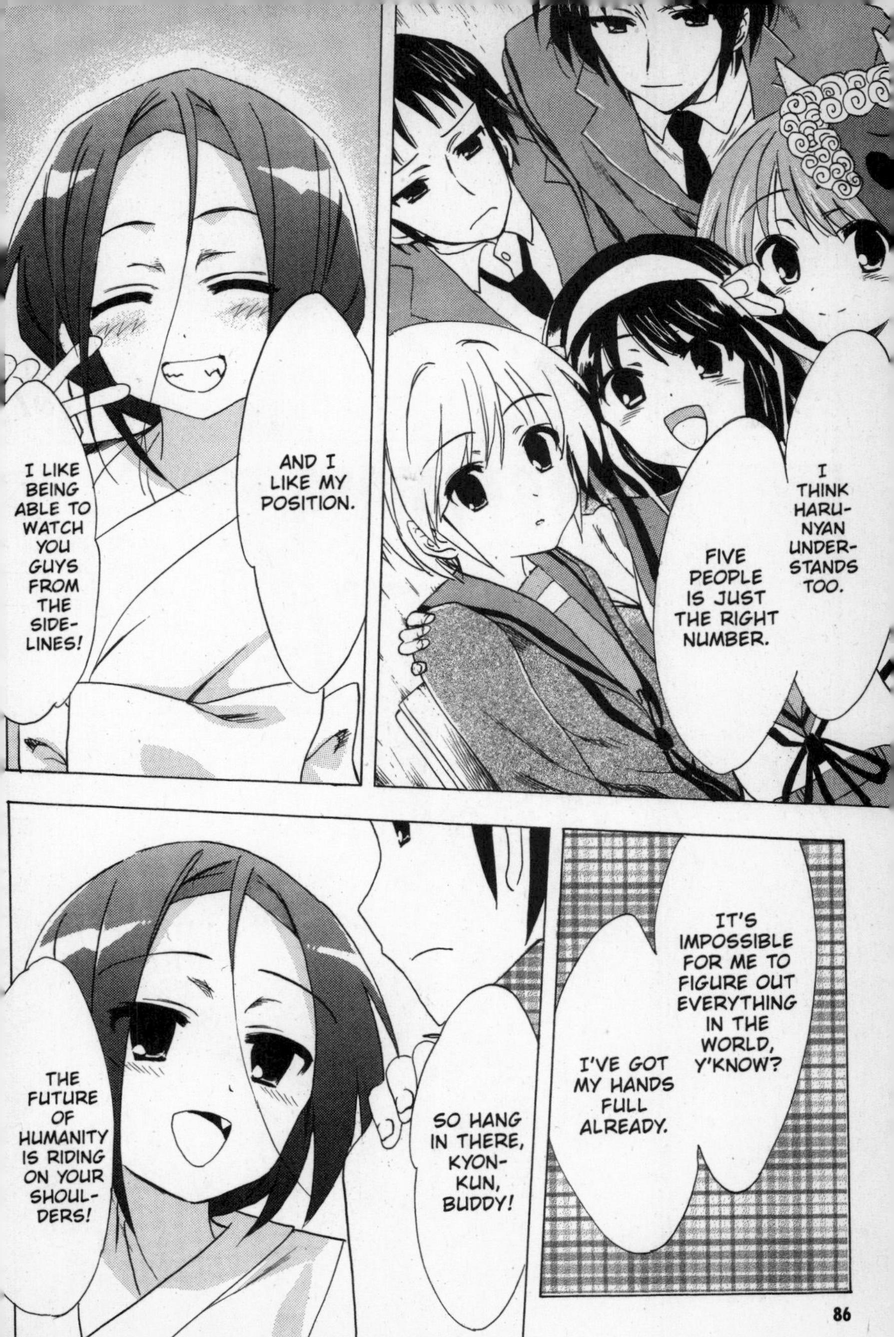
I THINK HARU-NYAN UNDER-STANDS TOO.
FIVE PEOPLE IS JUST THE RIGHT NUMBER.
AND I LIKE MY POSITION.
I LIKE BEING ABLE TO WATCH YOU GUYS FROM THE SIDE-LINES!
IT'S IMPOSSIBLE FOR ME TO FIGURE OUT EVERYTHING IN THE WORLD, Y'KNOW?
I'VE GOT MY HANDS FULL ALREADY.
SO HANG IN THERE, KYON-KUN, BUDDY!
THE FUTURE OF HUMANITY IS RIDING ON YOUR SHOULDERS!

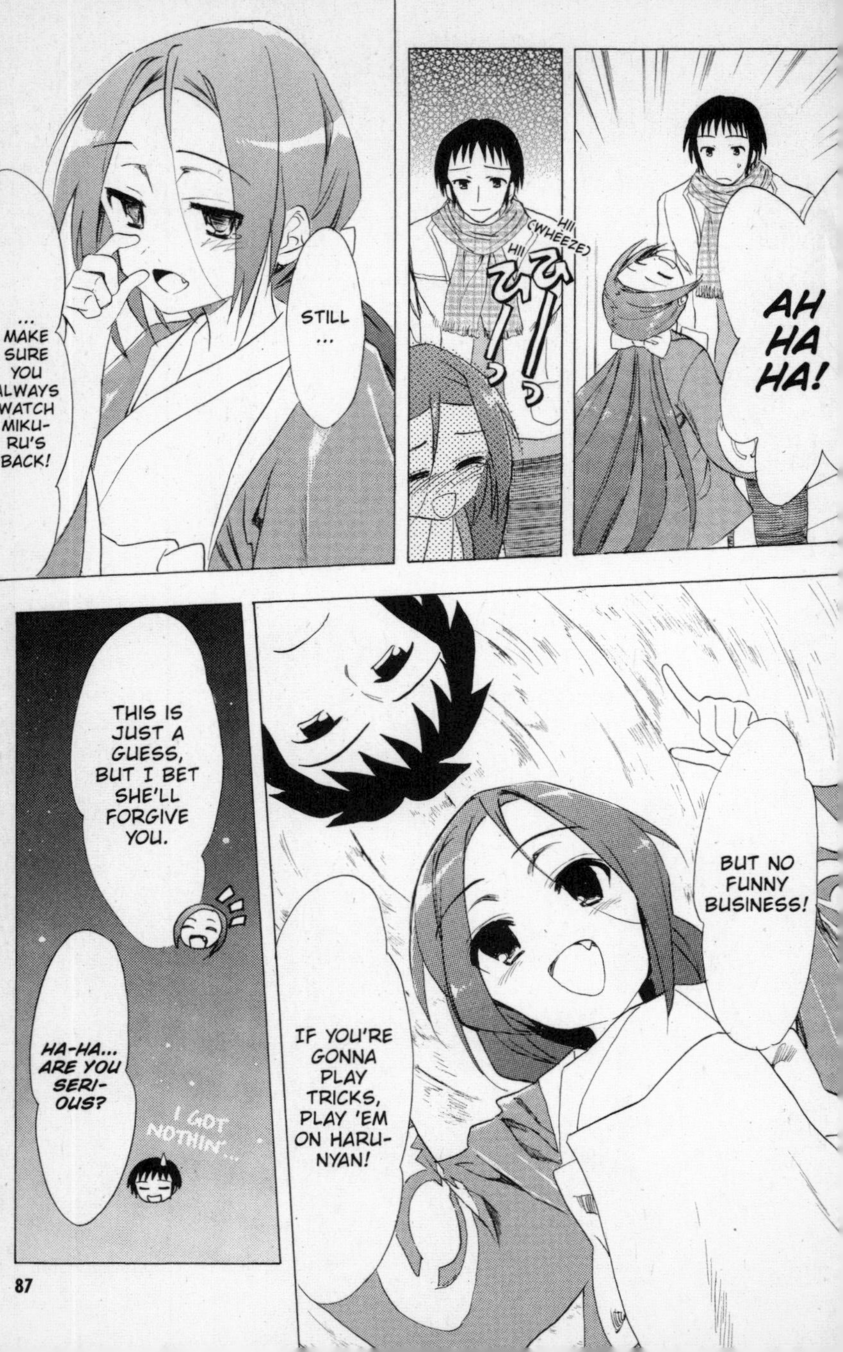
AH HA HA!
HII (WHEEZE) HII
ひーっ ひーっ
STILL ...
... MAKE SURE YOU ALWAYS WATCH MIKU-RU'S BACK!
BUT NO FUNNY BUSINESS!
IF YOU'RE GONNA PLAY TRICKS, PLAY 'EM ON HARU-NYAN!
THIS IS JUST A GUESS, BUT I BET SHE'LL FORGIVE YOU.
HA-HA... ARE YOU SERI-OUS?
I GOT NOTHIN'...

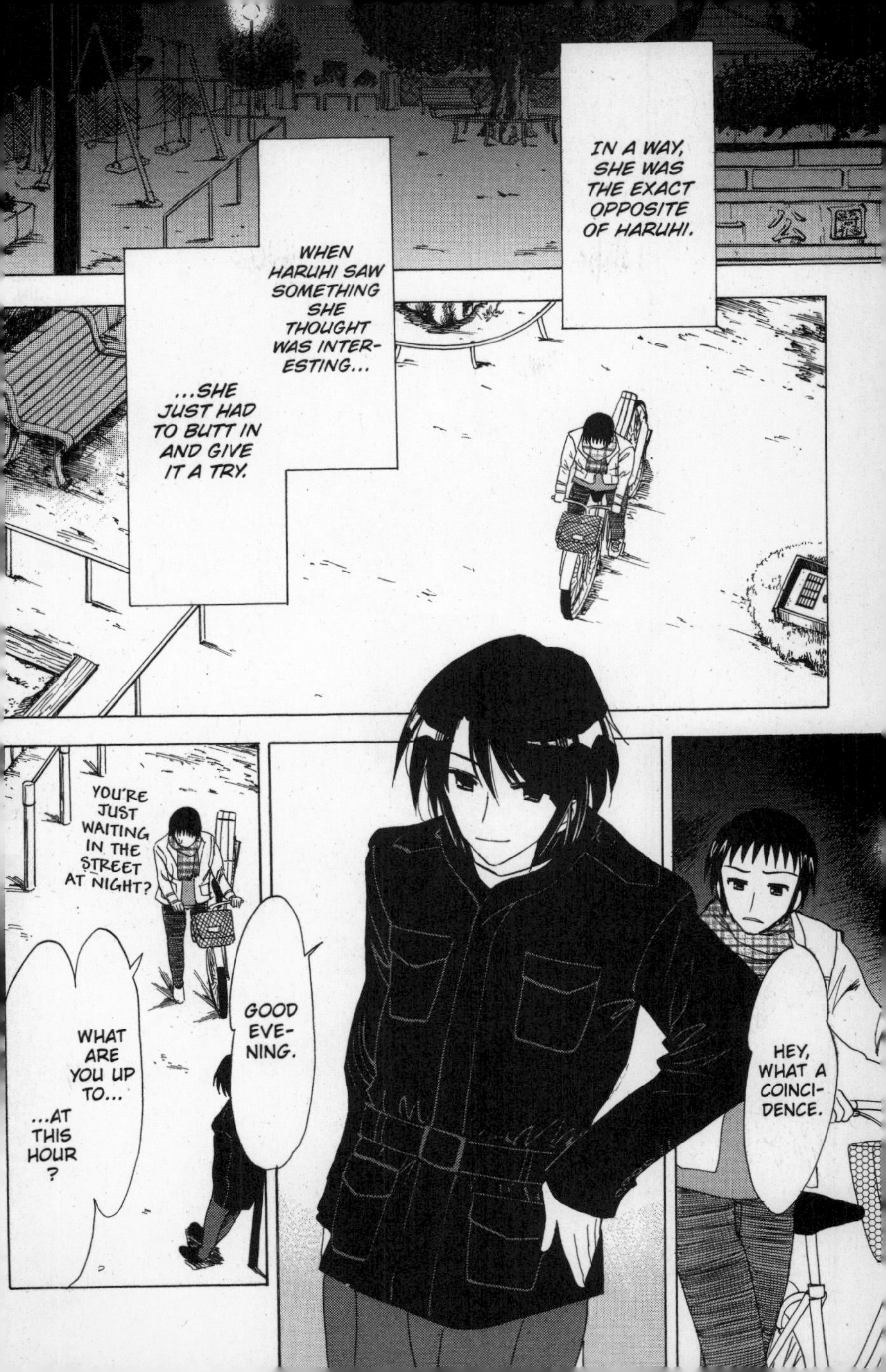
IN A WAY, SHE WAS THE EXACT OPPOSITE OF HARUHI.
WHEN HARUHI SAW SOMETHING SHE THOUGHT WAS INTER-ESTING...
...SHE JUST HAD TO BUTT IN AND GIVE IT A TRY.
HEY, WHAT A COINCI-DENCE.
GOOD EVE-NING.
YOU'RE JUST WAITING IN THE STREET AT NIGHT?
WHAT ARE YOU UP TO...
...AT THIS HOUR?

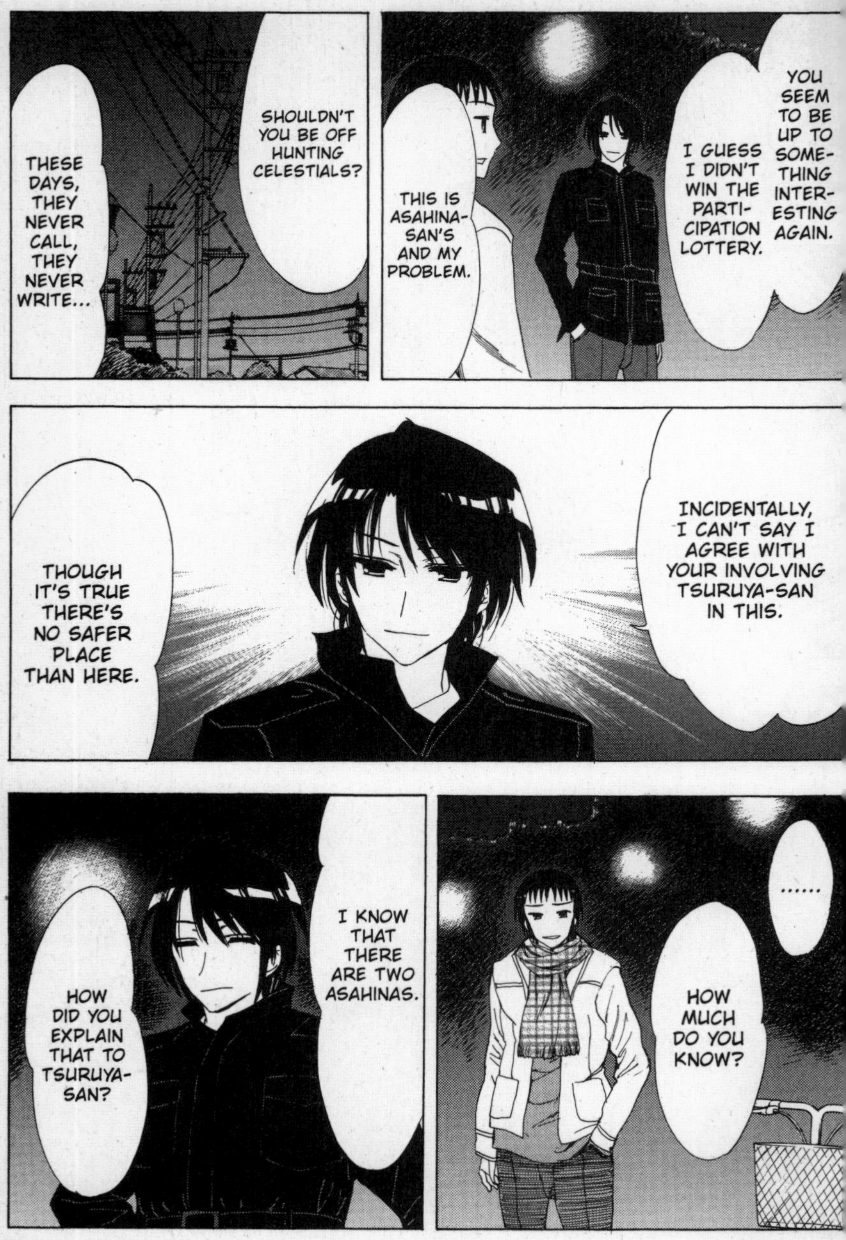
YOU SEEM TO BE UP TO SOMETHING INTERESTING AGAIN.
I GUESS I DIDN'T WIN THE PARTICIPATION LOTTERY.
THIS IS ASAHINA-SAN'S AND MY PROBLEM.
SHOULDN'T YOU BE OFF HUNTING CELESTIALS?
THESE DAYS, THEY NEVER CALL, THEY NEVER WRITE...
INCIDENTALLY, I CAN'T SAY I AGREE WITH YOUR INVOLVING TSURUYA-SAN IN THIS.
THOUGH IT'S TRUE THERE'S NO SAFER PLACE THAN HERE.
......
HOW MUCH DO YOU KNOW?
I KNOW THAT THERE ARE TWO ASAHINAS.
HOW DID YOU EXPLAIN THAT TO TSURUYA-SAN?

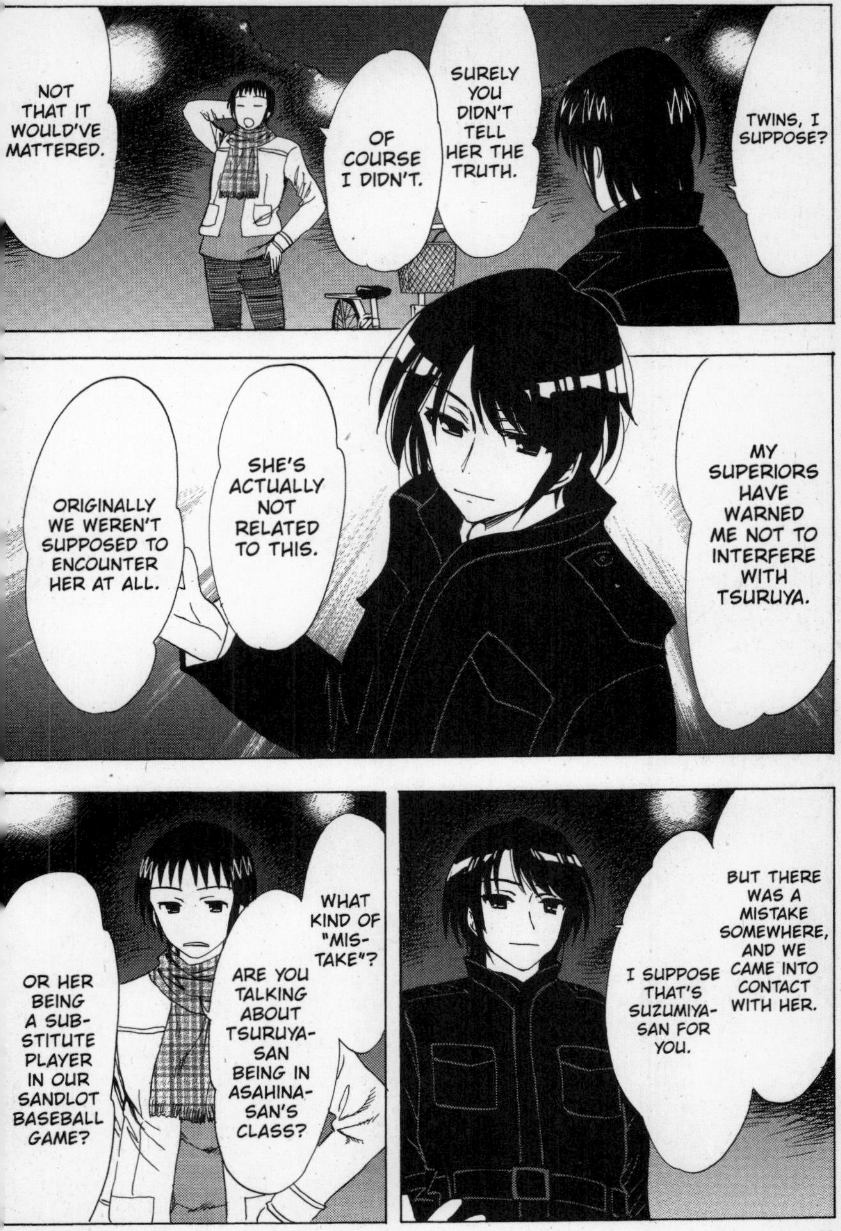
TWINS, I SUPPOSE?
SURELY YOU DIDN'T TELL HER THE TRUTH.
OF COURSE I DIDN'T.
NOT THAT IT WOULD'VE MATTERED.
MY SUPERIORS HAVE WARNED ME NOT TO INTERFERE WITH TSURUYA.
SHE'S ACTUALLY NOT RELATED TO THIS.
ORIGINALLY WE WEREN'T SUPPOSED TO ENCOUNTER HER AT ALL.
BUT THERE WAS A MISTAKE SOMEWHERE, AND WE CAME INTO CONTACT WITH HER.
I SUPPOSE THAT'S SUZUMIYA-SAN FOR YOU.
WHAT KIND OF "MIS-TAKE"?
ARE YOU TALKING ABOUT TSURUYA-SAN BEING IN ASAHINA-SAN'S CLASS?
OR HER BEING A SUB-STITUTE PLAYER IN OUR SANDLOT BASEBALL GAME?

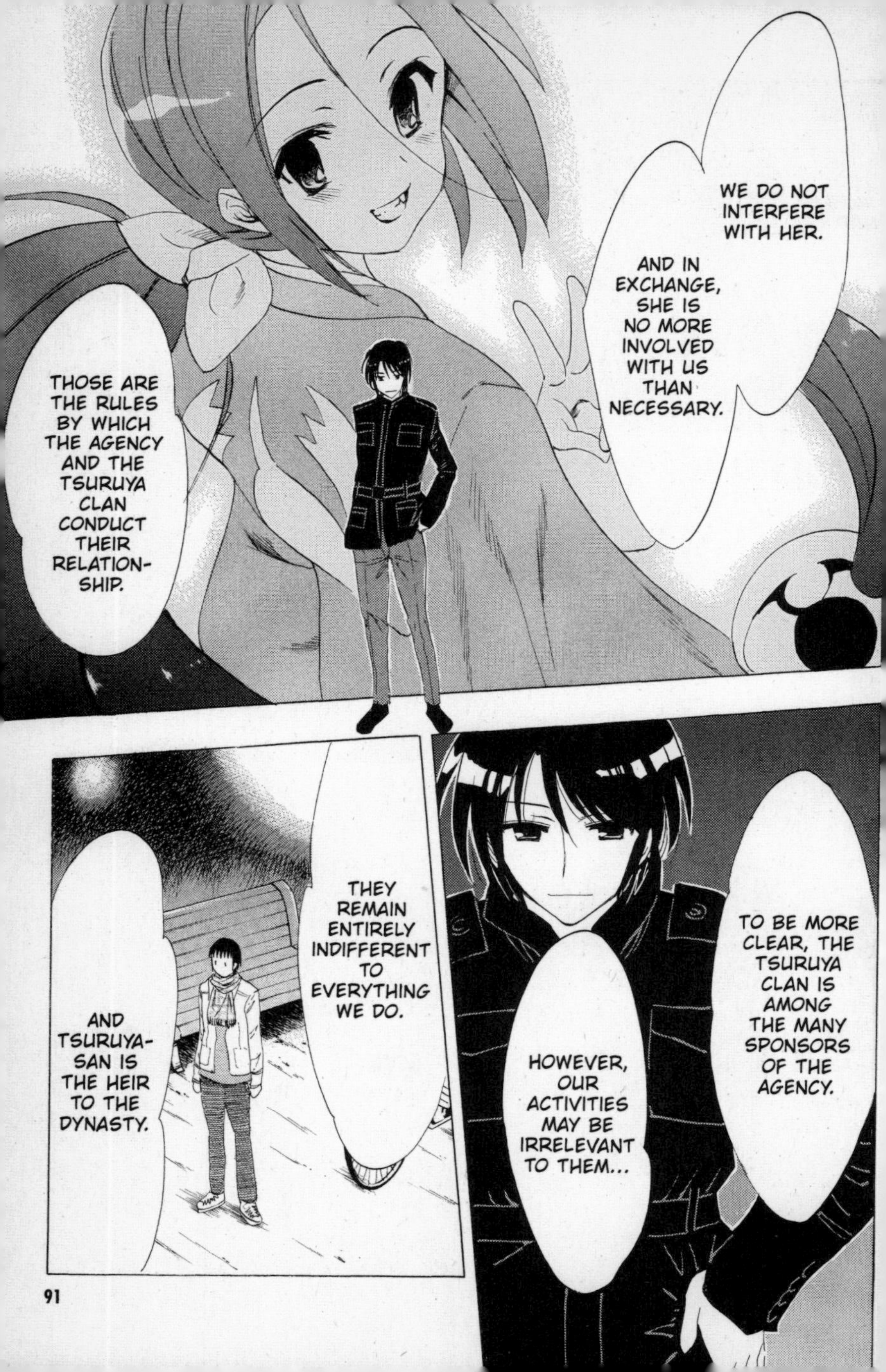
WE DO NOT INTERFERE WITH HER.
AND IN EXCHANGE, SHE IS NO MORE INVOLVED WITH US THAN NECESSARY.
THOSE ARE THE RULES BY WHICH THE AGENCY AND THE TSURUYA CLAN CONDUCT THEIR RELATION-SHIP.
TO BE MORE CLEAR, THE TSURUYA CLAN IS AMONG THE MANY SPONSORS OF THE AGENCY.
HOWEVER, OUR ACTIVITIES MAY BE IRRELEVANT TO THEM...
THEY REMAIN ENTIRELY INDIFFERENT TO EVERYTHING WE DO.
AND TSURUYA-SAN IS THE HEIR TO THE DYNASTY.

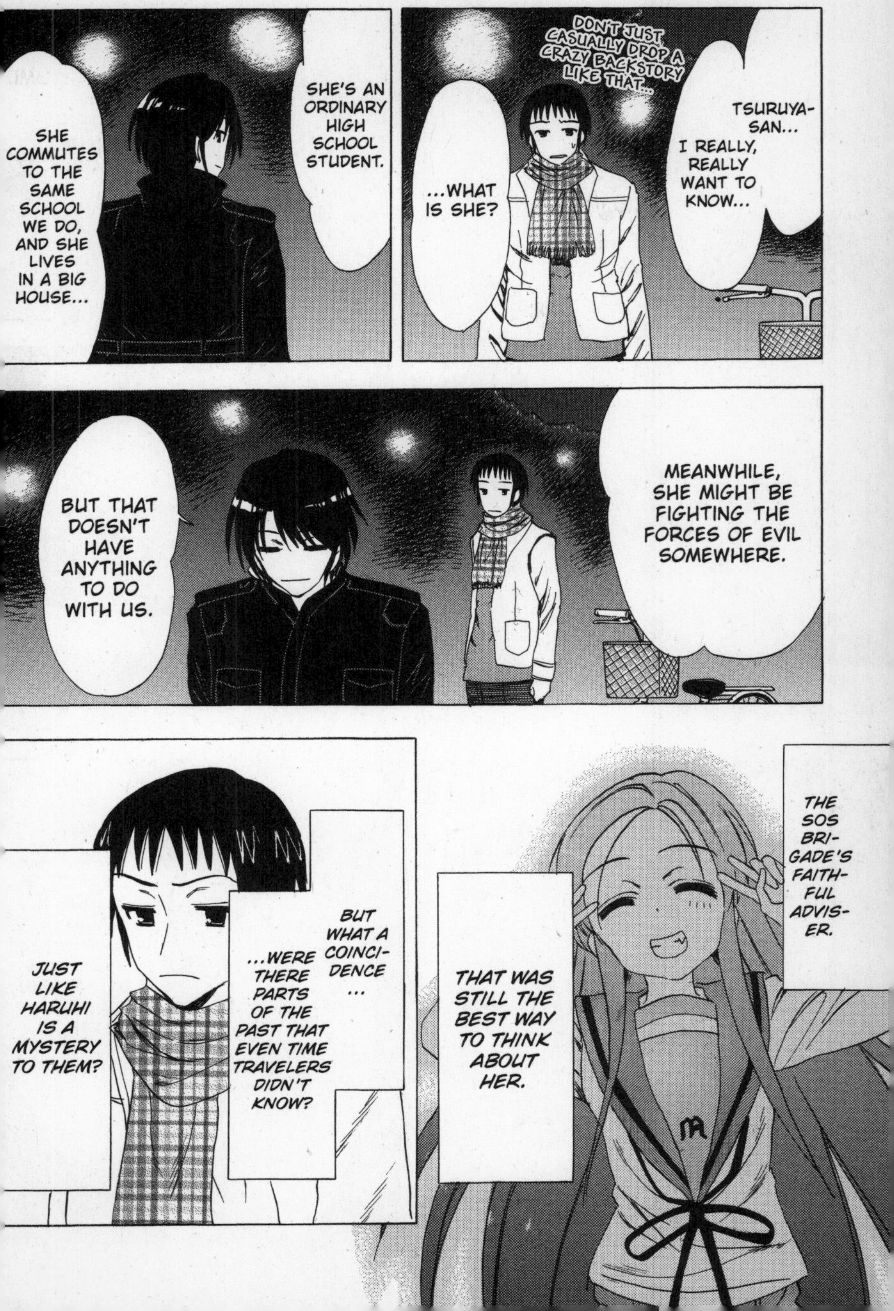
TSURUYA-SAN... I REALLY, REALLY WANT TO KNOW...
DON'T JUST CASUALLY DROP A CRAZY BACKSTORY LIKE THAT...
...WHAT IS SHE?
SHE'S AN ORDINARY HIGH SCHOOL STUDENT.
SHE COMMUTES TO THE SAME SCHOOL WE DO, AND SHE LIVES IN A BIG HOUSE...
MEANWHILE, SHE MIGHT BE FIGHTING THE FORCES OF EVIL SOMEWHERE.
BUT THAT DOESN'T HAVE ANYTHING TO DO WITH US.
THE SOS BRIGADE'S FAITHFUL ADVISER.
THAT WAS STILL THE BEST WAY TO THINK ABOUT HER.
BUT WHAT A COINCIDENCE...
...WERE THERE PARTS OF THE PAST THAT EVEN TIME TRAVELERS DIDN'T KNOW?
JUST LIKE HARUHI IS A MYSTERY TO THEM?

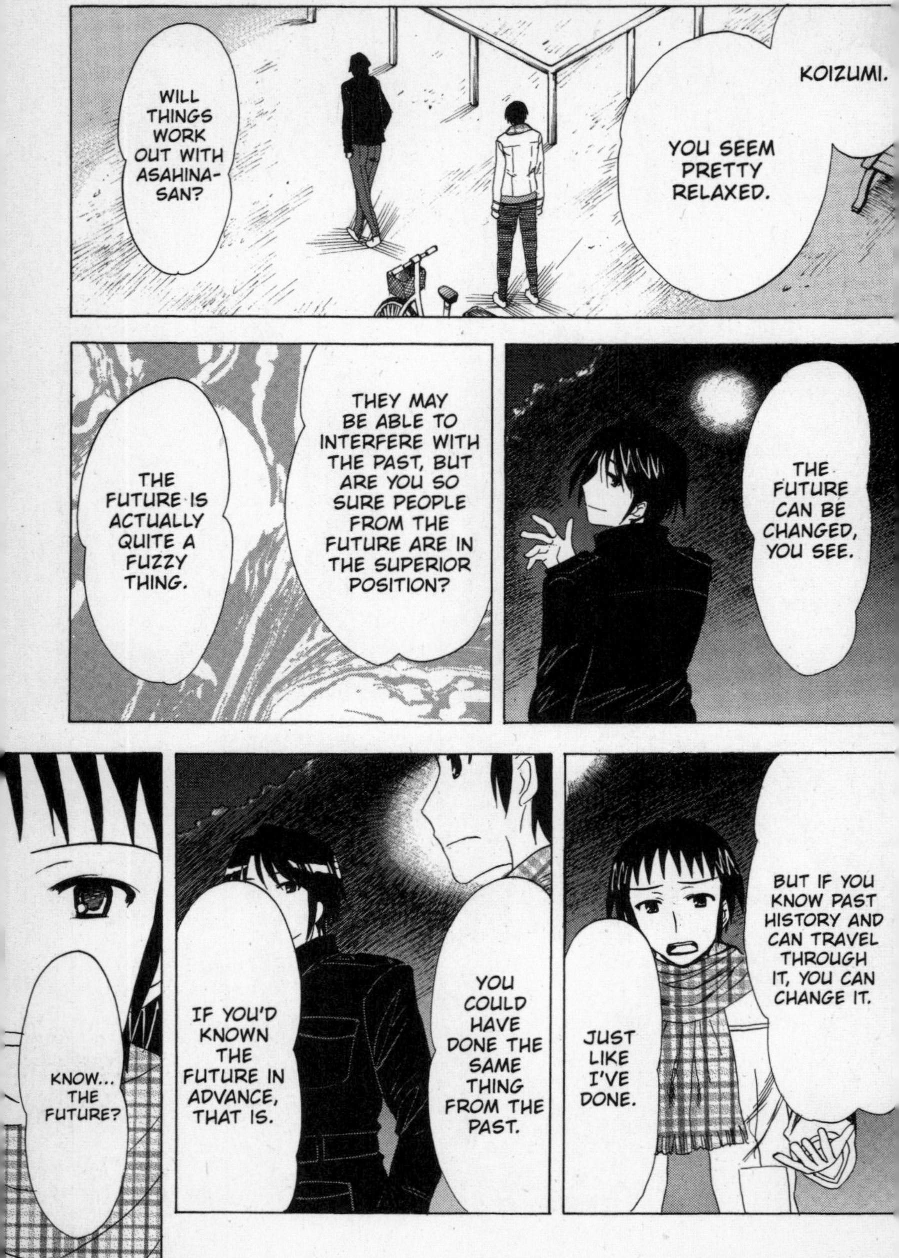
KOIZUMI.
YOU SEEM PRETTY RELAXED.
WILL THINGS WORK OUT WITH ASAHINA-SAN?
THE FUTURE CAN BE CHANGED, YOU SEE.
THEY MAY BE ABLE TO INTERFERE WITH THE PAST, BUT ARE YOU SO SURE PEOPLE FROM THE FUTURE ARE IN THE SUPERIOR POSITION?
THE FUTURE IS ACTUALLY QUITE A FUZZY THING.
BUT IF YOU KNOW PAST HISTORY AND CAN TRAVEL THROUGH IT, YOU CAN CHANGE IT.
JUST LIKE I'VE DONE.
YOU COULD HAVE DONE THE SAME THING FROM THE PAST.
IF YOU'D KNOWN THE FUTURE IN ADVANCE, THAT IS.
KNOW... THE FUTURE?

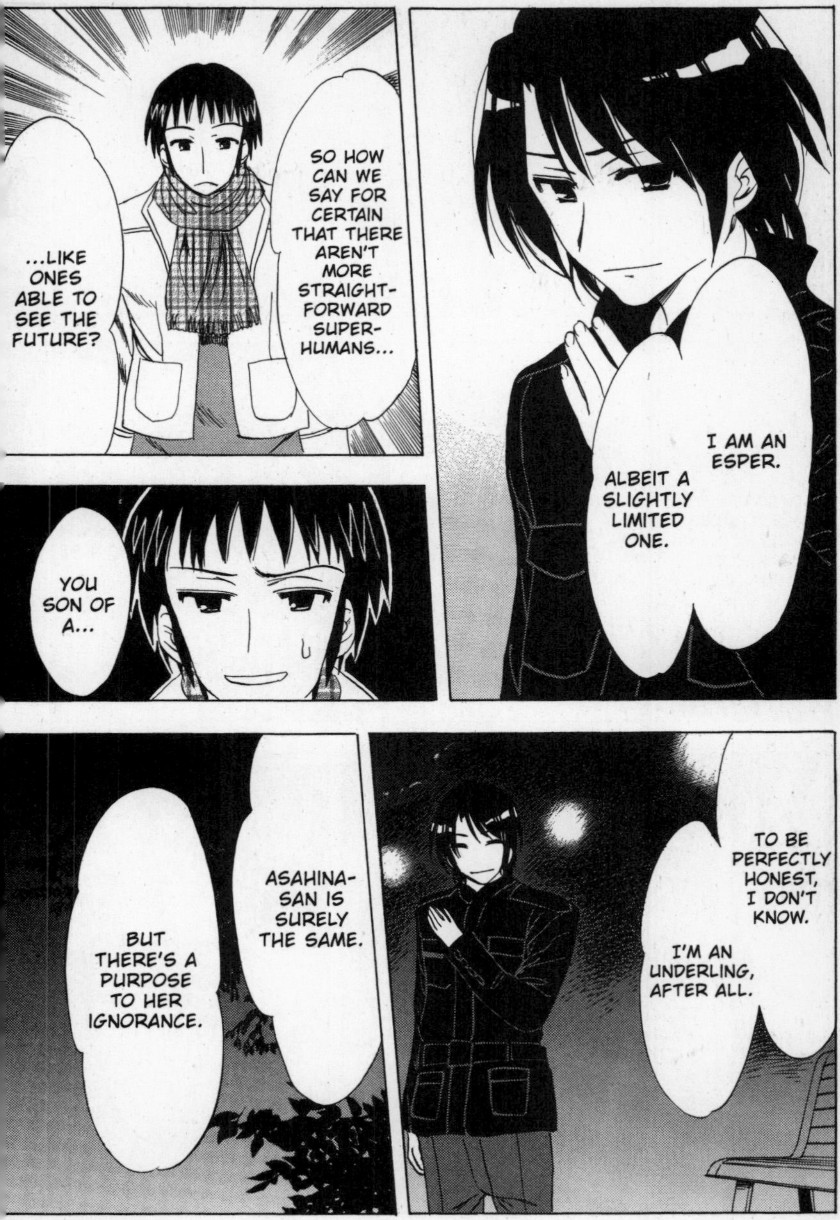
I AM AN ESPER.
ALBEIT A SLIGHTLY LIMITED ONE.
SO HOW CAN WE SAY FOR CERTAIN THAT THERE AREN'T MORE STRAIGHT-FORWARD SUPER-HUMANS...
...LIKE ONES ABLE TO SEE THE FUTURE?
YOU SON OF A...
TO BE PERFECTLY HONEST, I DON'T KNOW.
I'M AN UNDERLING, AFTER ALL.
ASAHINA-SAN IS SURELY THE SAME.
BUT THERE'S A PURPOSE TO HER IGNORANCE.

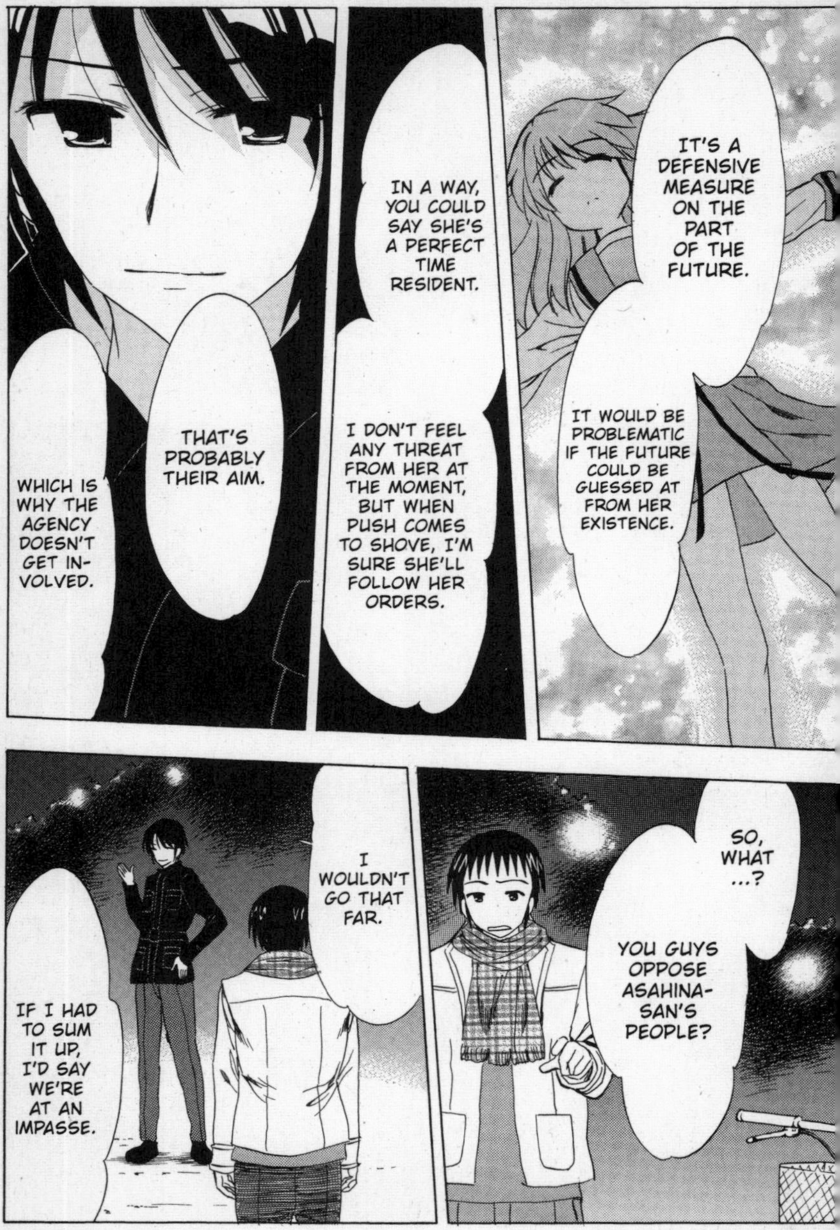
IT'S A DEFENSIVE MEASURE ON THE PART OF THE FUTURE.
IT WOULD BE PROBLEMATIC IF THE FUTURE COULD BE GUESSED AT FROM HER EXISTENCE.
IN A WAY, YOU COULD SAY SHE'S A PERFECT TIME RESIDENT.
I DON'T FEEL ANY THREAT FROM HER AT THE MOMENT, BUT WHEN PUSH COMES TO SHOVE, I'M SURE SHE'LL FOLLOW HER ORDERS.
THAT'S PROBABLY THEIR AIM.
WHICH IS WHY THE AGENCY DOESN'T GET INVOLVED.
SO, WHAT ...?
YOU GUYS OPPOSE ASAHINA-SAN'S PEOPLE?
I WOULDN'T GO THAT FAR.
IF I HAD TO SUM IT UP, I'D SAY WE'RE AT AN IMPASSE.

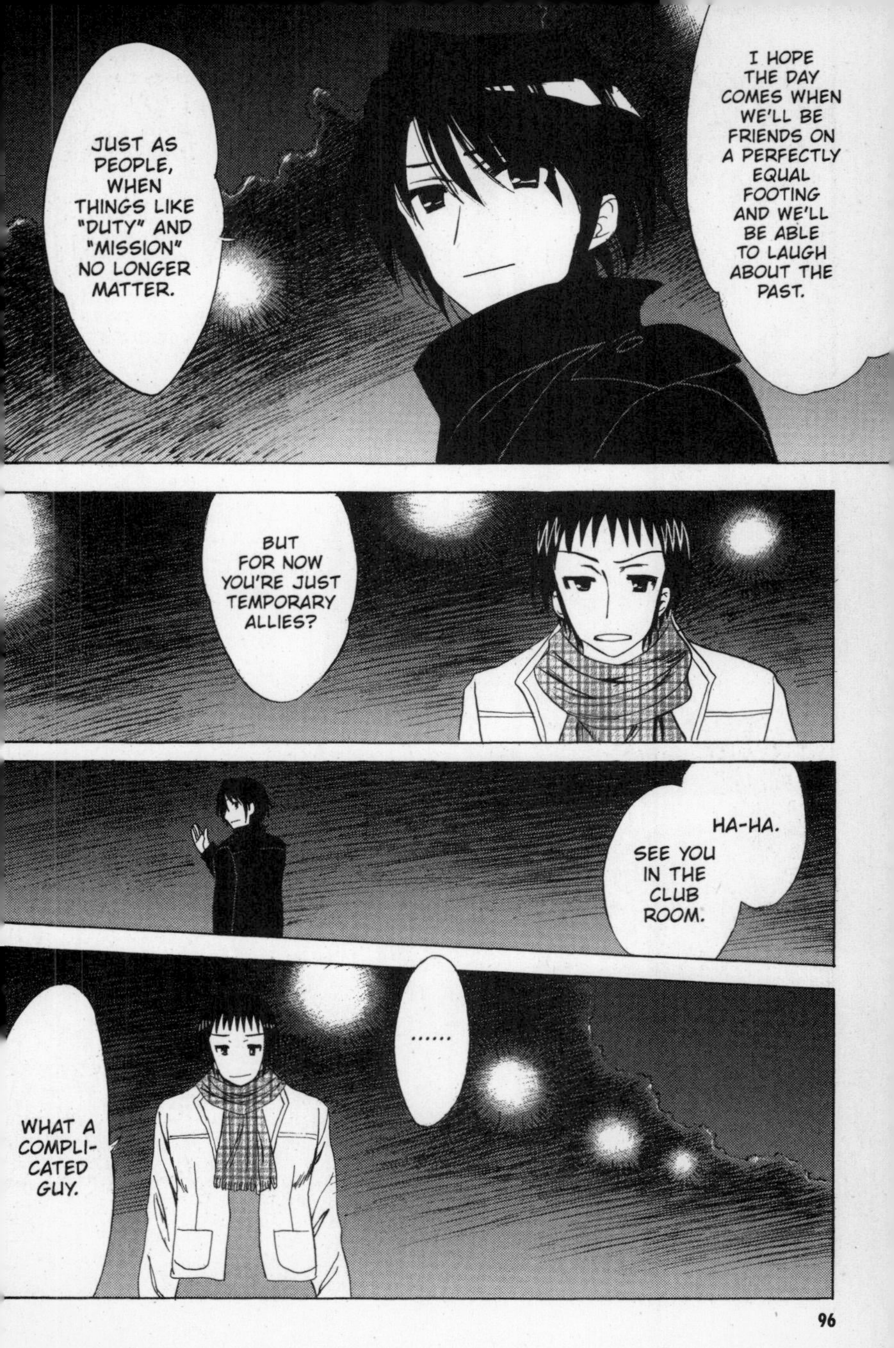
I HOPE THE DAY COMES WHEN WE'LL BE FRIENDS ON A PERFECTLY EQUAL FOOTING AND WE'LL BE ABLE TO LAUGH ABOUT THE PAST.
JUST AS PEOPLE, WHEN THINGS LIKE "DUTY" AND "MISSION" NO LONGER MATTER.
BUT FOR NOW YOU'RE JUST TEMPORARY ALLIES?
HA-HA.
SEE YOU IN THE CLUB ROOM.
......
WHAT A COMPLI-CATED GUY.

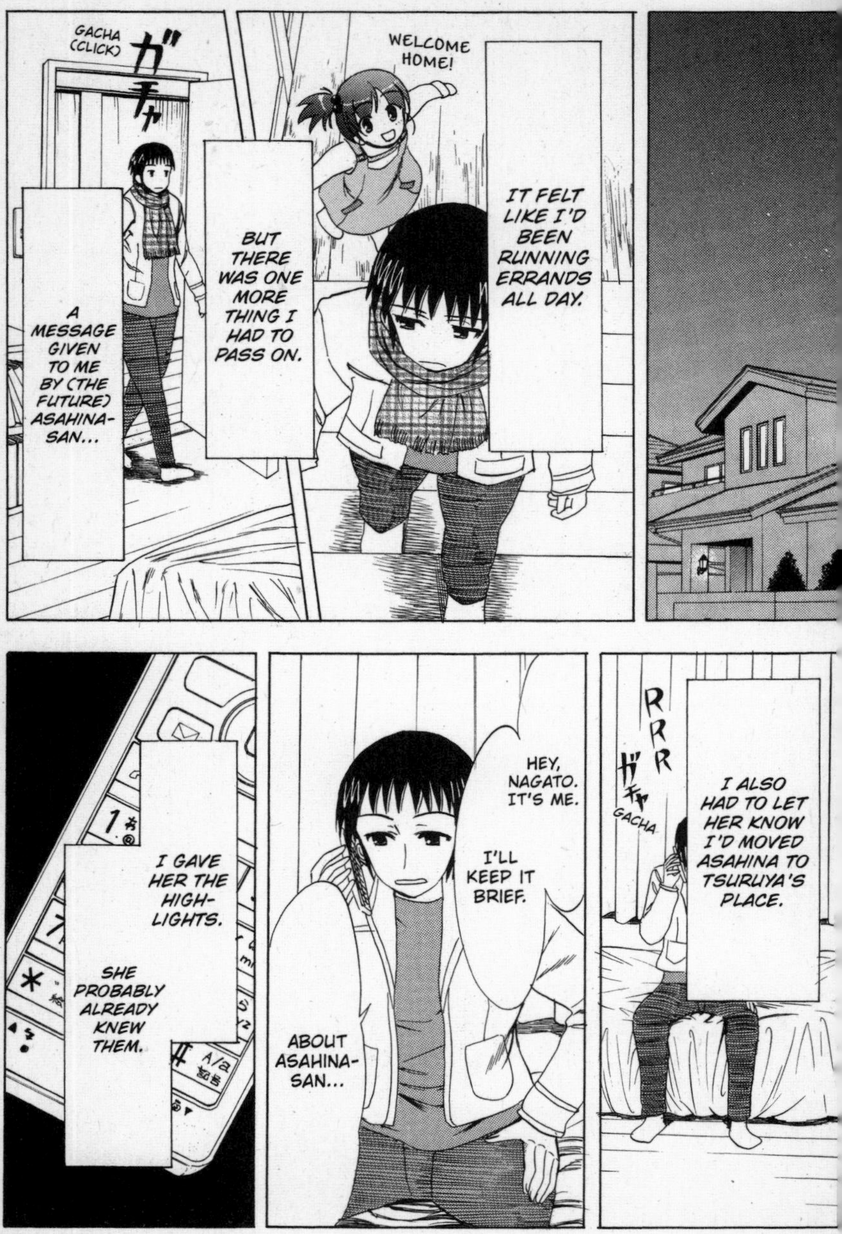
IT FELT LIKE I'D BEEN RUNNING ERRANDS ALL DAY.
WELCOME HOME!
BUT THERE WAS ONE MORE THING I HAD TO PASS ON.
GACHA (CLICK)
ガチャ
A MESSAGE GIVEN TO ME BY (THE FUTURE) ASAHINA-SAN...
I ALSO HAD TO LET HER KNOW I'D MOVED ASAHINA TO TSURUYA'S PLACE.
RRR
ガチャ
GACHA
HEY, NAGATO. IT'S ME.
I'LL KEEP IT BRIEF.
ABOUT ASAHINA-SAN...
I GAVE HER THE HIGH-LIGHTS.
SHE PROBABLY ALREADY KNEW THEM.

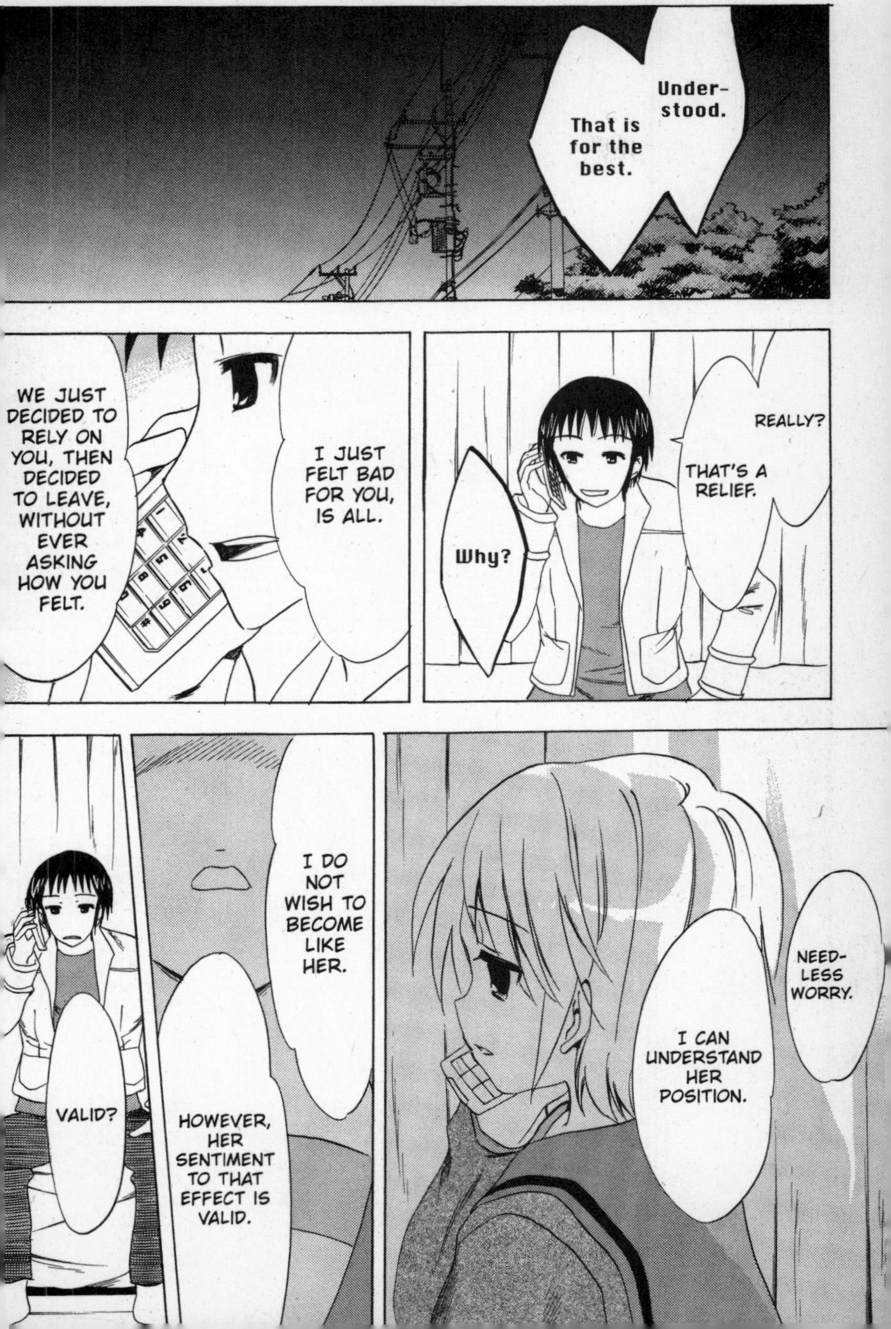
Under-stood.
That is for the best.
REALLY?
THAT'S A RELIEF.
Why?
I JUST FELT BAD FOR YOU, IS ALL.
WE JUST DECIDED TO RELY ON YOU, THEN DECIDED TO LEAVE, WITHOUT EVER ASKING HOW YOU FELT.
NEED-LESS WORRY.
I CAN UNDERSTAND HER POSITION.
I DO NOT WISH TO BECOME LIKE HER.
HOWEVER, HER SENTIMENT TO THAT EFFECT IS VALID.
VALID?

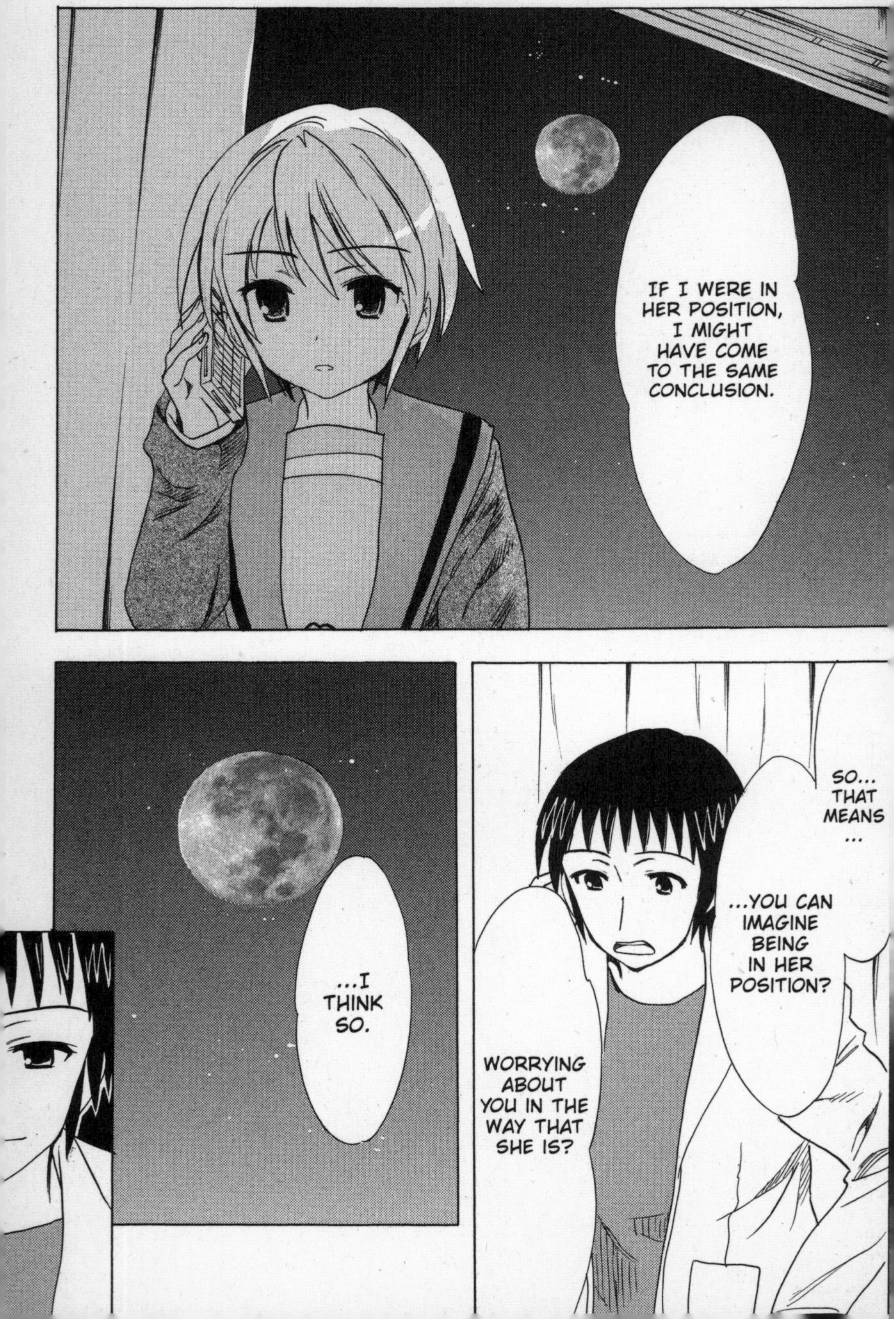
IF I WERE IN HER POSITION, I MIGHT HAVE COME TO THE SAME CONCLUSION.
SO... THAT MEANS ...
...YOU CAN IMAGINE BEING IN HER POSITION?
WORRYING ABOUT YOU IN THE WAY THAT SHE IS?
...I THINK SO.

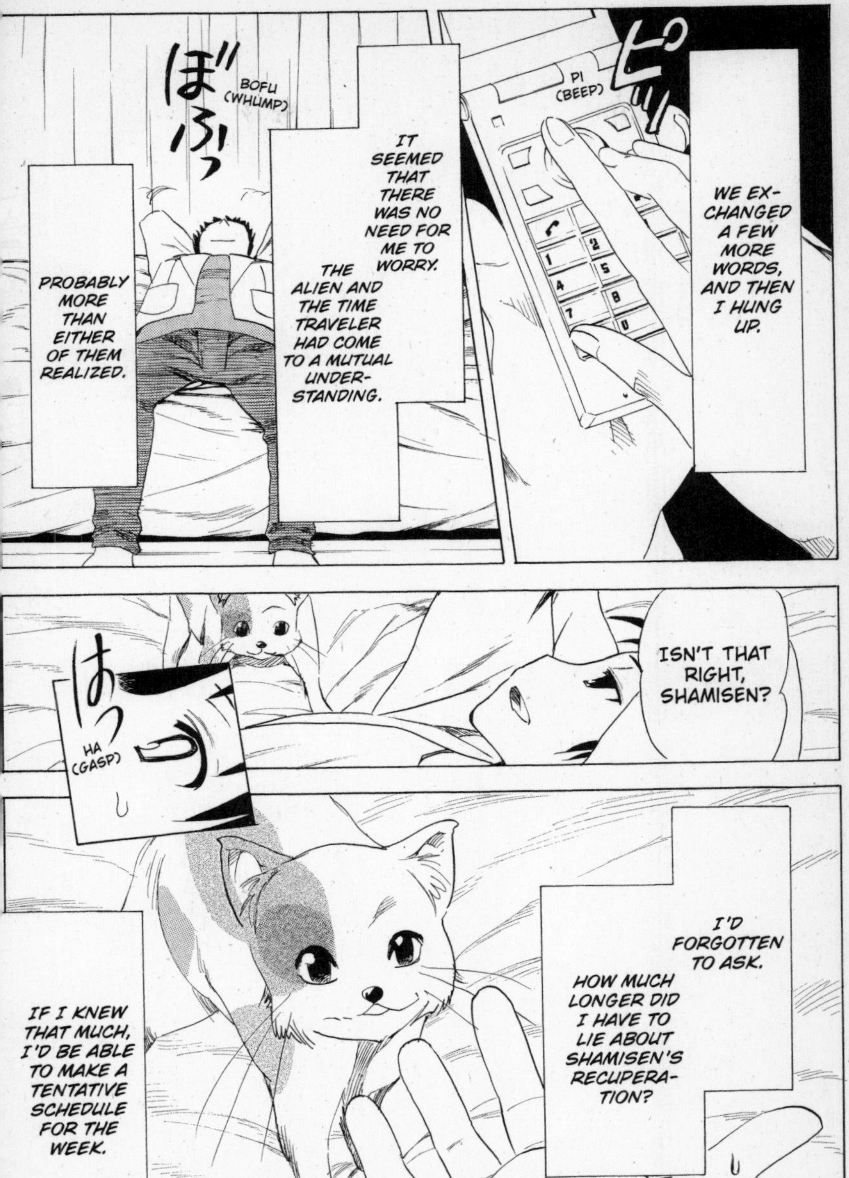
ピッ
PI (BEEP)
WE EXCHANGED A FEW MORE WORDS, AND THEN I HUNG UP.
ぼふっ
BOFU (WHUMP)
IT SEEMED THAT THERE WAS NO NEED FOR ME TO WORRY.
THE ALIEN AND THE TIME TRAVELER HAD COME TO A MUTUAL UNDERSTANDING.
PROBABLY MORE THAN EITHER OF THEM REALIZED.
ISN'T THAT RIGHT, SHAMISEN?
はっ
HA (GASP)
I'D FORGOTTEN TO ASK.
HOW MUCH LONGER DID I HAVE TO LIE ABOUT SHAMISEN'S RECUPERATION?
IF I KNEW THAT MUCH, I'D BE ABLE TO MAKE A TENTATIVE SCHEDULE FOR THE WEEK.

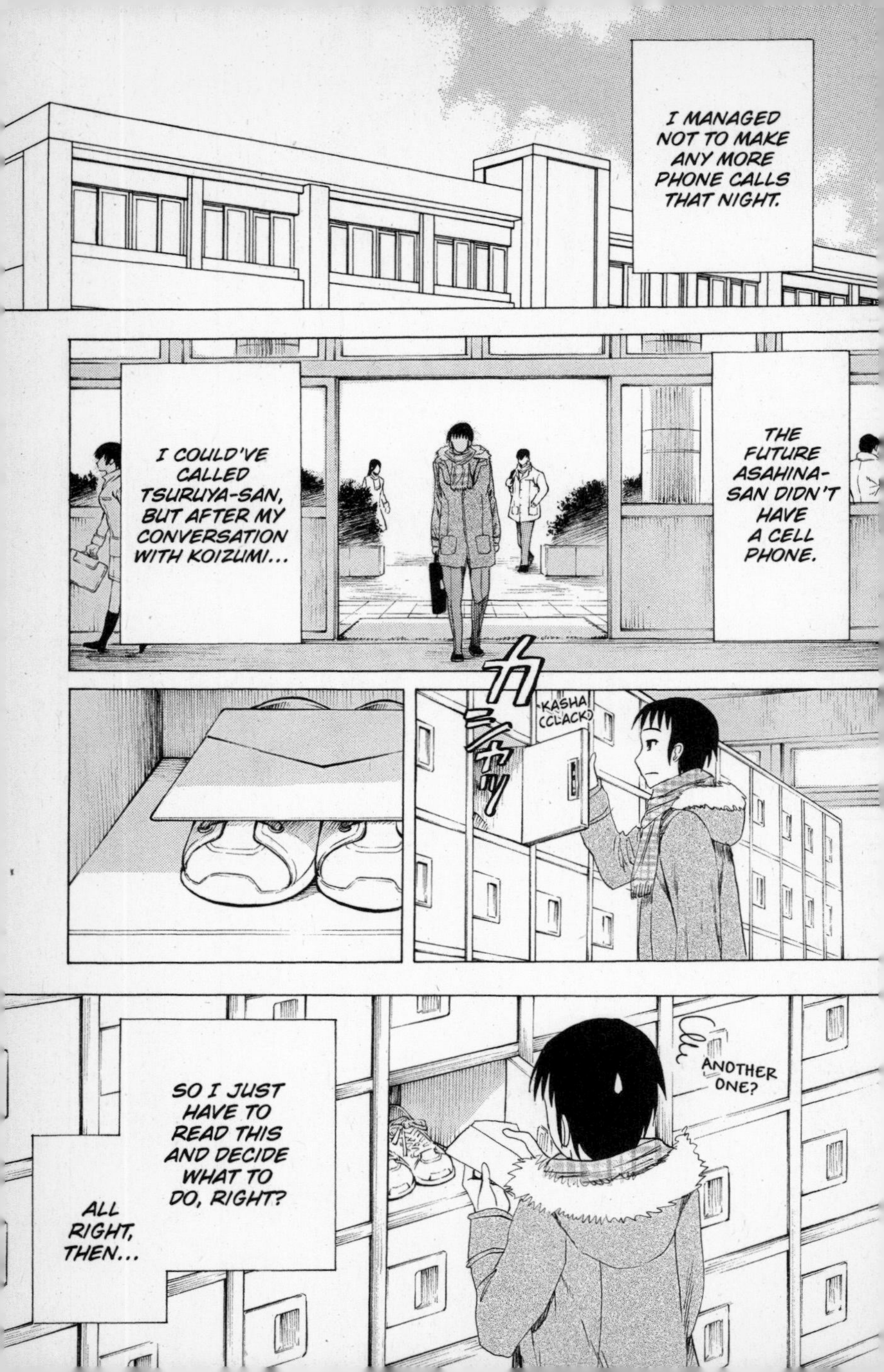

I MANAGED NOT TO MAKE ANY MORE PHONE CALLS THAT NIGHT.
THE FUTURE ASAHINA-SAN DIDN'T HAVE A CELL PHONE.
I COULD'VE CALLED TSURUYA-SAN, BUT AFTER MY CONVERSATION WITH KOIZUMI...
カシャッ
KASHA (CLACK)
ANOTHER ONE?
SO I JUST HAVE TO READ THIS AND DECIDE WHAT TO DO, RIGHT?
ALL RIGHT, THEN...

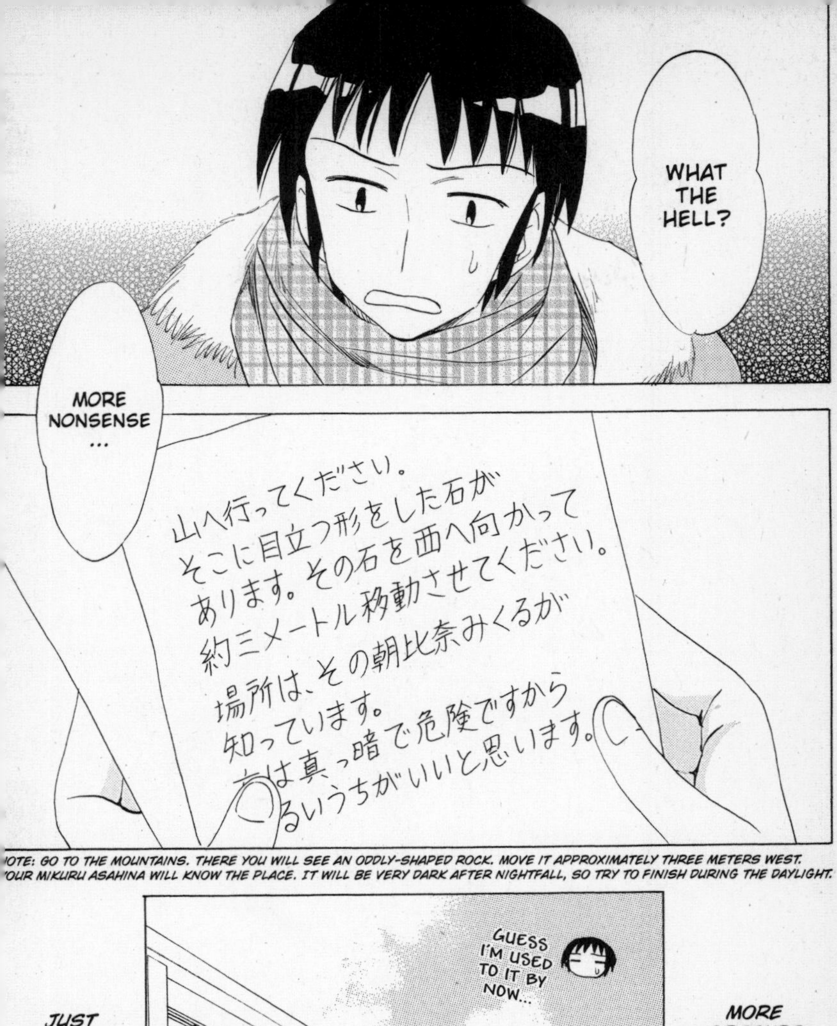
WHAT THE HELL?
MORE NONSENSE ...
山へ行ってください。
そこに目立つ形をした石が
あります。その石を西へ向かって
約三メートル移動させてください。
場所は、その朝比奈みくるが
知っています。
は真っ暗で危険ですから
るいうちがいいと思います。

NOTE: GO TO THE MOUNTAINS. THERE YOU WILL SEE AN ODDLY-SHAPED ROCK. MOVE IT APPROXIMATELY THREE METERS WEST. YOUR MIKURU ASAHINA WILL KNOW THE PLACE. IT WILL BE VERY DARK AFTER NIGHTFALL, SO TRY TO FINISH DURING THE DAYLIGHT.

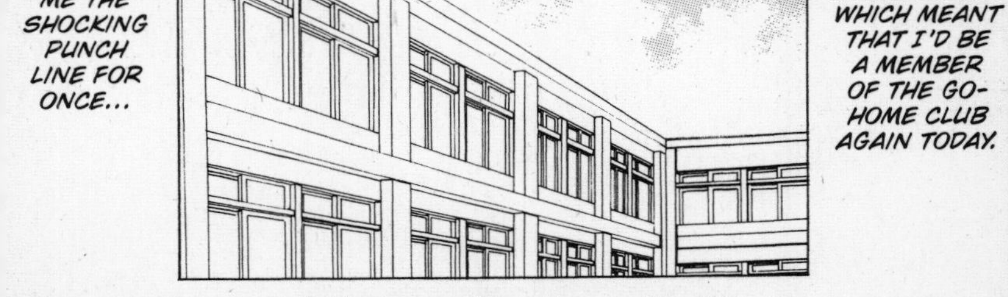
MORE OBSCURE DIRECTIONS... WHICH MEANT THAT I'D BE A MEMBER OF THE GO-HOME CLUB AGAIN TODAY.
GUESS I'M USED TO IT BY NOW...
JUST SPARE ME THE SHOCKING PUNCH LINE FOR ONCE...

THE INTRIGUES OF HARUHI SUZUMIYA IV : END

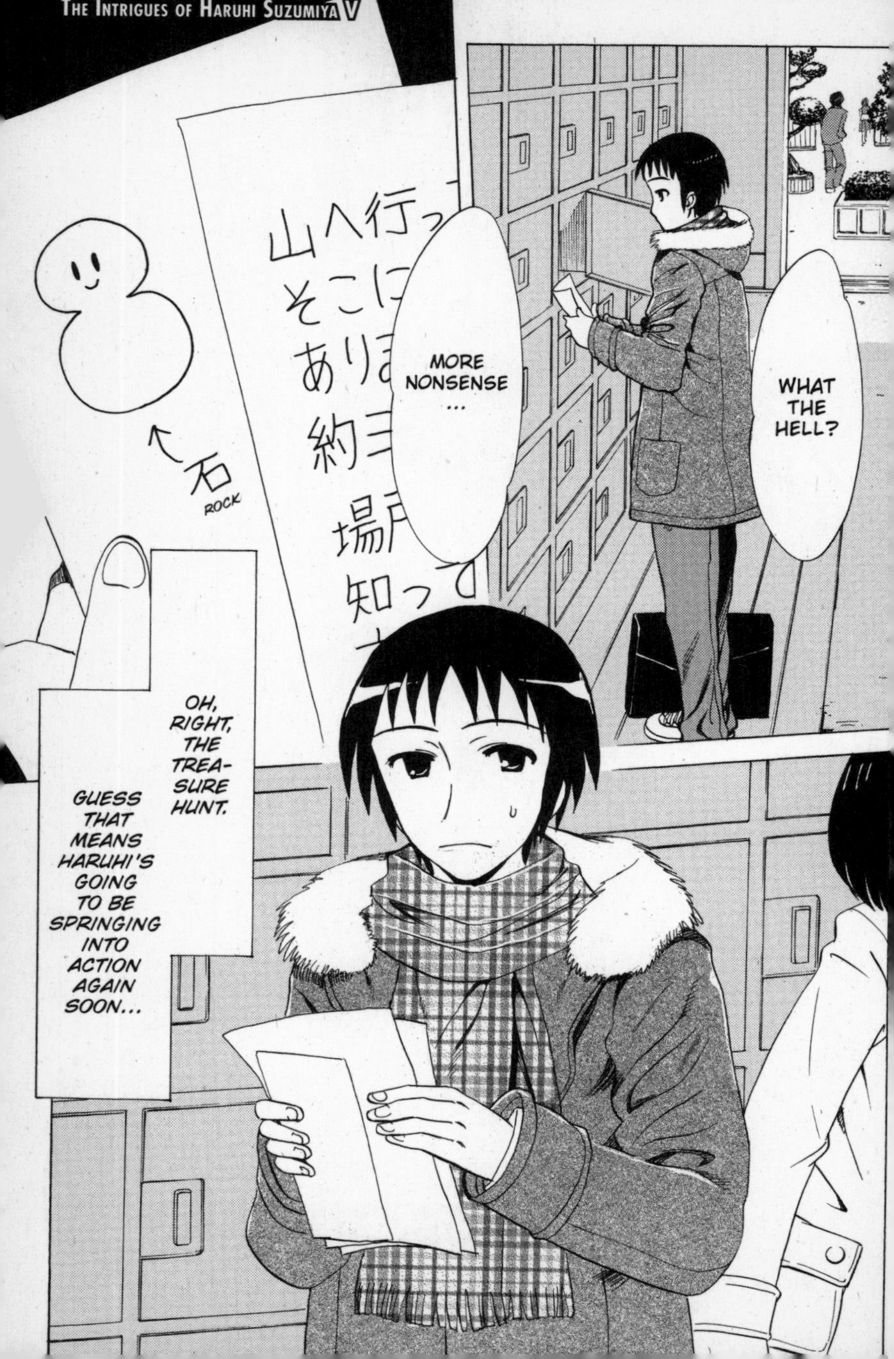
WHAT THE HELL?
MORE NONSENSE ...
山へ行っ
そこに
あり
約
場
知っ
石
ROCK
OH, RIGHT, THE TREASURE-HUNT.
GUESS THAT MEANS HARUHI'S GOING TO BE SPRINGING INTO ACTION AGAIN SOON...

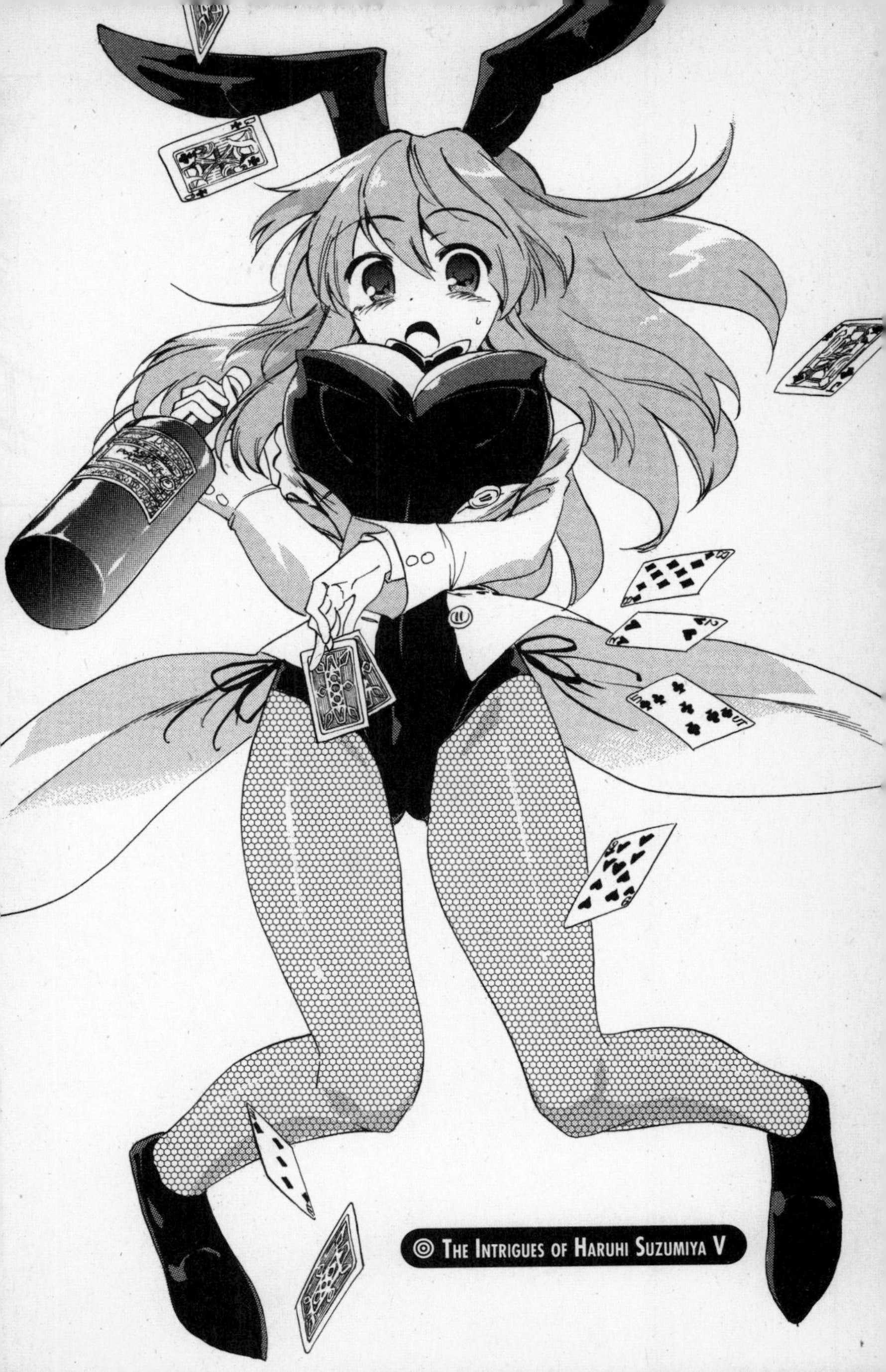
◎ The Intrigues of Haruhi Suzumiya V

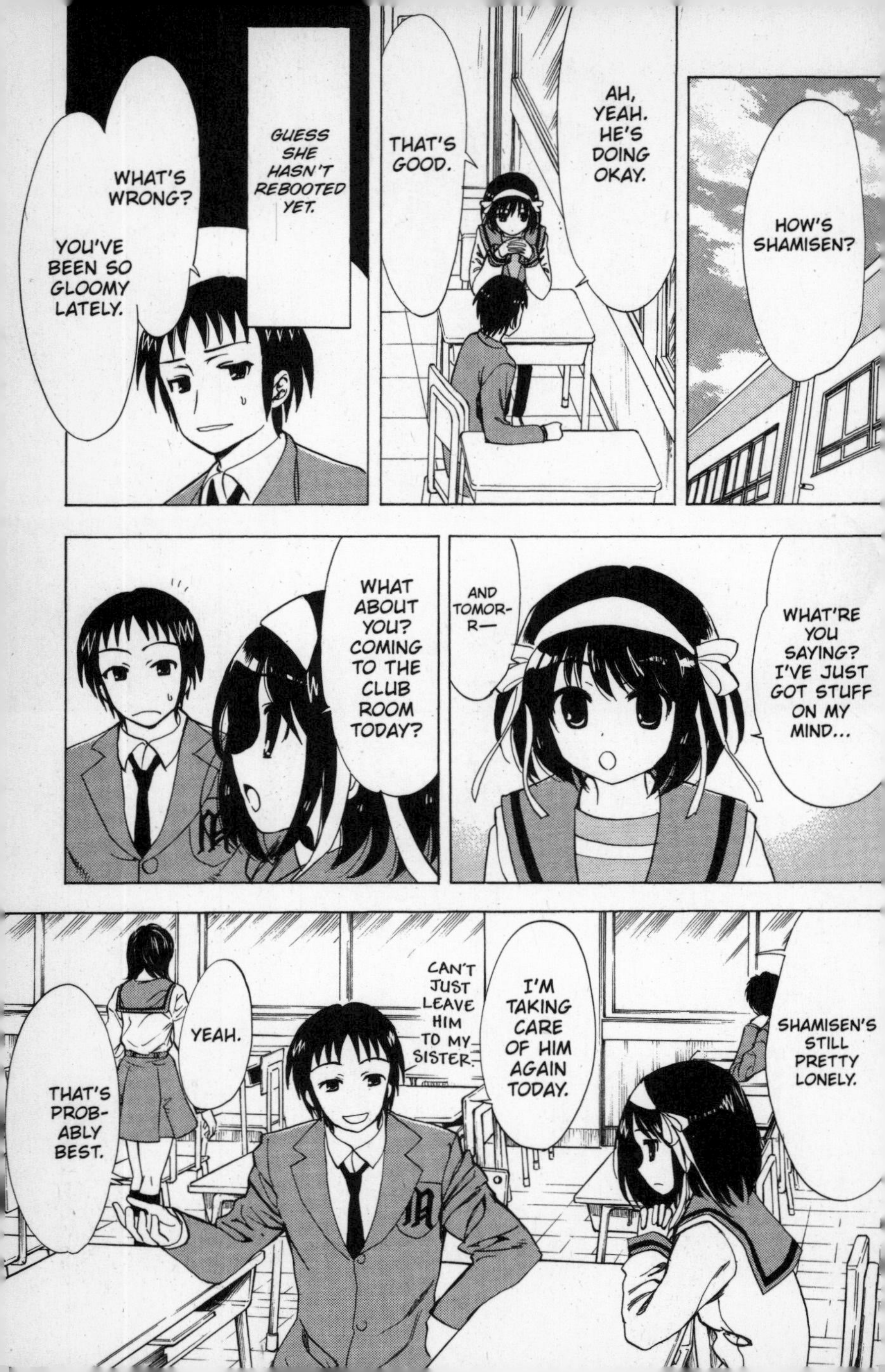
HOW'S SHAMISEN?
AH, YEAH. HE'S DOING OKAY.
THAT'S GOOD.
GUESS SHE HASN'T REBOOTED YET.
WHAT'S WRONG?
YOU'VE BEEN SO GLOOMY LATELY.
WHAT'RE YOU SAYING? I'VE JUST GOT STUFF ON MY MIND...
AND TOMOR- R—
WHAT ABOUT YOU? COMING TO THE CLUB ROOM TODAY?
SHAMISEN'S STILL PRETTY LONELY.
I'M TAKING CARE OF HIM AGAIN TODAY.
CAN'T JUST LEAVE HIM TO MY SISTER.
YEAH.
THAT'S PROBABLY BEST.

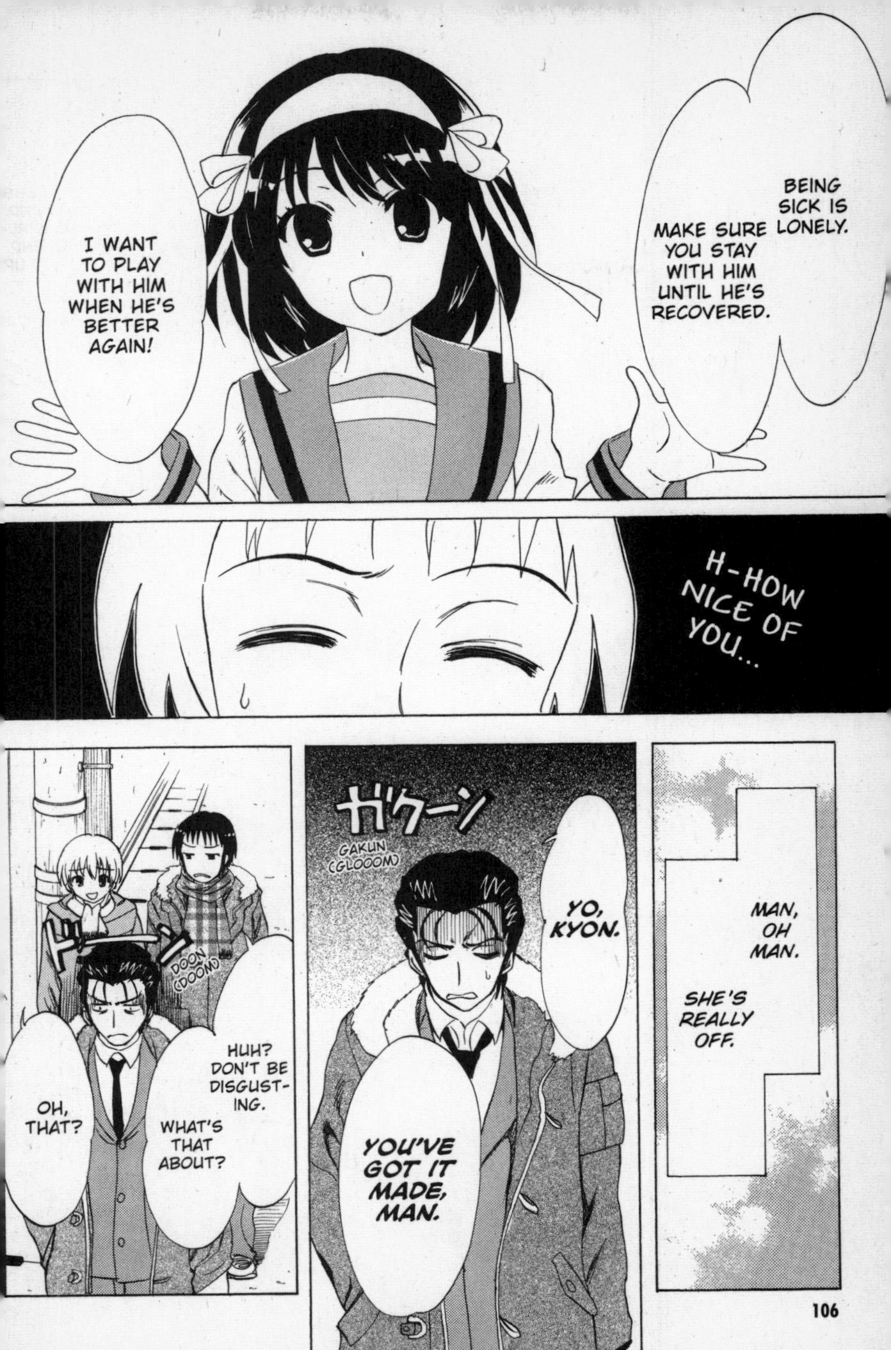
BEING SICK IS LONELY.
MAKE SURE YOU STAY WITH HIM UNTIL HE'S RECOVERED.
I WANT TO PLAY WITH HIM WHEN HE'S BETTER AGAIN!
H-HOW NICE OF YOU...
MAN, OH MAN.
SHE'S REALLY OFF.
ガクーン
GAKUN (GLOOOM)
YO, KYON.
YOU'VE GOT IT MADE, MAN.
DOON (DOON)
HUH? DON'T BE DISGUSTING.
WHAT'S THAT ABOUT?
OH, THAT?

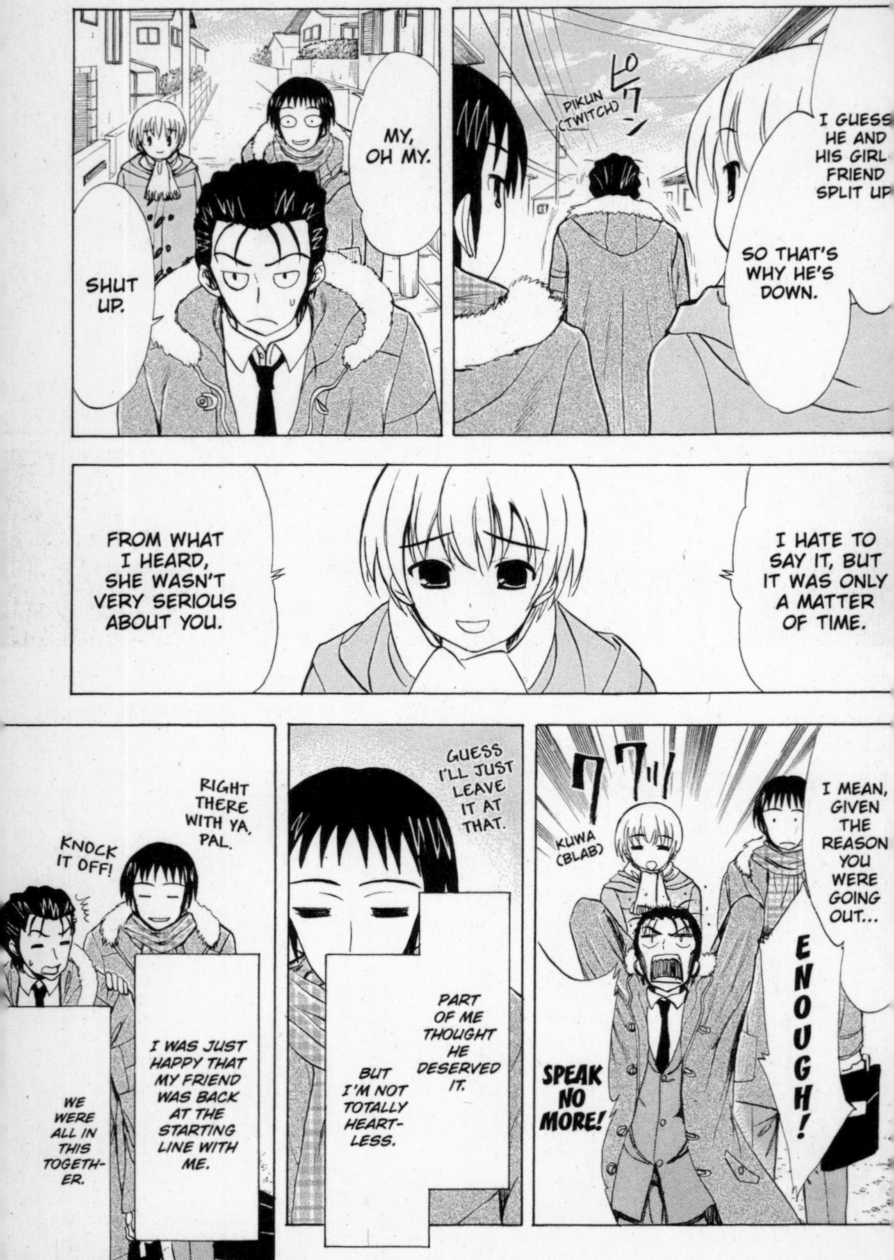
PIKUN (TWITCH)
I GUESS HE AND HIS GIRL FRIEND SPLIT UP
SO THAT'S WHY HE'S DOWN.
MY, OH MY.
SHUT UP.
I HATE TO SAY IT, BUT IT WAS ONLY A MATTER OF TIME.
FROM WHAT I HEARD, SHE WASN'T VERY SERIOUS ABOUT YOU.
I MEAN, GIVEN THE REASON YOU WERE GOING OUT...
KUWA (BLAB)
ENOUGH!
SPEAK NO MORE!
GUESS I'LL JUST LEAVE IT AT THAT.
PART OF ME THOUGHT HE DESERVED IT.
BUT I'M NOT TOTALLY HEART-LESS.
RIGHT THERE WITH YA, PAL.
KNOCK IT OFF!
I WAS JUST HAPPY THAT MY FRIEND WAS BACK AT THE STARTING LINE WITH ME.
WE WERE ALL IN THIS TOGETH-ER.

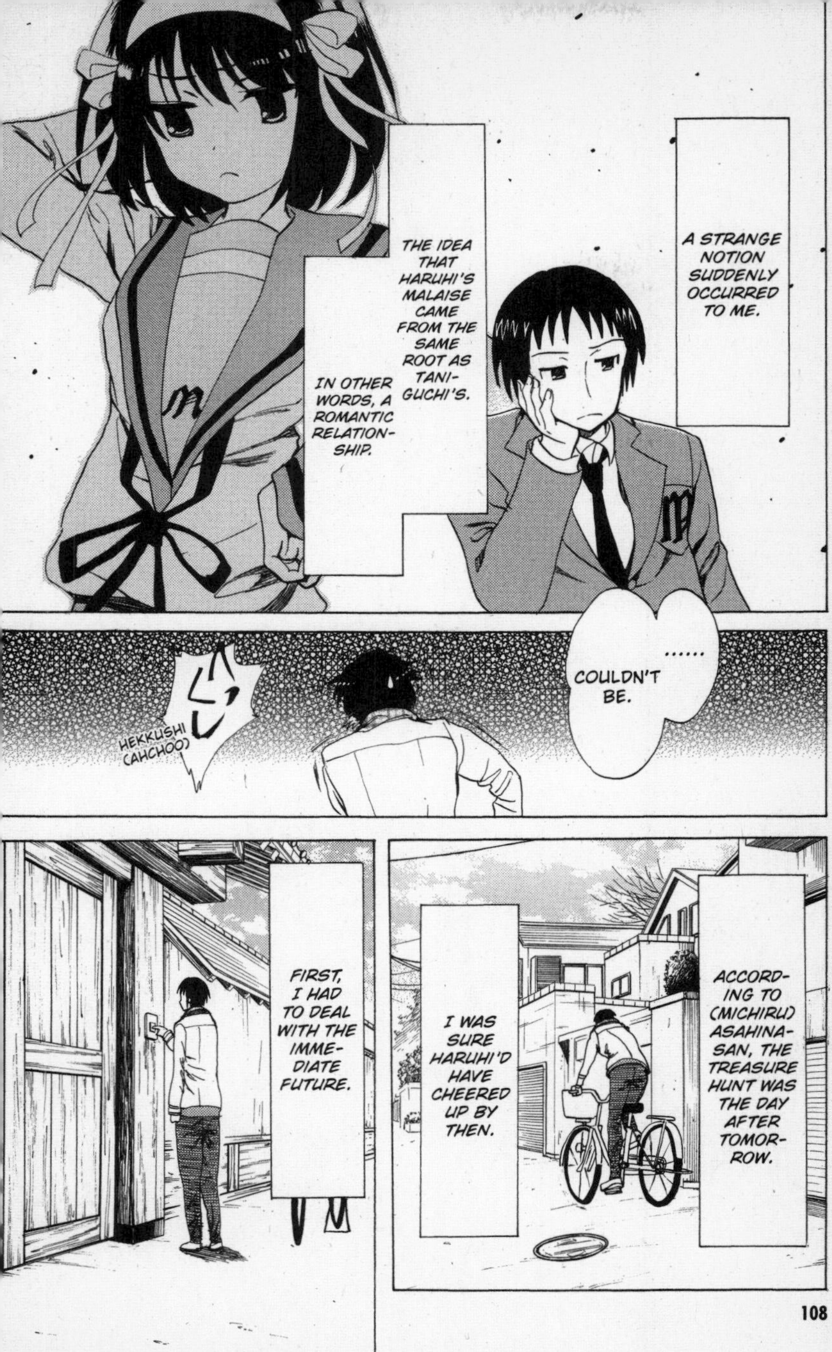
A STRANGE NOTION SUDDENLY OCCURRED TO ME.
THE IDEA THAT HARUHI'S MALAISE CAME FROM THE SAME ROOT AS TANI-GUCHI'S.
IN OTHER WORDS, A ROMANTIC RELATION-SHIP.
...... COULDN'T BE.
HEKKUSHI (AHCHOO)
ACCORD-ING TO (MICHIRU) ASAHINA-SAN, THE TREASURE HUNT WAS THE DAY AFTER TOMOR-ROW.
I WAS SURE HARUHI'D HAVE CHEERED UP BY THEN.
FIRST, I HAD TO DEAL WITH THE IMME-DIATE FUTURE.

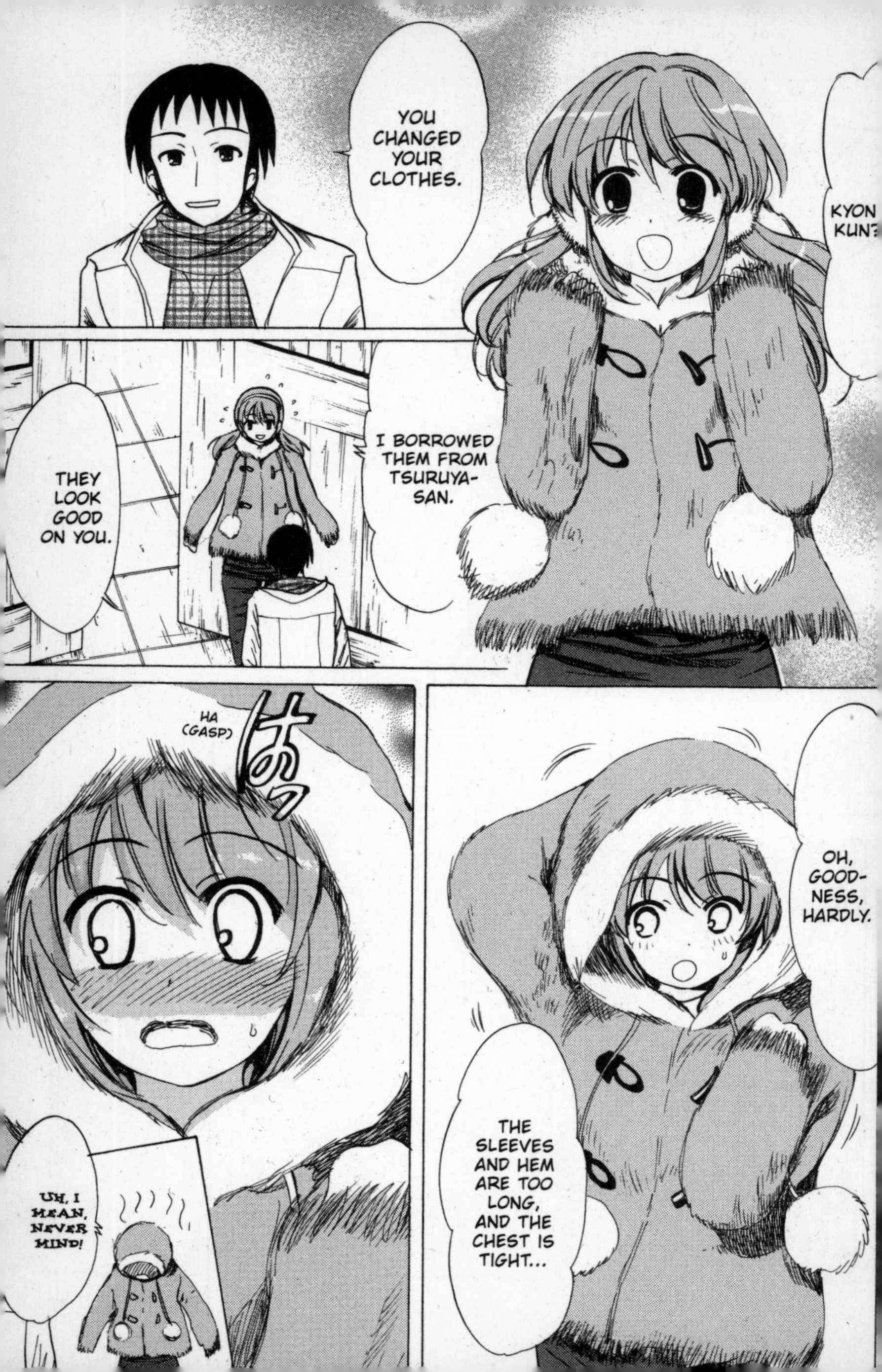
KYON KUN?
YOU CHANGED YOUR CLOTHES.
I BORROWED THEM FROM TSURUYA-SAN.
THEY LOOK GOOD ON YOU.
OH, GOOD-NESS, HARDLY.
THE SLEEVES AND HEM ARE TOO LONG, AND THE CHEST IS TIGHT...
HA (GASP)
UH, I MEAN, NEVER MIND!

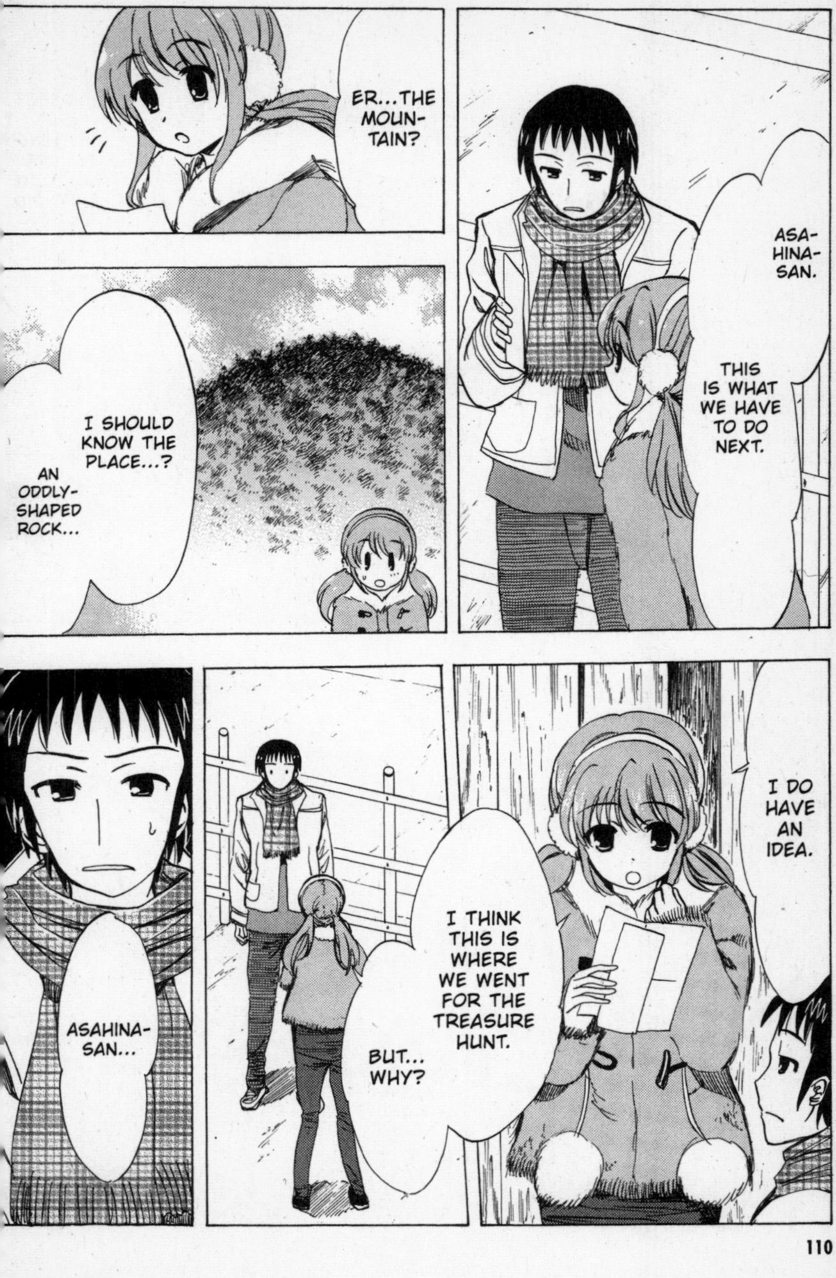
ASA-HINA-SAN.
THIS IS WHAT WE HAVE TO DO NEXT.
ER...THE MOUN-TAIN?
I SHOULD KNOW THE PLACE...?
AN ODDLY-SHAPED ROCK...
I DO HAVE AN IDEA.
I THINK THIS IS WHERE WE WENT FOR THE TREASURE HUNT.
BUT... WHY?
ASAHINA-SAN...

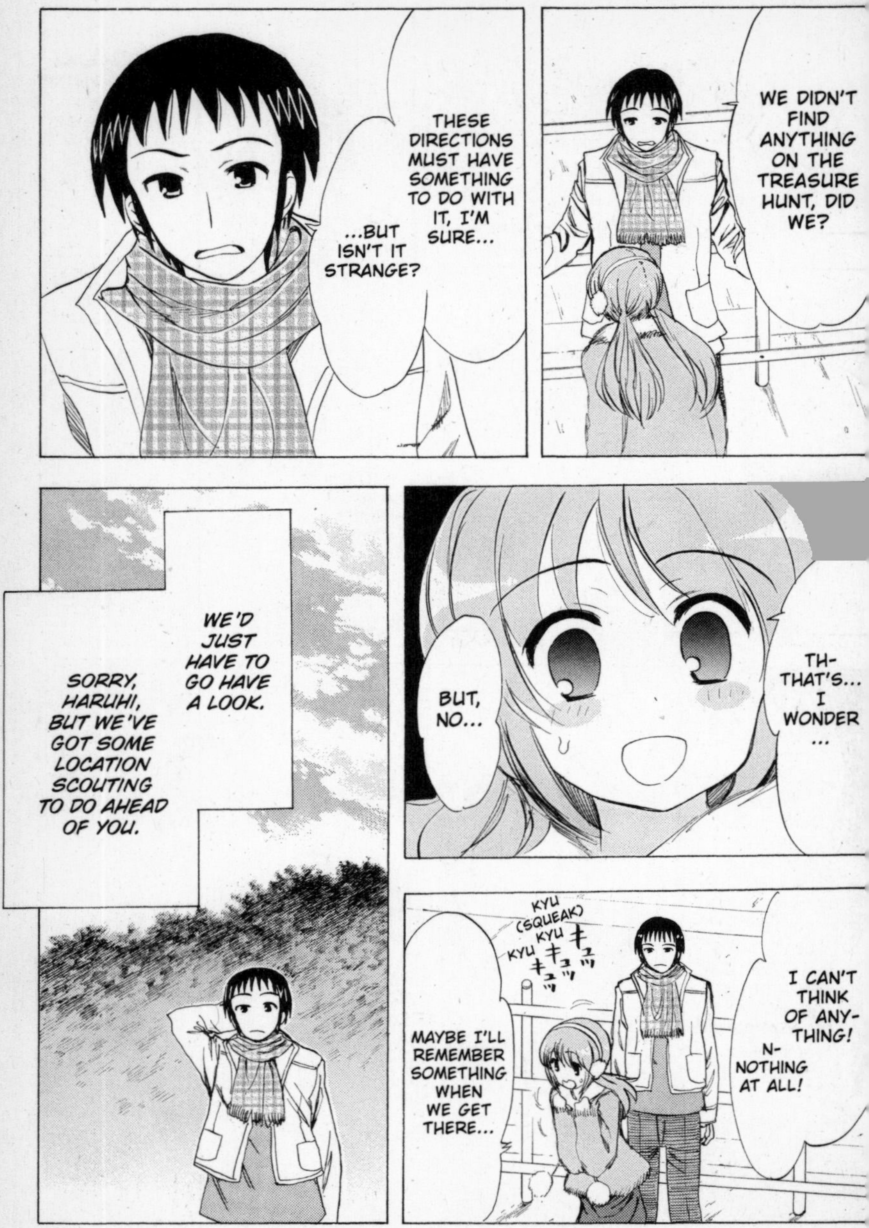
WE DIDN'T FIND ANYTHING ON THE TREASURE HUNT, DID WE?
THESE DIRECTIONS MUST HAVE SOMETHING TO DO WITH IT, I'M SURE...
...BUT ISN'T IT STRANGE?
TH-THAT'S... I WONDER ...
BUT, NO...
I CAN'T THINK OF ANY-THING!
N-NOTHING AT ALL!
KYU (SQUEAK) KYU KYU
MAYBE I'LL REMEMBER SOMETHING WHEN WE GET THERE...
WE'D JUST HAVE TO GO HAVE A LOOK.
SORRY, HARUHI, BUT WE'VE GOT SOME LOCATION SCOUTING TO DO AHEAD OF YOU.

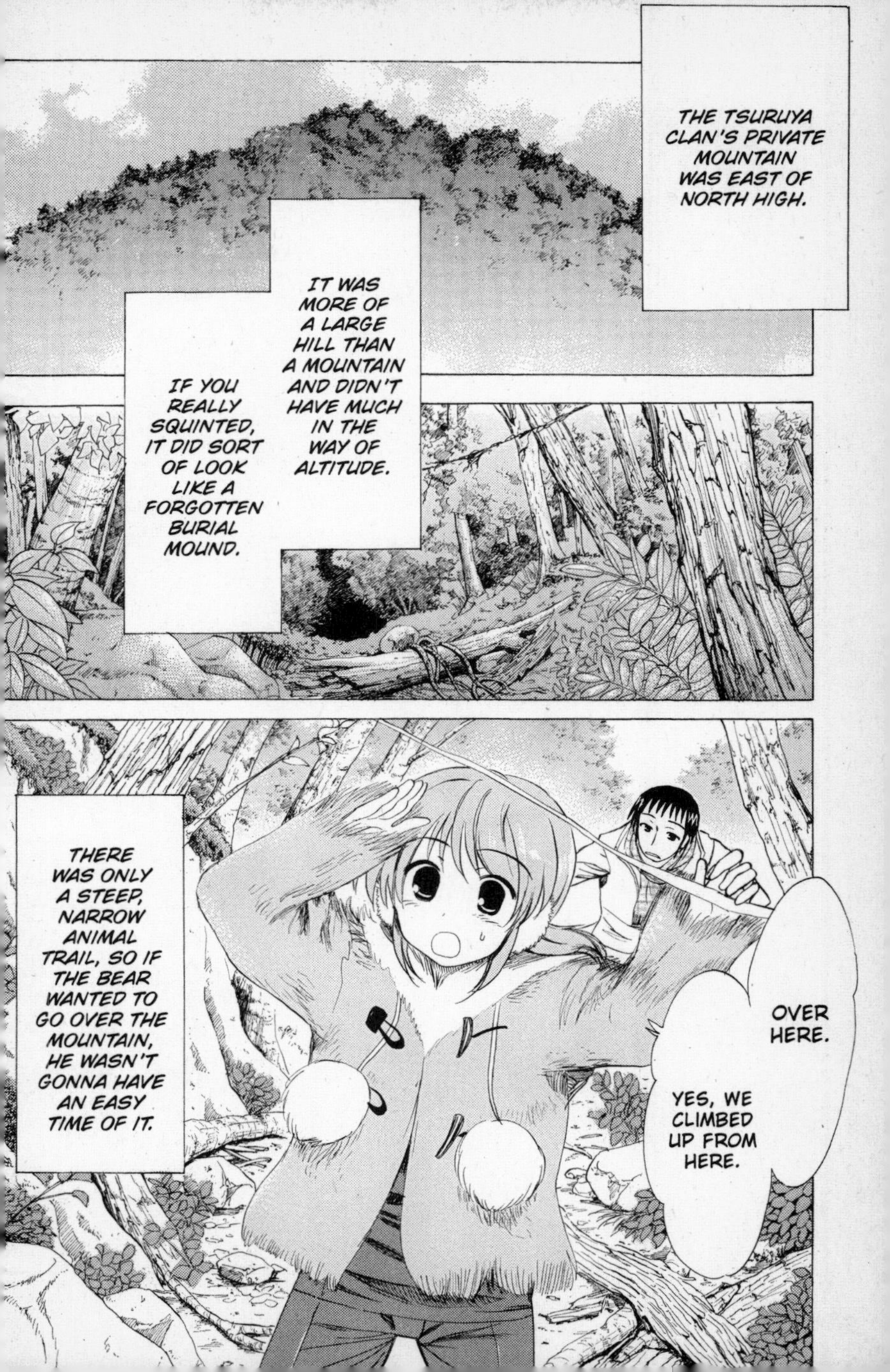
THE TSURUYA CLAN'S PRIVATE MOUNTAIN WAS EAST OF NORTH HIGH.
IT WAS MORE OF A LARGE HILL THAN A MOUNTAIN AND DIDN'T HAVE MUCH IN THE WAY OF ALTITUDE.
IF YOU REALLY SQUINTED, IT DID SORT OF LOOK LIKE A FORGOTTEN BURIAL MOUND.
OVER HERE.
YES, WE CLIMBED UP FROM HERE.
THERE WAS ONLY A STEEP, NARROW ANIMAL TRAIL, SO IF THE BEAR WANTED TO GO OVER THE MOUNTAIN, HE WASN'T GONNA HAVE AN EASY TIME OF IT.

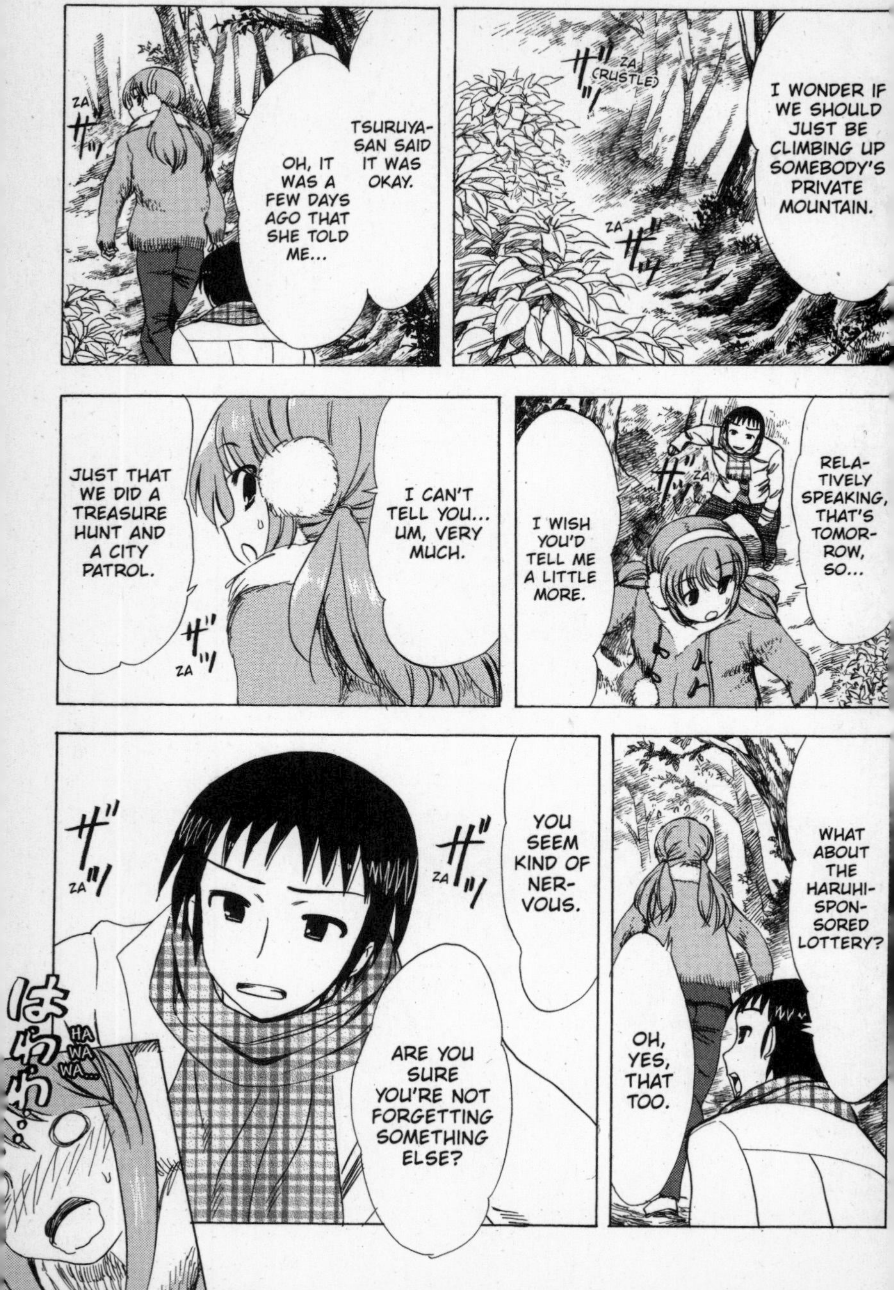
ZA (RUSTLE)
I WONDER IF WE SHOULD JUST BE CLIMBING UP SOMEBODY'S PRIVATE MOUNTAIN.
ZA
ZA
TSURUYA-SAN SAID IT WAS OKAY.
OH, IT WAS A FEW DAYS AGO THAT SHE TOLD ME...
RELATIVELY SPEAKING, THAT'S TOMORROW, SO...
ZA
I WISH YOU'D TELL ME A LITTLE MORE.
I CAN'T TELL YOU... UM, VERY MUCH.
JUST THAT WE DID A TREASURE HUNT AND A CITY PATROL.
ZA
WHAT ABOUT THE HARUHI-SPONSORED LOTTERY?
OH, YES, THAT TOO.
YOU SEEM KIND OF NERVOUS.
ZA
ZA
ARE YOU SURE YOU'RE NOT FORGETTING SOMETHING ELSE?
はわわ。
HAWAWA...

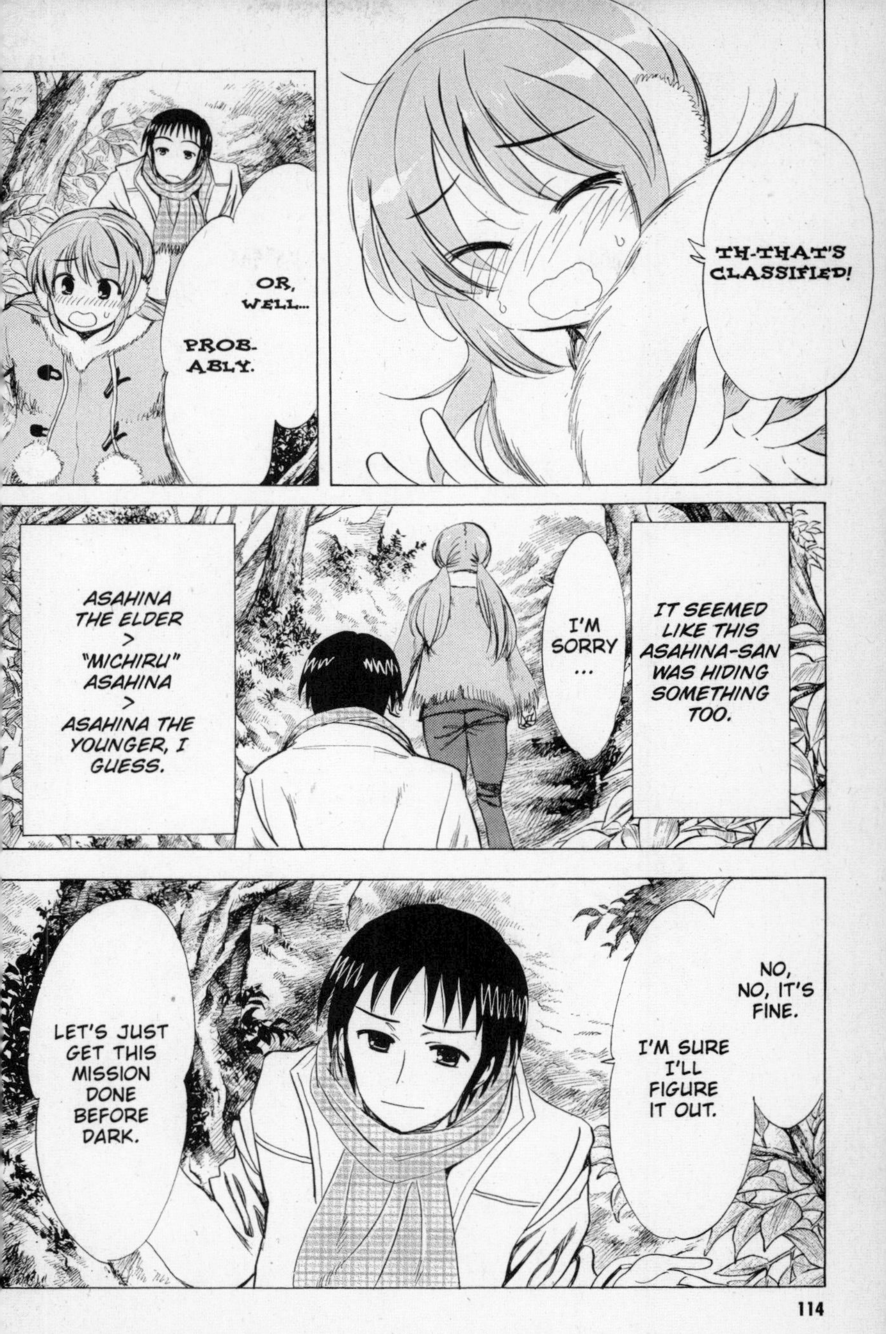
TH-THAT'S CLASSIFIED!
OR, WELL...
PROB-ABLY.
IT SEEMED LIKE THIS ASAHINA-SAN WAS HIDING SOMETHING TOO.
I'M SORRY ...
ASAHINA THE ELDER > "MICHIRU" ASAHINA > ASAHINA THE YOUNGER, I GUESS.
NO, NO, IT'S FINE.
I'M SURE I'LL FIGURE IT OUT.
LET'S JUST GET THIS MISSION DONE BEFORE DARK.

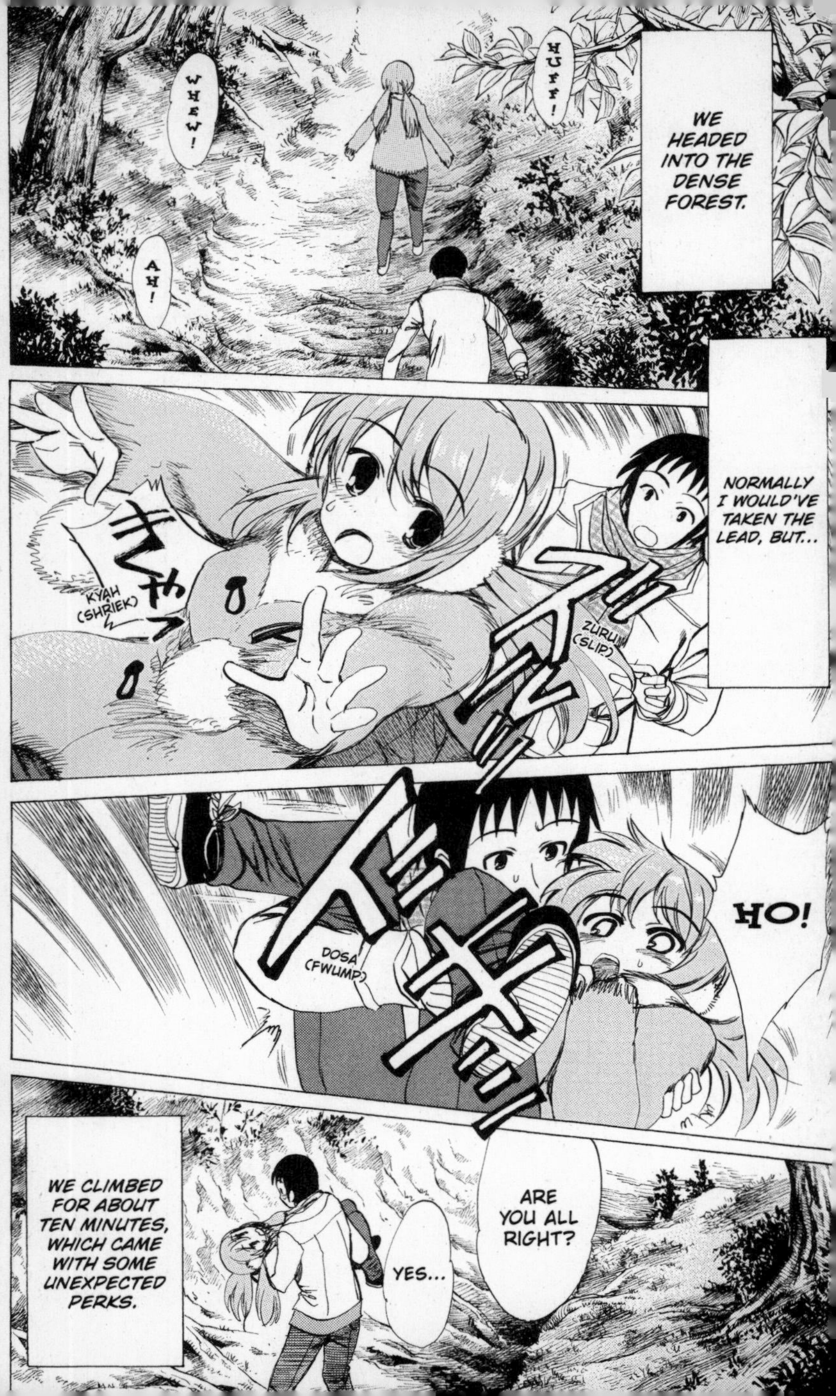
WE HEADED INTO THE DENSE FOREST.
HUFF!
WHEW!
AH!
NORMALLY I WOULD'VE TAKEN THE LEAD, BUT...
ZURU (SLIP)
KYAH (SHRIEK)
HO!
DOSA (FWUMP)
ARE YOU ALL RIGHT?
YES...
WE CLIMBED FOR ABOUT TEN MINUTES, WHICH CAME WITH SOME UNEXPECTED PERKS.

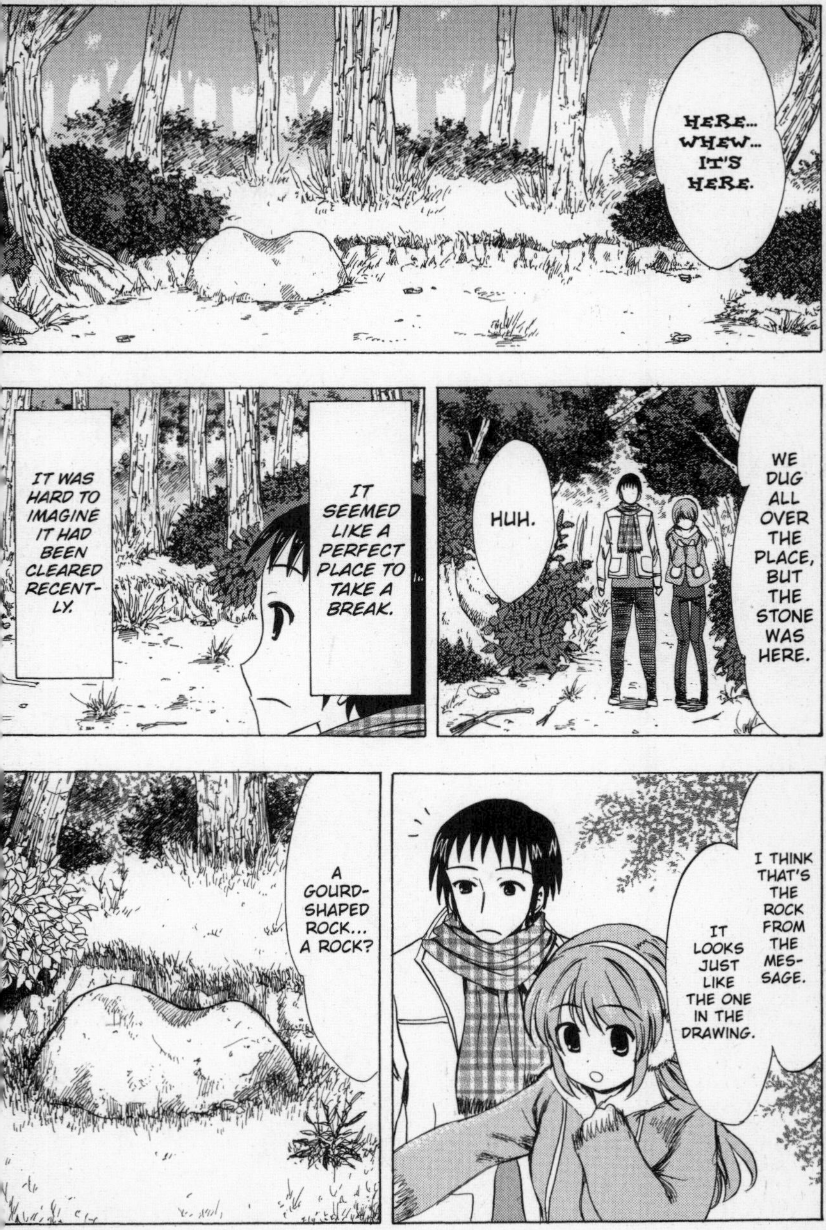
HERE... WHEW... IT'S HERE.
WE DUG ALL OVER THE PLACE, BUT THE STONE WAS HERE.
HUH.
IT SEEMED LIKE A PERFECT PLACE TO TAKE A BREAK.
IT WAS HARD TO IMAGINE IT HAD BEEN CLEARED RECENTLY.
I THINK THAT'S THE ROCK FROM THE MESSAGE.
IT LOOKS JUST LIKE THE ONE IN THE DRAWING.
A GOURD-SHAPED ROCK... A ROCK?

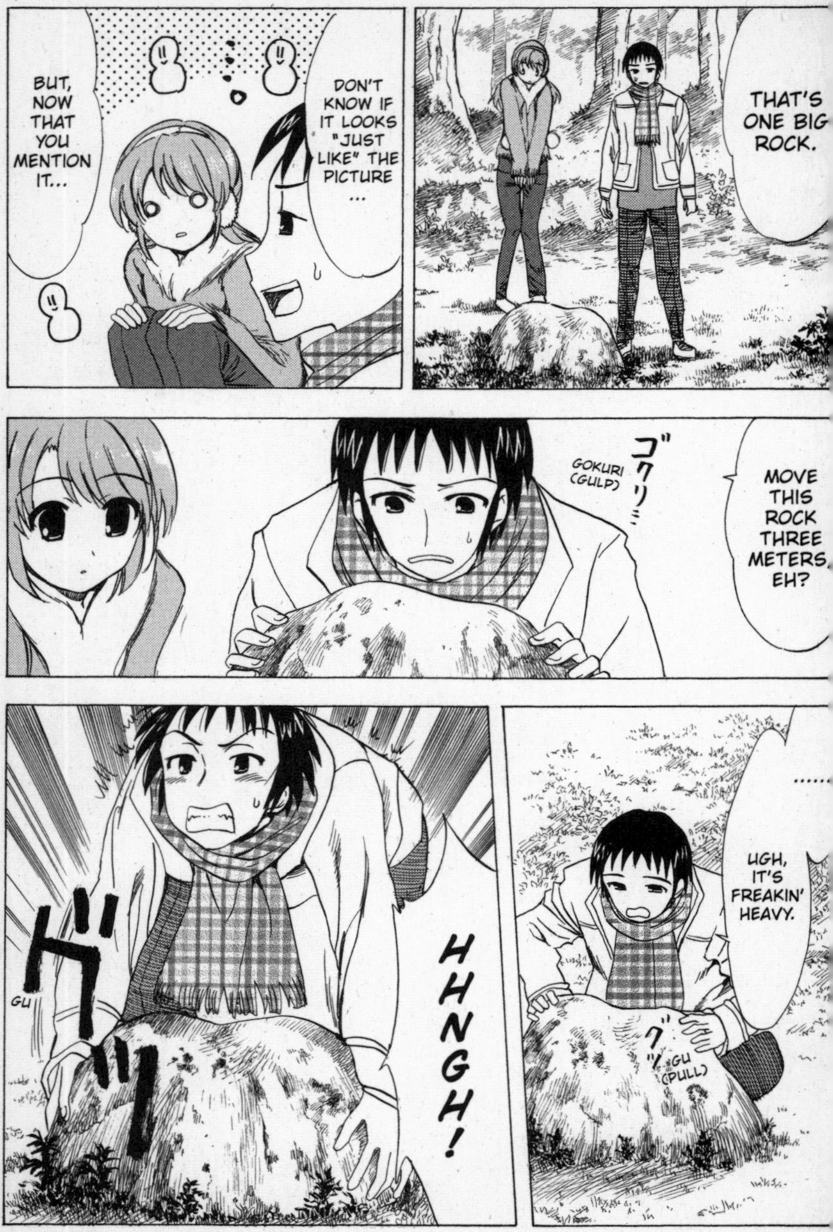
THAT'S ONE BIG ROCK.
DON'T KNOW IF IT LOOKS "JUST LIKE" THE PICTURE ...
BUT, NOW THAT YOU MENTION IT...
MOVE THIS ROCK THREE METERS, EH?
GOKURI (GULP)
......
UGH, IT'S FREAKIN' HEAVY.
GU (PULL)
HHNGH!
GU

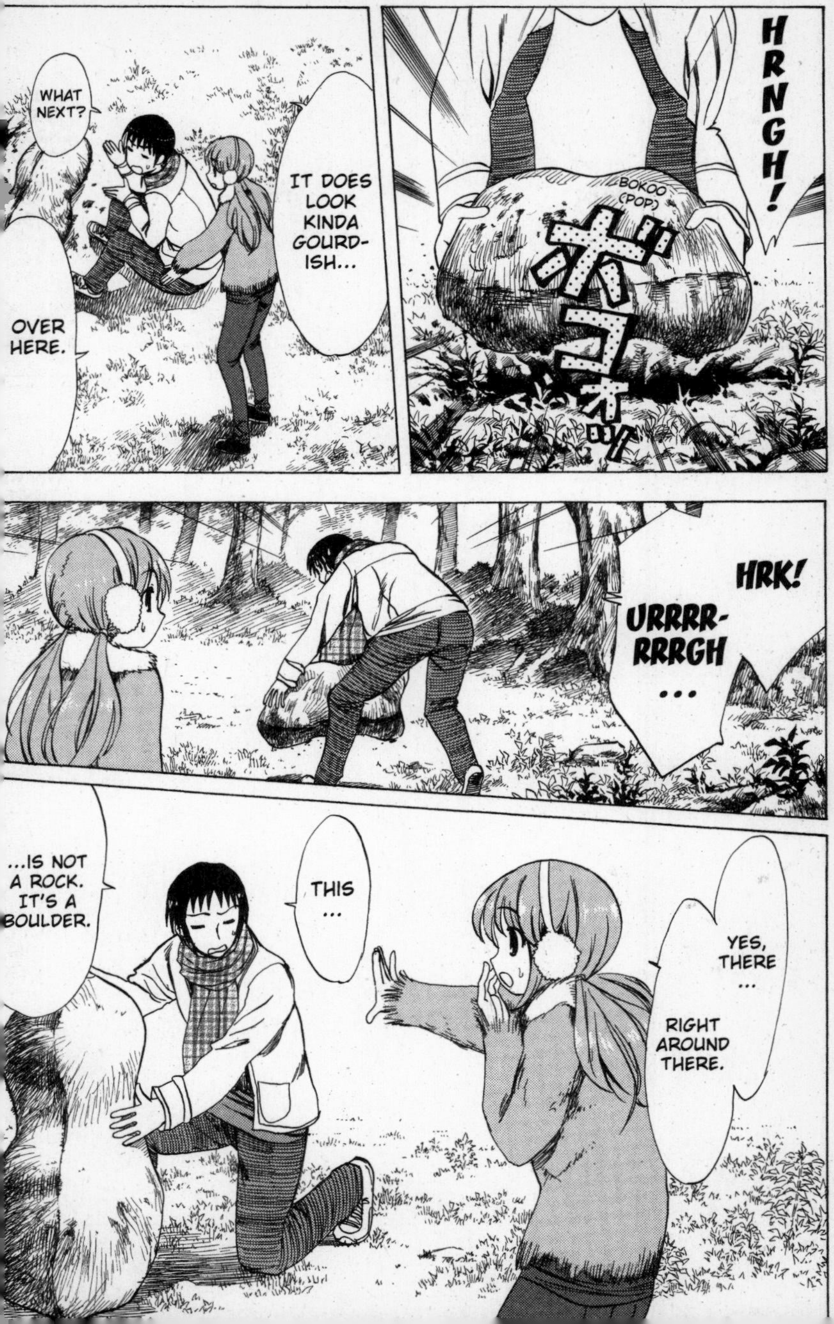
HRNGH!
BOKOO (POP)
IT DOES LOOK KINDA GOURD-ISH...
WHAT NEXT?
OVER HERE.
HRK!
URRRR-RRRGH ...
YES, THERE ...
RIGHT AROUND THERE.
THIS ...
...IS NOT A ROCK. IT'S A BOULDER.

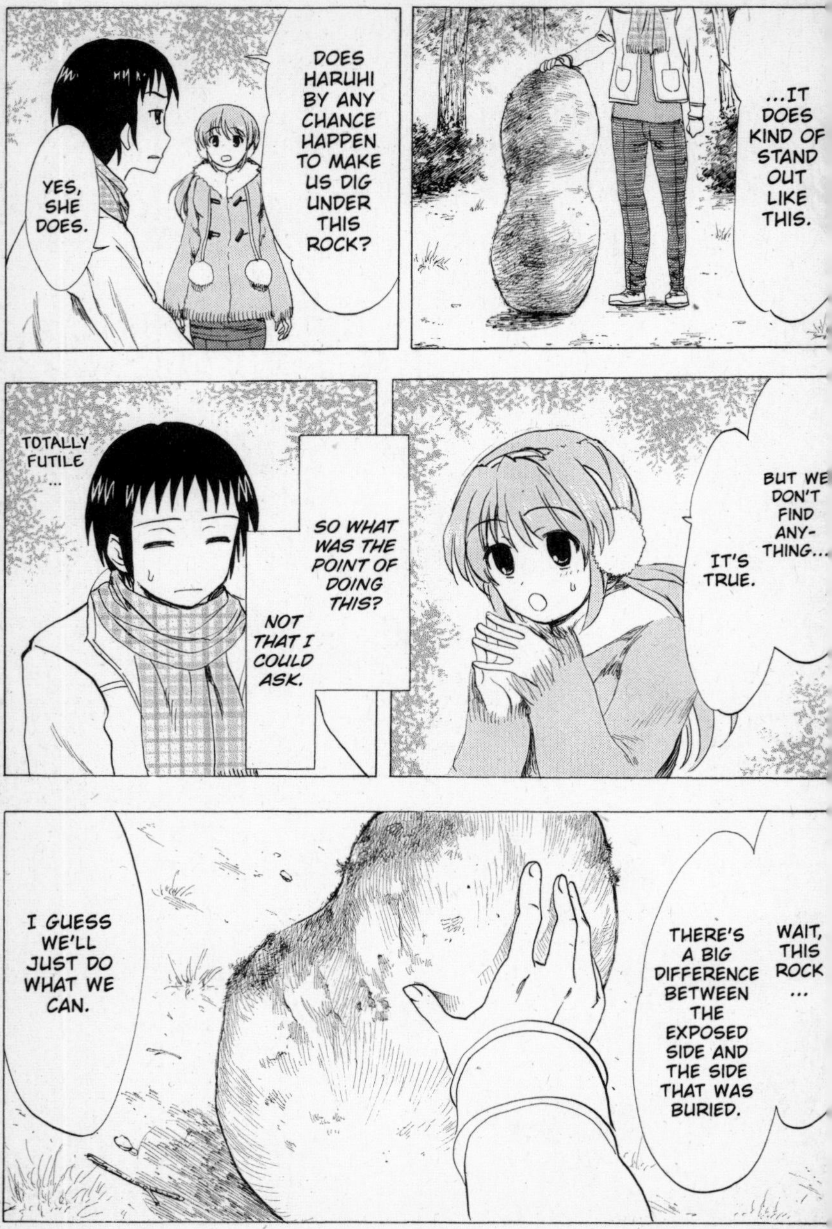
...IT DOES KIND OF STAND OUT LIKE THIS.
DOES HARUHI BY ANY CHANCE HAPPEN TO MAKE US DIG UNDER THIS ROCK?
YES, SHE DOES.
BUT WE DON'T FIND ANYTHING...
IT'S TRUE.
SO WHAT WAS THE POINT OF DOING THIS?
NOT THAT I COULD ASK.
TOTALLY FUTILE ...
WAIT, THIS ROCK ...
THERE'S A BIG DIFFERENCE BETWEEN THE EXPOSED SIDE AND THE SIDE THAT WAS BURIED.
I GUESS WE'LL JUST DO WHAT WE CAN.

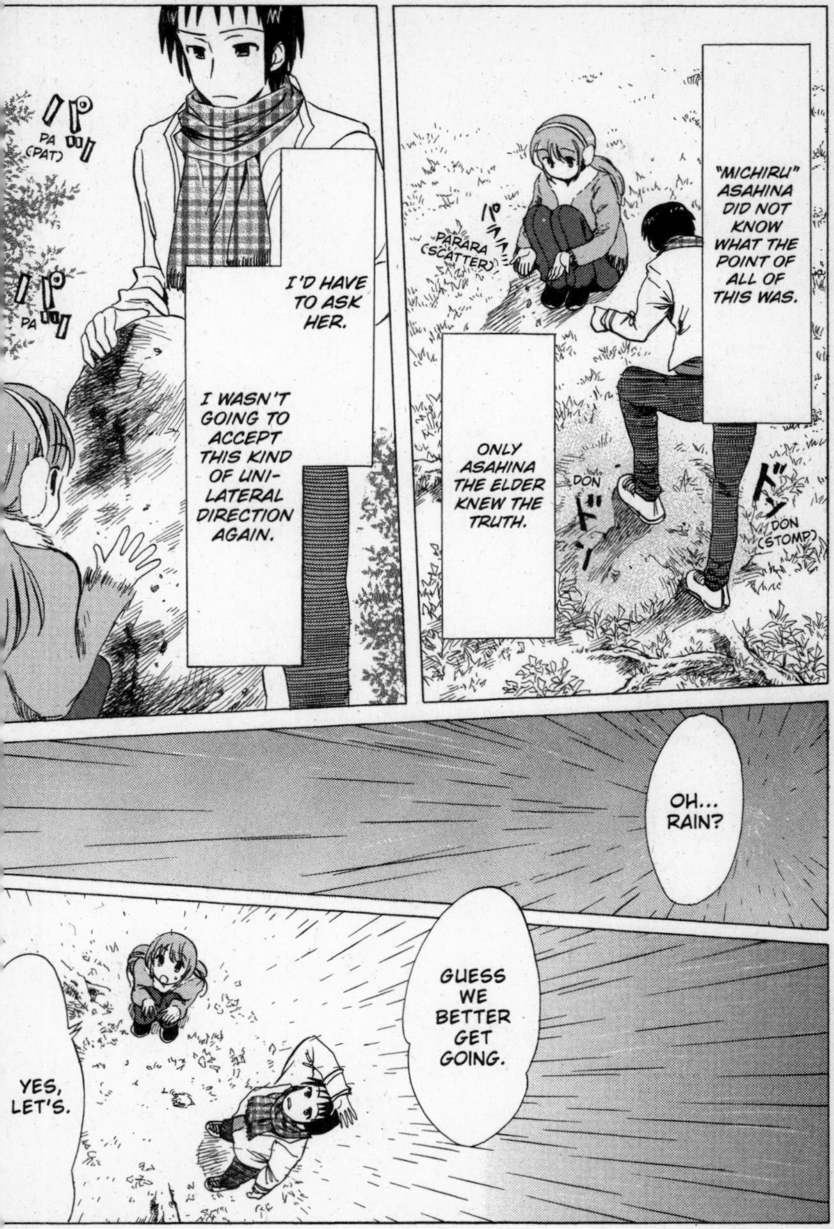
"MICHIRU" ASAHINA DID NOT KNOW WHAT THE POINT OF ALL OF THIS WAS.
PARARA (SCATTER)
ONLY ASAHINA THE ELDER KNEW THE TRUTH.
DON (STOMP)
DON
I'D HAVE TO ASK HER.
I WASN'T GOING TO ACCEPT THIS KIND OF UNI-LATERAL DIRECTION AGAIN.
PA (PAT)
PA
OH... RAIN?
GUESS WE BETTER GET GOING.
YES, LET'S.

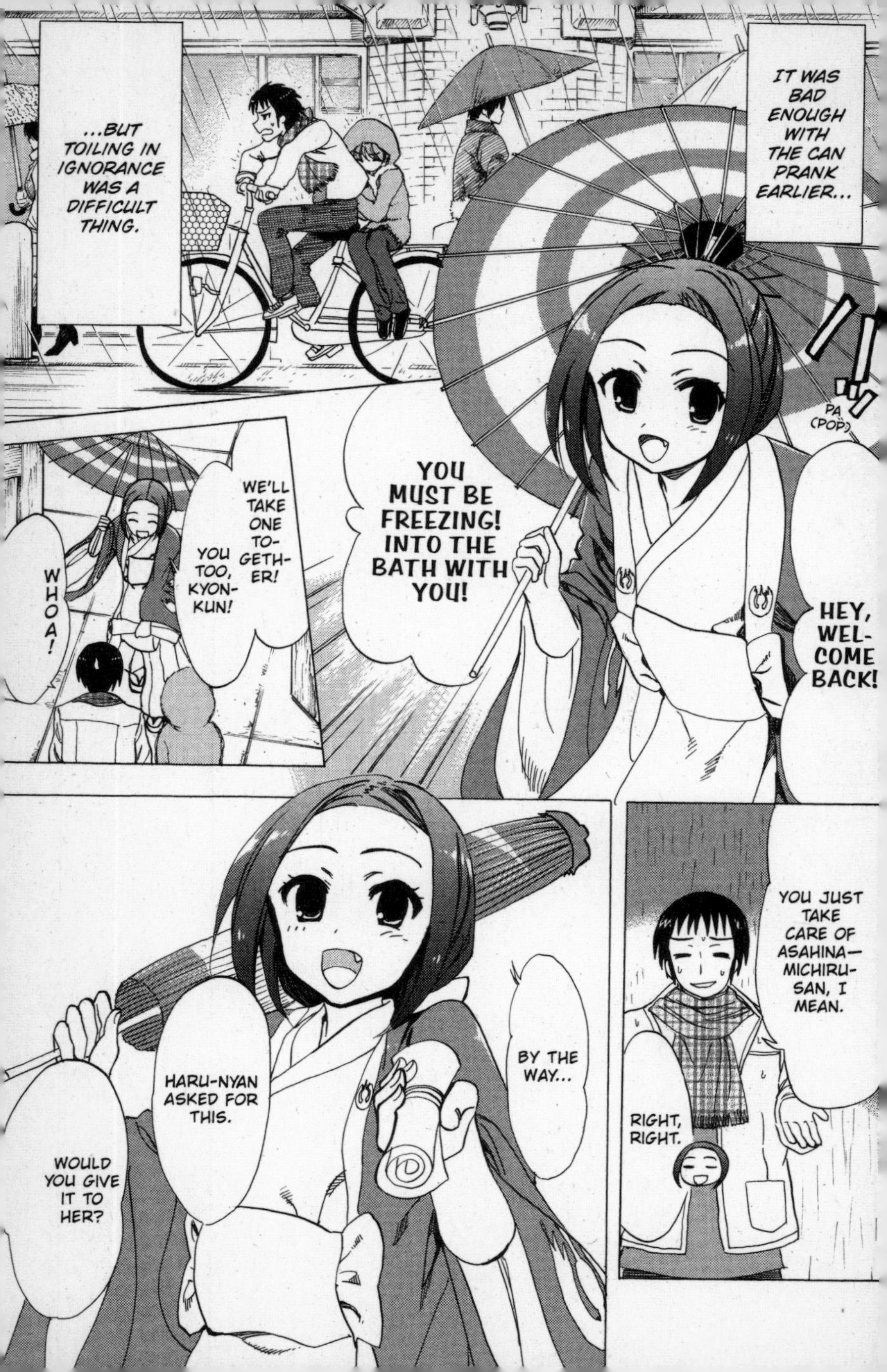
IT WAS BAD ENOUGH WITH THE CAN PRANK EARLIER...
...BUT TOILING IN IGNORANCE WAS A DIFFICULT THING.
PA (POP)
HEY, WELCOME BACK!
YOU MUST BE FREEZING! INTO THE BATH WITH YOU!
WE'LL TAKE ONE TOGETHER!
YOU TOO, KYON-KUN!
WHOA!
YOU JUST TAKE CARE OF ASAHINA—MICHIRU-SAN, I MEAN.
RIGHT, RIGHT.
BY THE WAY...
HARU-NYAN ASKED FOR THIS.
WOULD YOU GIVE IT TO HER?

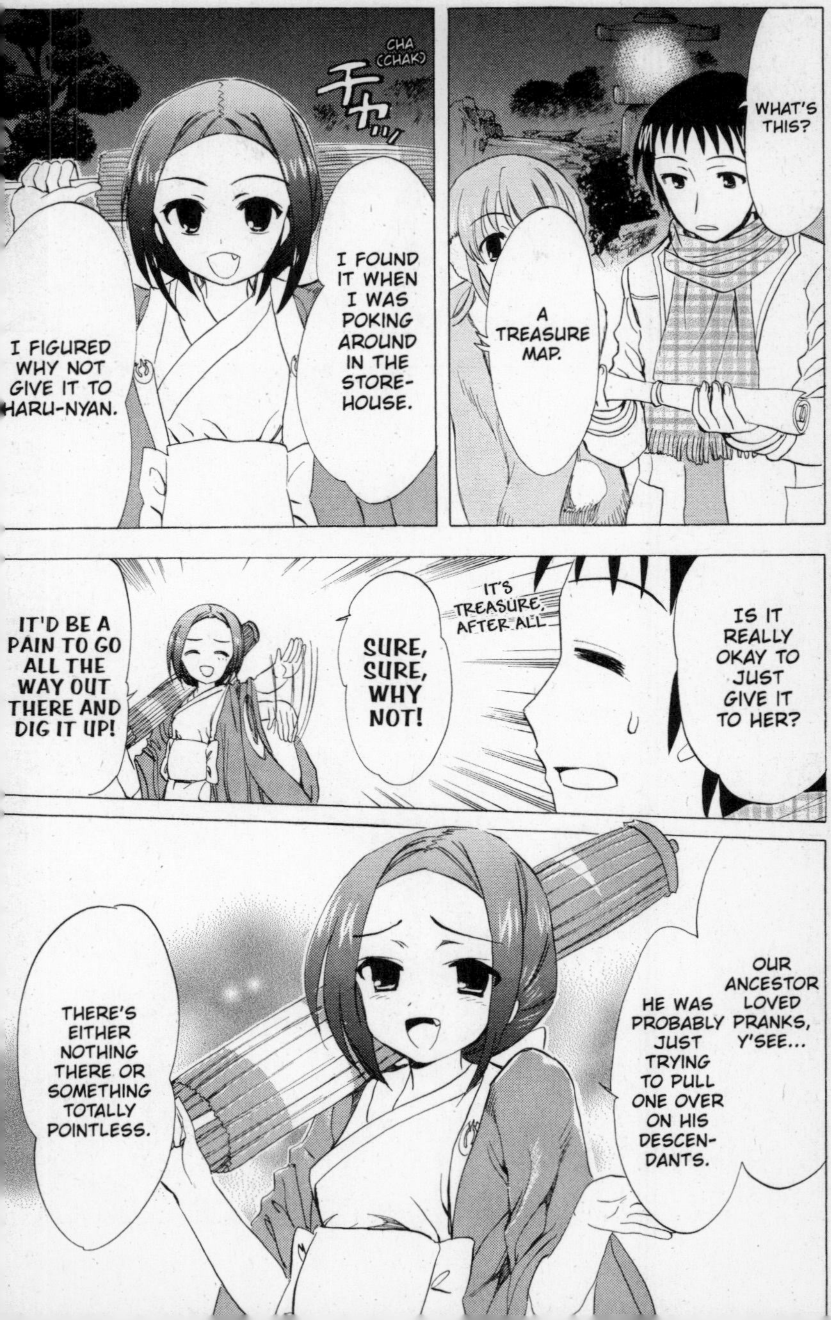
WHAT'S THIS?
A TREASURE MAP.
CHA (CHAK)
I FOUND IT WHEN I WAS POKING AROUND IN THE STORE-HOUSE.
I FIGURED WHY NOT GIVE IT TO HARU-NYAN.
IS IT REALLY OKAY TO JUST GIVE IT TO HER?
IT'S TREASURE, AFTER ALL
SURE, SURE, WHY NOT!
IT'D BE A PAIN TO GO ALL THE WAY OUT THERE AND DIG IT UP!
OUR ANCESTOR LOVED PRANKS, Y'SEE...
HE WAS PROBABLY JUST TRYING TO PULL ONE OVER ON HIS DESCEN-DANTS.
THERE'S EITHER NOTHING THERE OR SOMETHING TOTALLY POINTLESS.

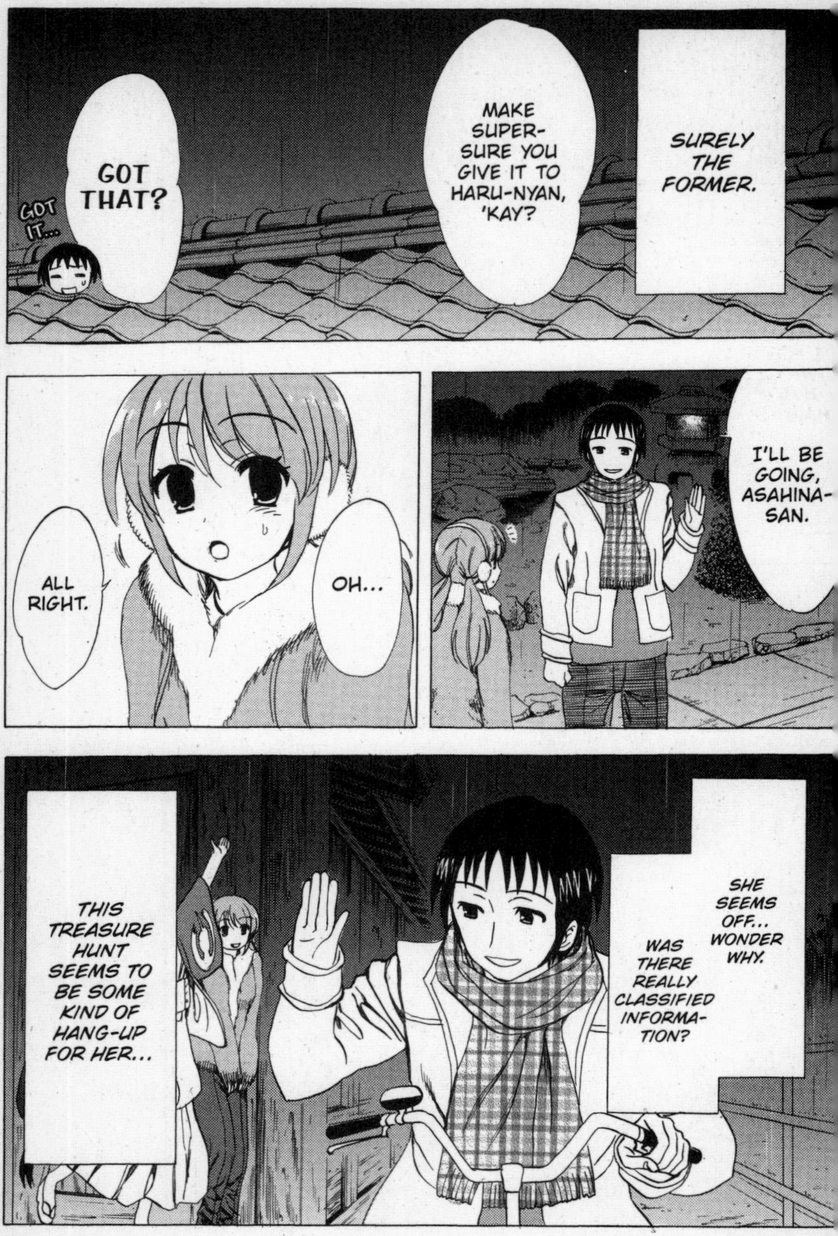
SURELY THE FORMER.
MAKE SUPER-SURE YOU GIVE IT TO HARU-NYAN, 'KAY?
GOT THAT?
GOT IT...
I'LL BE GOING, ASAHINA-SAN.
OH...
ALL RIGHT.
SHE SEEMS OFF... WONDER WHY.
WAS THERE REALLY CLASSIFIED INFORMATION?
THIS TREASURE HUNT SEEMS TO BE SOME KIND OF HANG-UP FOR HER...

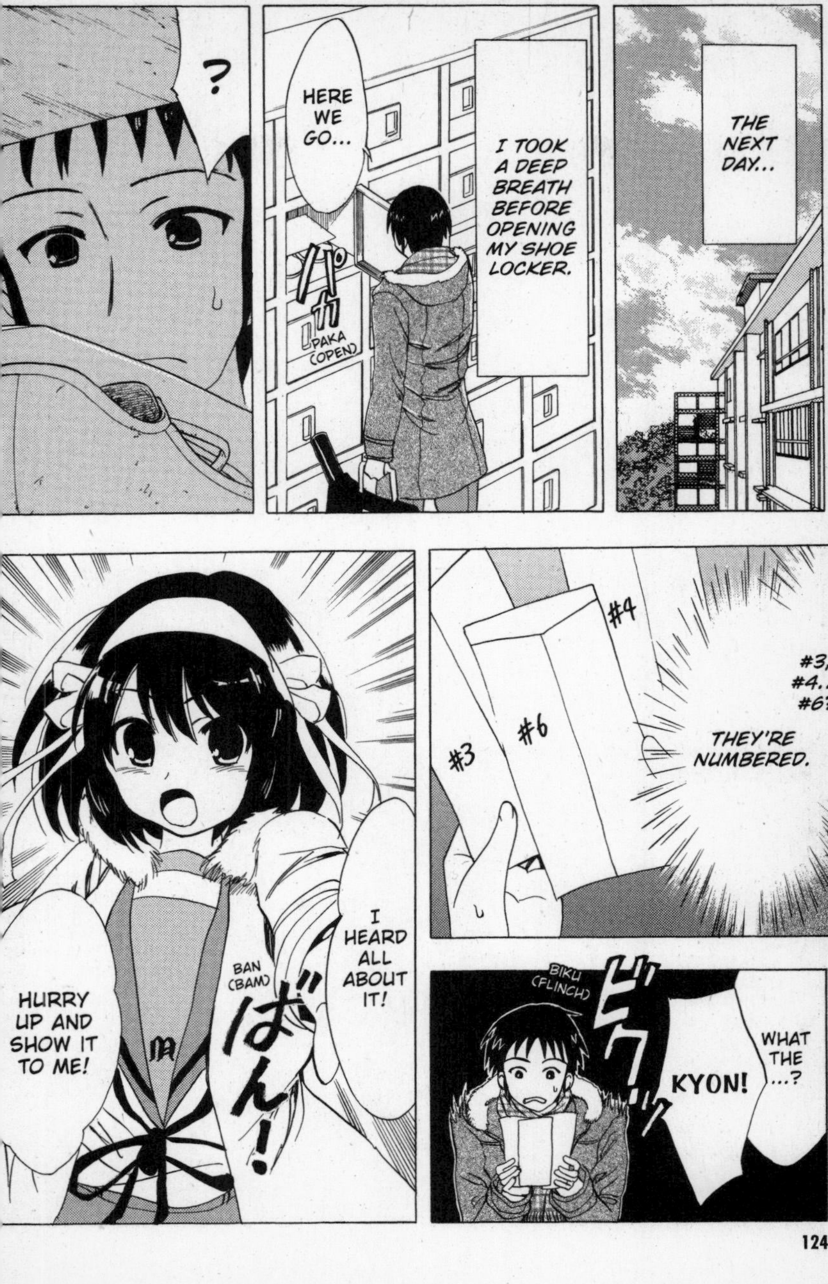
THE NEXT DAY...
I TOOK A DEEP BREATH BEFORE OPENING MY SHOE LOCKER.
HERE WE GO...
パカ
PAKA (OPEN)
?
#3, #4... #6?
THEY'RE NUMBERED.
#4
#6
#3
WHAT THE ...?
KYON!
ビクッ
BIKU (FLINCH)
I HEARD ALL ABOUT IT!
ばん!
BAN (BAM)
HURRY UP AND SHOW IT TO ME!

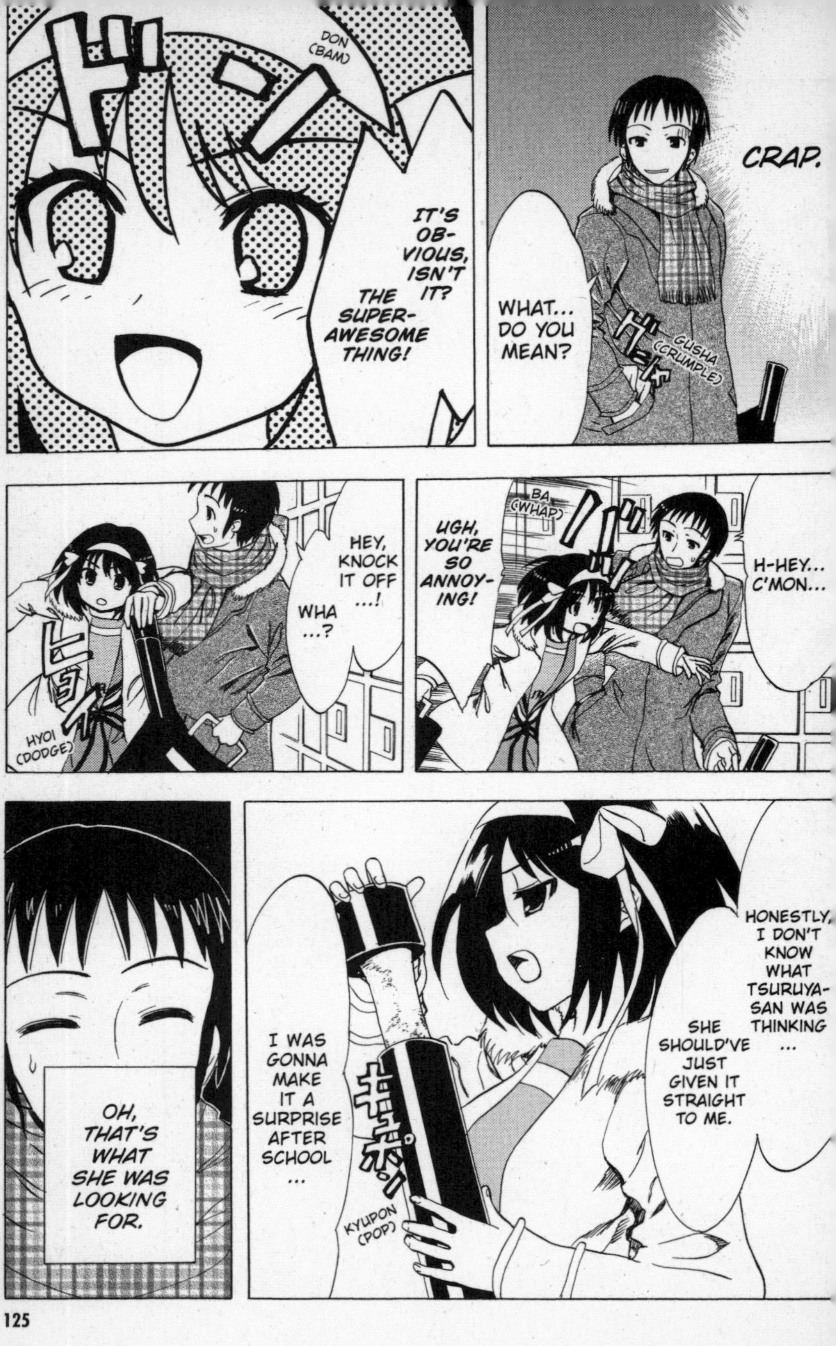
CRAP.
WHAT... DO YOU MEAN?
GUSHA (CRUMPLE)
DON (BAM)
IT'S OB- VIOUS, ISN'T IT?
THE SUPER- AWESOME THING!
H-HEY... C'MON...
UGH, YOU'RE SO ANNOY- ING!
BA (WHAP)
HEY, KNOCK IT OFF ...!
WHA ...?
HYOI (DODGE)
HONESTLY, I DON'T KNOW WHAT TSURUYA- SAN WAS THINKING ...
SHE SHOULD'VE JUST GIVEN IT STRAIGHT TO ME.
I WAS GONNA MAKE IT A SURPRISE AFTER SCHOOL ...
KYUPON (POP)
OH, THAT'S WHAT SHE WAS LOOKING FOR.

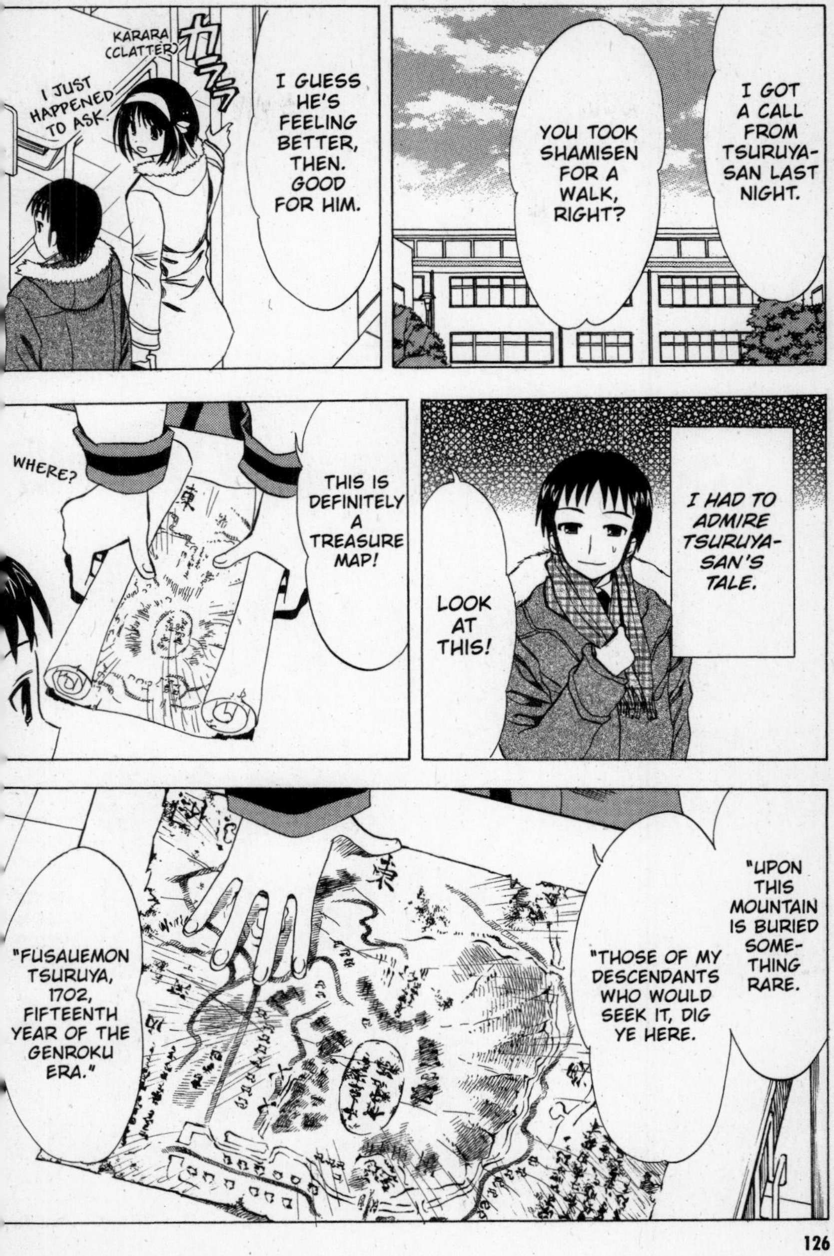
I GOT A CALL FROM TSURUYA-SAN LAST NIGHT.
YOU TOOK SHAMISEN FOR A WALK, RIGHT?
I GUESS HE'S FEELING BETTER, THEN. GOOD FOR HIM.
KARARA (CLATTER)
I JUST HAPPENED TO ASK.
I HAD TO ADMIRE TSURUYA-SAN'S TALE.
LOOK AT THIS!
THIS IS DEFINITELY A TREASURE MAP!
WHERE?
"UPON THIS MOUNTAIN IS BURIED SOMETHING RARE.
"THOSE OF MY DESCENDANTS WHO WOULD SEEK IT, DIG YE HERE.
"FUSAUEMON TSURUYA, 1702, FIFTEENTH YEAR OF THE GENROKU ERA."

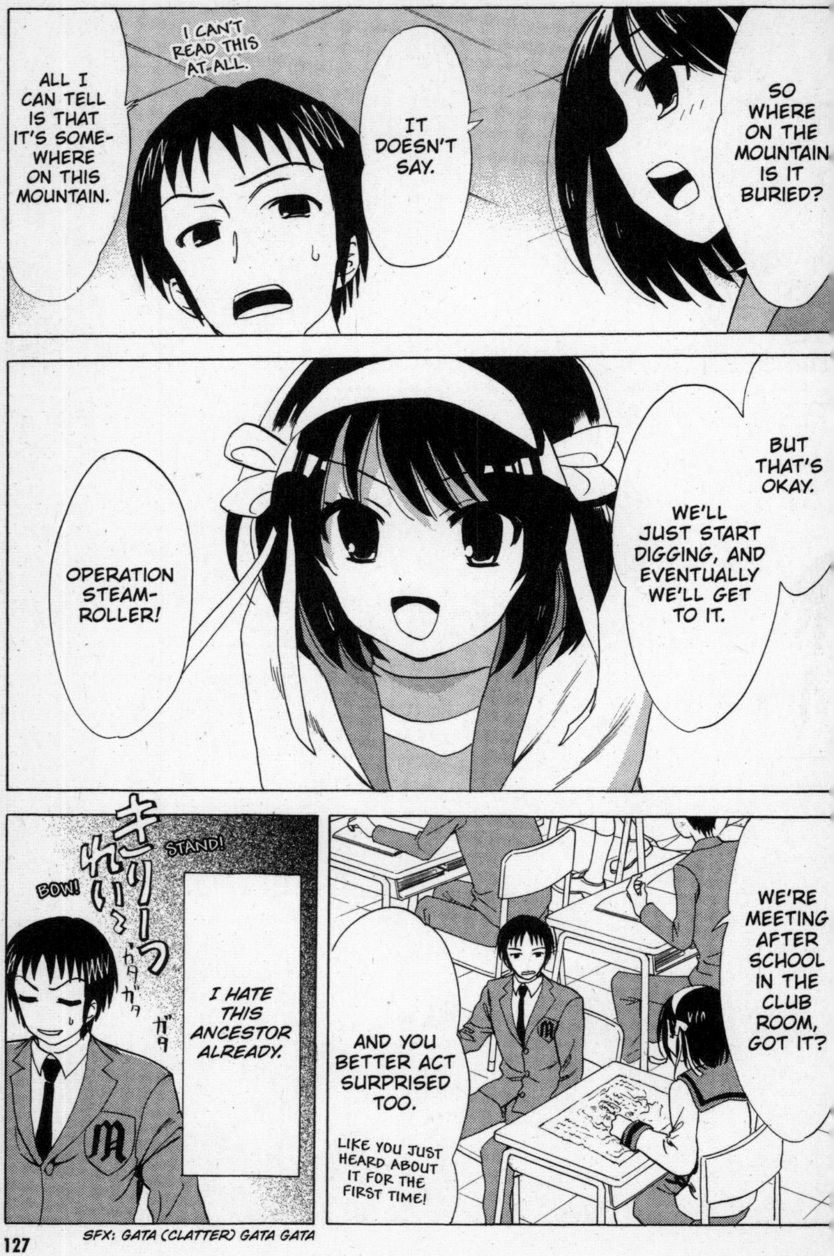
SO WHERE ON THE MOUNTAIN IS IT BURIED?
IT DOESN'T SAY.
I CAN'T READ THIS AT ALL.
ALL I CAN TELL IS THAT IT'S SOME-WHERE ON THIS MOUNTAIN.
BUT THAT'S OKAY.
WE'LL JUST START DIGGING, AND EVENTUALLY WE'LL GET TO IT.
OPERATION STEAM-ROLLER!
WE'RE MEETING AFTER SCHOOL IN THE CLUB ROOM, GOT IT?
AND YOU BETTER ACT SURPRISED TOO.
LIKE YOU JUST HEARD ABOUT IT FOR THE FIRST TIME!
きりーつ
STAND!
れい~
BOW!
ガタガタ
ガタ
I HATE THIS ANCESTOR ALREADY.

SFX: GATA (CLATTER) GATA GATA

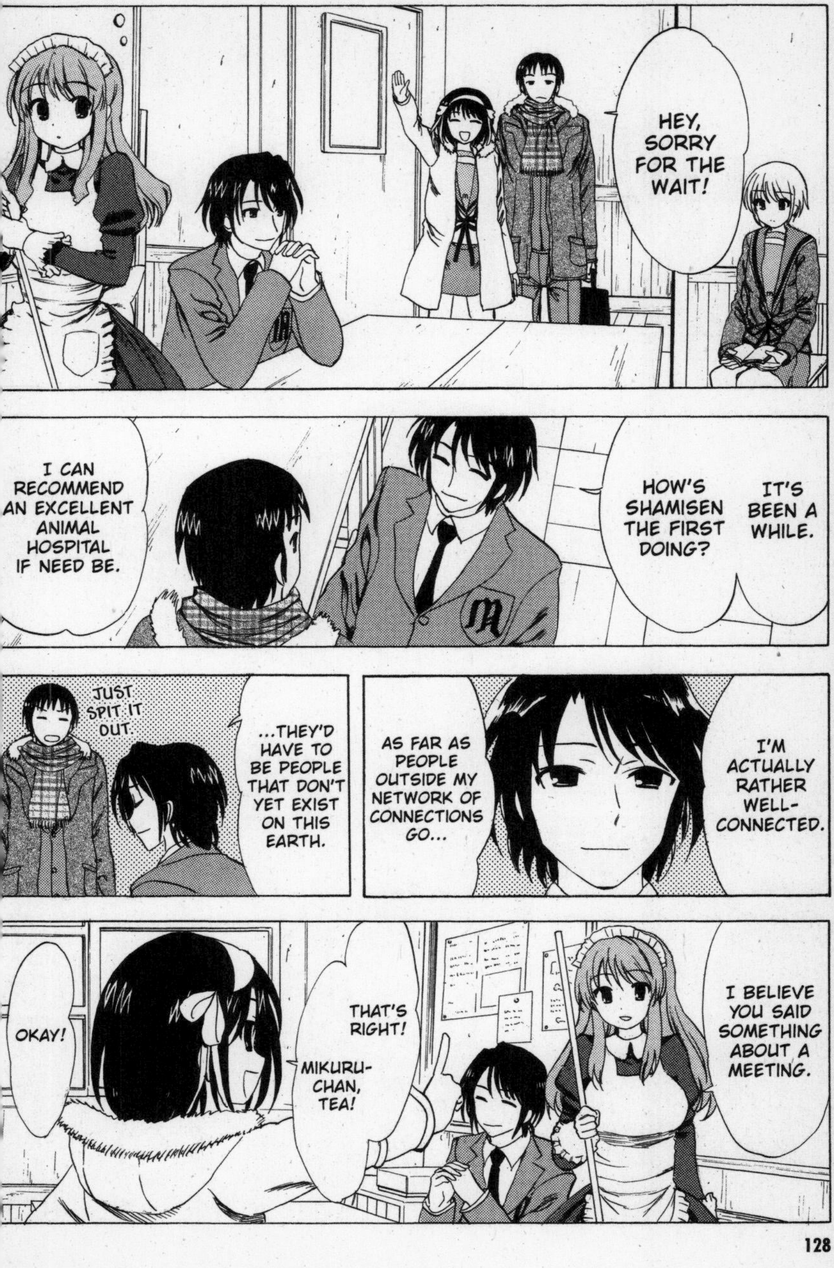
HEY, SORRY FOR THE WAIT!
IT'S BEEN A WHILE.
HOW'S SHAMISEN THE FIRST DOING?
I CAN RECOMMEND AN EXCELLENT ANIMAL HOSPITAL IF NEED BE.
I'M ACTUALLY RATHER WELL-CONNECTED.
AS FAR AS PEOPLE OUTSIDE MY NETWORK OF CONNECTIONS GO...
...THEY'D HAVE TO BE PEOPLE THAT DON'T YET EXIST ON THIS EARTH.
JUST SPIT IT OUT.
I BELIEVE YOU SAID SOMETHING ABOUT A MEETING.
THAT'S RIGHT!
MIKURU-CHAN, TEA!
OKAY!

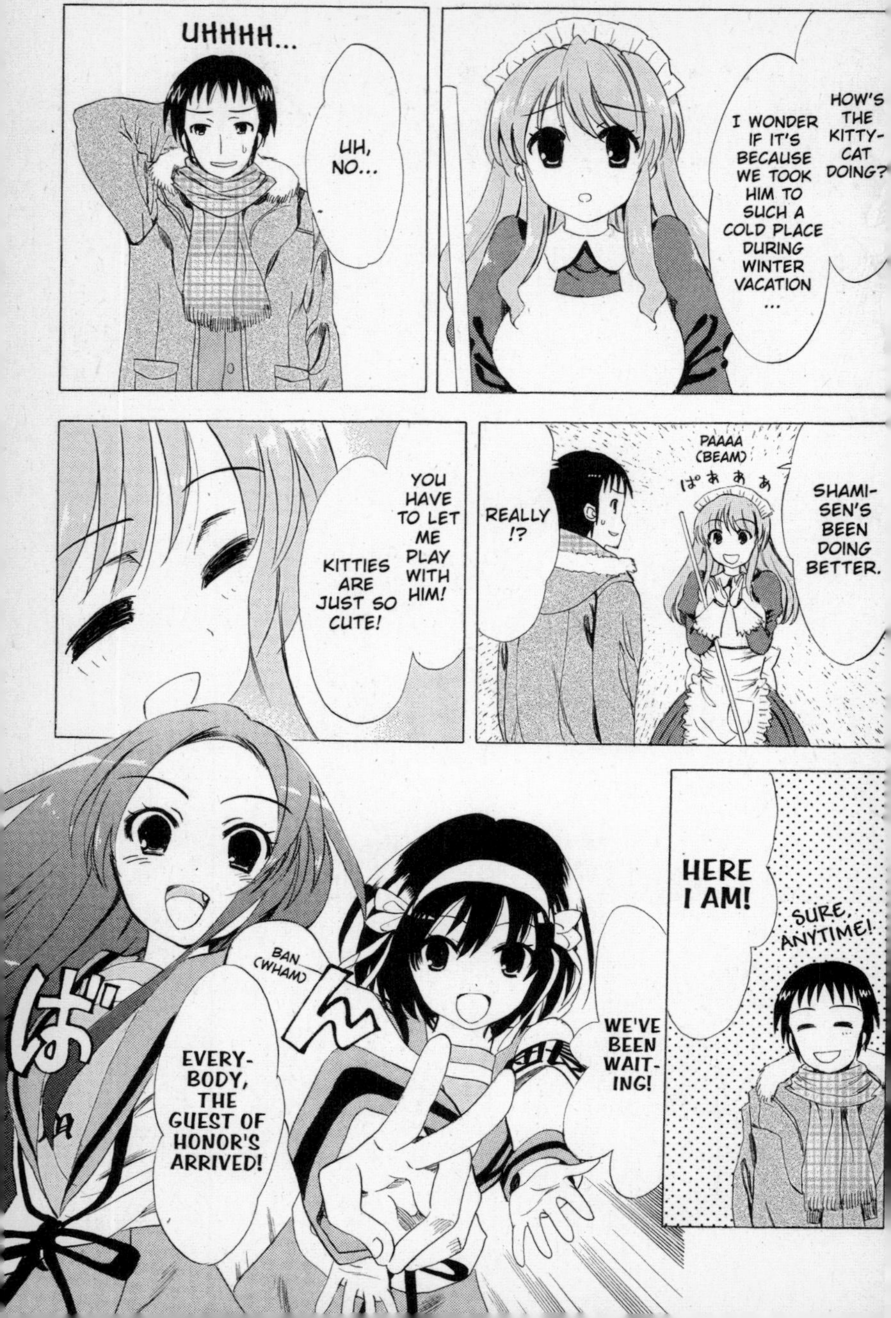
HOW'S THE KITTY-CAT DOING?
I WONDER IF IT'S BECAUSE WE TOOK HIM TO SUCH A COLD PLACE DURING WINTER VACATION ...
UHHHH...
UH, NO...
SHAMI-SEN'S BEEN DOING BETTER.
PAAAA (BEAM)
ぱあああ
REALLY !?
YOU HAVE TO LET ME PLAY WITH HIM!
KITTIES ARE JUST SO CUTE!
SURE, ANYTIME!
HERE I AM!
WE'VE BEEN WAIT-ING!
BAN (WHAM)
ばん
EVERY-BODY, THE GUEST OF HONOR'S ARRIVED!

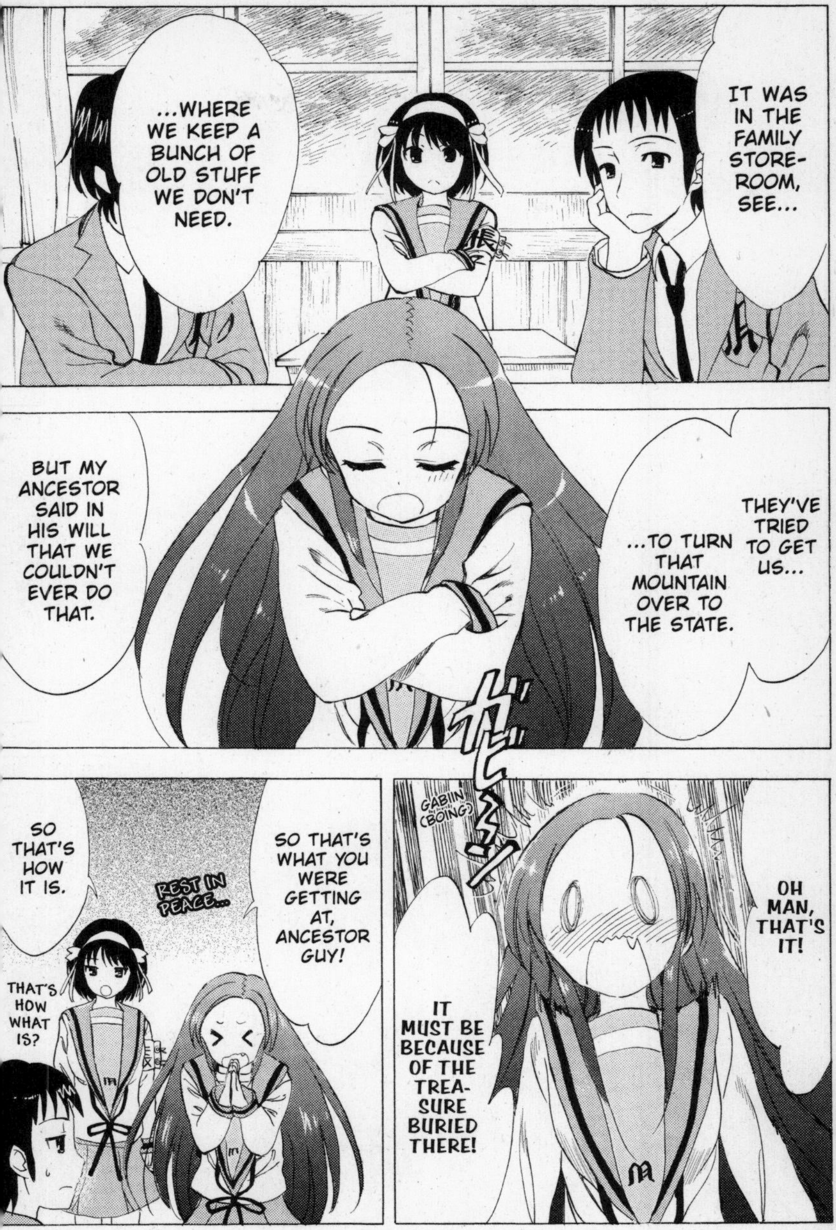
IT WAS IN THE FAMILY STORE-ROOM, SEE...
...WHERE WE KEEP A BUNCH OF OLD STUFF WE DON'T NEED.
THEY'VE TRIED TO GET US...
...TO TURN THAT MOUNTAIN OVER TO THE STATE.
BUT MY ANCESTOR SAID IN HIS WILL THAT WE COULDN'T EVER DO THAT.
GABIN (BOING)
OH MAN, THAT'S IT!
IT MUST BE BECAUSE OF THE TREA-SURE BURIED THERE!
SO THAT'S WHAT YOU WERE GETTING AT, ANCESTOR GUY!
REST IN PEACE...
SO THAT'S HOW IT IS.
THAT'S HOW WHAT IS?

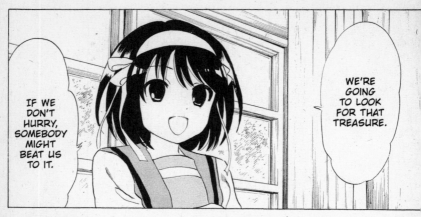

WE'RE GOING TO LOOK FOR THAT TREASURE.
IF WE DON'T HURRY, SOMEBODY MIGHT BEAT US TO IT.
MEET AT THE USUAL STATION, TOMORROW AT 9 A.M.!
オー!!
OOO (WHOOO)
IT WAS IMPOSSIBLE TO ACT SURPRISED AT THIS.
WHA...? TREA-SURE HUNT-ING?
TOMORROW? MOUNTAIN CLIMBING?
I'D BETTER MAKE SOME LUNCH-ES!
EXCEPT FOR HER.
WELL, WELL ...
THIS COULD INDEED BE FASCINATING, FROM AN ANTHROPO-LOGICAL AND ARCHAEO-LOGICAL PERSPECTIVE.
DO YOU ACTUALLY THINK THAT?

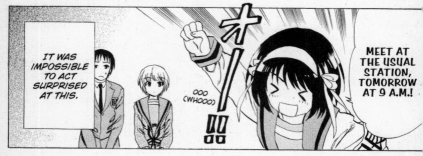

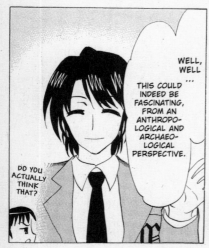

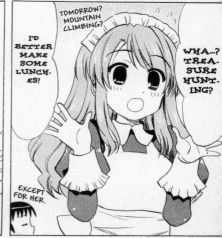

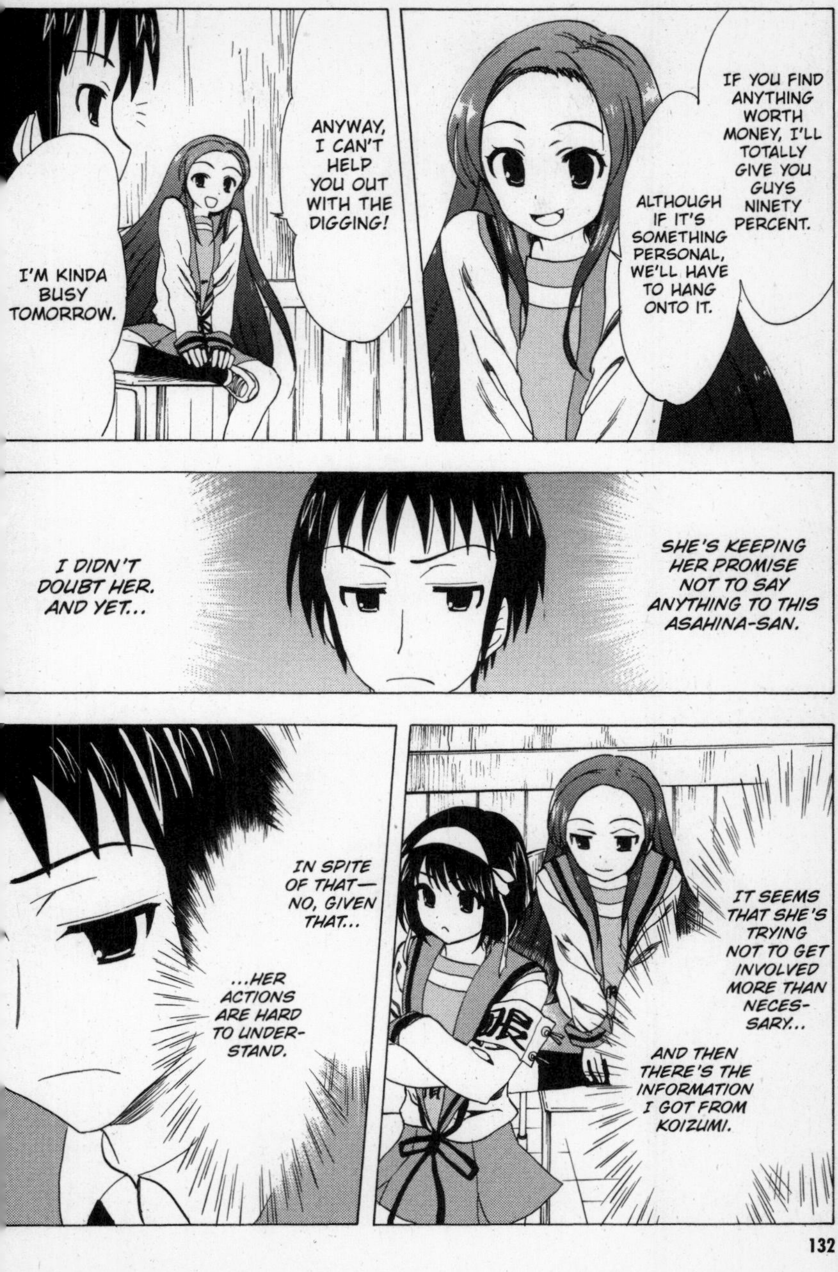
IF YOU FIND ANYTHING WORTH MONEY, I'LL TOTALLY GIVE YOU GUYS NINETY PERCENT.
ALTHOUGH IF IT'S SOMETHING PERSONAL, WE'LL HAVE TO HANG ONTO IT.
ANYWAY, I CAN'T HELP YOU OUT WITH THE DIGGING!
I'M KINDA BUSY TOMORROW.
SHE'S KEEPING HER PROMISE NOT TO SAY ANYTHING TO THIS ASAHINA-SAN.
I DIDN'T DOUBT HER. AND YET...
IT SEEMS THAT SHE'S TRYING NOT TO GET INVOLVED MORE THAN NECES-SARY...
AND THEN THERE'S THE INFORMATION I GOT FROM KOIZUMI.
IN SPITE OF THAT— NO, GIVEN THAT...
...HER ACTIONS ARE HARD TO UNDER-STAND.

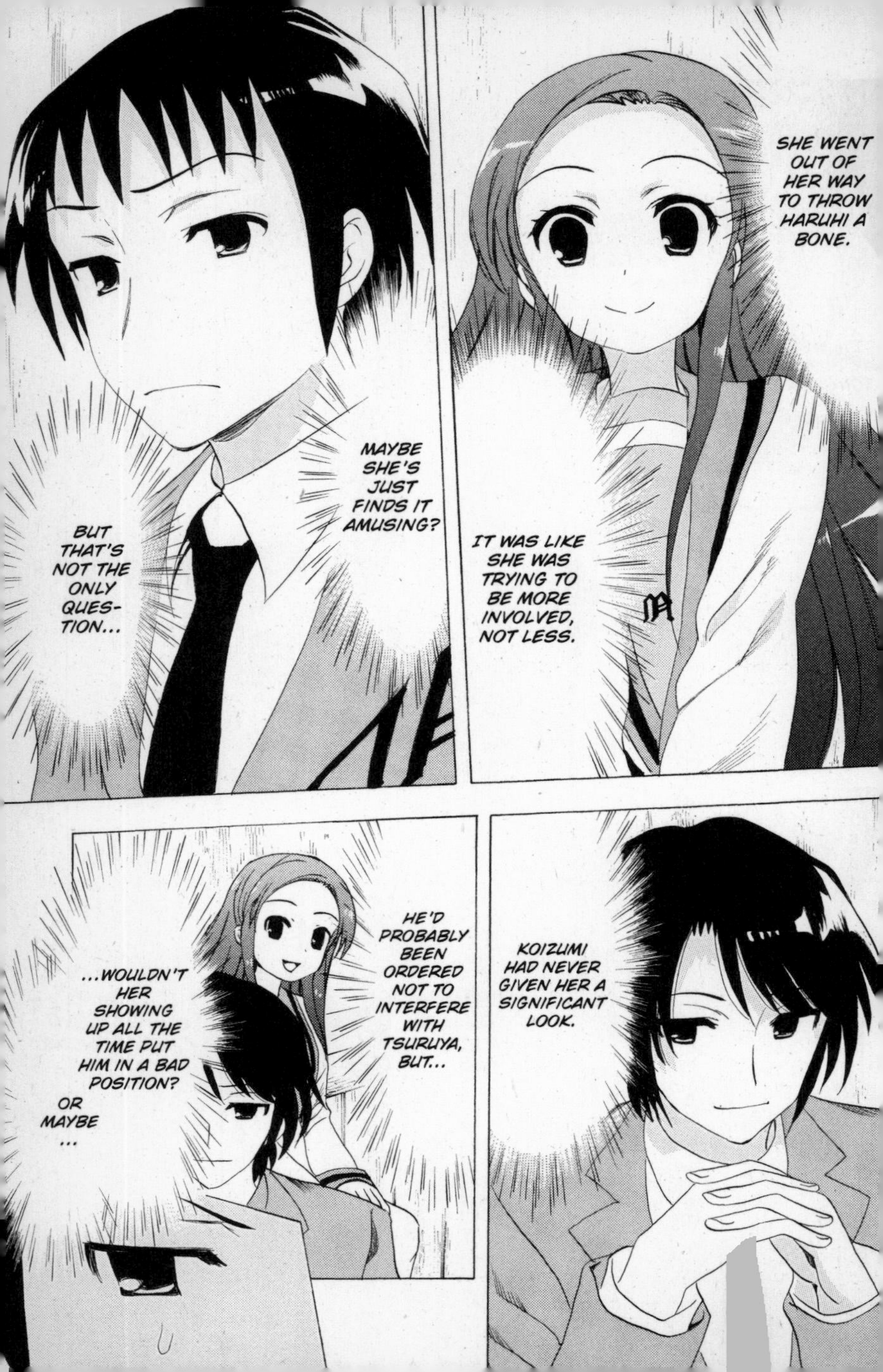
SHE WENT OUT OF HER WAY TO THROW HARUHI A BONE.
IT WAS LIKE SHE WAS TRYING TO BE MORE INVOLVED, NOT LESS.
MAYBE SHE'S JUST FINDS IT AMUSING?
BUT THAT'S NOT THE ONLY QUES-TION...
KOIZUMI HAD NEVER GIVEN HER A SIGNIFICANT LOOK.
HE'D PROBABLY BEEN ORDERED NOT TO INTERFERE WITH TSURUYA, BUT...
...WOULDN'T HER SHOWING UP ALL THE TIME PUT HIM IN A BAD POSITION?
OR MAYBE ...

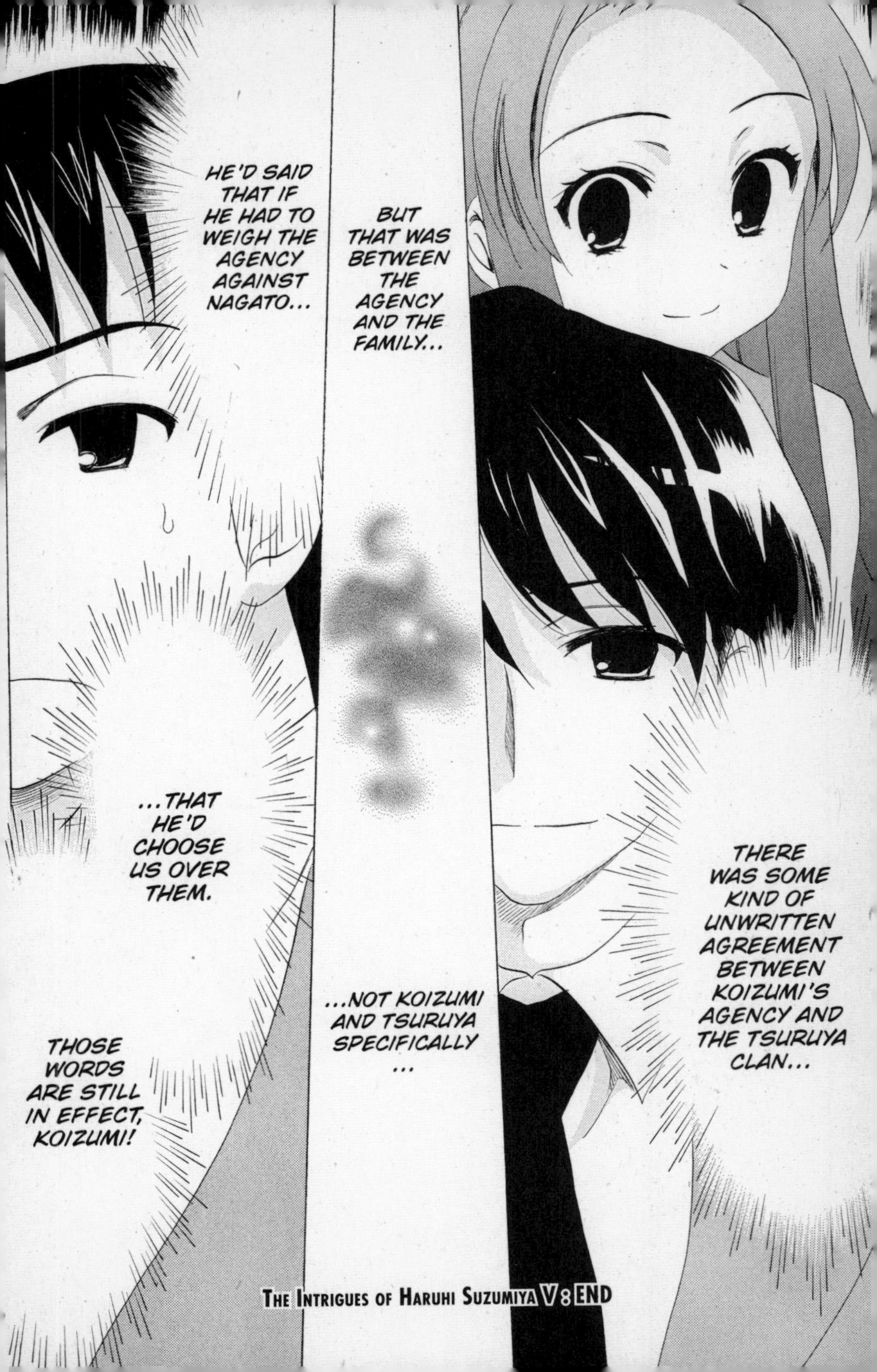
THERE WAS SOME KIND OF UNWRITTEN AGREEMENT BETWEEN KOIZUMI'S AGENCY AND THE TSURUYA CLAN...
BUT THAT WAS BETWEEN THE AGENCY AND THE FAMILY...
...NOT KOIZUMI AND TSURUYA SPECIFICALLY...
HE'D SAID THAT IF HE HAD TO WEIGH THE AGENCY AGAINST NAGATO...
...THAT HE'D CHOOSE US OVER THEM.
THOSE WORDS ARE STILL IN EFFECT, KOIZUMI!
THE INTRIGUES OF HARUHI SUZUMIYA V 8: END

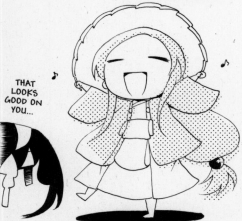

ASATTE, ASATTE,
SATE WA NANKIN
TAMASUDARE!

THAT
LOOKS
GOOD ON
YOU...

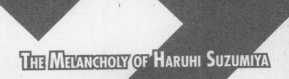

THE MELANCHOLY OF HARUHI SUZUMIYA

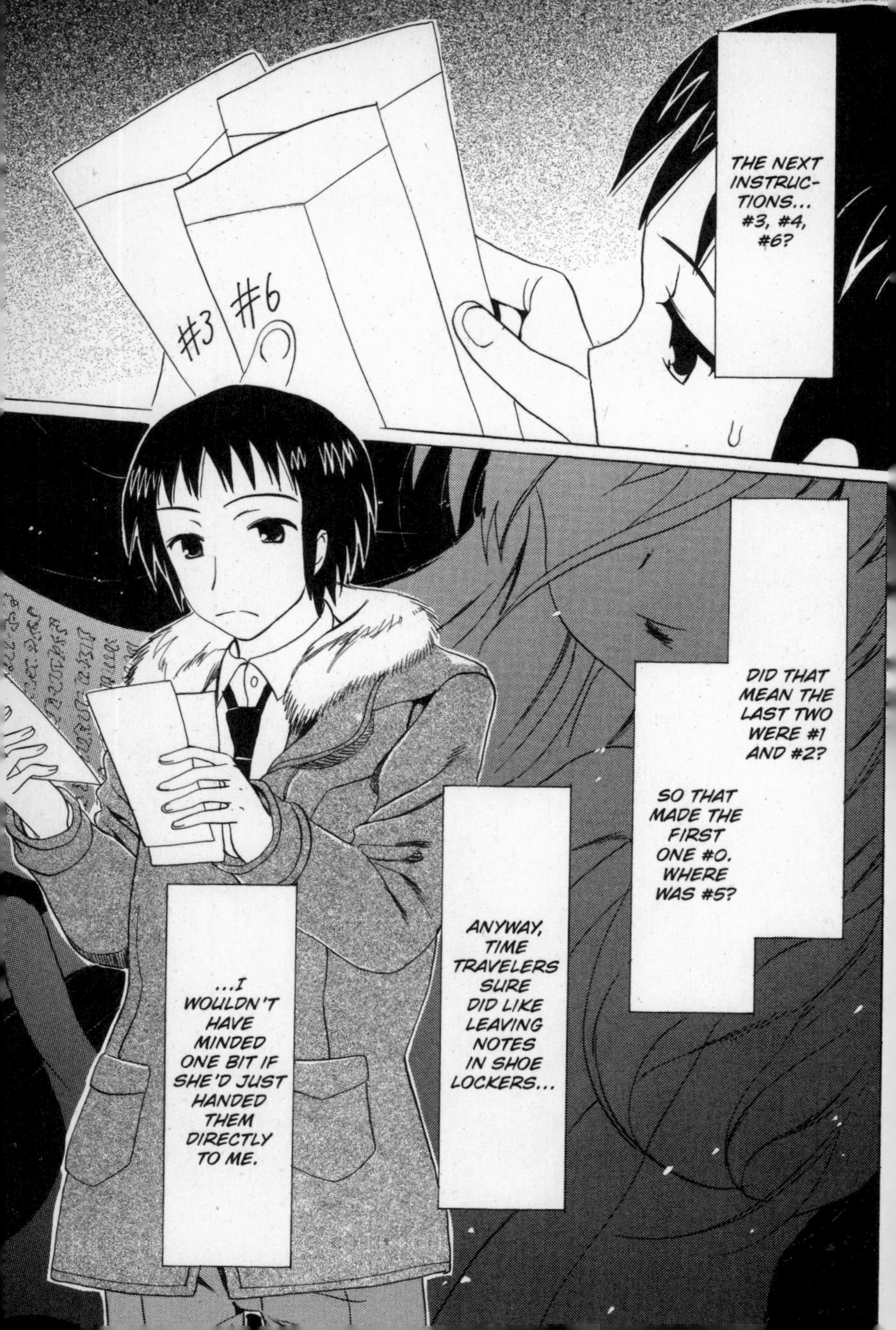
THE NEXT INSTRUCTIONS... #3, #4, #6?
#3
#6
DID THAT MEAN THE LAST TWO WERE #1 AND #2?
SO THAT MADE THE FIRST ONE #0. WHERE WAS #5?
ANYWAY, TIME TRAVELERS SURE DID LIKE LEAVING NOTES IN SHOE LOCKERS...
...I WOULDN'T HAVE MINDED ONE BIT IF SHE'D JUST HANDED THEM DIRECTLY TO ME.

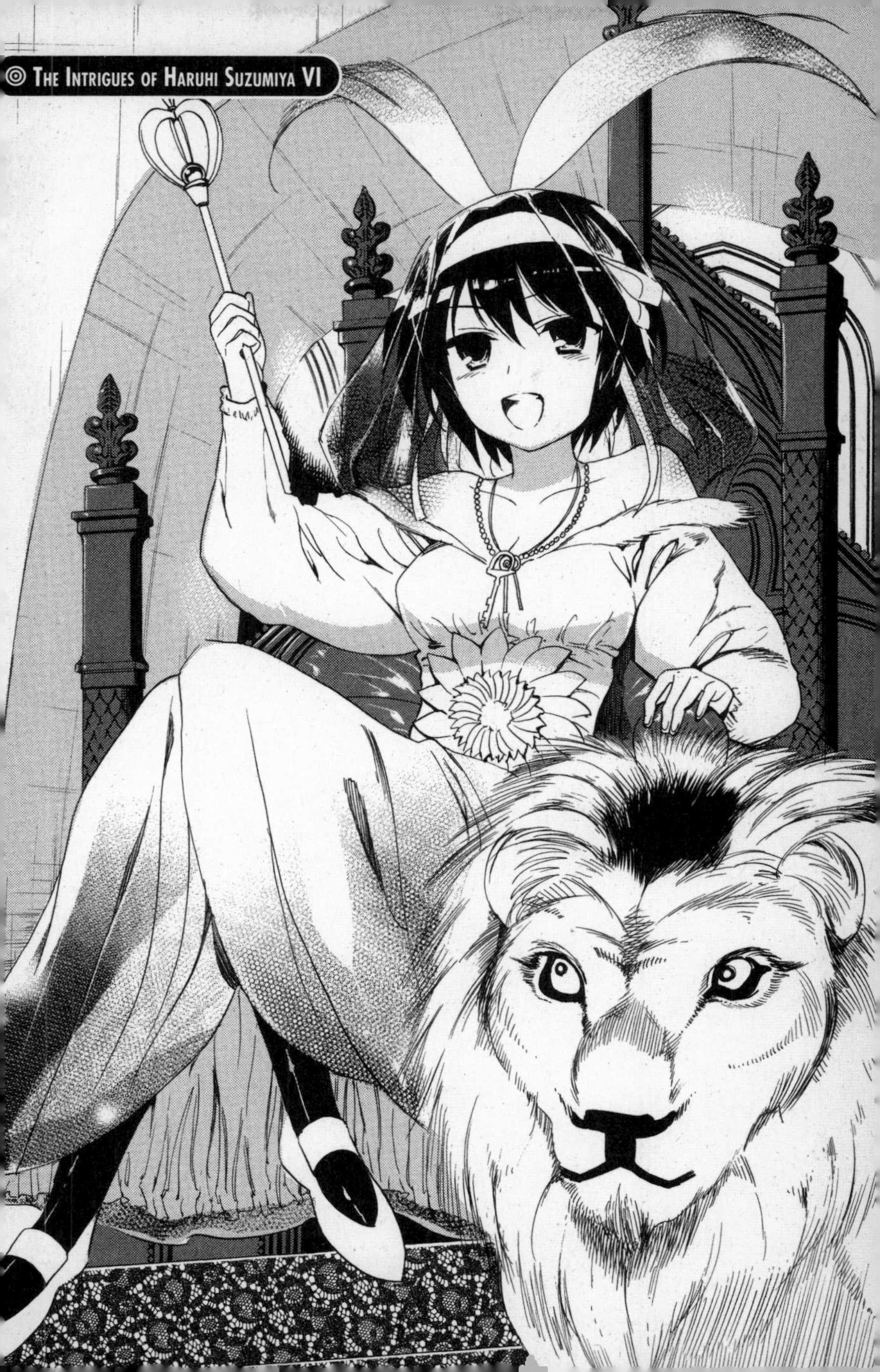

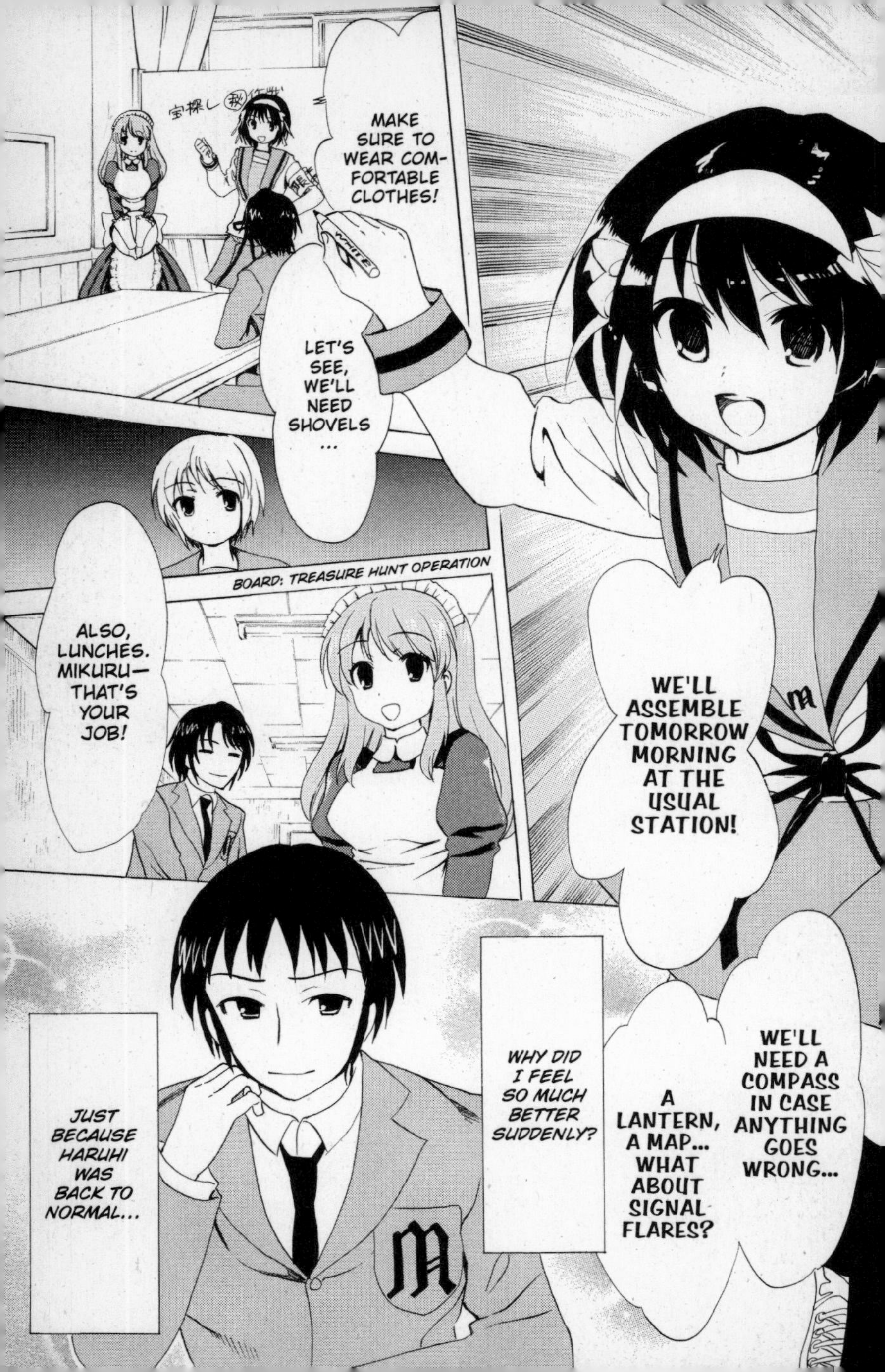
MAKE SURE TO WEAR COM-FORTABLE CLOTHES!
LET'S SEE, WE'LL NEED SHOVELS ...
WE'LL ASSEMBLE TOMORROW MORNING AT THE USUAL STATION!
ALSO, LUNCHES. MIKURU—THAT'S YOUR JOB!
BOARD: TREASURE HUNT OPERATION
WE'LL NEED A COMPASS IN CASE ANYTHING GOES WRONG...
A LANTERN, A MAP... WHAT ABOUT SIGNAL FLARES?
WHY DID I FEEL SO MUCH BETTER SUDDENLY?
JUST BECAUSE HARUHI WAS BACK TO NORMAL...

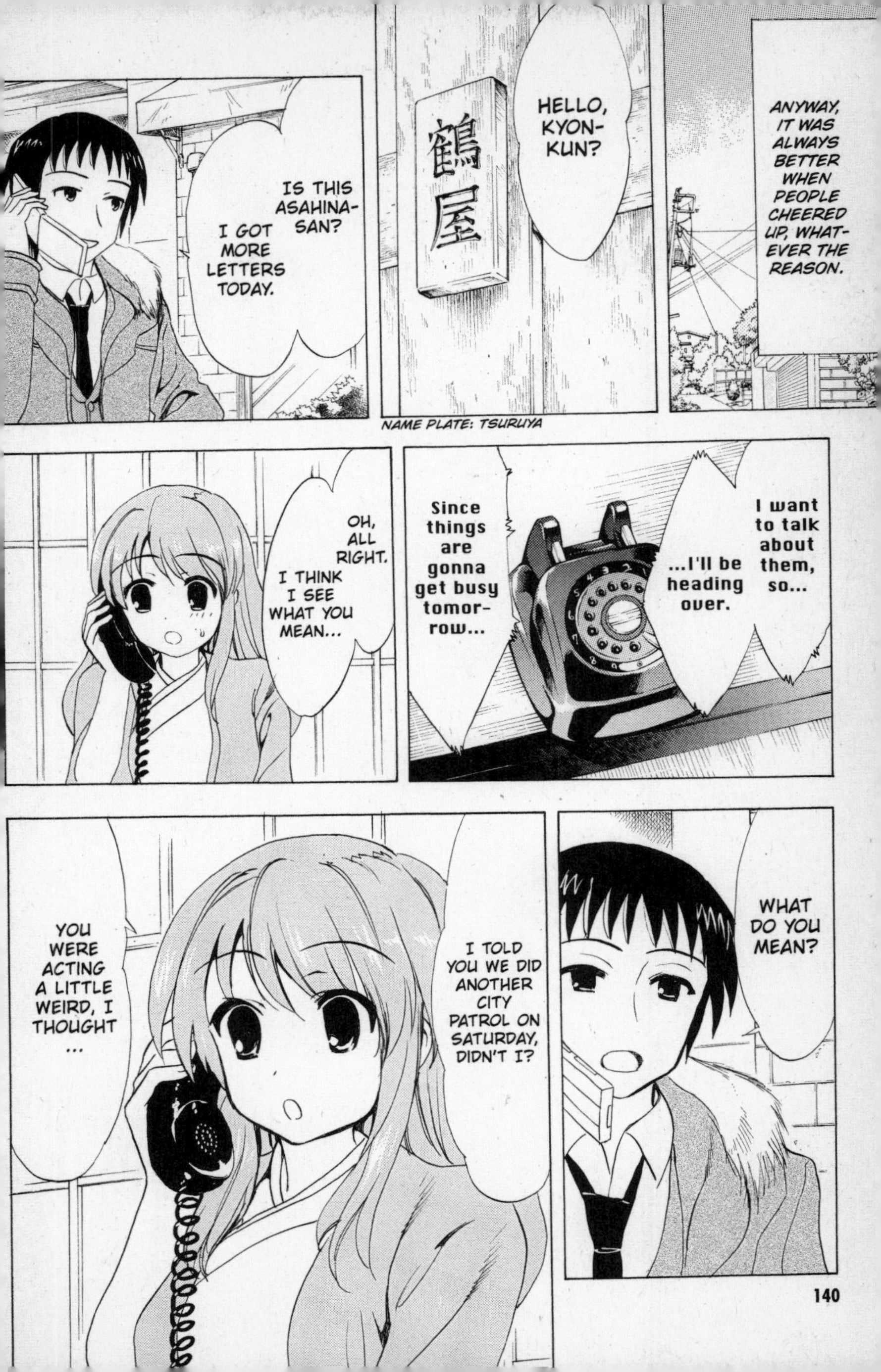
ANYWAY, IT WAS ALWAYS BETTER WHEN PEOPLE CHEERED UP, WHAT-EVER THE REASON.
HELLO, KYON-KUN?
鶴屋
IS THIS ASAHINA-SAN?
I GOT MORE LETTERS TODAY.
NAME PLATE: TSURUYA
I want to talk about them, so...
...I'll be heading over.
Since things are gonna get busy tomor-row...
OH, ALL RIGHT.
I THINK I SEE WHAT YOU MEAN...
WHAT DO YOU MEAN?
I TOLD YOU WE DID ANOTHER CITY PATROL ON SATURDAY, DIDN'T I?
YOU WERE ACTING A LITTLE WEIRD, I THOUGHT ...

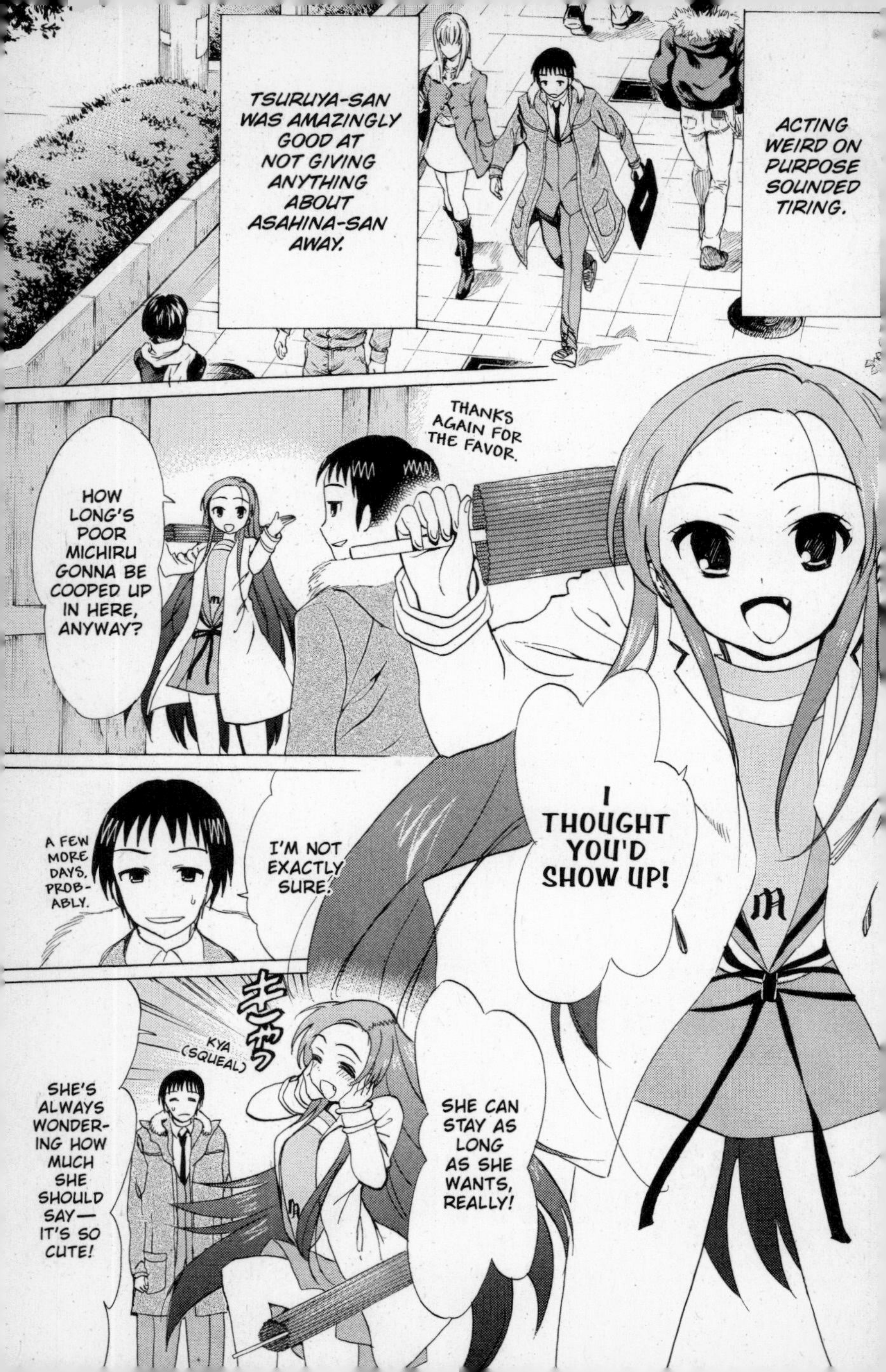
ACTING WEIRD ON PURPOSE SOUNDED TIRING.
TSURUYA-SAN WAS AMAZINGLY GOOD AT NOT GIVING ANYTHING ABOUT ASAHINA-SAN AWAY.
I THOUGHT YOU'D SHOW UP!
THANKS AGAIN FOR THE FAVOR.
HOW LONG'S POOR MICHIRU GONNA BE COOPED UP IN HERE, ANYWAY?
I'M NOT EXACTLY SURE.
A FEW MORE DAYS, PROB-ABLY.
キャ
KYA (SQUEAL)
SHE CAN STAY AS LONG AS SHE WANTS, REALLY!
SHE'S ALWAYS WONDER-ING HOW MUCH SHE SHOULD SAY— IT'S SO CUTE!

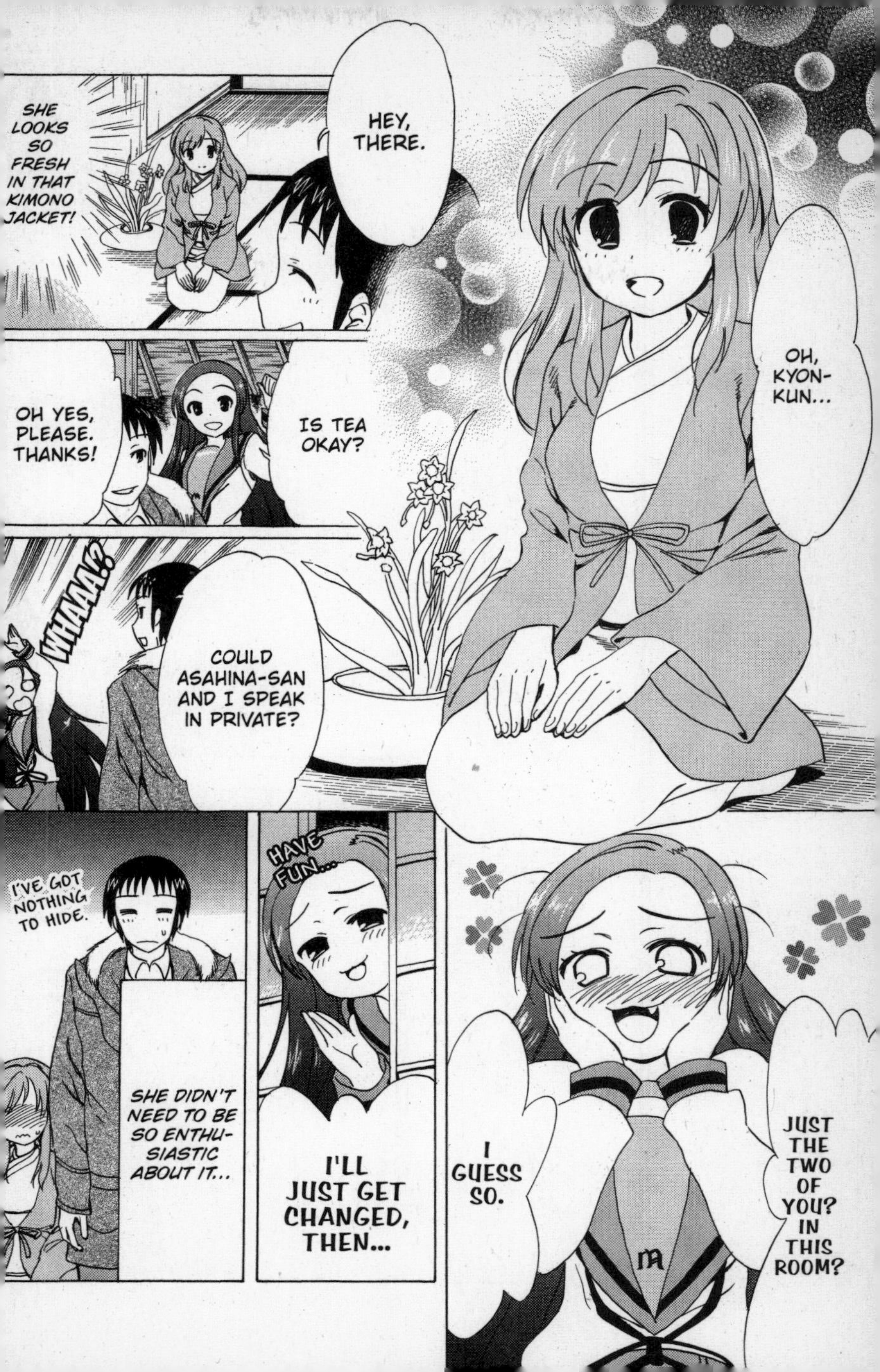
OH, KYON-KUN...
HEY, THERE.
SHE LOOKS SO FRESH IN THAT KIMONO JACKET!
IS TEA OKAY?
OH YES, PLEASE. THANKS!
COULD ASAHINA-SAN AND I SPEAK IN PRIVATE?
WHAAA!?
JUST THE TWO OF YOU? IN THIS ROOM?
I GUESS SO.
HAVE FUN...
I'LL JUST GET CHANGED, THEN...
I'VE GOT NOTHING TO HIDE.
SHE DIDN'T NEED TO BE SO ENTHU-SIASTIC ABOUT IT...

NOTE: SATURDAY, THE DAY AFTER TOMORROW: GO SOUTH TO THE PEDESTRIAN BRIDGE IN [XXXX] COUNTY, [XXXX] WARD BY DUSK. THERE, IN FRONT OF THE BRIDGE, YOU WILL SEE SOME PANSIES. PICK UP THE OBJECT THAT'S BEEN DROPPED THERE AND SEND IT ANONYMOUSLY TO THE ADDRESS BELOW. THE OBJECT IS A PORTABLE STORAGE DEVIC

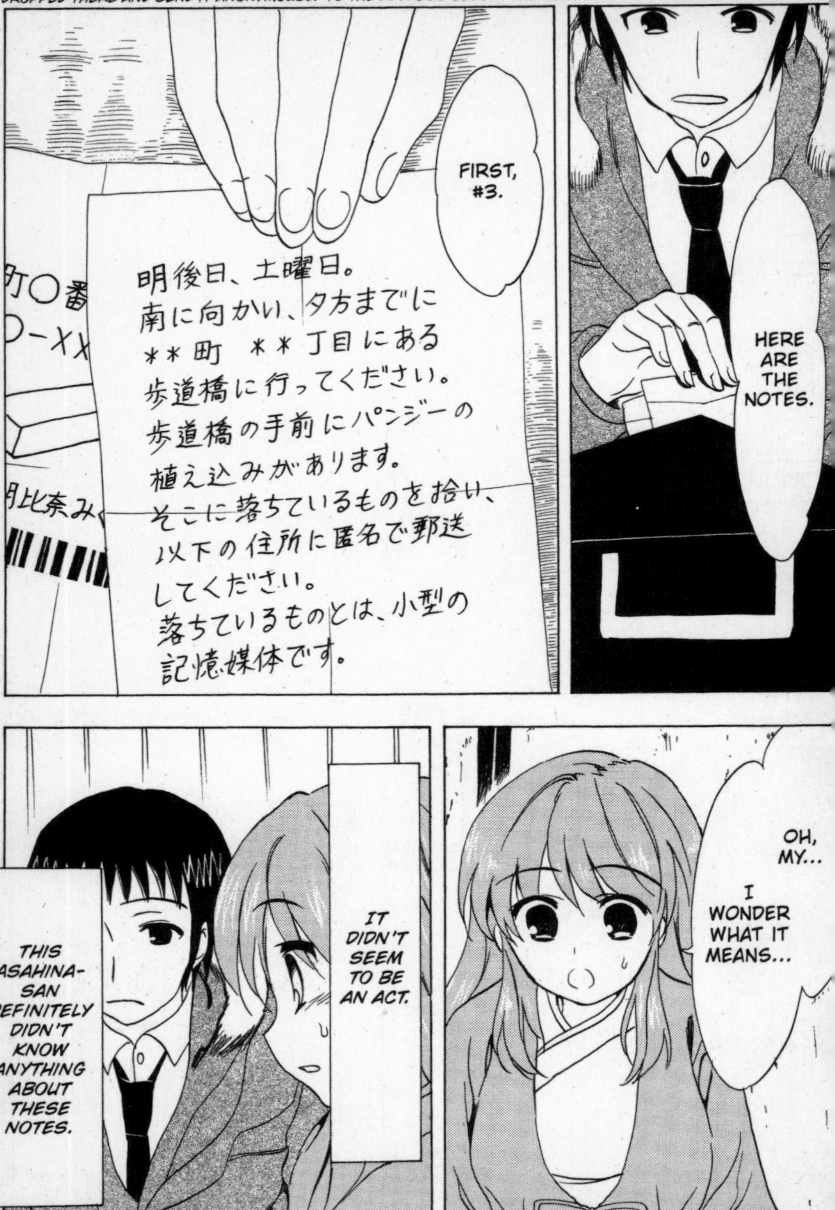
HERE ARE THE NOTES.
FIRST, #3.
明後日、土曜日。
南に向かい、夕方までに
＊＊町　＊＊丁目にある
歩道橋に行ってください。
歩道橋の手前にパンジーの
植え込みがあります。
そこに落ちているものを拾い、
以下の住所に匿名で郵送
してください。
落ちているものとは、小型の
記憶媒体です。
OH, MY...
I WONDER WHAT IT MEANS...
THIS ASAHINA-SAN DEFINITELY DIDN'T KNOW ANYTHING ABOUT THESE NOTES.
IT DIDN'T SEEM TO BE AN ACT.

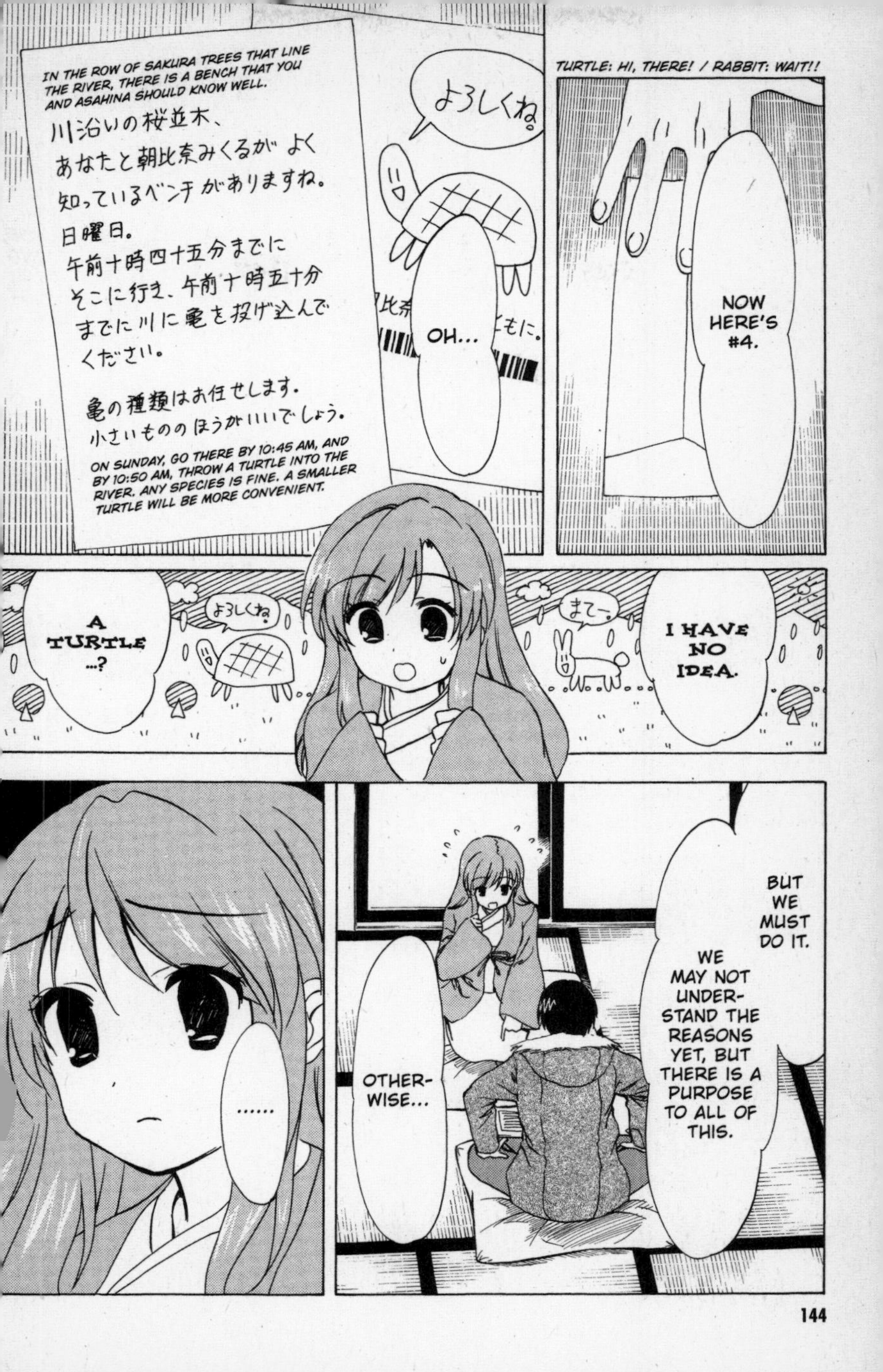
TURTLE: HI, THERE! / RABBIT: WAIT!!
NOW HERE'S #4.
よろしくね。
OH...
IN THE ROW OF SAKURA TREES THAT LINE THE RIVER, THERE IS A BENCH THAT YOU AND ASAHINA SHOULD KNOW WELL.
川沿いの桜並木、
あなたと朝比奈みくるが よく
知っているベンチ があリますね。
日曜日。
午前十時四十五分までに
そこに行き、午前十時五十分
までに川に亀を投げ込んで
ください。
亀の種類はお任せします。
小さいもののほうがいいでしょう。
ON SUNDAY, GO THERE BY 10:45 AM, AND BY 10:50 AM, THROW A TURTLE INTO THE RIVER. ANY SPECIES IS FINE. A SMALLER TURTLE WILL BE MORE CONVENIENT.
I HAVE NO IDEA.
まてー。
よろしくね。
A TURTLE ...?
BUT WE MUST DO IT.
WE MAY NOT UNDER-STAND THE REASONS YET, BUT THERE IS A PURPOSE TO ALL OF THIS.
OTHER-WISE...
......

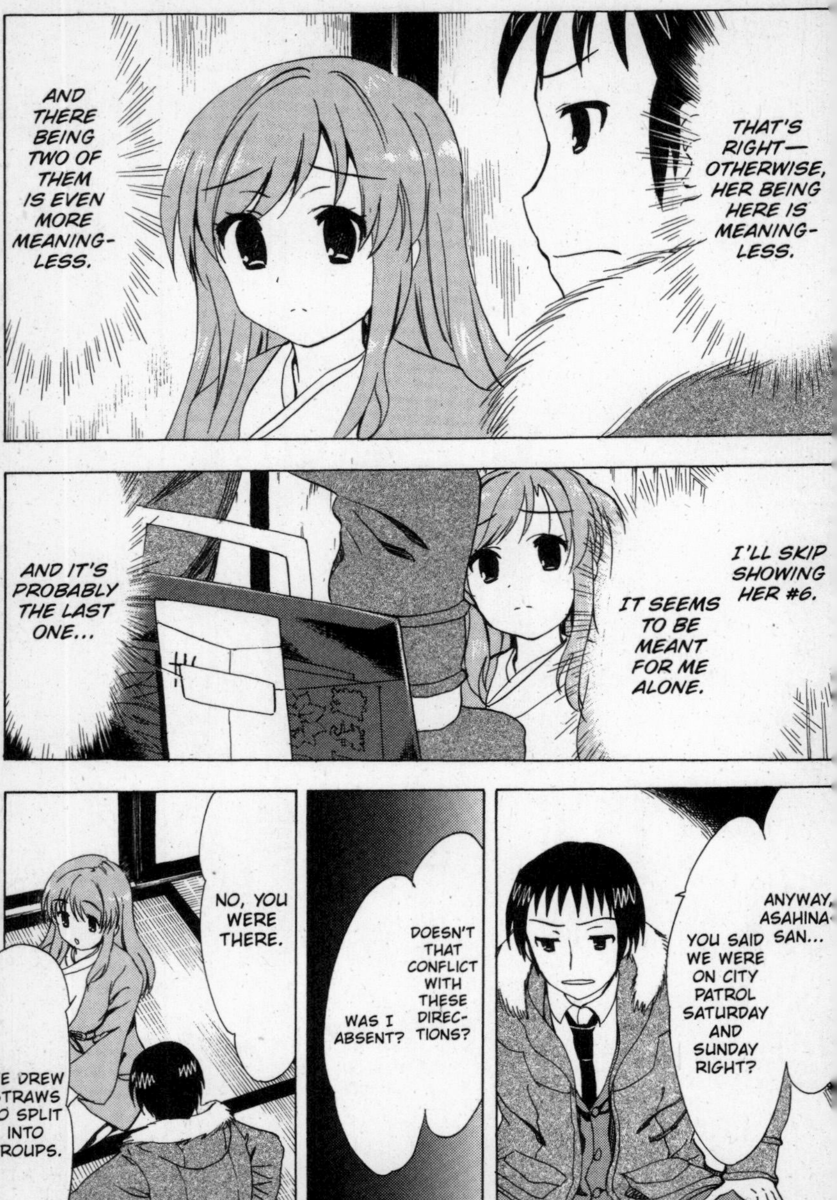
THAT'S RIGHT— OTHERWISE, HER BEING HERE IS MEANING-LESS.
AND THERE BEING TWO OF THEM IS EVEN MORE MEANING-LESS.
I'LL SKIP SHOWING HER #6.
IT SEEMS TO BE MEANT FOR ME ALONE.
AND IT'S PROBABLY THE LAST ONE...
ANYWAY, ASAHINA-SAN...
YOU SAID WE WERE ON CITY PATROL SATURDAY AND SUNDAY RIGHT?
DOESN'T THAT CONFLICT WITH THESE DIREC-TIONS?
WAS I ABSENT?
NO, YOU WERE THERE.
WE DREW STRAWS TO SPLIT INTO GROUPS.

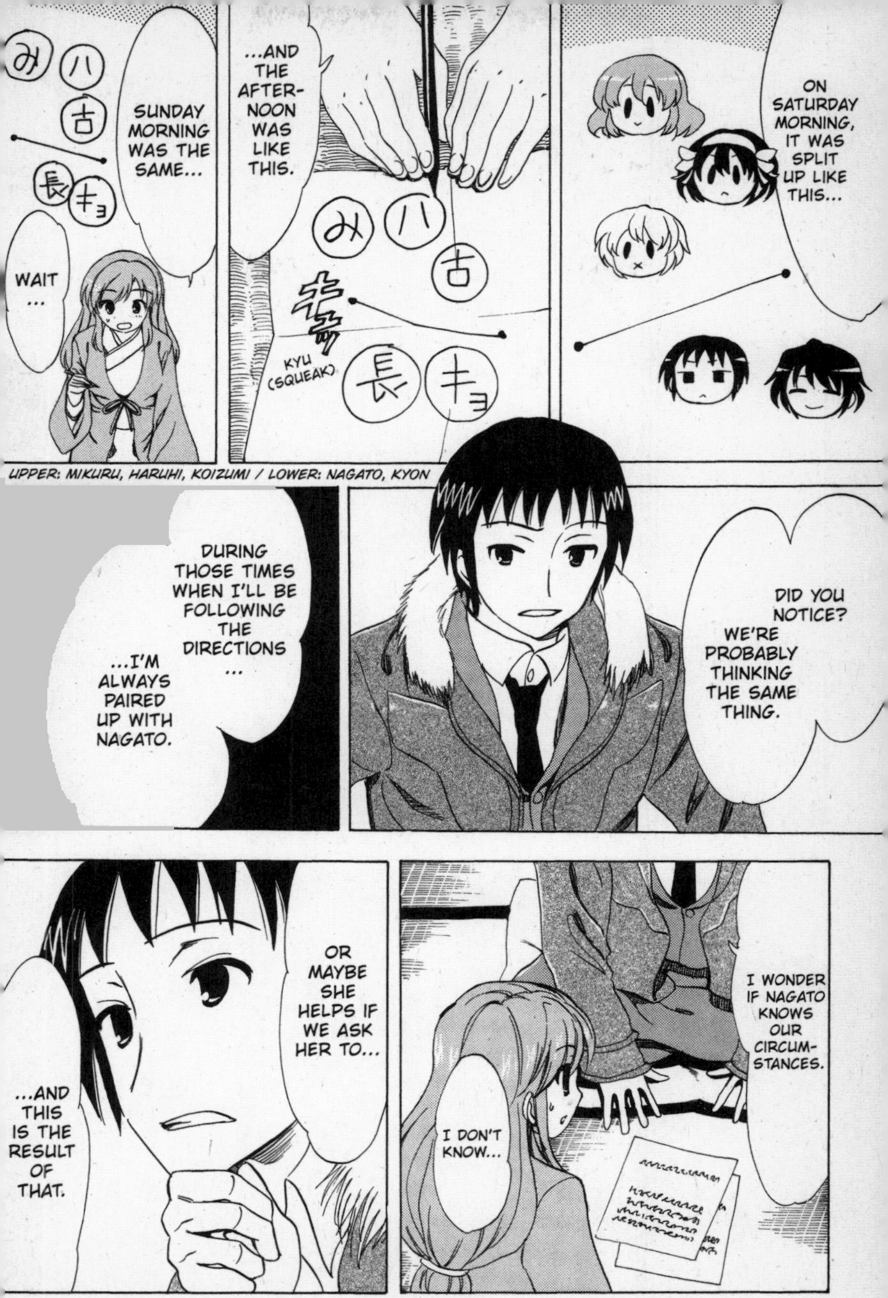

ON SATURDAY MORNING, IT WAS SPLIT UP LIKE THIS...
...AND THE AFTERNOON WAS LIKE THIS.
み ハ 古
長 キョ
キュ
KYU (SQUEAK)
SUNDAY MORNING WAS THE SAME...
み ハ 古
長 キョ
WAIT ...
UPPER: MIKURU, HARUHI, KOIZUMI / LOWER: NAGATO, KYON
DID YOU NOTICE? WE'RE PROBABLY THINKING THE SAME THING.
DURING THOSE TIMES WHEN I'LL BE FOLLOWING THE DIRECTIONS ...
...I'M ALWAYS PAIRED UP WITH NAGATO.
I WONDER IF NAGATO KNOWS OUR CIRCUMSTANCES.
I DON'T KNOW...
OR MAYBE SHE HELPS IF WE ASK HER TO...
...AND THIS IS THE RESULT OF THAT.

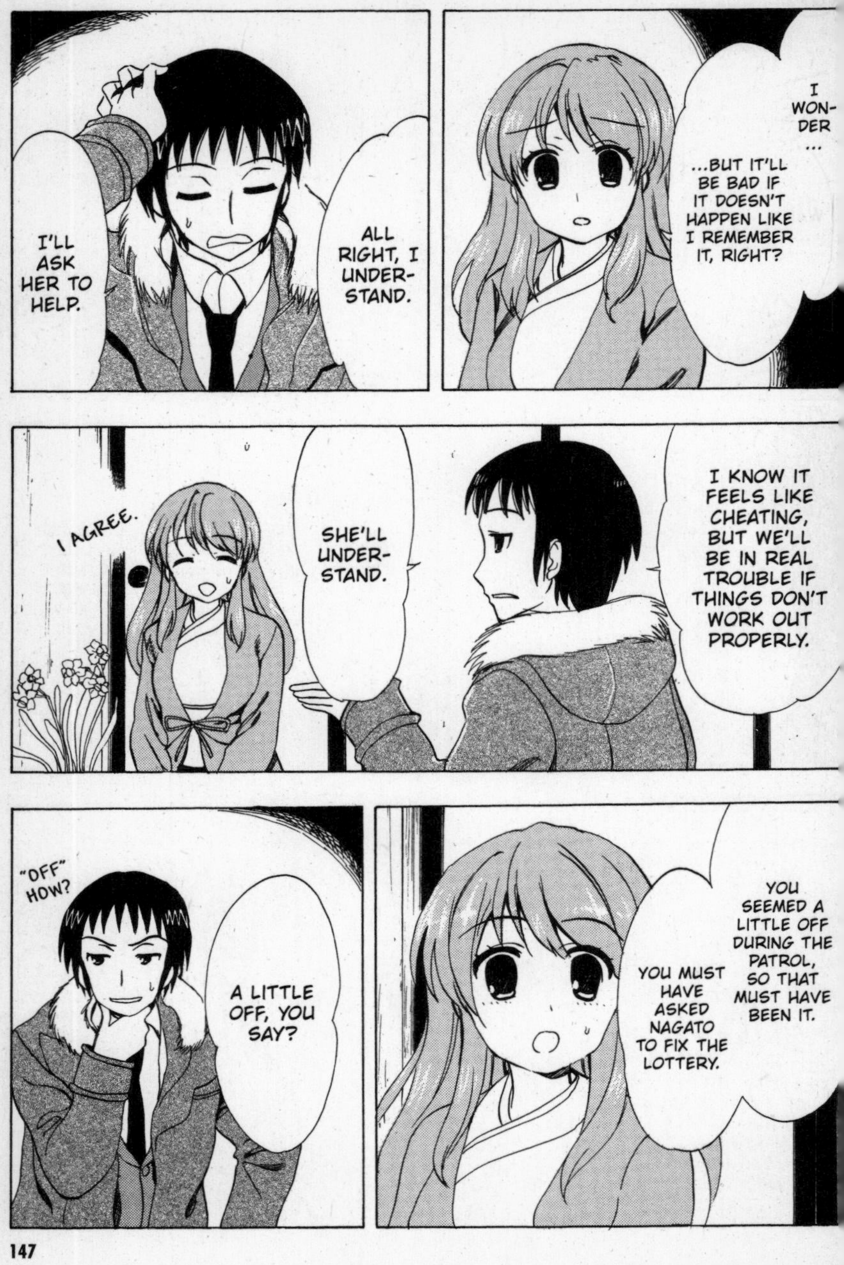
I WONDER...
...BUT IT'LL BE BAD IF IT DOESN'T HAPPEN LIKE I REMEMBER IT, RIGHT?
ALL RIGHT, I UNDERSTAND.
I'LL ASK HER TO HELP.
I KNOW IT FEELS LIKE CHEATING, BUT WE'LL BE IN REAL TROUBLE IF THINGS DON'T WORK OUT PROPERLY.
SHE'LL UNDERSTAND.
I AGREE.
YOU SEEMED A LITTLE OFF DURING THE PATROL, SO THAT MUST HAVE BEEN IT.
YOU MUST HAVE ASKED NAGATO TO FIX THE LOTTERY.
A LITTLE OFF, YOU SAY?
"OFF" HOW?

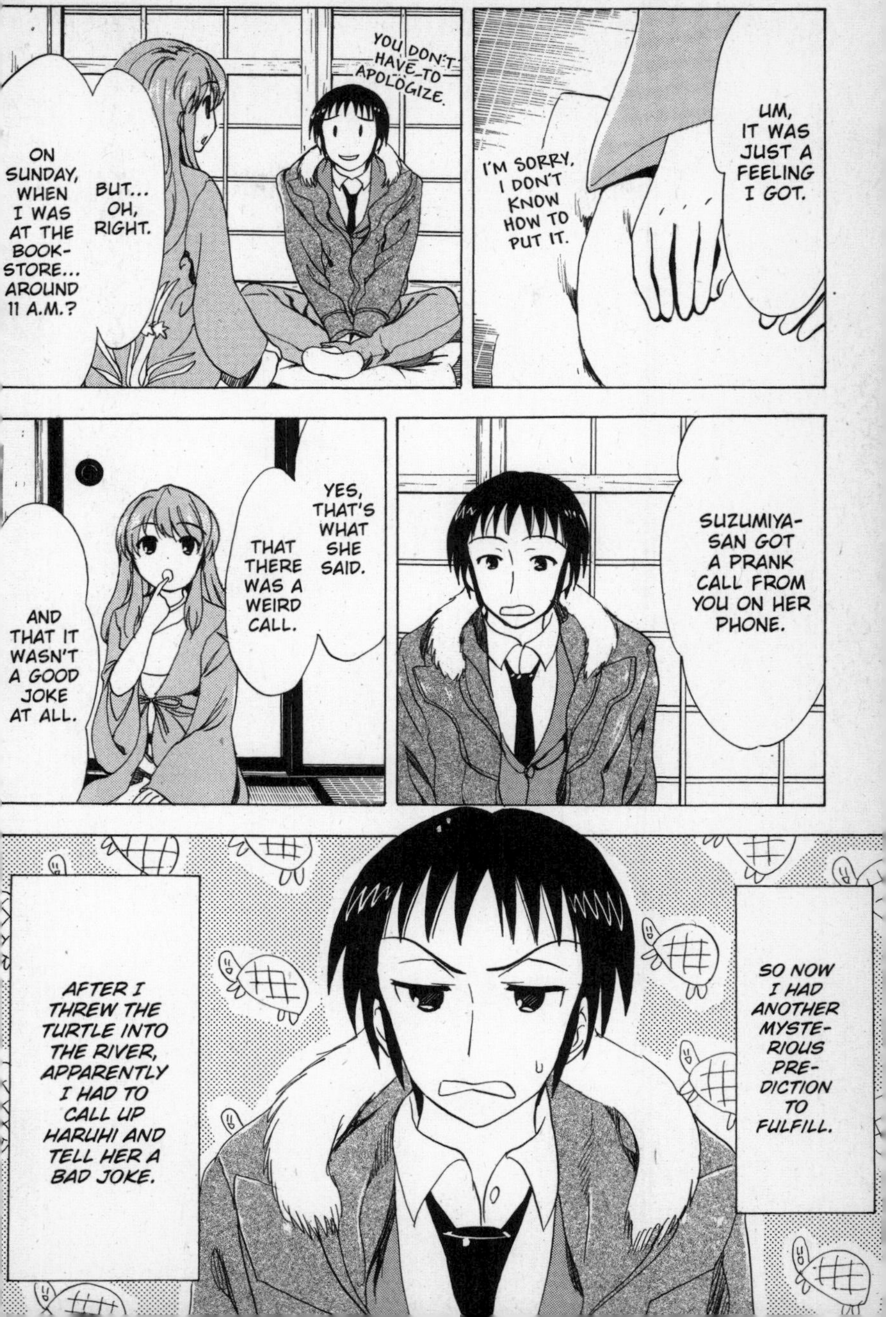
UM, IT WAS JUST A FEELING I GOT.
I'M SORRY, I DON'T KNOW HOW TO PUT IT.
YOU DON'T HAVE TO APOLOGIZE.
BUT... OH, RIGHT.
ON SUNDAY, WHEN I WAS AT THE BOOKSTORE... AROUND 11 A.M.?
SUZUMIYA-SAN GOT A PRANK CALL FROM YOU ON HER PHONE.
YES, THAT'S WHAT SHE SAID.
THAT THERE WAS A WEIRD CALL.
AND THAT IT WASN'T A GOOD JOKE AT ALL.
SO NOW I HAD ANOTHER MYSTERIOUS PREDICTION TO FULFILL.
AFTER I THREW THE TURTLE INTO THE RIVER, APPARENTLY I HAD TO CALL UP HARUHI AND TELL HER A BAD JOKE.

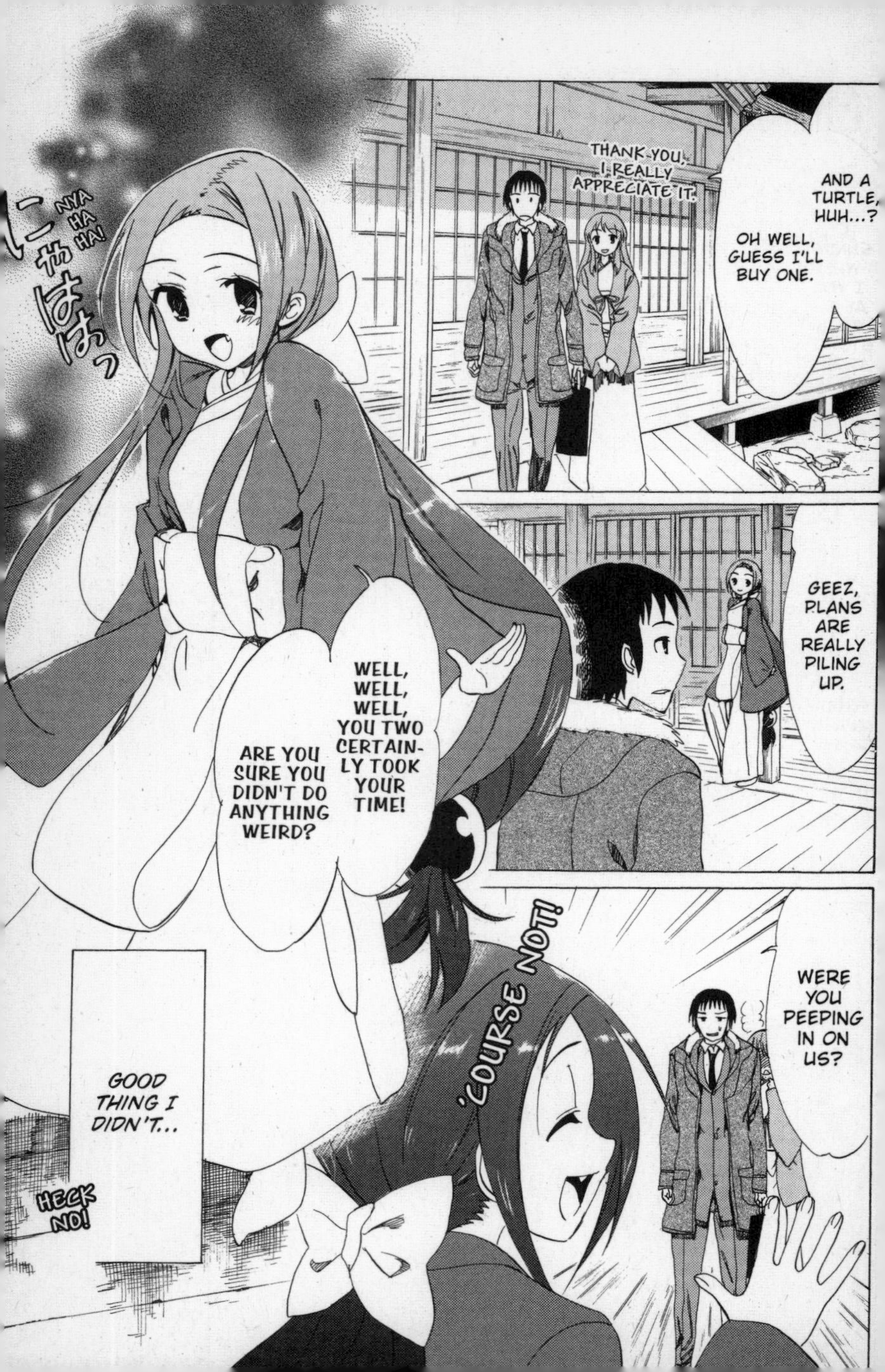
AND A TURTLE, HUH...? OH WELL, GUESS I'LL BUY ONE.
THANK YOU, I REALLY APPRECIATE IT.
GEEZ, PLANS ARE REALLY PILING UP.
WERE YOU PEEPING IN ON US?
'COURSE NOT!
にゃははっ
NYA HA HA!
WELL, WELL, WELL, YOU TWO CERTAIN-LY TOOK YOUR TIME!
ARE YOU SURE YOU DIDN'T DO ANYTHING WEIRD?
GOOD THING I DIDN'T...
HECK NO!

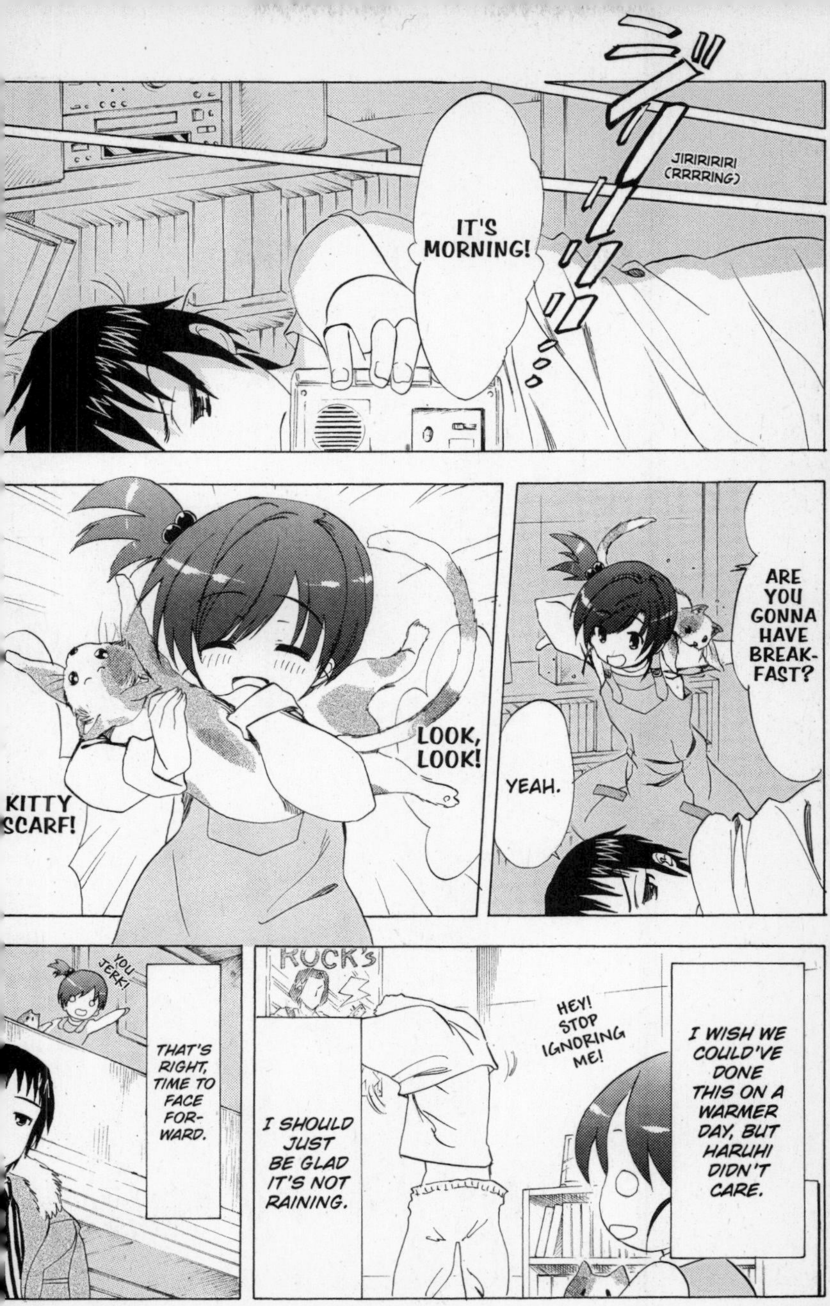
JIRIRIRIRI (RRRRING)
IT'S MORNING!
ARE YOU GONNA HAVE BREAK-FAST?
YEAH.
LOOK, LOOK!
KITTY SCARF!
I WISH WE COULD'VE DONE THIS ON A WARMER DAY, BUT HARUHI DIDN'T CARE.
HEY! STOP IGNORING ME!
ROCK's
I SHOULD JUST BE GLAD IT'S NOT RAINING.
THAT'S RIGHT, TIME TO FACE FOR-WARD.
YOU JERK!

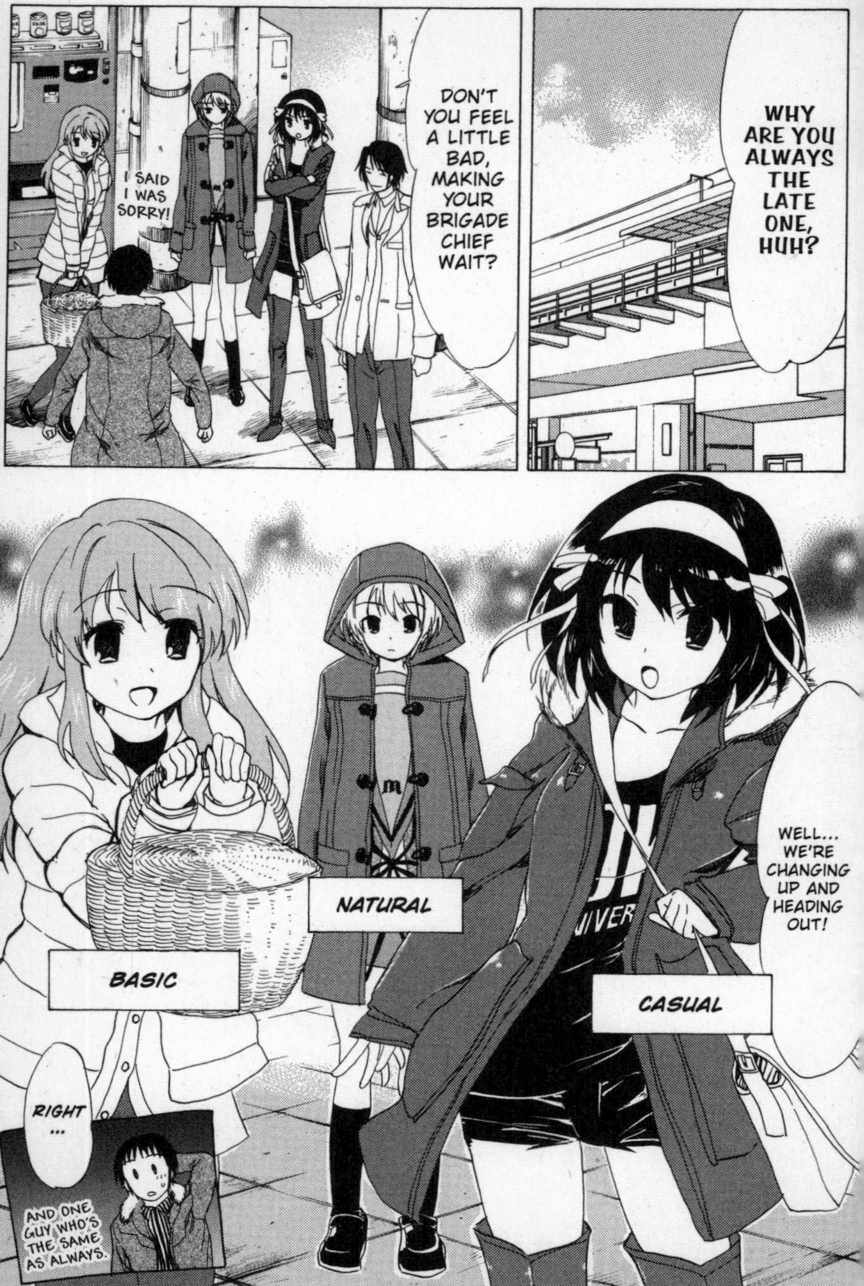
WHY ARE YOU ALWAYS THE LATE ONE, HUH?
DON'T YOU FEEL A LITTLE BAD, MAKING YOUR BRIGADE CHIEF WAIT?
I SAID I WAS SORRY!
WELL... WE'RE CHANGING UP AND HEADING OUT!
CASUAL
NATURAL
BASIC
RIGHT...
AND ONE GUY WHO'S THE SAME AS ALWAYS.

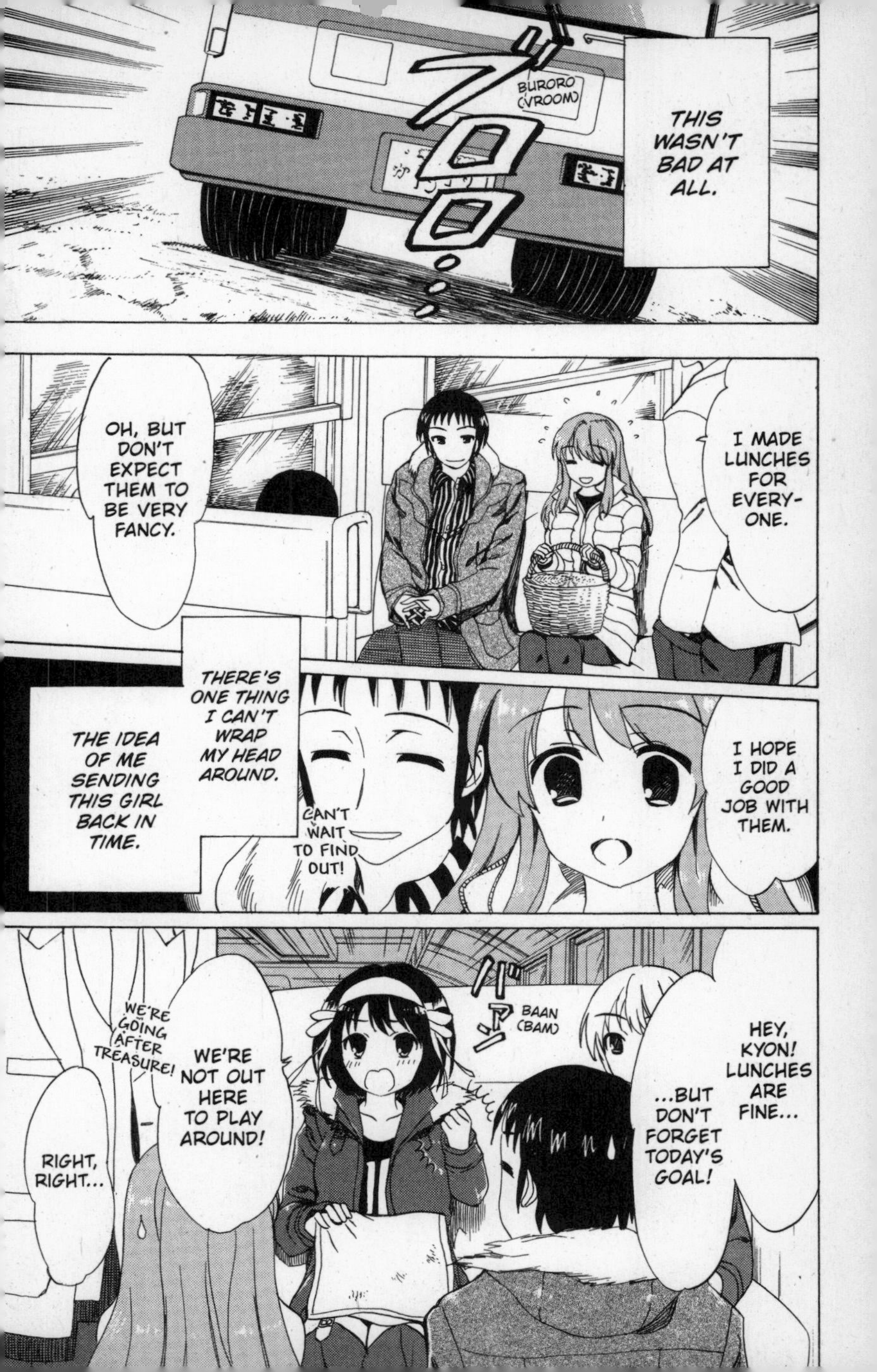
THIS WASN'T BAD AT ALL.
BURORO (VROOM)
I MADE LUNCHES FOR EVERY-ONE.
OH, BUT DON'T EXPECT THEM TO BE VERY FANCY.
I HOPE I DID A GOOD JOB WITH THEM.
CAN'T WAIT TO FIND OUT!
THERE'S ONE THING I CAN'T WRAP MY HEAD AROUND.
THE IDEA OF ME SENDING THIS GIRL BACK IN TIME.
HEY, KYON! LUNCHES ARE FINE...
...BUT DON'T FORGET TODAY'S GOAL!
BAAN (BAM)
WE'RE NOT OUT HERE TO PLAY AROUND!
WE'RE GOING AFTER TREASURE!
RIGHT, RIGHT...

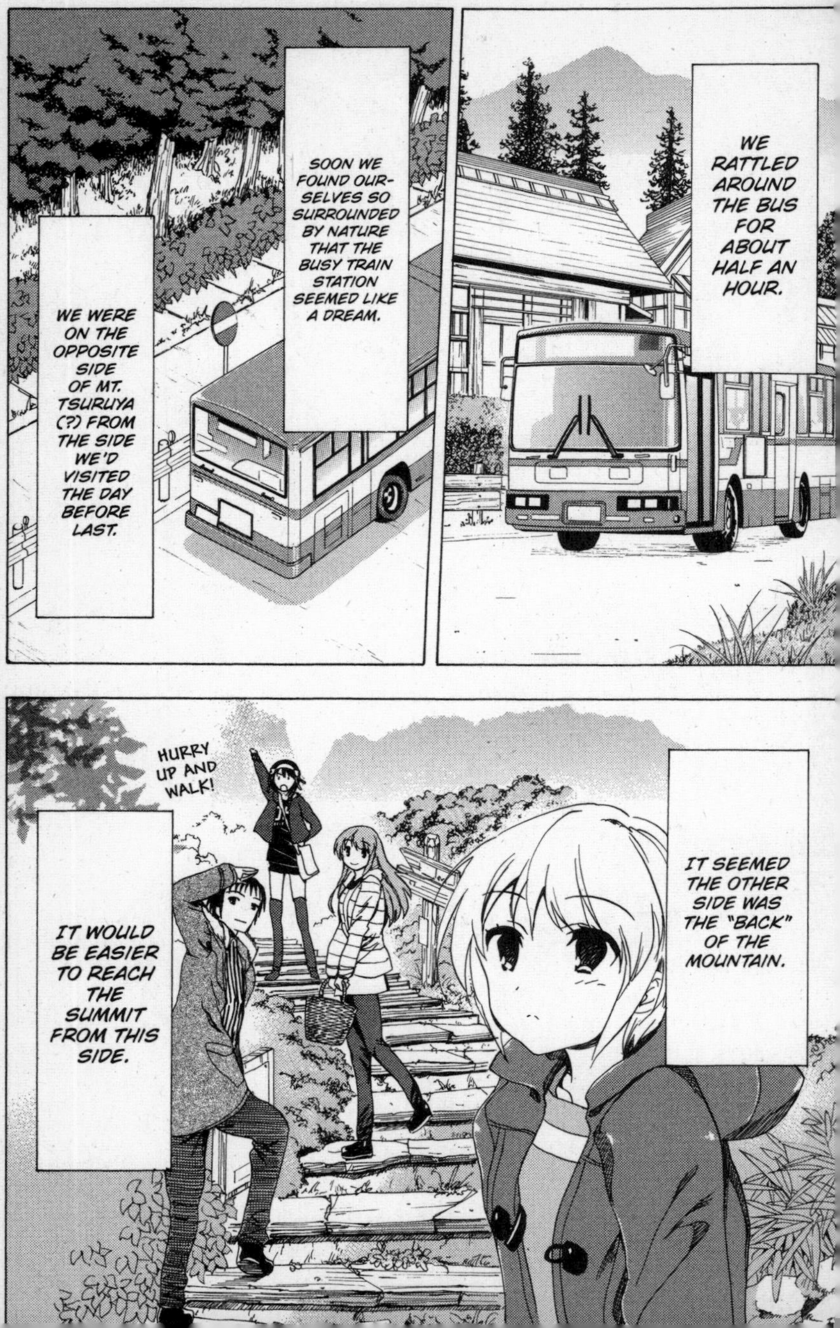
WE RATTLED AROUND THE BUS FOR ABOUT HALF AN HOUR.
SOON WE FOUND OUR-SELVES SO SURROUNDED BY NATURE THAT THE BUSY TRAIN STATION SEEMED LIKE A DREAM.
WE WERE ON THE OPPOSITE SIDE OF MT. TSURUYA (?) FROM THE SIDE WE'D VISITED THE DAY BEFORE LAST.
IT SEEMED THE OTHER SIDE WAS THE "BACK" OF THE MOUNTAIN.
HURRY UP AND WALK!
IT WOULD BE EASIER TO REACH THE SUMMIT FROM THIS SIDE.

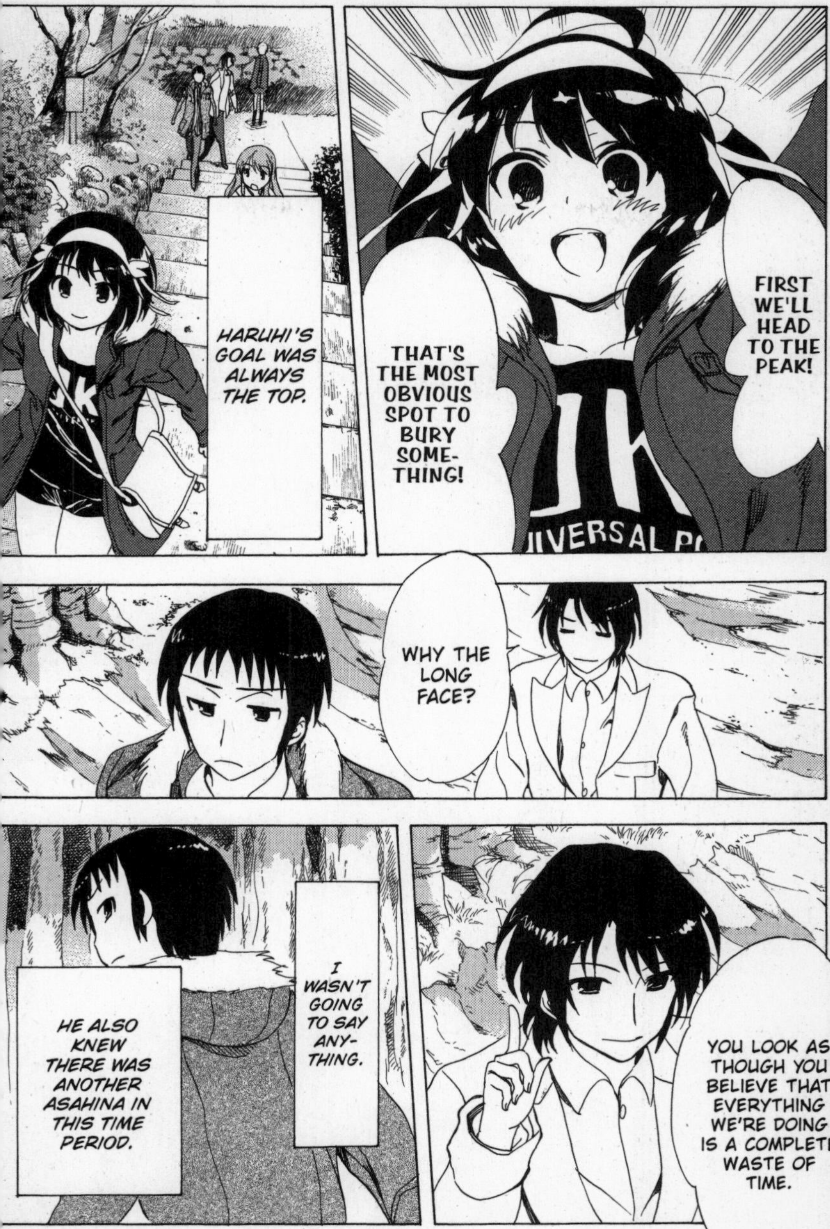
FIRST WE'LL HEAD TO THE PEAK!
THAT'S THE MOST OBVIOUS SPOT TO BURY SOME-THING!
HARUHI'S GOAL WAS ALWAYS THE TOP.
WHY THE LONG FACE?
YOU LOOK AS THOUGH YOU BELIEVE THAT EVERYTHING WE'RE DOING IS A COMPLETE WASTE OF TIME.
I WASN'T GOING TO SAY ANY-THING.
HE ALSO KNEW THERE WAS ANOTHER ASAHINA IN THIS TIME PERIOD.

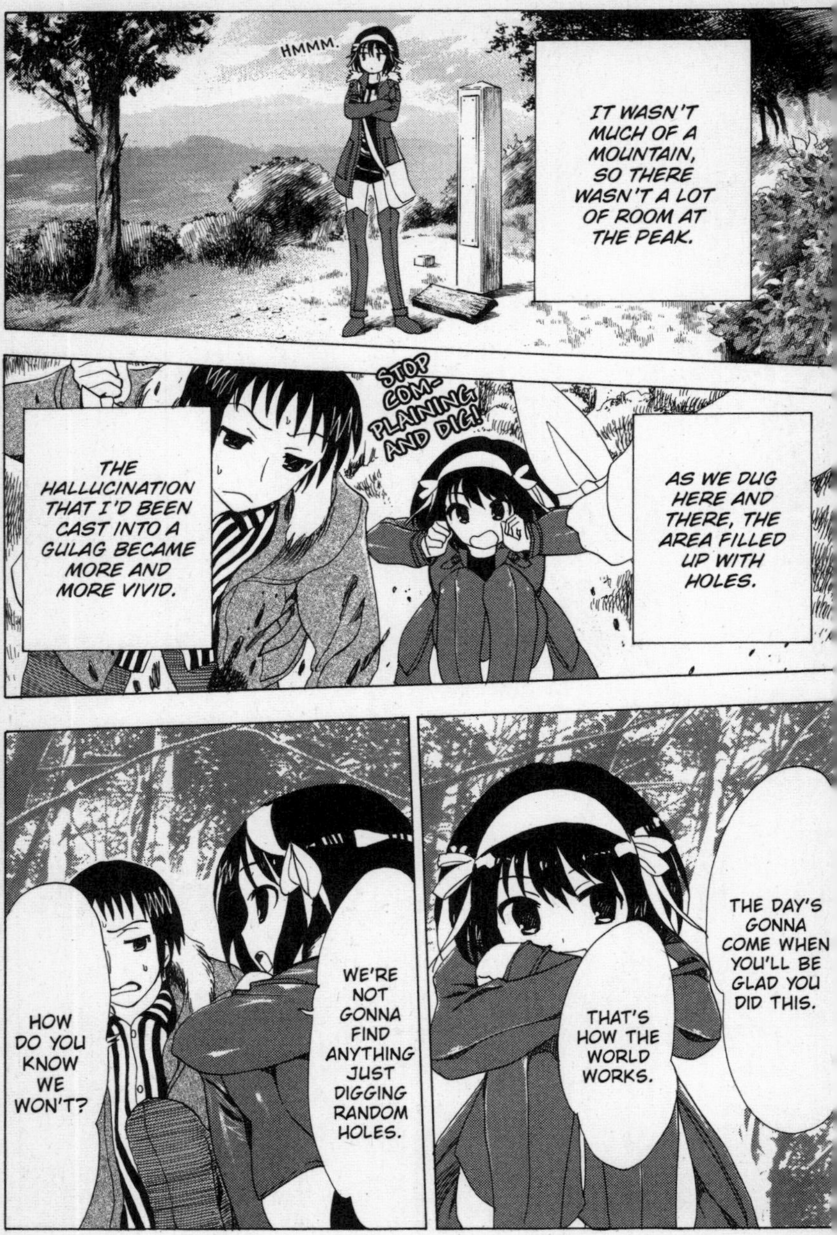
IT WASN'T MUCH OF A MOUNTAIN, SO THERE WASN'T A LOT OF ROOM AT THE PEAK.
HMMM.
AS WE DUG HERE AND THERE, THE AREA FILLED UP WITH HOLES.
STOP COM-PLAINING AND DIG!
THE HALLUCINATION THAT I'D BEEN CAST INTO A GULAG BECAME MORE AND MORE VIVID.
THE DAY'S GONNA COME WHEN YOU'LL BE GLAD YOU DID THIS.
THAT'S HOW THE WORLD WORKS.
WE'RE NOT GONNA FIND ANYTHING JUST DIGGING RANDOM HOLES.
HOW DO YOU KNOW WE WON'T?

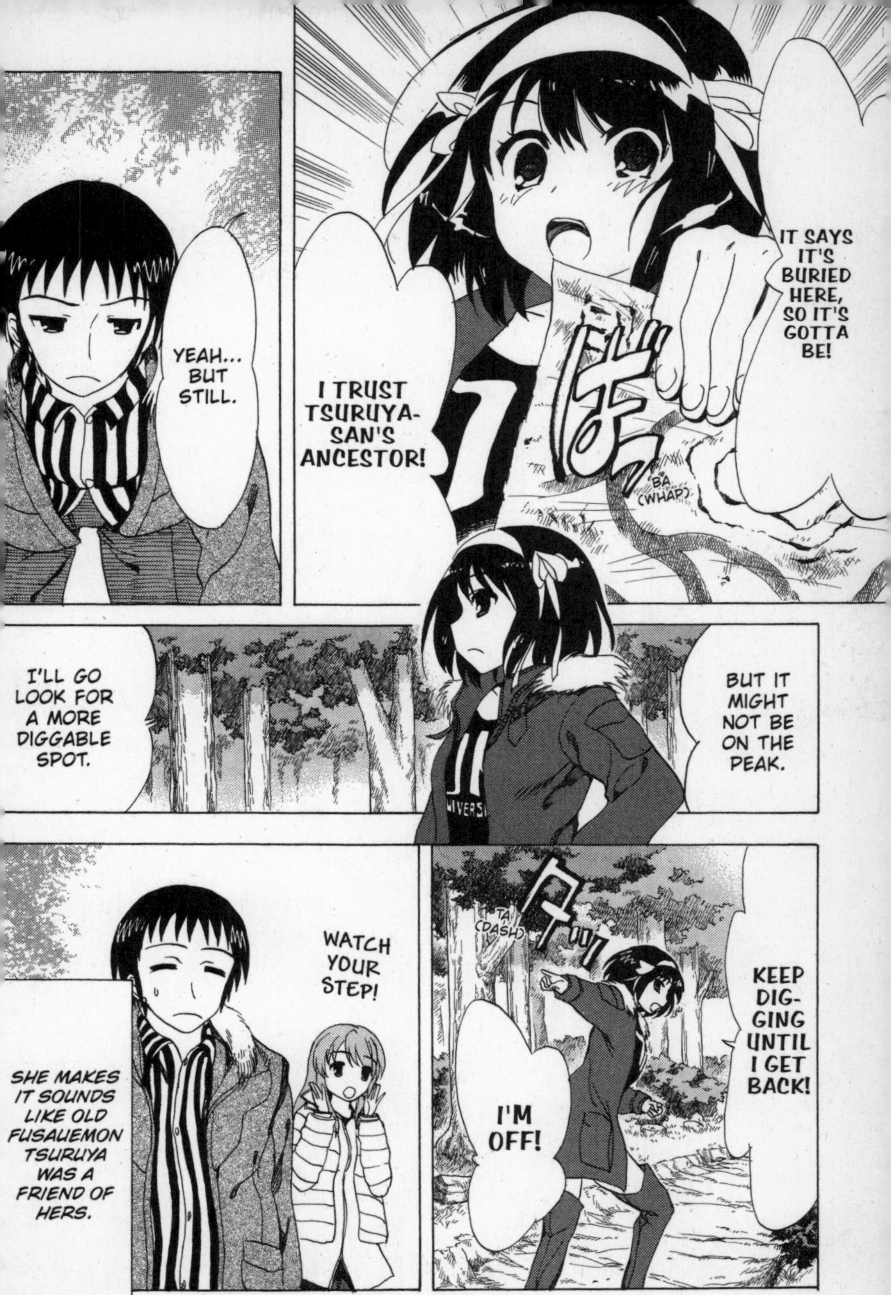
IT SAYS IT'S BURIED HERE, SO IT'S GOTTA BE!
BA (WHAP)
I TRUST TSURUYA-SAN'S ANCESTOR!
YEAH... BUT STILL.
BUT IT MIGHT NOT BE ON THE PEAK.
I'LL GO LOOK FOR A MORE DIGGABLE SPOT.
KEEP DIG-GING UNTIL I GET BACK!
TA (DASH)
I'M OFF!
WATCH YOUR STEP!
SHE MAKES IT SOUNDS LIKE OLD FUSAUEMON TSURUYA WAS A FRIEND OF HERS.

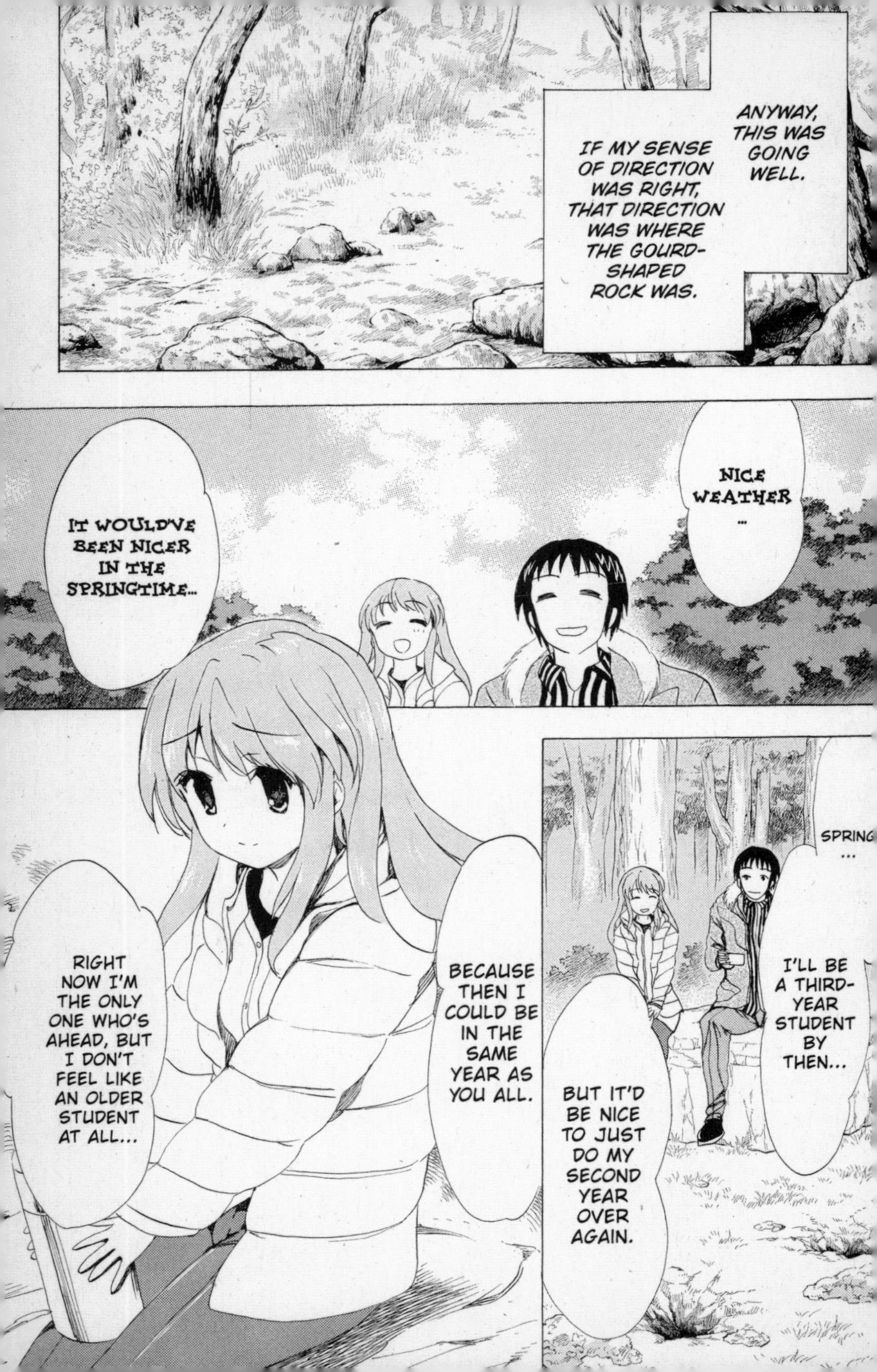
ANYWAY, THIS WAS GOING WELL.
IF MY SENSE OF DIRECTION WAS RIGHT, THAT DIRECTION WAS WHERE THE GOURD-SHAPED ROCK WAS.
NICE WEATHER...
IT WOULD'VE BEEN NICER IN THE SPRINGTIME...
SPRING...
I'LL BE A THIRD-YEAR STUDENT BY THEN...
BUT IT'D BE NICE TO JUST DO MY SECOND YEAR OVER AGAIN.
BECAUSE THEN I COULD BE IN THE SAME YEAR AS YOU ALL.
RIGHT NOW I'M THE ONLY ONE WHO'S AHEAD, BUT I DON'T FEEL LIKE AN OLDER STUDENT AT ALL...

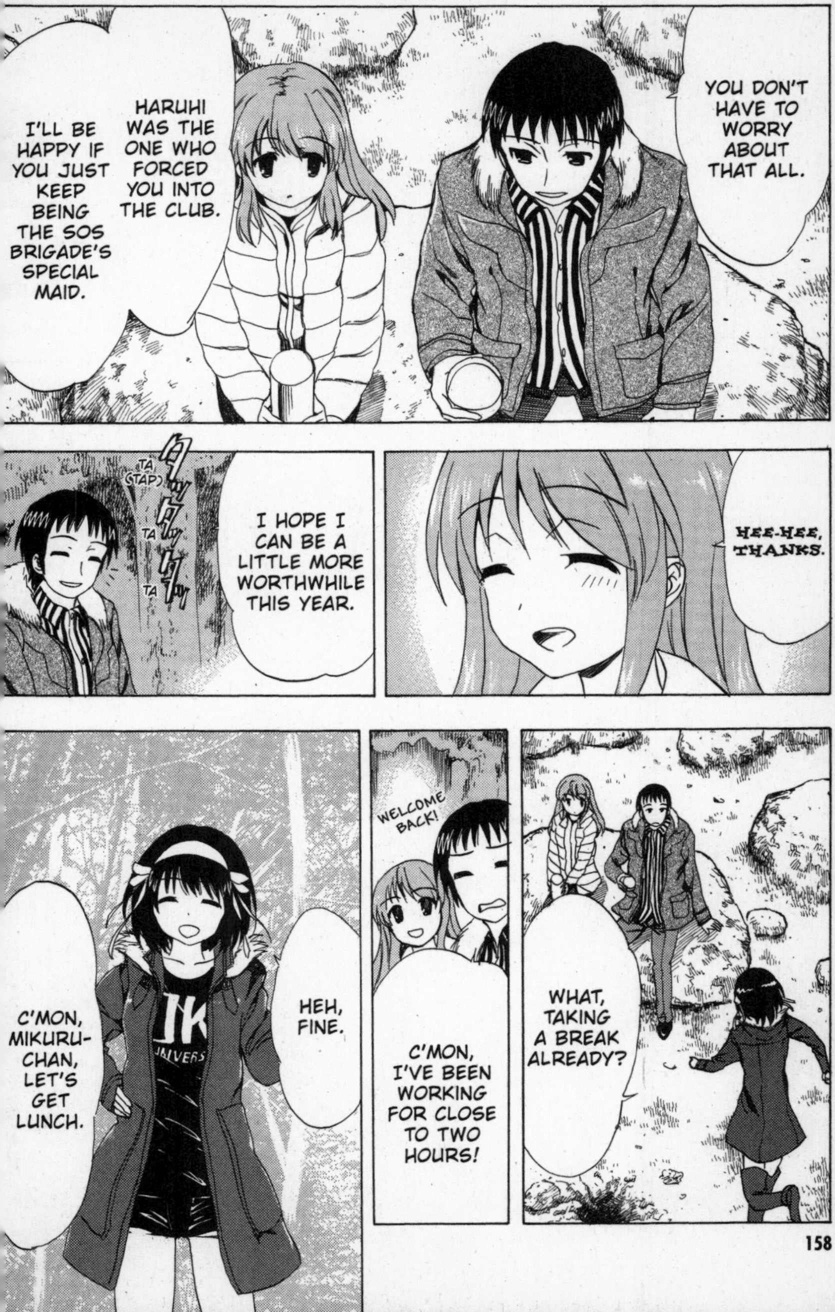
YOU DON'T HAVE TO WORRY ABOUT THAT ALL.
HARUHI WAS THE ONE WHO FORCED YOU INTO THE CLUB.
I'LL BE HAPPY IF YOU JUST KEEP BEING THE SOS BRIGADE'S SPECIAL MAID.
HEE-HEE, THANKS.
TA (TAP) TA TA
I HOPE I CAN BE A LITTLE MORE WORTHWHILE THIS YEAR.
WHAT, TAKING A BREAK ALREADY?
WELCOME BACK!
C'MON, I'VE BEEN WORKING FOR CLOSE TO TWO HOURS!
HEH, FINE.
C'MON, MIKURU-CHAN, LET'S GET LUNCH.

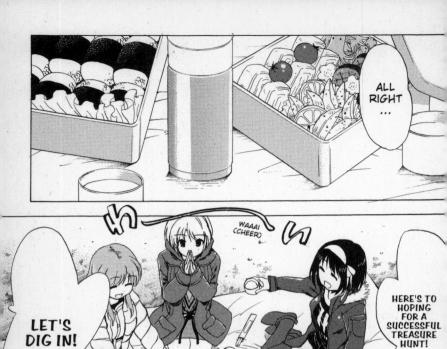

ALL RIGHT...

WAAA! (CHEER)

LET'S DIG IN!

HERE'S TO HOPING FOR A SUCCESSFUL TREASURE HUNT!

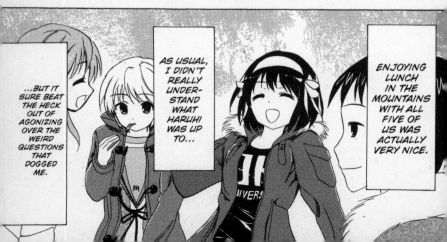

...BUT IT SURE BEAT THE HECK OUT OF AGONIZING OVER THE WEIRD QUESTIONS THAT DOGGED ME.

AS USUAL, I DIDN'T REALLY UNDERSTAND WHAT HARUHI WAS UP TO...

ENJOYING LUNCH IN THE MOUNTAINS WITH ALL FIVE OF US WAS ACTUALLY VERY NICE.

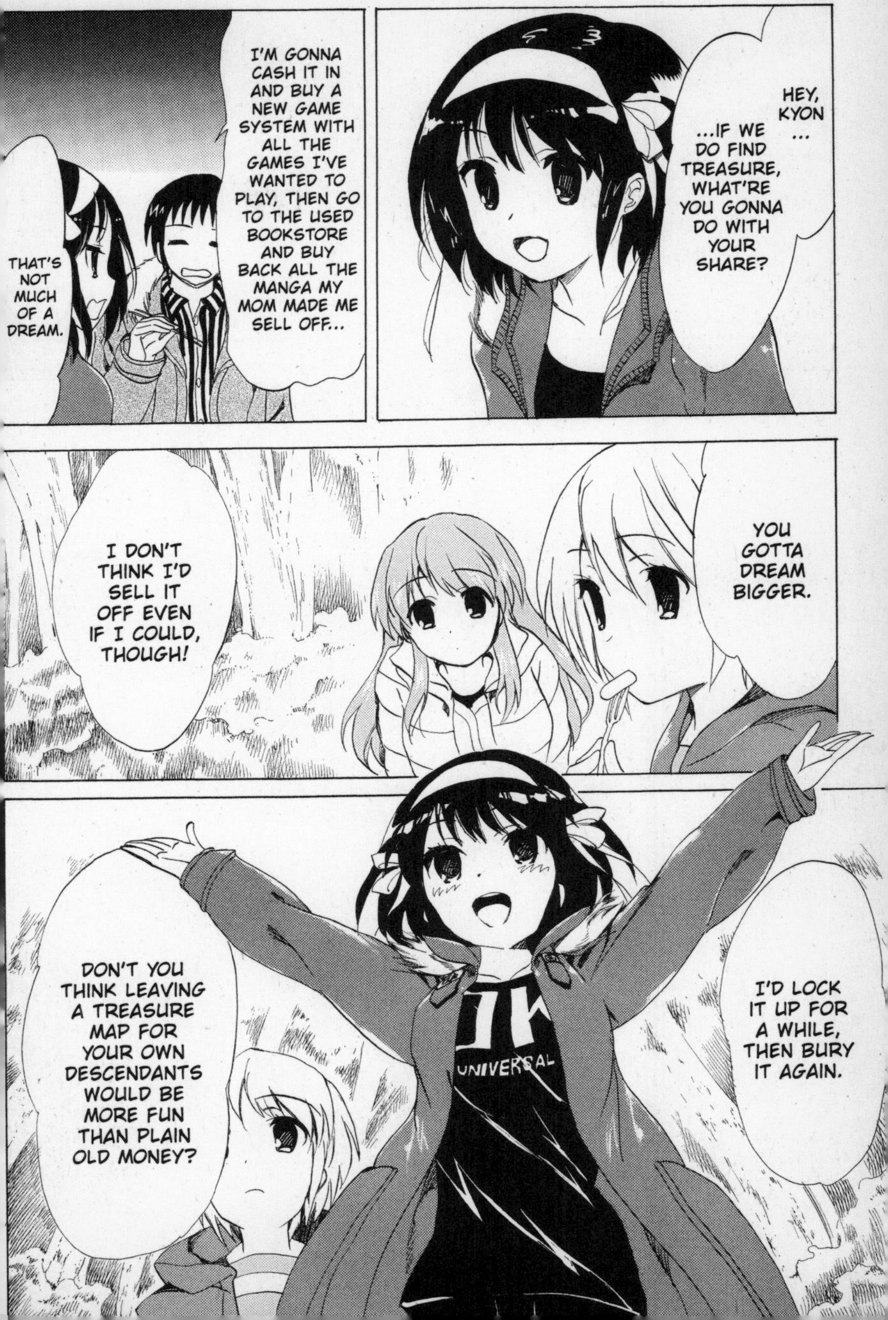
HEY, KYON ...
...IF WE DO FIND TREASURE, WHAT'RE YOU GONNA DO WITH YOUR SHARE?
I'M GONNA CASH IT IN AND BUY A NEW GAME SYSTEM WITH ALL THE GAMES I'VE WANTED TO PLAY, THEN GO TO THE USED BOOKSTORE AND BUY BACK ALL THE MANGA MY MOM MADE ME SELL OFF...
THAT'S NOT MUCH OF A DREAM.
YOU GOTTA DREAM BIGGER.
I DON'T THINK I'D SELL IT OFF EVEN IF I COULD, THOUGH!
I'D LOCK IT UP FOR A WHILE, THEN BURY IT AGAIN.
UNIVERSAL
DON'T YOU THINK LEAVING A TREASURE MAP FOR YOUR OWN DESCENDANTS WOULD BE MORE FUN THAN PLAIN OLD MONEY?

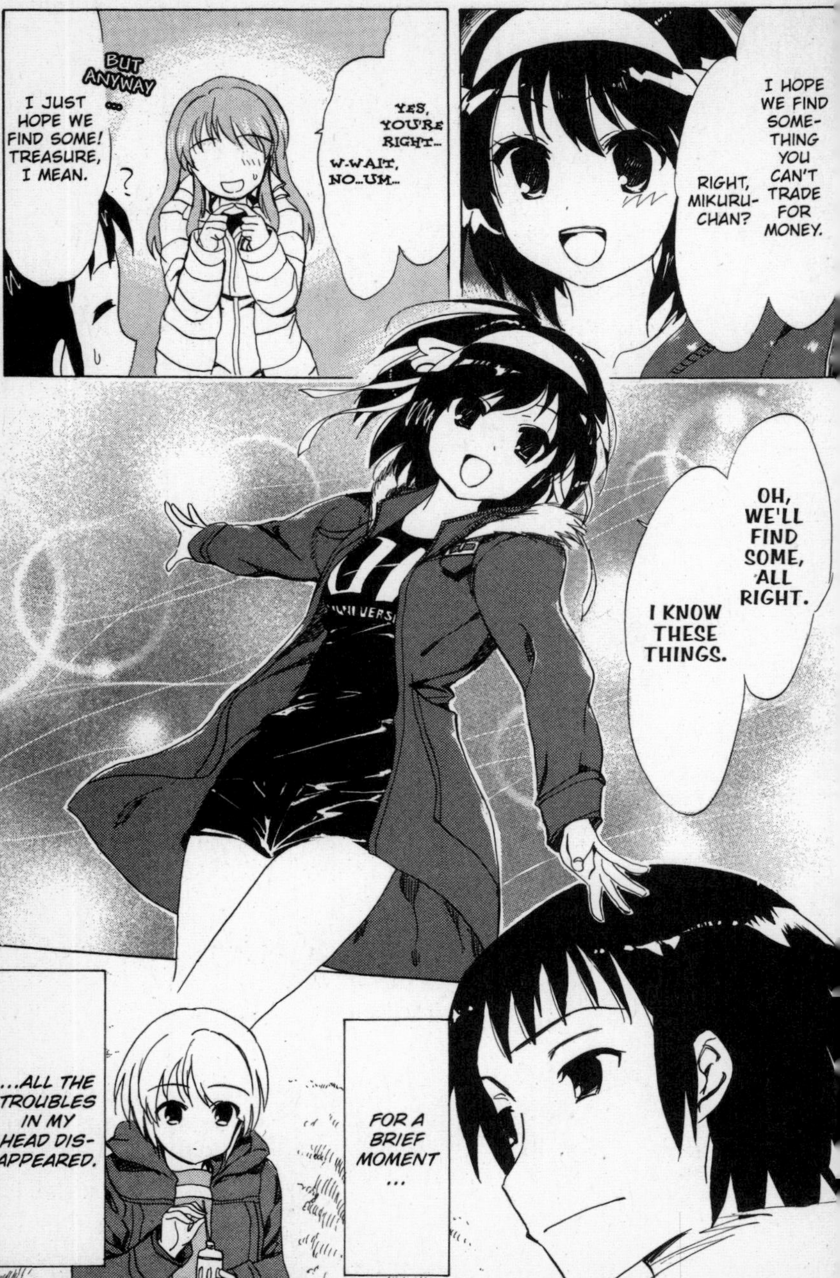
I HOPE WE FIND SOME-THING YOU CAN'T TRADE FOR MONEY.
RIGHT, MIKURU-CHAN?
YES, YOU'RE RIGHT...
W-WAIT, NO...UM...
BUT ANYWAY...
I JUST HOPE WE FIND SOME! TREASURE, I MEAN.
?
OH, WE'LL FIND SOME, ALL RIGHT.
I KNOW THESE THINGS.
FOR A BRIEF MOMENT...
...ALL THE TROUBLES IN MY HEAD DIS-APPEARED.

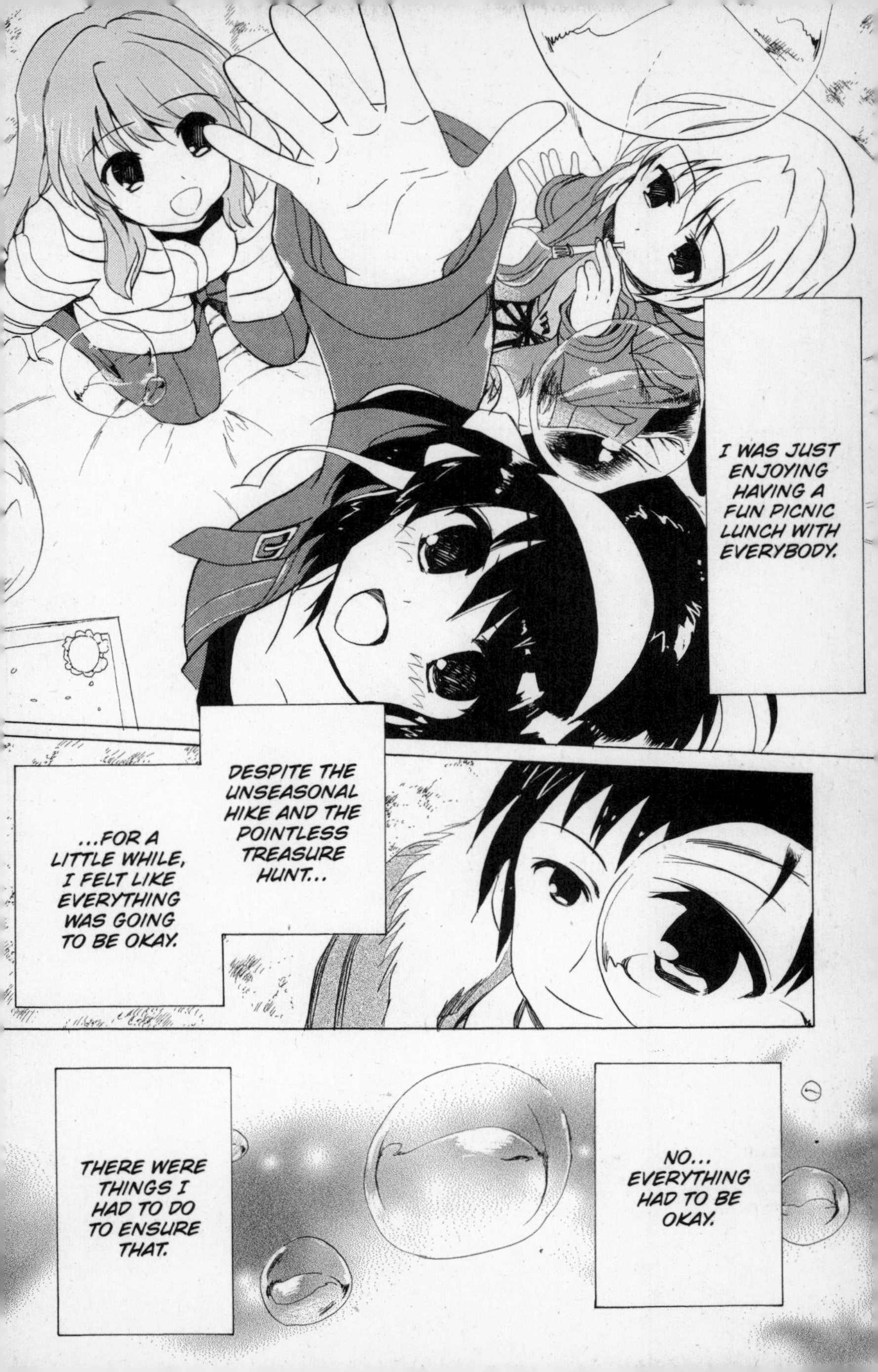
I WAS JUST ENJOYING HAVING A FUN PICNIC LUNCH WITH EVERYBODY.
DESPITE THE UNSEASONAL HIKE AND THE POINTLESS TREASURE HUNT...
...FOR A LITTLE WHILE, I FELT LIKE EVERYTHING WAS GOING TO BE OKAY.
NO... EVERYTHING HAD TO BE OKAY.
THERE WERE THINGS I HAD TO DO TO ENSURE THAT.

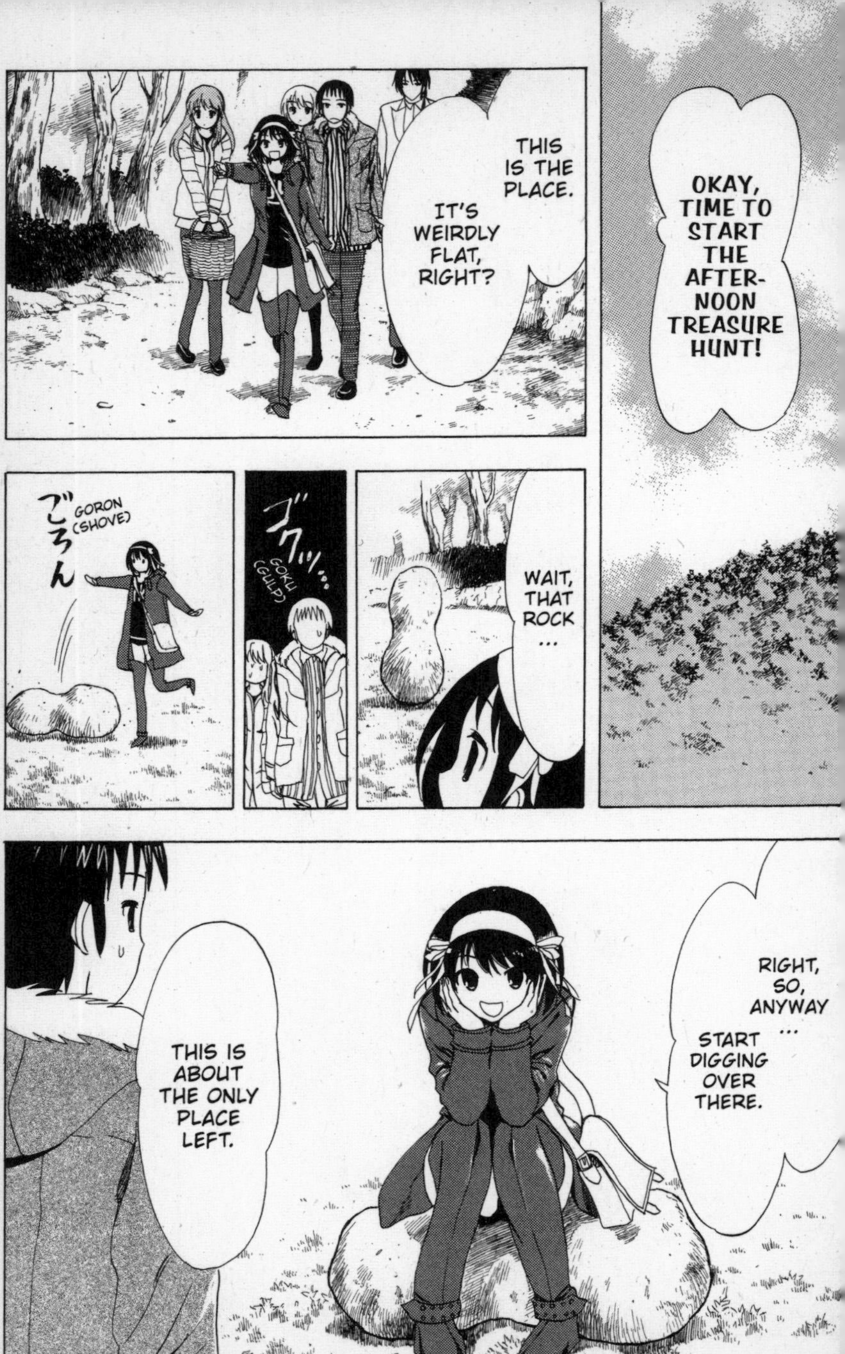
OKAY, TIME TO START THE AFTERNOON TREASURE HUNT!
THIS IS THE PLACE.
IT'S WEIRDLY FLAT, RIGHT?
WAIT, THAT ROCK ...
ゴクッ…
GOKU (GULP)
ごろん
GORON (SHOVE)
RIGHT, SO, ANYWAY ...
START DIGGING OVER THERE.
THIS IS ABOUT THE ONLY PLACE LEFT.

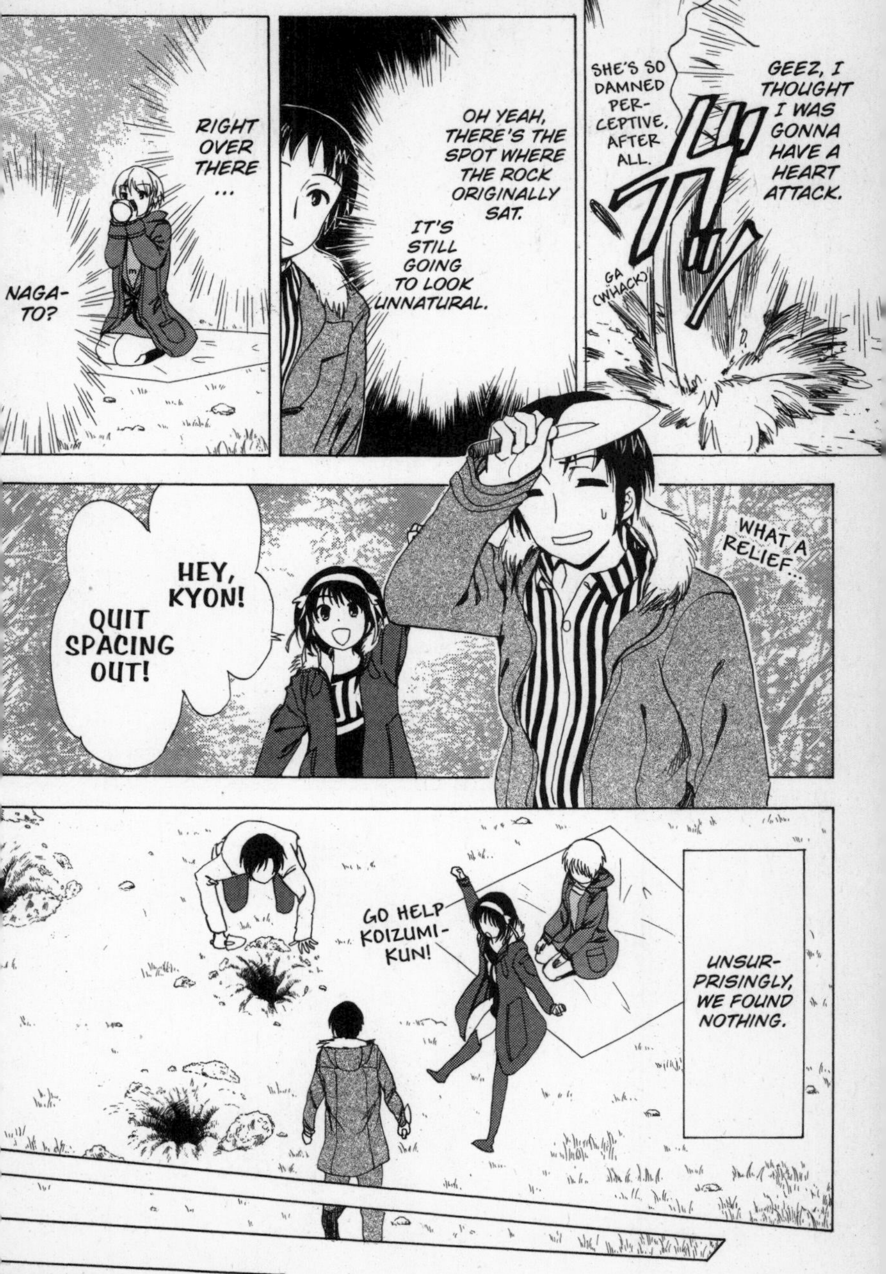
GEEZ, I THOUGHT I WAS GONNA HAVE A HEART ATTACK.
SHE'S SO DAMNED PER-CEPTIVE, AFTER ALL.
GA (WHACK)
OH YEAH, THERE'S THE SPOT WHERE THE ROCK ORIGINALLY SAT.
IT'S STILL GOING TO LOOK UNNATURAL.
RIGHT OVER THERE ...
NAGA-TO?
WHAT A RELIEF...
HEY, KYON!
QUIT SPACING OUT!
UNSUR-PRISINGLY, WE FOUND NOTHING.
GO HELP KOIZUMI-KUN!

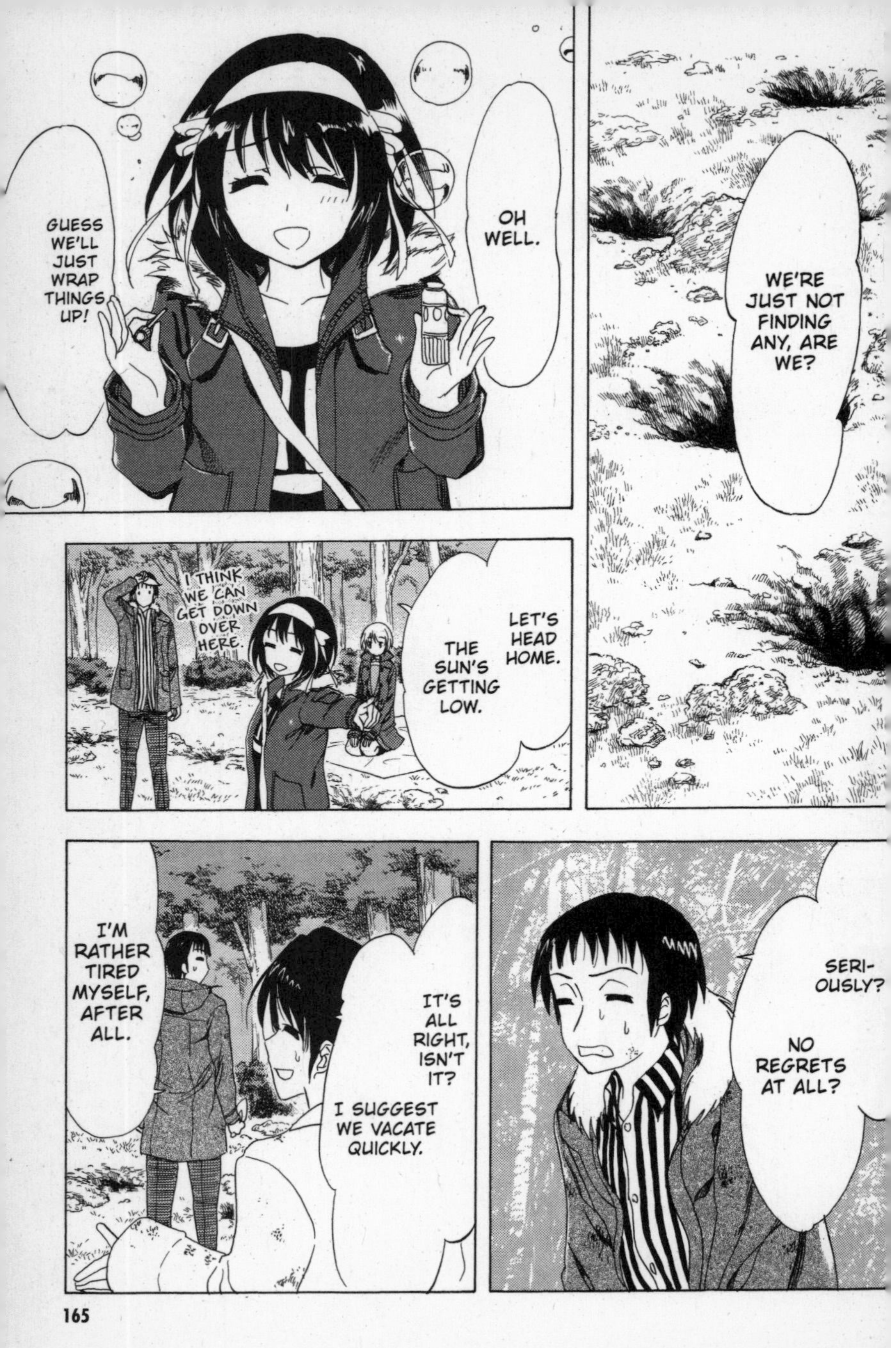
WE'RE JUST NOT FINDING ANY, ARE WE?
OH WELL.
GUESS WE'LL JUST WRAP THINGS UP!
LET'S HEAD HOME.
THE SUN'S GETTING LOW.
I THINK WE CAN GET DOWN OVER HERE.
SERI-OUSLY?
NO REGRETS AT ALL?
IT'S ALL RIGHT, ISN'T IT?
I SUGGEST WE VACATE QUICKLY.
I'M RATHER TIRED MYSELF, AFTER ALL.

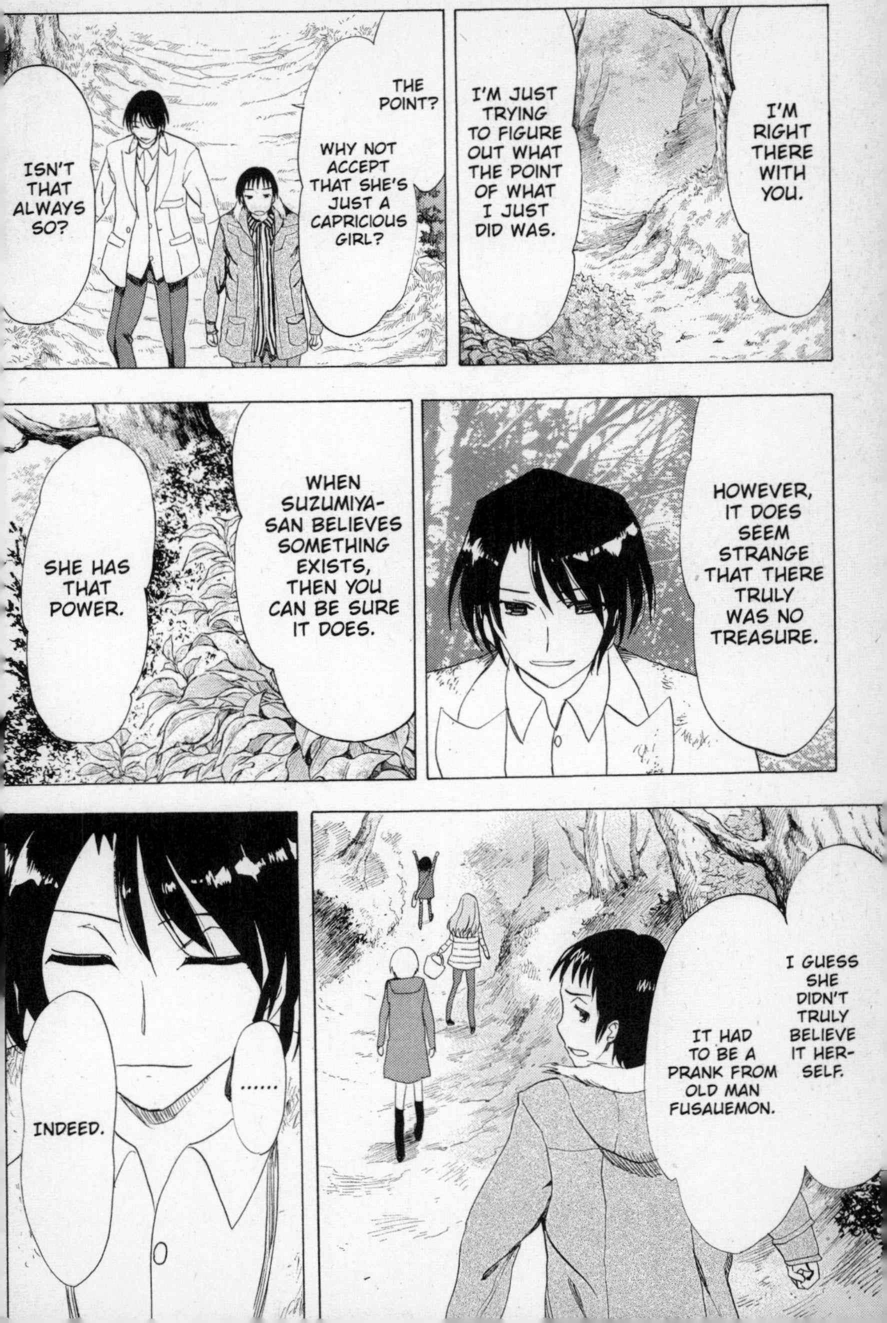
I'M RIGHT THERE WITH YOU.
I'M JUST TRYING TO FIGURE OUT WHAT THE POINT OF WHAT I JUST DID WAS.
THE POINT?
WHY NOT ACCEPT THAT SHE'S JUST A CAPRICIOUS GIRL?
ISN'T THAT ALWAYS SO?
HOWEVER, IT DOES SEEM STRANGE THAT THERE TRULY WAS NO TREASURE.
WHEN SUZUMIYA-SAN BELIEVES SOMETHING EXISTS, THEN YOU CAN BE SURE IT DOES.
SHE HAS THAT POWER.
I GUESS SHE DIDN'T TRULY BELIEVE IT HER-SELF.
IT HAD TO BE A PRANK FROM OLD MAN FUSAUEMON.
......
INDEED.

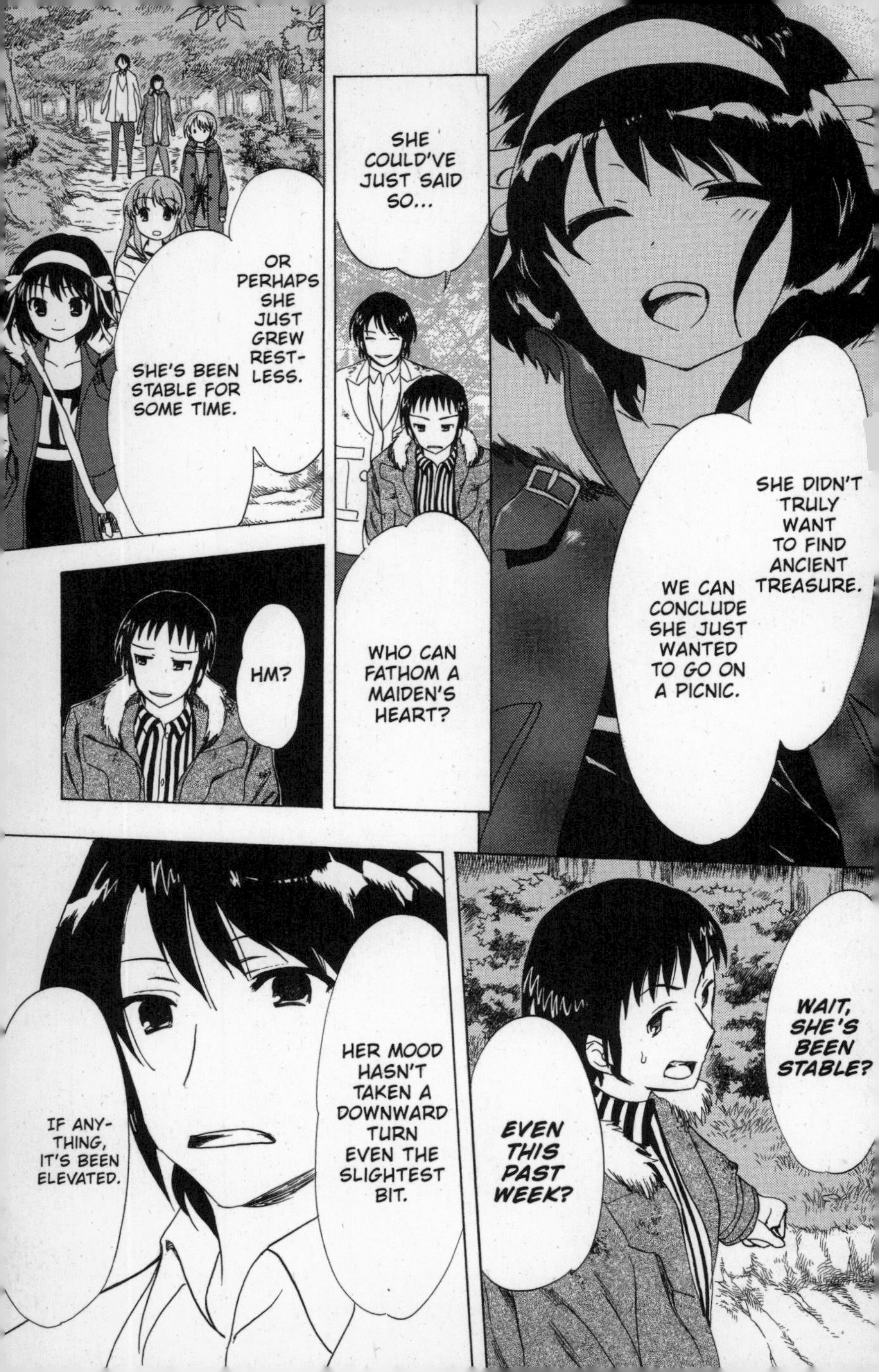
SHE DIDN'T TRULY WANT TO FIND ANCIENT TREASURE.
WE CAN CONCLUDE SHE JUST WANTED TO GO ON A PICNIC.
SHE COULD'VE JUST SAID SO...
WHO CAN FATHOM A MAIDEN'S HEART?
OR PERHAPS SHE JUST GREW REST-LESS.
SHE'S BEEN STABLE FOR SOME TIME.
HM?
WAIT, SHE'S BEEN STABLE?
EVEN THIS PAST WEEK?
HER MOOD HASN'T TAKEN A DOWNWARD TURN EVEN THE SLIGHTEST BIT.
IF ANY-THING, IT'S BEEN ELEVATED.

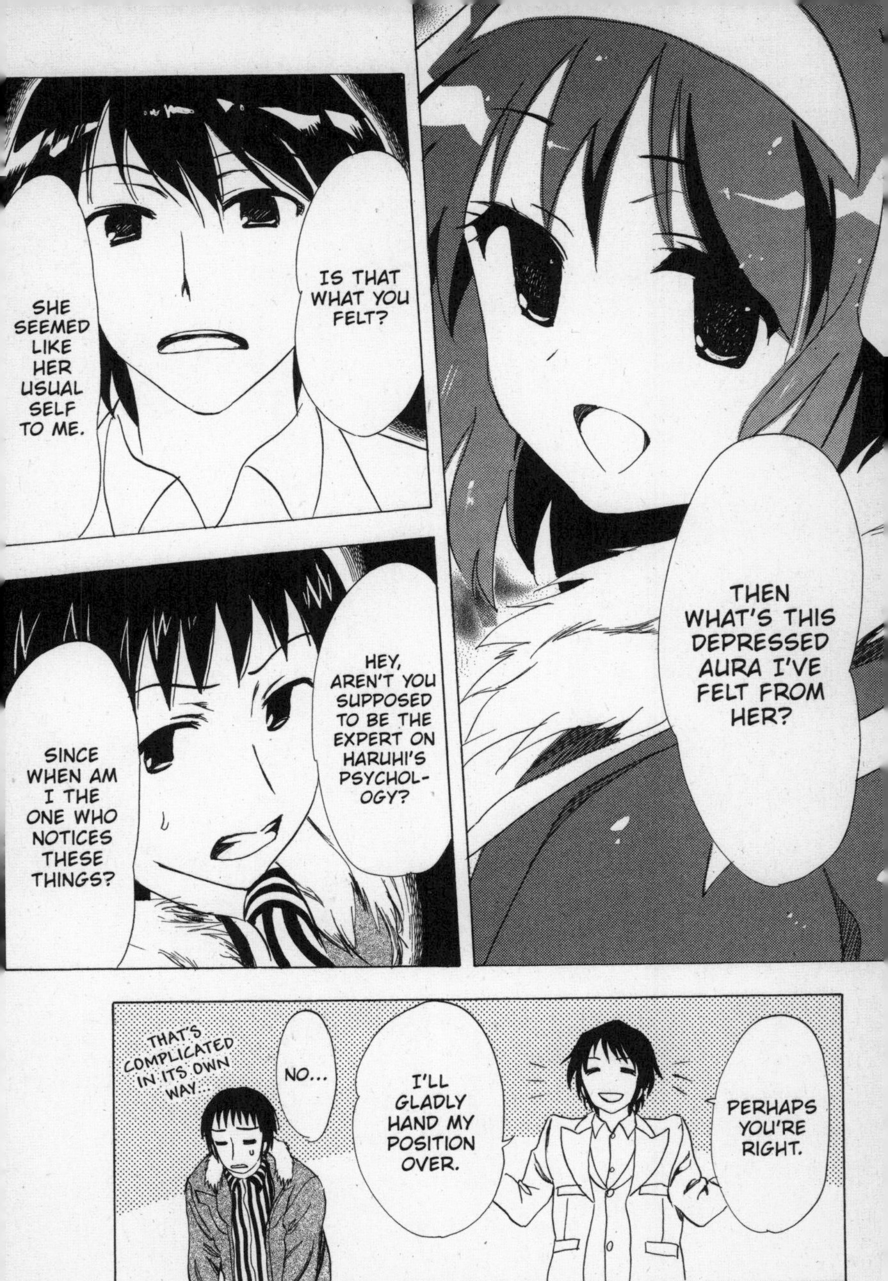
THEN WHAT'S THIS DEPRESSED AURA I'VE FELT FROM HER?
IS THAT WHAT YOU FELT?
SHE SEEMED LIKE HER USUAL SELF TO ME.
HEY, AREN'T YOU SUPPOSED TO BE THE EXPERT ON HARUHI'S PSYCHOL-OGY?
SINCE WHEN AM I THE ONE WHO NOTICES THESE THINGS?
PERHAPS YOU'RE RIGHT.
I'LL GLADLY HAND MY POSITION OVER.
NO...
THAT'S COMPLICATED IN ITS OWN WAY.

THE INTRIGUES OF HARUHI SUZUMIYA VI : END

TRANSLATION NOTES

Page 21

Beyond the Pale of Vengeance (*Onshuu No Kanata Ni*) by Kan Kikuchi is an early 20th-century Japanese novel based on the life of a 19th-century monk as he tries to make amends for the sins of his past. At one point, the protagonist digs a tunnel through a mountain by hand as penance for his misdeeds.

Page 135

Nankin tamasudare is a type of traditional Japanese street performance. The perfomer chants a poem while manipulating a loosely-woven screen made of sticks to resemble the object they are describing in each verse chant. While the poem has a number of variations based on the performer, each verse begins with *"asate, asate, sate wa nankin tamasudare"* ("Hurry, hurry, hurry, it's the Nankin Tamasudare").

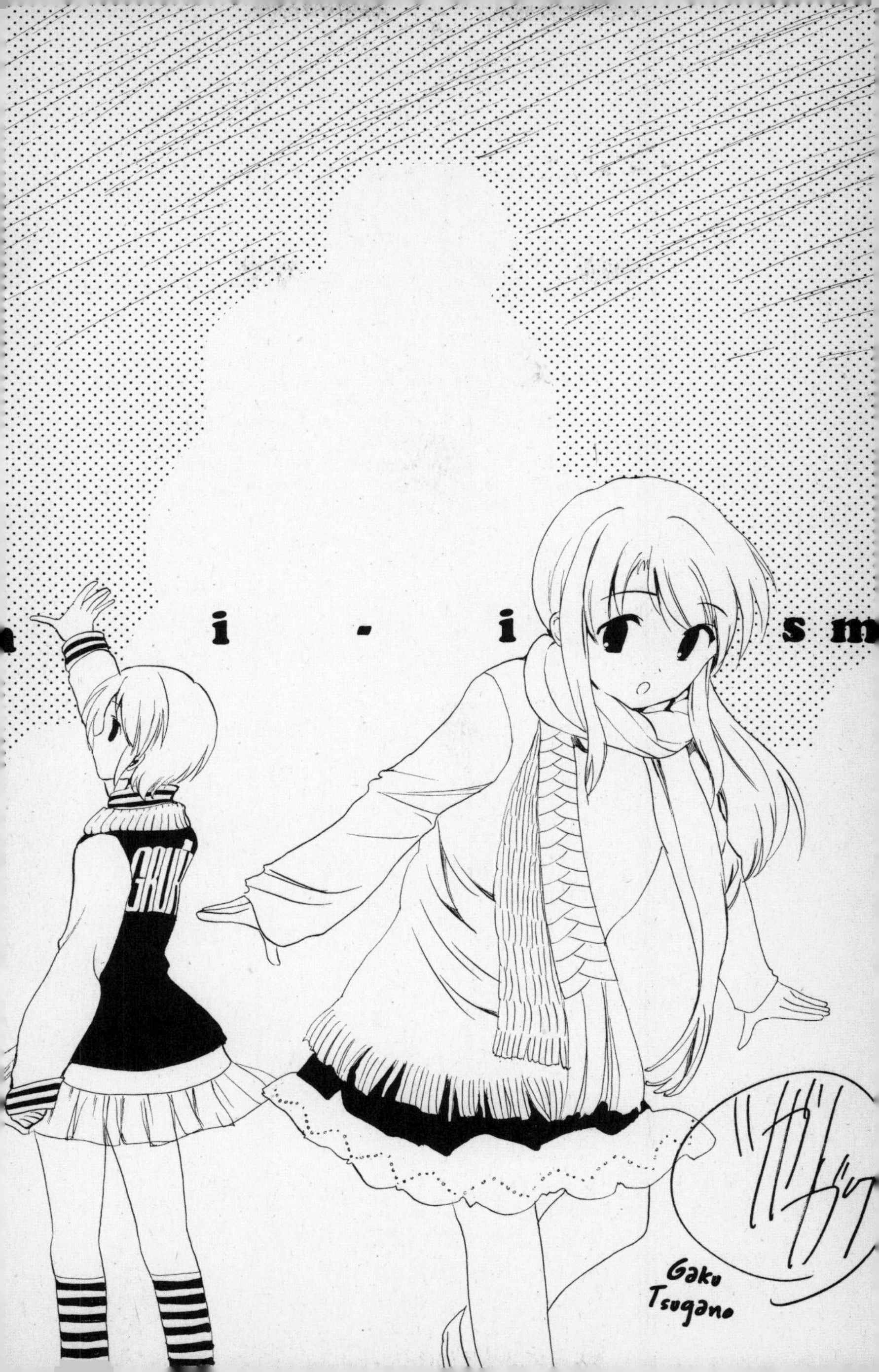
a i - i sm
Gaku Tsugano

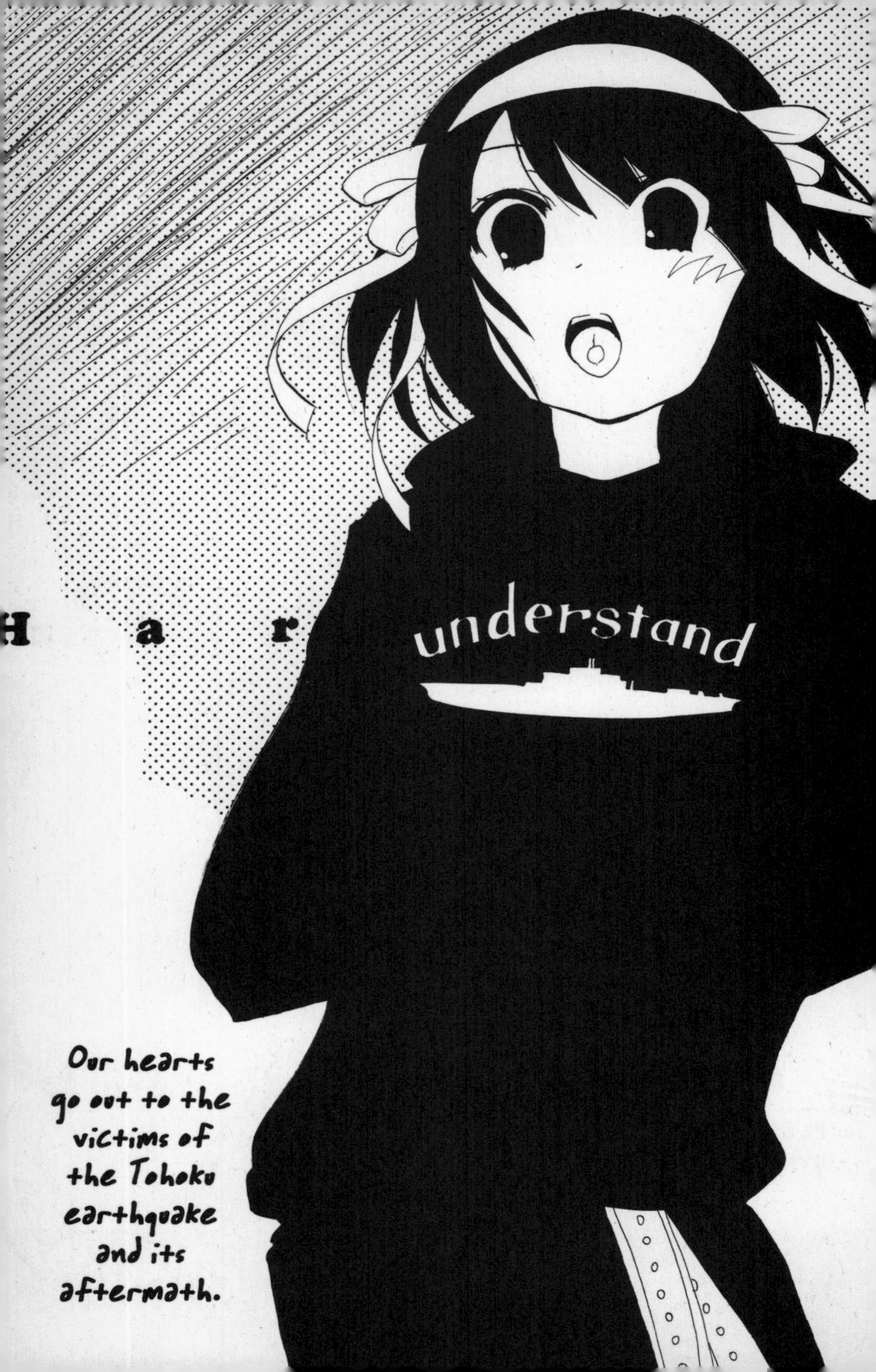
H a r
understand
Our hearts go out to the victims of the Tohoku earthquake and its aftermath.

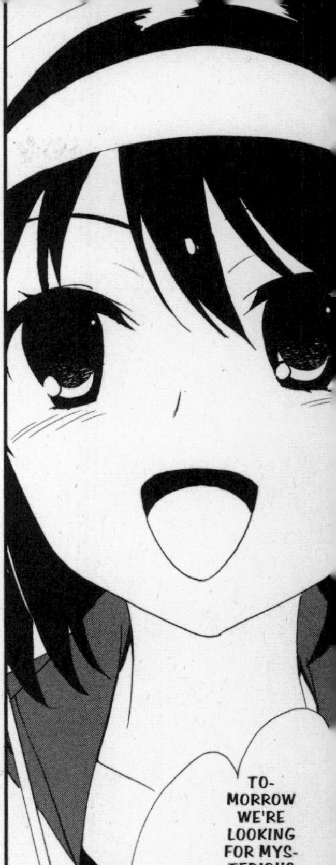
TO-MORROW WE'RE LOOKING FOR MYS-TERIOUS PHENOM-ENA IN THE CITY!
DON'T BE LATE!

HARUHI SPRINGS INTO ACTION!!

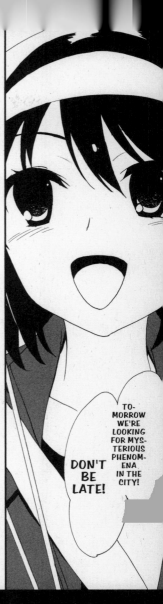

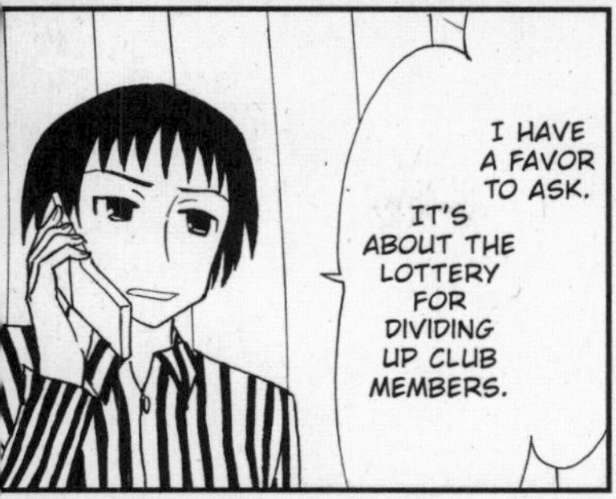
I HAVE A FAVOR TO ASK.
IT'S ABOUT THE LOTTERY FOR DIVIDING UP CLUB MEMBERS.

MEANWHILE, KYON HAS HIS HANDS FULL WITH CARRYING OUT ASAHINA THE ELDER'S INSTRUCTIONS...

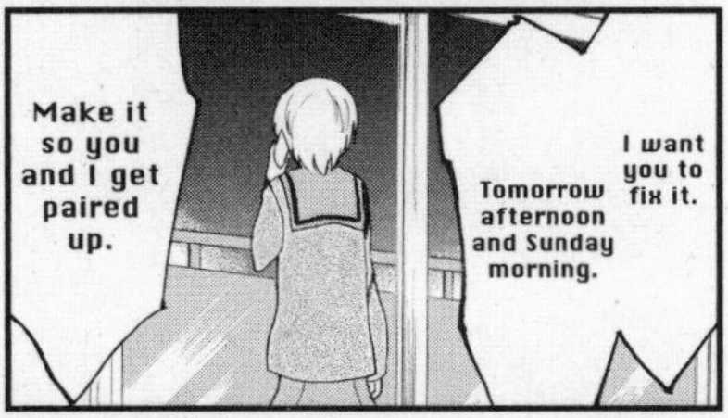
I want you to fix it.
Tomorrow afternoon and Sunday morning.
Make it so you and I get paired up.

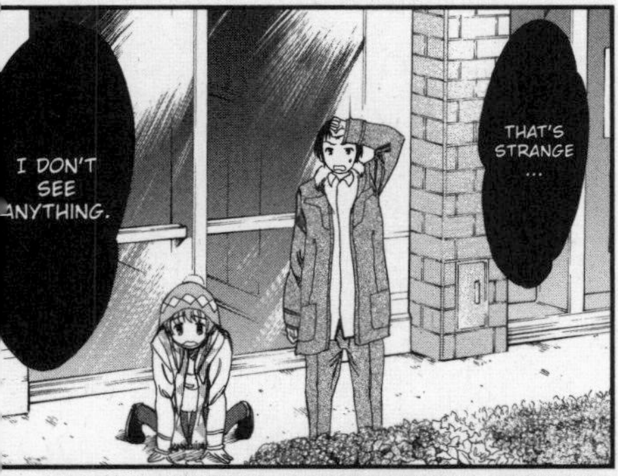
THAT'S STRANGE ...
I DON'T SEE ANYTHING.

...TRYING TO FIND THE PORTABLE STORAGE DEVICE WITH MIKURU (MICHIRU)...

VOLUME 15 AVAILABLE SOON!

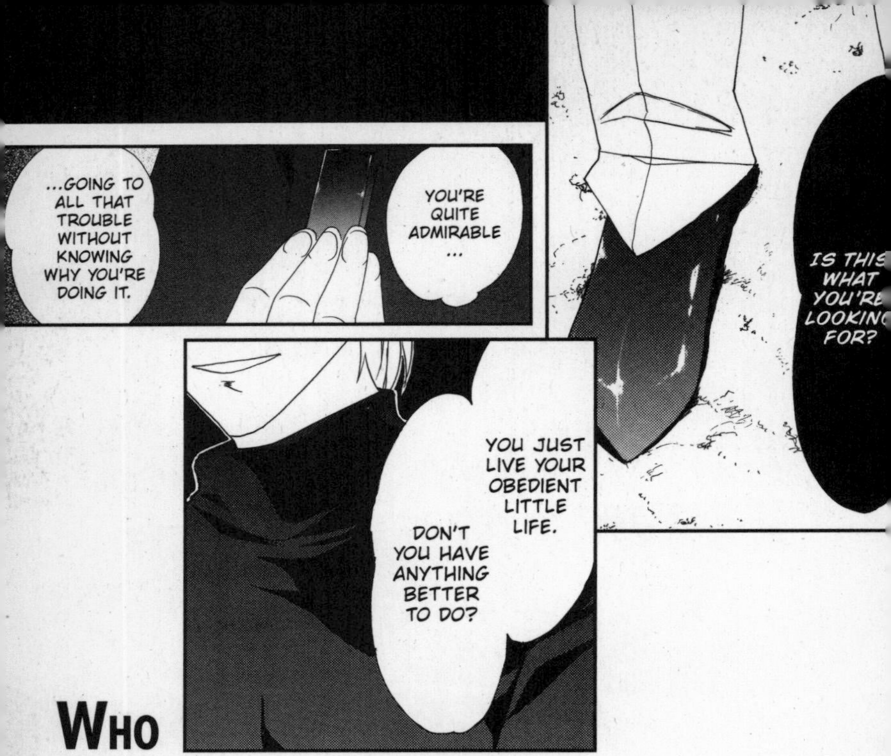
IS THIS WHAT YOU'RE LOOKING FOR?
YOU'RE QUITE ADMIRABLE ...
...GOING TO ALL THAT TROUBLE WITHOUT KNOWING WHY YOU'RE DOING IT.
YOU JUST LIVE YOUR OBEDIENT LITTLE LIFE.
DON'T YOU HAVE ANYTHING BETTER TO DO?

SUDDENLY, A STRANGE MAN APPEARS!!

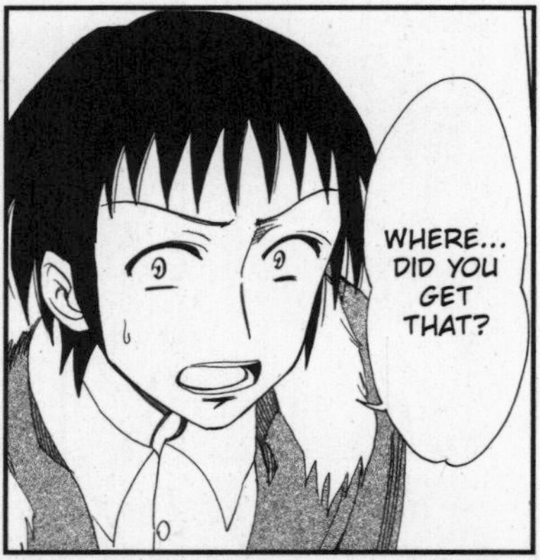
WHERE... DID YOU GET THAT?

WHO IS HE ...!?

THE CLIMAX OF THE "INTRIGUES"!

Can't wait for the next volume? You don't have to!

Keep up with the latest chapters of some of your favorite manga every month online in the pages of YEN PLUS!

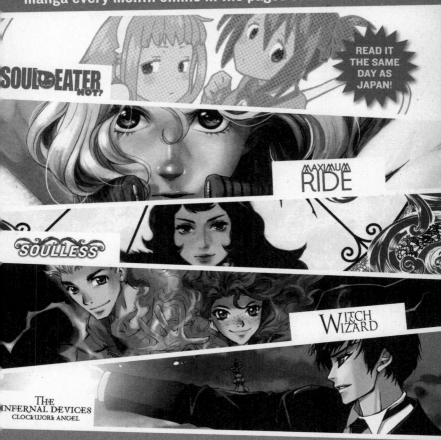

READ IT THE SAME DAY AS JAPAN!

SOUL EATER NOT?

MAXIMUM RIDE

SOULLESS

WITCH & WIZARD

THE INFERNAL DEVICES CLOCKWORK ANGEL

Visit us at
ww.yenplus.com
for details!

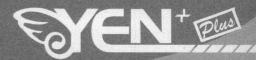

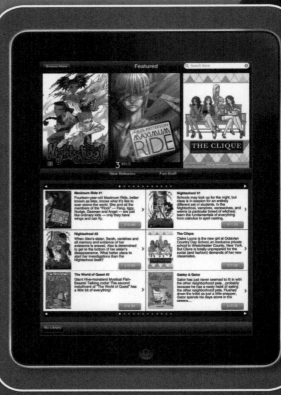
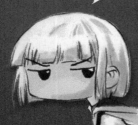

WELCOME TO IKEBUKURO, WHERE TOKYO'S WILDEST CHARACTERS GATHER!!

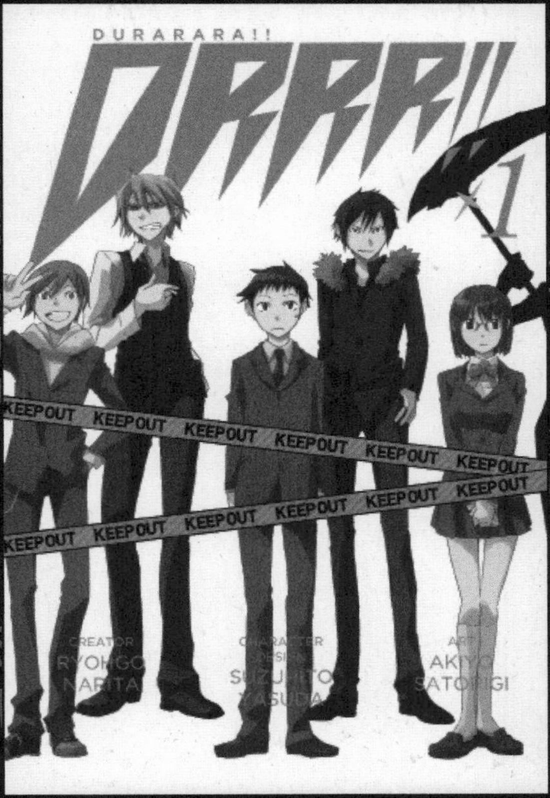

DURARARA!!

DRRR!!

AS THEIR PATHS CROSS, THIS ECCENTRIC CAST WEAVES A TWISTED, CRACKED LOVE STORY...

AVAILABLE NOW!!

To become the ultimate weapon, one boy must eat the souls of 99 humans...

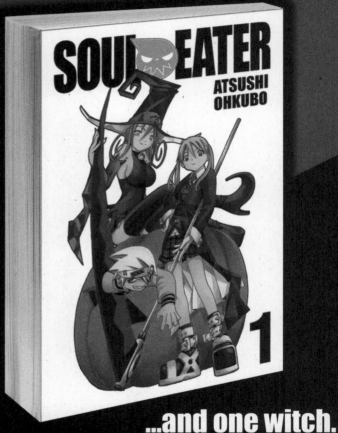

SOUL EATER

ATSUSHI OHKUBO

1

...and one witch.

Maka is a scythe meister, working to perfect her demon scythe until it is good enough to become Death's Weapon—the weapon used by Shinigami-sama, the spirit of Death himself. And if that isn't strange enough, her scythe also has the power to change form—into a human-looking boy!

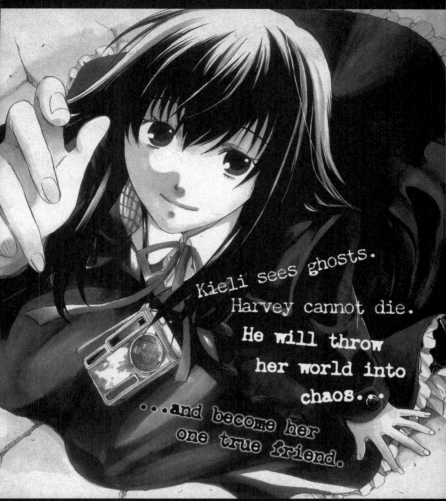

Kieli sees ghosts.
Harvey cannot die.
He will throw
her world into
chaos...
...and become her
one true friend.

STORY BY **Yukako Kabei**
ART BY **Shiori Teshirogi**

KIELI

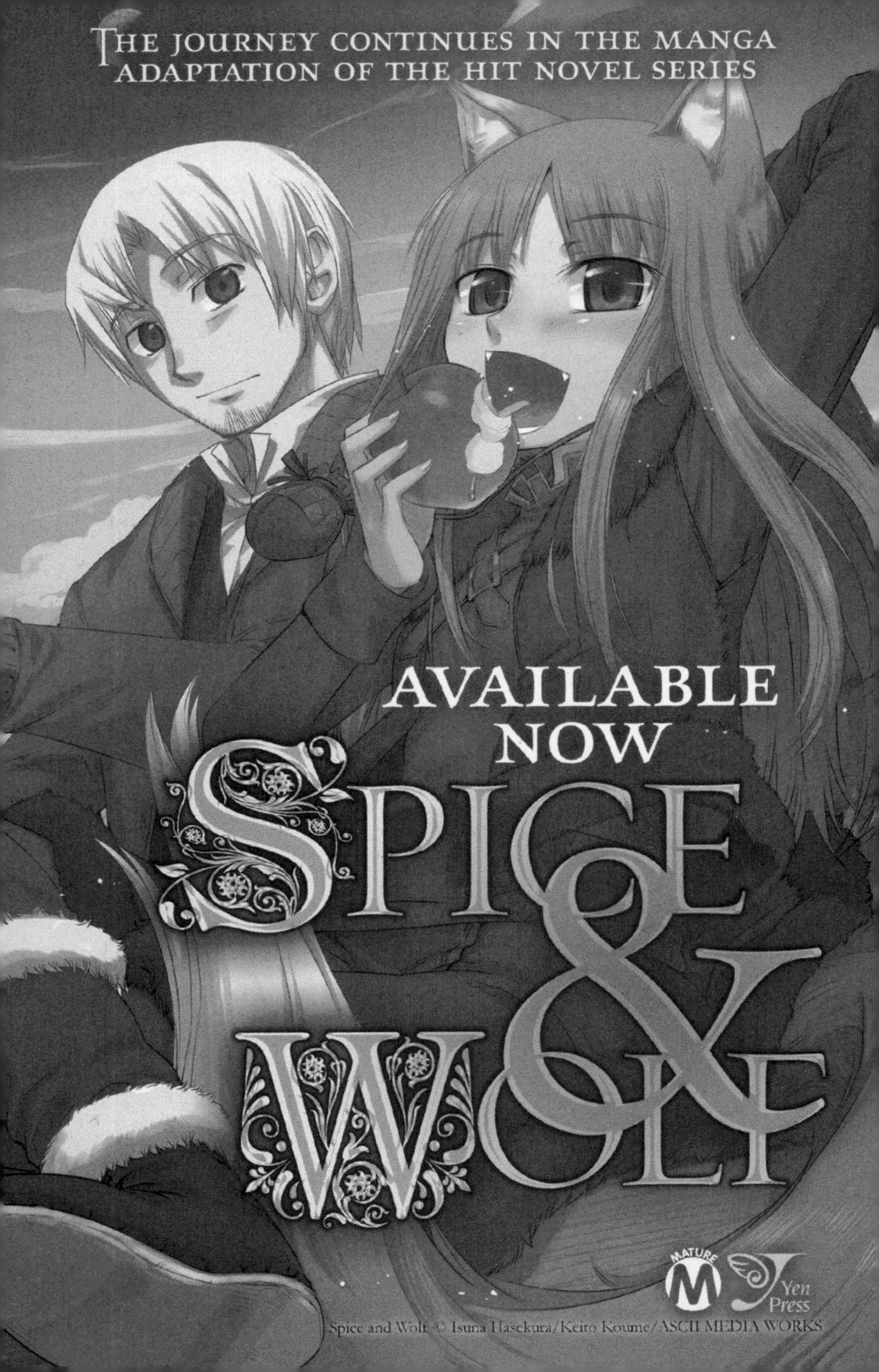
THE JOURNEY CONTINUES IN THE MANGA
ADAPTATION OF THE HIT NOVEL SERIES
AVAILABLE
NOW
SPICE
&
WOLF
MATURE
M
Yen
Press
Spice and Wolf © Isuna Hasekura/Keito Koume/ASCII MEDIA WORKS

THE MELANCHOLY ⬛⬛⬛⬛⬛YA

P9-AEW-860

Original Story: Nagaru Tanigawa
Manga: Gaku Tsugano
Character Design: Noizi Ito

Translation: Paul Starr
Lettering: Alexis Eckerman

SUZUMIYA HARUHI NO YUUTSU Volume 14 © Nagaru TANIGAWA • Noizi ITO 2011 © Gaku TSUGANO 2011. First published in Japan in 2011 by KADOKAWA SHOTEN CO., LTD., Tokyo. English translation rights arranged with KADOKAWA SHOTEN CO., LTD., Tokyo through Tuttle-Mori Agency, Inc., Tokyo.

English translation © 2012 by Hachette Book Group, Inc.

Yen Press
Hachette Book Group
237 Park Avenue, New York, NY 10017

www.HachetteBookGroup.com
www.YenPress.com

Yen Press is an imprint of Hachette Book Group, Inc. The Yen Press name and logo are trademarks of Hachette Book Group, Inc.

First Yen Press Edition: December 2012

ISBN: 978-0-316-22905-0

10 9 8 7 6 5 4 3 2 1

BVG

Printed in the United States of America